ADVANCES IN ECONOMETRICS

Volume 1 ● 1982

ADVANCES IN ECONOMETRICS

A Research Annual

Editors: R. L. BASMANN
Department of Economics
Texas A & M University

GEORGE F. RHODES, JR.
Department of Economics
Colorado State University

VOLUME 1 ● 1982

JAI PRESS INC.

Greenwich, Connecticut   *London, England*

CONTENTS

LIST OF CONTRIBUTORS

C. L. Flinn

Department of Economics
University of Wisconsin–Madison

J. J. Heckman

Department of Economics
University of Chicago

Dale W. Jorgenson

Department of Economics
Harvard University

Takeaki Kariya

Department of Mathematics and
Statistics, University of Pittsburgh,
Institute of Economic
Research, Hitotsubashi
University, Japan

Lawrence J. Lau

Department of Economics
Stanford University

Louis Phlips

Center for Operations Research
and Economics, Universite
Catholique de Louvin, France

J. D. Sargan

London School of Economics
and Political Science
University of London

Frans Spinnewyn

Center for Operations Research
and Economics, Universite
Catholique de Louvin, France

Thomas M. Stoker

Sloan School of Management
Massachusetts Institute of
Technology

INTRODUCTION

Our criteria for papers published in *Advances in Econometrics* are two:

- Papers shall make original contributions in economics and econometrics that lay major new foundations for continued study, and
- Papers shall be sufficiently long and writing style sufficiently mature and complete that they are self-contained. They should be readable and should not require more than occasional reference to previous works.

Papers in this first volume exceed our standards and establish hallmark standards for papers in future volumes. It is a pleasure to offer them to the social science profession.

R. L. Basmann
George F. Rhodes, Jr.
Series Editors

PART I
STUDIES OF CONSUMER AND
WORKER BEHAVIOR

RATIONALITY VERSUS MYOPIA IN DYNAMIC DEMAND SYSTEMS

Louis Phlips and Frans Spinnewyn

ABSTRACT

This chapter starts with a survey, in Section I, of work done in the Hout-hakker–Taylor tradition in the area of dynamic demand systems. Section II establishes the observational equivalence of myopic demand systems (whether static or dynamic) with systems derived under the assumption of intertemporal utility maximization. Theoretical standing can thus be given to myopic systems and, in particular, to models of durable goods that use purchase prices instead of user costs. Along the way, new estimates of the marginal propensities to consume of the average American consumer, based on rational intertemporal behavior, are given, together with estimates of his rate of time preference and his real rate of interest on human and nonhuman wealth during the period 1929–1966.

This chapter starts with a survey, in Section I, of work done in the Houthakker–Taylor tradition in the area of dynamic demand systems. These systems are said to be "dynamic" because they are based on

Advances in Econometrics, volume 1, pages 3–33.
ISBN: 0-89232-138-5

(endogenously determined) changes in tastes. They are also said to be "myopic" because they are derived on the assumption of instantaneous utility maximization. The strengths and weaknesses of this type of models are discussed in some detail.

Section II establishes the observational equivalence of myopic demand systems (whether static or dynamic) with systems derived under the assumption of intertemporal utility maximization. Myopic systems can thus be given theoretical standing, at least in the sense that they provide a handy way of estimating rational intertemporal behavior. In the present state of the art they probably provide the simplest way of estimating demand systems with a sound intertemporal foundation.

By the same token, observational equivalence is shown to exist between approaches that put purchases of durables in the utility function and more orthodox formulations in which the services rendered by durables appear as arguments in the utility function. Theoretical standing can thus be given to models of durable goods that use purchase prices instead of user costs. The vexing problems resulting from the difficulty of measuring user costs can thus be circumvented.

Along the way new estimates of the marginal propensities to consume of the average American consumer, based on rational intertemporal behavior, are given, together with estimates of his rate of time preference and his real rate of interest on human and nonhuman wealth during the period 1929–1966.

I. MYOPIC MODELS

A. The State Variable Approach

The state variable approach originates from the now widely used single equation partial adjustment models for durable goods of the 1950s. These models can typically be written in reduced form as

$$x_{it} = \beta_{0i} + \beta_{1i} s_{it} + \beta_{2i} y_t + \alpha_i p_{it-1} + \eta_{it} \qquad (1)$$

where x_{it} represents purchases of durable good i, p_{it} is the (relative) price, y_t is disposable income (per capita), and s_{it-1} is the existing stock. This reduced form corresponds to a partial adjustment equation

$$x_{it} = \kappa_i (s_{it}^* - s_{it-1}) + \delta_i s_{it-1} \qquad (2)$$

where κ_i is the adjustment coefficient and δ_i is the constant rate of depreciation, and an equation explaining desired stock s_{it}^* as

$$s_{it}^* = a_{0i} + a_{1i} p_{it} + a_{2i} y_t + \varepsilon_{it} \qquad (3)$$

Pioneering work along these lines is reported in Harberger (1960), with

Chow's (1960) analysis of the demand for automobiles as a particularly interesting example.

Two features are worth emphasizing, in view of our discussion in Section II of intertemporal models. First, the coefficient α_i, which measures the impact of physical stocks on current purchases in Eq. (1), turns out to be a negative number: the higher your stock, the smaller your purchases. (This is the so-called stock effect.) Second, this coefficient is equal to the difference between the rate of depreciation and the adjustment coefficient

$$\alpha_i = \delta_i - \kappa_i \qquad (4)$$

so that $\kappa_i = \delta_i - \alpha_i$. With α_i negative, it may thus happen that $\delta_i - \alpha_i = 1$, in which case adjustment to desired stock would be immediate and complete: we would be back in the static case, in which purchases (x_{it}) are equal to the sum of replacement purchases $(\delta_i s_{it-1})$ and desired changes in the stock $(s_{it}^* - s_{it-1})$.

The first edition of Houthakker and Taylor's *Consumer Demand in the United States* generalized the demand for durables analysis, as sketched above, to the case of nondurable goods and introduced what we call the state variable approach. Redefine s_{it} as a state variable reflecting past purchases of commodity i. More precisely, let s_{it} be the solution of the difference equation

$$s_{it} = x_{it} + (1 - \delta_i)s_{it-1} \qquad (5)$$

Then s_{it} can stand either for a physical stock, as above, or for a "psychological stock of habits." And its initial value s_{it-1} would appear in the reduced form [equation (1)] for nondurable goods as well as for durables. But now α_i would take a positive value for nondurables, i.e., when measuring the (positive) impact of habit formation on current purchases, while δ_i becomes the rate at which habits wear off. Needless to say, κ_i would necessarily be smaller than one, so that habit formation is seen to imply a partial adjustment. By the same token, Eq. (1) becomes what Farrell (1952), following Marshall (1920, Appendix H, §3), called an irreversible demand equation.

In the second (1970) edition of their book, Houthakker and Taylor present a further generalization, which will be continuously referred to in this paper. It shows that estimating equations of the same form as Eq. (1) can be obtained as the result of constrained utility maximization. Define an instantaneous "dynamic" utility function as

$$u_t = u(x_{1t}, \ldots, x_{nt}; s_{it}, \ldots, s_{nt}) \qquad (6)$$

in which state variables appear as parameters, there being one state variable corresponding to the purchases of each commodity. The utility so defined incorporates taste changes, through the presence of the state variables, and yet its functional form does not change over time. This is exactly the idea underlying the recent Stigler–Becker (1977) paper, in which "stocks of habits" are called "consumption capital," while habit formation is baptized "addiction." As Pollak (1978) rightly remarks, there is no more explanatory power in a household production model that postulates the accumulation of a specific but unobservable consumption capital than in our habit formation model with state variables.

The introduction of state variables into the utility function is an elegant way of taking adjustment costs, whether psychological or not, into account. As is well known, partial adjustment models have been rationalized as the optimal reaction of an agent to the adjustment costs of implementing a plan. (See Eisner and Strotz, 1963 and Lucas, 1967, on adjustment costs in production, or Griliches, 1967.) For a consumer, it suffices to interpret partial adjustment as a trade-off between the costs of not attaining the utility maximizing solution that neglects transaction costs and the costs of adjusting to the new position. The costs of change are a function of past behavior, which can be summarized in state variables. Instead of introducing transaction costs explicitly into the problem, it is convenient to capture their effect implicitly by state variables as in equation (6).

Assume, indeed, that $f(x_t, s_t) \leq 0$ is the transactions technology. Then, maximizing

$$u^*(x_{1t}, \ldots, x_{nt})$$

subject to

$$f(x_t, s_t) \leq 0$$
$$p_t' x_t \leq y_t$$

is equivalent to maximizing

$$u(x_{1t}, \ldots, x_{nt}; s_{1t}, \ldots, s_{nt}) = u^*(x_{1t}, \ldots, x_{nt}) - \mu f(x_t, s_t)$$

subject to the constraint $p_t' x_t \leq y_t$.

The state variables in the dynamic utility function [equation (6)] may therefore capture a wide range of dynamic elements that characterize the consumer's choice: the stock effect of durable goods and the addiction effect, but also "learning by doing" effects, adjustment effects, and so on. It is, then, not surprising that the maximization of (6), under the usual budget constraint

$$y_t = \sum_i p_{it} x_{it} \tag{7}$$

where y_t represents total expenditures and p_{it} are current purchase prices, leads to demand equations that are observationally equivalent with those obtained from the partial adjustment model—at least when the utility function is specified in an appropriate way. It should be emphasized that this maximization (with respect to x_{it}) is carried out instantaneously in each period.

What are the strengths and weaknesses of this type of dynamic utility maximization?

The applied economist should be impressed by the possibility that is offered to simultaneously compute not only a complete set of both short- and long-run price and income elasticities but also a set of depreciation rates and adjustment coefficients (using $\delta_i - \alpha_i$). The short-run elasticities are computed from the demand equations obtained by maximizing the dynamic utility function. "Short-run" is indeed synonymous with partial adjustment. The long-run elasticities are derived from the same demand equations, after imposing the condition $s_{it} - s_{it-1} = 0$, or equivalently

$$x_{it} = \delta_i \, s_{it-1} \tag{8}$$

which amounts to saying that purchases are for replacement purposes only.

The theoretician, on the other hand, might derive some intellectual satisfaction from the fact that the first-order conditions

$$\frac{\partial u}{\partial x_{it}} = \lambda_t p_{it} \qquad i = 1, \ldots, n \tag{9}$$

appear to be identical with the reduced forms one obtains by imposing a partial adjustment mechanism on the long-run equilibrium conditions (which in turn are formally identical with the static equilibrium conditions), as shown in detail in Phlips (1974, Chapter 6). A theoretical foundation for partial adjustments and the resulting distributed lags is thus available. It is not irrational for a consumer to distribute his response over time so as to approach his (static or long-run) equilibrium position gradually. On the contrary, by doing so he is maximizing utility.

The very same theoretician might immediately add, though, that this sort of models is far from attaining the theoretical standing he is used to. And recall that these models are presented as "models for durable goods," while what is being done is simply—we quote from Brown and Deaton (1972:1225)—to "graft dynamic considerations into the static utility model rather than rooting them in an intertemporal maximization process."

The objection could be made more precise with the following arguments. The consumer who behaves according to equations (6)–(8) is looking backward but not forward. At each moment in time, he maximizes an instantaneous utility function in which the influence of past decisions is embedded. When he buys a durable, he takes his initial stock (s_{it-1}) into account but ignores the obvious fact that it is going to be there tomorrow, whether he still likes it or not, that it will need repairing or replacement, etc. The consumer who is developing habits acts in the same "myopic" way: when smoking an additional cigarette, he closes his eyes to the sign saying "this may be dangerous to your health."

Pollak (1975) characterized the demand behavior obtained by maximizing the instantaneous utility function subject to the budget constraint as "naive" habit formation. The consumer recognizes that his current satisfaction depends on past behavior, so that his current behavior will also be influenced by what he purchased in the past. But he fails to take the effect of his current choice on the formation of his future tastes into account. Pollak opposes "rational" habit formation to "naive" habit formation. The rational consumer is aware of the endogenous process in which future tastes are formed. In making a current plan, he therefore allows for the effects of his current choice on his future possibilities.

The use of the traditional budget constraint [equation (7)] might be criticized on similar grounds. It implies that the allocation of income between total expenditures (y_t) and savings is treated as exogenously given. Shouldn't one explain this allocation together with the allocation of y_t among n commodities, possibly including time? Shouldn't one then use a wealth constraint rather than an income constraint?

While these objections are entirely valid from a theoretical point of view, it is our contention that, in practical econometric applications, the use of myopic models may be justified in some cases. Section II will indeed show that (1) some popular models are observationally equivalent with models derived from intertemporal utility maximization under a wealth constraint and (2) it is possible to derive the (intertemporally) correct parameters and elasticities from the corresponding myopic ones for those models.

Myopic models have other features that are often considered with suspicion. To begin with, a theoretician may be disturbed by the presence of quantities purchased rather than consumption services (or stocks of durables, to the extent that these are proportional to the services provided) in the utility function. We are not too unhappy about this, for two reasons.

A first link between purchases and services consumed is provided by the interpretation of myopic models in terms of partial adjustments to long-run equilibria. In the long run, $(s_{it} - s_{it-1})$ being zero, quantities purchased are equal to depreciation, which is equal to consumption, as noted in equation (8). Instantaneous utility maximization then provides a short-run rationalization of the partial adjustment, with the help of current purchases, to long-run desired *consumption*. And the shape of the time path of purchases captures a phenomenon that would be hard to specify in a model written in terms of services or stocks, namely the sequential realization of a consumption plan through a series of purchases in a specific order.

A second link between purchases, services, and stocks will be illustrated in the next section. It is simply the fact that, in some of the currently popular models at least, it amounts to the same whether one uses purchases, services, or stocks as arguments in the utility function. To show this, we shall take what is a special case from a dynamic point of view, i.e., the static case without habit formation and with immediate adjustment (to which standard theory explicitly or implicitly refers) and which implies the restriction $\delta_i - \alpha_i = 1$.

The state variable approach, as presented earlier, has a further feature that results from the use of purchases as decision variables for all commodities: durable and nondurable goods are treated in a symmetric way, so that durables have, by definition, a (negative) stock effect, whereas nondurables are habit forming. The former are not "allowed" to be habit forming, whereas the availability of physical stocks for commodity j is not given a chance to influence the degree of habit formation of commodity i. In fact, however, psychological and physical factors may interact. Habit formation may arise from nonpsychological costs of adjusting to the changing economic environment. The physical depreciation of durable goods may be reduced if one gets experienced in using these. For nondurable goods, the expertise acquired in consuming may work as a stock effect (the experienced cook can make marvellous dishes with simple ingredients). On the other hand, goods may lose much of their appeal once their snob effect or demonstration effect disappears. In practice, it may therefore be difficult to distinguish between psychological and physical stocks. The only thing one can take for granted is that current satisfaction depends on past behavior. Whether past behavior has a positive or negative effect on current purchases may be impossible to ascertain *a priori*.

Let us emphasize, though, that some analytical refinements can and have been introduced successfully by, for example, Taylor (1974) and Spinnewyn (1981a), at the cost, however, of a number of additional assumptions and of increasing considerably the dimensionality of the problem from the point of view of estimation. It is not clear whether the additional information gained outweighs the much greater complexity of the computations. It is not even clear whether the additional parameters can be identified. On the other hand, it must be recognized that the estimated values of the δ and α coefficients, in the model presented earlier, have to be interpreted, at least in the case of durables, as reflecting the net combined effect of a psychological and a physical factor. For example, a positive α_i indicates that, on balance, habit formation dominated the stock effect. Or a particularly large δ_i might be a combination of physical depreciation and "economic" depreciation, where the latter includes the speed at which habits wear off. All this is not intellectually satisfactory and yet defendable on grounds of computational efficiency.

B. Particular Specifications

For the sake of completeness, and by way of illustration of the above, it may be worthwhile to recall a few dynamic specifications that have proven their usefulness in applied work.

A dynamic version of the linear expenditure system is obtained by introducing variable minimum required quantities γ_{it} into the instantaneous Stone–Geary utility function, which becomes

$$u_t = \sum_i \beta_i \ln(x_{it} - \gamma_{it}) \tag{10}$$

and defining γ_{it} as

$$\gamma_{it} = \theta_i + \alpha_i s_{it-1} \tag{11}$$

The specification of γ_{it} as a linear function of the state variables is the only way of specifying a demand system that is both linear (in the variables) and theoretically plausible, i.e., compatible with utility maximization (Phlips, 1974, Chapter 7).

From the point of view of the preceding discussion, this model has the interesting feature that it can be interpreted as incorporating a partial adjustment, for each commodity, to its optimal stock in the long run, *and* that the adjustment coefficients κ_i are equal to $\delta_i - \alpha_i$.

It can also be easily shown to be equivalent to a dynamic linear expenditure system defined in terms of stocks (and therefore of the consumption of services) in the special case where $\kappa_i = 1$ or, equivalently, $\alpha_i = -(1 - \delta_i)$. Indeed, under this assumption one finds

$$\begin{aligned} x_{it} - \gamma_{it} &= x_{it} - \theta_i - \alpha_i s_{it-1} \\ &= s_{it} + \alpha_i s_{it-1} - \theta_i - \alpha_i s_{it-1} \\ &= s_{it} - \theta_i \end{aligned} \tag{12}$$

on using equation (5). The coefficients θ_i can be interpreted as measuring physical minimum quantities. Using purchases or stocks is equivalent in a static framework without delayed responses. Using purchases opens additional perspectives when responses are delayed, without excluding the possibility that the behavior described by a theoretically "correct" model for durable goods might show up in the data.

Houthakker and Taylor (1970) preferred to dynamize the once popular quadratic utility function by writing it as

$$u_t = x_t'a + s_{t-1}'b + \frac{1}{2}x_t'Ax_t + x_t'Bs_{t-1} + \frac{1}{2}s_{t-1}'Cs_{t-1} \tag{13}$$

where A, B, and C are diagonal matrices. This function was chosen because of the linearity of the first-order derivative and therefore of the first-order conditions.

Here, the diagonal matrix of adjustment coefficients K turns out to be

$$K = \hat{\delta} + A^{-1}B \tag{14}$$

where $\hat{\delta}$ is the diagonal matrix of depreciation rates. Again, the speed of adjustment depends on the interplay of depreciation and the impact of the state variables on current purchases.

Notice that the quadratic utility function [equation (13)] could be rewritten as

$$u_t = (x_t - \gamma_t)'d + \frac{1}{2}(x_t - \gamma_t)'D(x_t - \gamma_t) \tag{13a}$$

with $A = D$, $B = -\hat{\alpha}D$ and $C = \hat{\alpha}^2 D$, which establishes, on using Eq. (12), the equivalence between the use of stocks and the use of purchases, under the assumption that

$$K = I = \hat{\delta} + A^{-1}B = \hat{\delta} - D^{-1}\hat{\alpha}D = \hat{\delta} - \hat{\alpha}$$

The quadratic utility function has the well-known drawback of having marginal utilities that may become zero or negative. In a dynamic framework, this translates into the fact that satiation income is never far on the consumer's horizon, so that the marginal utility of income (λ_t) must decline more sharply than in the linear expenditure system, as shown in Weiserbs (1974). Furthermore, the latter system beats the former in terms of forecasting performance (Taylor and Weiserbs, 1972), so that we shall concentrate in what follows on the linear expenditure system.

II. RATIONAL MODELS

We now turn to intertemporal models, which are the main topic of this chapter. Our interest is in intertemporal models with taste changes and durables. By definition, such models view the consumer as being conscious of the implications, for the development of future preferences, of past and current consumption decisions. In this sense, "rational habit formation'' is involved and the models (or the consumers) under analysis are said to be rational.

Before entering these (complicated) matters, it is useful and perhaps necessary to discuss the static intertemporal allocation model. Indeed, we want to analyze the relations between the consumption–savings decision and the allocation of a given consumption budget among n commodities. In particular, we want to know under which conditions the two problems can be separated. These conditions have been extensively analyzed in the static case without taste changes.

A natural question will then be to ask whether they extend to the dynamic case with myopic and/or rational habit formation. Once this question is answered, we will move to the practical problem of the estimation of demand systems derived under the assumption of rational habit formation. Many a reader will be surprised, with us, to discover that the myopic dynamic demand systems presented in Section I,A are observationally equivalent with the corresponding rational dynamic systems.

We abstract throughout from the uncertainty that naturally arises in an intertemporal framework and therefore assume that the consumer has either perfect information or deterministic expectations.

A.   Decentralization with Unchanging Tastes

Let x_t be an n-vector of purchases at period t and w_{FT} final financial wealth, which may yield satisfaction as the bequest. With an intertemporal utility function

$$U = U(x_1, \ldots, x_T, \ldots, w_{Ft}) \qquad (15)$$

and a wealth constraint, it is possible to simultaneously solve the allocation problem of y_t among the n commodities at each period t, and the allocation problem of income in year t between total consumption (or expenditures) y_t and savings: it suffices to find the optimal time path $\{x_{it}\}$ and to aggregate over the n commodities to find optimal total consumption. This is the approach followed by Lluch (1973) in the construction of the so-called "extended linear expenditure system," in which an equation explaining y_t in terms of exogenous income is added to the static linear expenditure system.

Generally, demand analysis proceeds otherwise. Most models dealing with the consumer's demand for goods and services at a disaggregated level study the allocation of a *given* budget y_t among different uses. It is therefore assumed that the intertemporal consumer choice can be *decentralized*. Once the budgets (y_t) are allocated to the different periods, the consumer is supposed to be able to allocate his budget of a particular period among the different goods and services without reconsidering the entire intertemporal optimization procedure.

Decentralization of the intertemporal decision problem is, indeed, an attractive property for the empirically oriented economist. The computation of the budget to be assigned to a particular period may be difficult, requiring much information that is not directly necessary for the study of the allocation of the budget to the goods and services of a particular period. Because the budget of any period can be observed, a large part of the information that in one way or another determines the observed demand behavior can therefore be discarded by considering demand conditional on the budget assigned.

If the formal definition in Blackorby, Primont, and Russell (1975) of decentralizability is applied to an intertemporal decision problem, one can say that decisions can be decentralized over time if in any period only prices of the current period are needed to determine demand, once the budget is known. Using a result of Gorman (1971), we know that decentralizability of decisions over time is then identical to requiring weak separability of the intertemporal utility function with respect to commodities relating to different periods.

Under separability, the allocation of an observed budget y_t can be considered as the second stage in a two-stage budgeting procedure. The empirically oriented demand analyst has, as such, no direct interest in the way budgets are assigned intertemporally. Yet, from a theoretical point of view, it is illuminating to be more explicit about this first stage.

It is impossible to allocate budgets intertemporally without some information about what is happening at the second stage. But it is sometimes possible to summarize this information in an efficient way, such that the intertemporal allocation procedure is simplified. Price aggregation turns out to be important. In an intemporal context, price aggregation may be defined as the possibility of computing the budget assigned to any period by knowing only the value of price indices (for all periods) in addition to initial wealth.

Let y_t be the budget and r_t be the interest rate. In discrete time and with a finite horizon T, an optimal budget allocation is the solution to

$$\max_{y_1, \ldots, y_{T-1}, w_{FT}} V(y_1, \ldots, y_t, \ldots, y_{T-1}, w_{FT}) \tag{16}$$

subject to

$$w_{Ft+1} = (1 + r_t)(w_{Ft} - y_t) \qquad t = 1, \ldots, T - 1 \tag{17}$$

where V is the intertemporal indirect utility function.

Several assumptions have to be made to formulate the first-stage allocation problem in this way. First of all, weak separability of the instantaneous direct utility function makes it possible to define an indirect representation $v(y_t, p_t)$. This is a natural way to derive an objective function in terms of budgets such as equation (16) representing the original preferences [equation (15)]. The prices are not explicitly introduced in the objective function [equation (16)]. But if we assume these to be constant, it is not necessary to do so.

One also assumes that the consumption–savings decision can be separated from the portfolio problem, in which the investment of wealth in different assets is considered. In other words, the interest rate r_t summarizes the information on the investment opportunities and this information is all one needs for the consumption–savings decisions. This problem is adequately dealt with by Samuelson (1969), Hakansson (1970), and others and will not be considered here.

Wealth and total expenditures are defined in equation (17) in such a way that there is no exogenous income nor exogenous expenditures. However, under the assumption that one can borrow or lend in the current period for any future period and that the borrowing rate is equal to the lending rate, it is always possible to take the discounted value of such exogenous outlays or receipts. This value can be considered to be part of initial wealth.

It does not suffice to represent preferences by a utility function in terms of budgets, as in equation (16): the functional structure of this utility function has to be further simplified if one wants to obtain closed form solutions. Since Phelps (1962), utility functions that are homothetic and additive in the budgets have received great attention.

If the intertemporal objective function is homothetic in the budgets, it follows that the budgets are proportional to initial wealth. This can be proved as follows (see also Mirrlees, 1974).

If $V(y_1, \ldots, y_t, \ldots, y_{T-1}, w_{FT})$ is homothetic, there exists by definition a positive increasing transformation of V, which is positively homogeneous of degree one. A feasible plan that maximizes the normalization F will also maximize V, since the transformation is increasing.

Now let $y_1, \ldots, y_t, \ldots, y_{T-1}, w_{FT}$ be an optimal plan for initial wealth w_{F1}. It follows from the wealth constraint [Equation (17)] that $ky_1, \ldots, ky_t, \ldots, ky_{T-1}, kw_{FT}$ is feasible for kw_{F1}. But it is also optimal. For consider any other feasible plan $k\bar{y}_1, \ldots, k\bar{y}_{T-1}, k\bar{w}_{FT}$. Then

$$F(k\bar{y}_1, \ldots, k\bar{w}_{FT}) = kF(\bar{y}_1, \ldots, \bar{w}_{FT}) \leq kF(y_1, \ldots, w_{FT}) =$$

$$F(ky, \ldots, kw_{FT})$$

The inequality follows from the feasibility of $\bar{y}_1, \ldots, \bar{w}_{FT}$ and the optimality of $y_1, \ldots, w_{FT}$ for initial wealth w_{F1}.

If, then, $y_t = f_t(w_{Ft})$ is the optimal plan for $t = 1, \ldots, T - 1$, we have $ky_t = f_t(kw_{Ft}) = kf_t(w_{Ft})$, so that f_t is homogeneous of degree one. It follows that (for y_t nonnegative)

$$y_t = \xi_t w_{Ft} \tag{18}$$

Add the assumption of additivity to the assumption of homotheticity and suppose V also to be increasing and strictly quasi-concave: you obtain the "Bergson family," which can be written as

$$V = \sum_t C(t) \left(\frac{1}{a}\right) y_t^a + C^*(T) \left(\frac{1}{a}\right) w_{FT}^a \tag{19}$$

for $a < 1$, and as

$$V = \sum_t C(t) \ln y_t + C^*(T) \ln w_{FT} \tag{20}$$

for $a \to 0$. For these functions there exist closed form solutions.

A solution is obtained recursively (e.g., Samuelson, 1969). Let

$$\beta(t) = \frac{C(t + 1)}{C(t)}$$

rewrite $C^*(T)$ for convenience as $C(T)\xi_T^{a-1}$, and consider the case where $a \neq 0$.

At time $t - 1$ we have to find y_{T-1} such that

$$\left(\frac{1}{a}\right) y_{T-1}^a + \beta(T - 1)\xi_T^{a-1} \left(\frac{1}{a}\right) w_{FT}^a \tag{21}$$

is maximized subject to $w_{FT} = (1 + r_{T-1})(w_{FT-1} - y_{T-1})$. Since $y_{T-1} = \xi_{T-1} w_{FT-1}$, we have that

$$w_{FT} = (1 + r_{T-1})(1 - \xi_{T-1}) w_{FT-1}$$

Substitution into (21) yields, at $T - 1$,

$$\left(\frac{1}{a}\right) w_{FT-1}^a [\xi_{T-1}^a + \beta(T - 1)\xi_T^{a-1}(1 + r_{T-1})^a (1 - \xi_{T-1})^a] \tag{22}$$

The first-order condition for ξ_{T-1} is

$$\xi_{T-1}^{a-1} - \beta(T - 1)\xi_T^{a-1}(1 + r_{T-1})^a (1 - \xi_{T-1})^{a-1} = 0$$

so that

$$\xi_{T-1} = \frac{b_{T-1} \xi_T}{1 + b_{T-1}\xi_T}$$

where

$$b_{T-1} = [\beta(T - 1)]^{1/(a-1)} (1 + r_{T-1})^{a/(a-1)}$$

Substituting the first-order condition into equation (22) and multiplying by $\beta(T - 2)$ yields the optimal value of the utility from $T - 1$ onward, as seen at $T - 2$

$$\beta(T - 2)\left(\frac{1}{a}\right)\xi_{T-1}^{a-1}\, w_{FT-1}^{a}$$

which is of the same form as the bequest function in equation (21).

At time $T - 2$, we can again take equation (21) as the objective, after adjusting the time subscripts and repeat the procedure. For each period t we therefore obtain

$$\xi_t = \frac{b_t\, \xi_{t+1}}{1 + b_t\, \xi_{t+1}} \tag{23}$$

where

$$b_t = \beta(t)^{1/(a-1)}\, (1 + r_t)^{a/(a-1)}$$

We may also look at the limiting value of ξ, when the interest rate (and β) are constant and the horizon is infinitely far. If b exceeds unity, we obtain

$$\xi = 1 - b^{-1} = 1 - \beta^{-1/(a-1)}\, (1 + r)^{-a(a-1)}$$

In the logarithmic case [equation (20)], we have $a = 0$ and therefore $b_t = \beta^{-1}$ so that in the limit $\xi = 1 - \beta$. The argument is essentially the same as for $a \neq 0$. But the utility from t onward has the form

$$\xi_t^{-1} \ln w_{Ft} + A_t \tag{24}$$

where A_t is a constant that does not affect the allocation process.

Up to now, prices were supposed to be constant. With variable prices, additive and homothetic instantaneous utility functions have a corresponding indirect utility function of the form

$$\left(\frac{1}{a}\right)\left[\frac{y_t}{\pi(p_t)}\right]^{a}$$

where $\pi(p_t)$ is a price index. Assume in addition that the intertemporal utility function is the discounted sum of the instantaneous (indirect) utility functions, with a constant discount rate. Then $C(t)$ can be specified as

$$C(t) = \rho^t\, [\pi(p_t)]^{-a}$$

so that

$$\beta(t) = \frac{C(t + 1)}{C(t)} = \rho\left[\frac{\pi(p_{t+1})}{\pi(p_t)}\right]^{-a}$$

$$b_t = \rho^{1/(a-1)} \left[\frac{\pi(p_t)}{\pi(p_{t+1})} (1 + r_t) \right]^{a/(a-1)}$$

$$= \rho^{1/(a-1)} (1 + r_t^*)^{a/(a-1)}$$

where r_t^*, the real interest rate, is the solution to

$$(1 + r_t^*) = \frac{\pi(p_t)}{\pi(p_{t+1})} (1 + r_t)$$

Under these assumptions, the real interest rate (approximately the nominal interest rate r_t less the price inflation given by the price indices of the two periods) summarizes all the information about price changes.

The usefulness of the Bergson family of utility functions for the practical solution of our first-stage allocation problem is thus established. True, these functions are highly unrealistic when defined in terms of quantities consumed or purchased. Nevertheless, they can be used in applied demand analysis through a change in variables, i.e., when defined in terms of transformed quantities, such as the committed quantities ($z_{it} = x_{it} - \gamma_i$), which appear in the Stone–Geary instantaneous utility function (10). The intertemporal utility function is weakly separable in z, once the instantaneous utility function is written with these committed quantities as arguments. And the wealth constraint can also be redefined in terms of z.

Indeed, let the uncommitted expenditures (or supernumerary income) be

$$e_t = p_t' z_t \tag{25}$$

The indirect utility function is then

$$\left(\frac{1}{a} \right) \left(\frac{e_t}{\pi(p_t)} \right)^a$$

Let $w_{HT} = 0$ and define w_{HT} recursively as

$$w_{Ht} = Y_t - p_t' \gamma + \frac{1}{1 + r_t} w_{Ht+1}$$

for $t = 1, \ldots , T - 1$, where Y_t is exogenous labor income. The wealth constraint

$$w_{Ft+1} = (1 + r_t)(w_{Ft} + Y_t - y_t)$$

can then be rewritten as

$$w_{Ft+1} + w_{Ht+1} = (1 + r_t)(w_{Ft} + w_{Ht} - y_t + p_t'\gamma)$$

or as

$$w_{t+1} = (1 + r_t)(w_t - e_t) \tag{26}$$

where $w_t = w_{Ft} + w_{Ht}$. Equation (26) is in the same form as equation (17). The variable w_{Ht} will be given a concrete meaning later on [see Eq. (34)]. What we wanted to show is that, by redefining the problem in terms of uncommitted expenditures e_t and an extended wealth concept w_t, the results obtained for our original problem, defined in eqs. (16) and (17), can be applied to the new problem. This insight will turn out to be very useful when we will tackle the corresponding problem with changing tastes in the next section.

B.   Decentralization with Changing Tastes

The intertemporal utility function ceases to be separable when instantaneous utility is made to depend upon past purchases through the introduction of state variables as in equation (6). This formulation indeed endogenizes taste changes, with the result that marginal rates of substitution in one period cease to be independent of purchases in another period. Is intertemporal decentralization therefore impossible when tastes change in the way described in Section I? Do the myopic models of Section I lack theoretical standing?

The orthodox attitude is to answer that, indeed, decentralization becomes impossible and to treat the first-stage and the second-stage allocation problem simultaneously. As indicated earlier, this amounts to solving the intertemporal model with respect to each argument in the direct utility function, i.e., finding the optimal path for each x_{it} and adding up optimal expenditures $p_{it} x_{it}$ over all i in each period, to find the intertemporally optimal budgets (total expenditures). This is the approach followed by Lluch (1974) and Phlips (1974, Chapter X).

Another attitude is to claim that decentralization is still possible, simply because the (static) concept of decentralizability defined earlier is too narrowly defined when it requires the information of current prices to be sufficient to explain demand behavior once the budget is known. Why shouldn't past purchases (determined by past prices) be allowed to enter the problem through their impact on stocks?

Blackorby et al. (1975) introduced asymmetric restrictions on the structure of the utility functions. One can expect these to be particularly interesting in an intertemporal setting, because time runs in one direction. Myopic models could then be rationalized on the basis of what Phlips (1975) called "forward" separability (as distinguished from "backward" separability). More formally, write equation (15) as

$$U = U[u_{T-1}(x_{T-1}, u_{T-2}), w_{FT}]$$

with $u_t = u_t(x_t, u_{t-1})$ for $t \leq T - 1$. Once an intertemporal allocation of the budgets is determined in a first stage (a difficult problem compared to the assignment of the budgets considered in Section II,A), the instantaneous utility function can then be maximized subject to the familiar budget constraint. For the allocation of the preassigned budget among the different commodities, all one needs is current prices and past purchases, which is precisely the additional information used in dynamic demand systems.

But even in an intertemporal setting with time running in one direction, asymmetric separability imposes severe restrictions on the endogenous process in which tastes are formed. Forward separability implies, by definition, that the effect of past purchases can be aggregated into one indicator, u_{t-1}, which, in the terminology used earlier, can be considered as a stock. Indeed, both the physical or psychological stocks and the instantaneous utility level of the previous period depend on past behavior and determine (together with current purchases) the instantaneous utility of the current period. But unlike the state variable approach, which associates one state variable with each commodity, forward separability channels all particular dynamic links through the same gate. This special structure of the intertemporal utility function introduces dynamic elements and yet allows myopia in the allocation of a given budget. Of course, foresightedness will be required in the choice of an optimal intertemporal plan for the budgets.

Although myopic behavior in the allocation of a given budget can thus be justified, even if current tastes change endogenously, forward separability will in many instances be too restrictive to deal with the dynamic links in the preference structure. Indeed, in the dynamic instantaneous utility functions introduced in Section I, each commodity is linked to the past in its own way. In that case, even in allocating a preassigned budget, the rational consumer has to look both backward and forward. Unlike the case with forward separability, myopia in the allocation of the budget becomes naive. Or, alternatively, forward separability could be said to be present only if the instantaneous utility function were treated as if it represented an intertemporal preference ordering, which is of course hard to swallow: the rational consumer will be aware of the effect of current purchases on future tastes.

The attitude taken in this chapter is to fully recognize the absence of separability and yet to point at the possibility of decentralizing. This possibility arises, as shown in Spinnewyn (1979a) when intertemporal models with state variables can be made formally equivalent with intertemporal models without state variables, so that rational habit formation ceases to be a problem *sui generis*.

When such formal equivalence exists, it is worth being investigated. First of all, it is a fact that all empirical knowledge of demand behavior, whether static or dynamic, is based on the assumption of decentralizability. If the latter can be shown also to exist in the dynamic case, then the myopic models of Section I can be given a sound theoretical basis. Second, decentralizability simplifies considerably the empirical implementation of intertemporal models.

Formal equivalence can be obtained whenever it is possible (1) to rewrite the nonseparable intertemporal utility function so that it becomes weakly separable with respect to new variables, and (2) to redefine accordingly the cost of consumption and consequently to enlarge the wealth constraint in such a way that the latter takes the same form as the static wealth constraint defined in equation (17). The only difficulty is to find the appropriate change in variables.

The reader will have guessed that the appropriate change in variables is to write the utility function in terms of $z_{it} = x_{it} - \gamma_{it}$. As for the enlargement of the wealth constraint under rational habit formation, we closely follow the procedure outlined in Spinnewyn (1979). The generalization presented here specializes to the type of dynamic models described in Section I.

We start from

$$x_{it} = s_{it} - (1 - \delta_i)s_{it-1} \tag{27}$$

$$\gamma_{it} = \theta_i + \alpha_i s_{it-1} \tag{28}$$

$$w_{Ft+1} = (1 + r_t)(w_{Ft} + Y_t - y_t) \tag{29}$$

How is the wealth equation (29) to be enlarged to take account of rational habit formation?

First rewrite it as

$$p'_t x_t + i_t w_{Ft+1} = w_{Ft} + Y_t \tag{29a}$$

where $i_t = 1/(1 + r_t)$. Now, let the n-vector μ_{t+1} be the value attached to induced consumption from $t + 1$ onward per unit of stock. As there is no distinction between physical and psychological stocks, μ_{it+1} is defined as either the value attached to a stock of habits, when good i is perishable, or the value of a combined physical and psychological stock, when i is durable and habit forming. Then

$$\mu'_{t+1}s_t = \mu'_{t+1} x_t + \mu'_{t+1}(I - \hat{\delta})s_{t-1} \tag{30}$$

is to be added to the value of financial wealth at $t + 1$, with a corresponding subtraction, so that Eq. (29a) remains valid. This gives

$$c'_t x_t + i_t(w_{Ft+1} + \mu'_{t+1}s_t) = w_{Ft} + Y_t + i_t\mu'_{t+1}(I - \hat{\delta})s_{t-1} \tag{31}$$

in which $c'_t = p'_t - i_t\mu'_{t+1}$ is the corrected price vector of the quantities purchased. It can be interpreted as a vector of rental prices for units of physical or psychological stocks. In allocating his budget, the rational consumer uses c_t', not p_t', to evaluate the cost of his purchases.

Now rewrite equation (31) in terms of committed expenditures. To this effect, it suffices to subtract $c_t'\gamma_t$ on both sides, using Eq. (28) and remembering that $z_t = x_t - \gamma_t$. This gives

$$c_t'z_t + i_t(w_{Ft+1} + \mu_{t+1}'s_t) = w_{Ft} + Y_t + [i_t\mu_{t+1}'(I - \hat{\delta}) - c_t'\alpha]s_{t-1} - c_t'\theta$$

or

$$c_t'z_t + i_t(w_{Ft+1} + \mu_{t+1}'s_t) = w_{Ft} + Y_t + \mu_t's_{t-1} - c_t'\theta \qquad (32)$$

where

$$\mu_t' = i_t\mu_{t+1}'(I - \hat{\delta}) - c_t'\hat{\alpha} \qquad (33)$$

Finally, we introduce human wealth w_{Ht} into the wealth equation. Define w_{Ht} by the recurrence relation

$$w_{HT} = (Y_t - c_t'\theta) + i_t w_{Ht+1} \qquad (34)$$

$c_t'\theta$ is the cost of exogenous physically necessary consumption. Equation (34) thus defines human wealth as the discounted sum of the excess of exogenous labor income over the cost of exogenous physically necessary consumption. Now add $i_t w_{Ht+1}$ to both sides of (32) to obtain

$$c_t'z_t + i_t(w_{Ft+1} + w_{Ht+1} + \mu_{t+1}'s_t) = w_{Ft} + w_{Ht} + \mu_t's_{t-1}$$

or

$$
\begin{aligned}
w_{t+1} &= (1 + r_t)(w_t - c_t'z_t) \\
&= (1 + r_t)(w_t - e_t)
\end{aligned} \qquad (35)
$$

where total wealth w_t is defined as

$$w_t = w_{Ft} + w_{Ht} + \mu_t's_{t-1} \qquad (36)$$

and

$$e_t = c_t'z_t \qquad (37)$$

is now supernumerary income evaluated at the true prices c_t'.

What is the relationship between these true prices and the purchase prices p_t'? Consider Eq. (33), which defines μ_t', and remember that $c_t' = p_t' - i_t\mu_{t+1}'$. On combining these two equations, we see that

$$\mu_t' = i_t\mu_{t+1}'(I - \hat{\delta} + \hat{\alpha}) - p_t'\hat{\alpha}$$

If, furthermore, prices and the rate of interest are expected to be constant, then the rational consumer evaluates μ' as

$$\mu' = -p'\hat{\alpha}[I - i(I + \hat{\alpha} - \hat{\delta})]^{-1}$$

and c' as

$$c' = p'[I + \hat{\alpha}(rI + \hat{\delta} - \hat{\alpha})^{-1}]$$

In other words, for each commodity i in the system, c_{it} is evaluated as

$$c_{it} = p_{it}\varepsilon_i \tag{38}$$

with

$$\varepsilon_i = \frac{r + \delta_i}{r + \delta_i - \alpha_i}$$

Notice that the correction factor ε_i is very close to the myopic factor $\delta_i/(\delta_i - \alpha_i)$, which transforms the parameters β_i and θ_i of the short-run dynamic Stone–Geary utility function Eq. (10) into the corresponding parameters of the utility function, which rationalizes the myopic linear expenditure system in the long run.

It is illuminating to consider the value of μ' and c' under the assumption of total and immediate adjustment (such that $I = \hat{\delta} - \hat{\alpha}$). Then

$$\mu' = p'(I - \hat{\delta})$$

i.e., μ_i is the value of the depreciated stock of durable i, while

$$c_{it} = p_{it}\left[\frac{r + \delta_i}{1 + r}\right]$$

i.e., c_i is the discrete version of the traditional rental price of durable goods. This provides a justification for also interpreting c_i as a rental price when there is habit formation as in equation (31).

Note, finally, that μ_i is positive when $\alpha_i < 0$ (the stock effect dominates) and negative when $\alpha_i > 0$ (habit formation dominates) in the general case.

C.   The Linear Expenditure System with Rational Habit Formation

Equation (35) is in the same form as the static wealth constraint (17). It is also in the form required for an application of the usual dynamic programming techniques, if we take e_t as the budget whose optimal path is to be determined and c_t as the vector of true prices. Suppose the instantaneous indirect utility function of a rational consumer is Stone–Geary

$$v_t = \ln e_t - \sum_i \beta_i \ln c_{it}$$
$$= \ln(e_t / \prod_i c_{it}^{\beta_i})$$

so that the optimal time path for e_t is found by maximizing

$$\sum_{t=0}^{T-1}\left[\rho^t\left(\ln e_t - \sum_i \beta_i \ln c_{it}\right)\right] + \rho^T \xi_T \ln w_T \tag{39}$$

This indirect intertemporal utility function belongs to the logarithmic Bergson family and has therefore all the properties required. In particular, it is separable in e_t. A straightforward application of the recursive procedure outlined in Section II.A gives, in the limit, $\xi = (1 - \rho)$ or

$$\dot{e}_t = \xi w_t = (1 - \rho)w_t \tag{40}$$

The single dot notation indicates that the consumer behaves rationally, i.e., looks both forward and backward.

The linear expenditure system with rational habit formation takes the form

$$\dot{x}_{it} = \gamma_{it} + \frac{\dot{\beta}_i}{c_{it}} \dot{e}_t \tag{41}$$

where $\dot{\beta}_i$ is the marginal propensity to consume commodity i of a rational consumer who accumulates stocks and habits.

D. Observational Equivalence with Myopic Models

The variables $\dot{e}_t$ and c_{it} are not observable. However, the linear expenditure system with rational habit formation is easily transformed into a system that is observationally equivalent with the myopic linear expenditure system. Multiply system (41) by p_{it}, use (38) to obtain

$$p_{it} \dot{x}_{it} = p_{it} \gamma_{it} + \frac{\dot{\beta}_i}{\varepsilon_i} \dot{e}_t$$

and sum over all commodities, so that

$$\sum_i p_{it} \dot{x}_{it} = \sum_i p_{it} \gamma_{it} + \dot{e}_t \sum_i \left(\frac{\dot{\beta}_i}{\varepsilon_i}\right)$$

or

$$\dot{e}_t = (y_t - \sum_i p_{it} \gamma_{it})/\sum_i \left(\frac{\dot{\beta}_i}{\varepsilon_i}\right)$$

Then

$$p_{it} \dot{x}_{it} = p_{it} \gamma_{it} + \beta_i (\dot{y}_t - \sum_j p_{jt}\gamma_{jt}) \tag{42}$$

with

$$\beta_i = \left(\frac{\dot{\beta}_i}{\varepsilon_i}\right)/\sum_j \left(\frac{\dot{\beta}_j}{\varepsilon_j}\right) \tag{43}$$

System (42) is equivalent with the myopic demand version of the linear expenditure system discussed in Section I.B. The instantaneous maximization of $u = \sum_i \beta_i \ln(x_{it} - \gamma_{it})$ subject to $y_t = p_t' x_t$, where y_t is on its optimal path (i.e., $y_t = \dot{y}_t$) is thus equivalent to the maximization of $\sum_{\tau=t}^{T} \rho^{T-\tau} \sum_i \dot{\beta}_i \ln(x_{i\tau} - \gamma_{i\tau})$ plus the utility of final bequests, subject to the wealth equation (35), if the consumer's expectations are constant and the horizon is sufficiently far away.

Observational equivalence (i.e., equivalence in terms of a regression model) is obtained when system (42) is rewritten as

$$p_{it} x_{it} = p_{it} \gamma_{it} + \beta_i (y_t - \sum_j p_{jt} \gamma_j) + \eta_{it} \qquad (44)$$

where η_{it} is an error term, on the assumption that $y_t = \dot{y}_t$. Under this assumption, the condition that $\sum_i \eta_{it} = 0$, with the implied singularity of the contemporaneous variance–covariance matrix, can be maintained. However, if $y_t \neq \dot{y}_t$, then this condition ceases to be applicable, as the budget constraint has no longer to be satisfied exactly. And the value of $\sum_i \eta_{it}$ could be interpreted as an estimate of the "intertemporal" error made by the observed consumers, to the extent that they are not entirely rational in solving their first-stage allocation problem. There seems to be no possibility of making y_t endogenous. Nor is it possible to estimate $\dot{e}_t$, using (40) as an estimating equation, simultaneously with system (44), as $\dot{e}_t$ is defined in terms of true prices c_t. The logic of decentralizability suggests, however, that it is observed y_t that has to be allocated, whether it contains an intertemporal error or not.

Equation (43) is homogeneous of degree zero in $\dot{\beta}_i$. We can therefore compute $\dot{\beta}_i$ as

$$\dot{\beta}_i = \frac{\varepsilon_i \beta_i}{\sum_i \varepsilon_i \beta_i} \qquad (45)$$

where β_i is the short-run marginal propensity to consume that is estimated in the myopic linear expenditure system. Conversely, β_i can be reinterpreted as reflecting the behavior of a rational rather than a myopic consumer: this consumer can be thought of as transforming his true $\dot{\beta}_i$ coefficients into β_i when confronted with purchase prices p_t instead of correct prices c_t.

When confronted with purchase prices p_t, the consumer will give relatively less weight, in the myopic short-run utility function, to commodities that are strongly habit forming (high α_i) or for which habits are wearing off slowly (small δ_i). He knows that future consumption of these commodities will be stimulated through habit formation, so that he reduces the short-run marginal propensities to consume. The converse is true for commodities that are weakly habit forming (low α_i) and for which habits are wearing off quickly (high δ_i) or for which the stock effect dominates (α_i is negative). In other words, the rational consumer corrects the inadequate information provided by the observed budget constraint by readjusting the short-run marginal propensities to consume.

The reader may wonder whether the other structural parameters (α, δ_i and θ_i) of the dynamic linear expenditure system remain unchanged under rational habit formation. In fact they do. To see this, remember that the estimating equations of the myopic linear expenditure system are nothing but the first-order conditions, so that the marginal utility of money λ_t appears explicitly, and remember that the budget constraint is imposed through an iteration on λ_t. These equations are

$$x_{it} = K_{i0} + K_{i1} x_{it-1} + K_{i2} \left(\frac{1}{\lambda_t p_{it}}\right) + K_{i3} \left(\frac{1}{\lambda_{t-1} p_{it-1}}\right) \tag{46}$$

On the other hand, the marginal utility of money is

$$\lambda_t = \frac{1}{y_t - p'_t \gamma_t} \tag{47}$$

Using Eq. (41), which defines the rational linear expenditure system, we find the rational $\dot{\lambda}_t$ to be

$$\dot{\lambda}_t = \frac{1}{\dot{e}_t} \tag{48}$$

$$= \sum_i \left(\frac{\dot{\beta}_i}{\varepsilon_i}\right) / (y_t - p'_t \gamma_t) = \sum_i \left(\frac{\dot{\beta}_i}{\varepsilon_i}\right) \lambda_t$$

$\dot{\lambda}_t$ is thus proportional to λ_t. Inserting $\dot{\lambda}_t$ in the estimating equations (46), and replacing p_{it} and p_{it-1}, by c_{it} and c_{it-1}, we see that only K_{i2} and K_{i3} are affected, and that they change in the same proportion. A look at the equations that define the structural parameters in terms of the regression coefficients will convince the reader that α_i, θ_i, and δ_i are unchanged:

$$\delta_i = \frac{2(K_{i2} + K_{i3})}{K_{i2} - K_{i3}} \qquad \alpha_i = \delta_i - \frac{2(1 - K_{i1})}{1 + K_{i1}}$$

$$\beta_i = \frac{K_{i2} - K_{i3}}{1 + K_{i1}} \qquad \theta_i = \frac{K_{i0}(K_{i2} - K_{i3})}{(1 + K_{i1})(K_{i2} + K_{i3})} \tag{49}$$

All information about the future is thus summarized in the $\dot{\beta}$ coefficients. And all these coefficients are needed to define $\dot{\lambda}_t$. This multiplier can thus be said to subsume all future information. An analogous idea was used by Heckman and MaCurdy (1979) in their analysis of a life cycle model of female labor supply.

Table 1 reproduces estimates of the structural parameters β_i, α_i and δ_i. These estimates are taken from Phlips and Pieraerts (1979) and were computed using Abbott and Ashenfelter's corrected data (see Pencavel,

Table 1

Commodity group	β	α	δ
Durables	0.261	0.353	0.712
Food	0.248	0.014	0.245
Clothing	0.078	0.148	0.168
Other nondurables	0.089	0.387	0.511
Housing services	0.082	0.692	0.778
Transportation services	0.029	−0.012	0.038
Other services	0.102	0.170	0.148
Leisure	0.108	0.553	0.719

1979) on expenditures for seven commodity groups and on hours worked in the U.S. during the period 1929–1967.

Table 2 gives the corresponding values of ε and $\dot{\beta}$ for $r^* = 0.03, 0.05$, and 0.10.

The values taken by ε are surprisingly high. "Transportation services" is the only item for which the user cost is lower than the purchase price. Our interpretation is as follows. We notice, first, that the consumer's choice is limited, in every period, since he has first to satisfy habitual (i.e., committed) consumption. The true prices (user costs) are used to allocate uncommitted expenditures. On the other hand, the rational consumer recognizes that current consumption will induce future habitual consumption through its effect on future habit stocks. He knows therefore that, in his free choice for consumption now, he commits himself to consumption in the future. If a household switches from a black and white to a color TV set, or if it buys a second car, or if the housewife enters the labor market, it will be difficult to abandon the new consumption pattern, even when the car or the TV set has to be replaced, or when the family situation has changed. The rational consumer will

Table 2

Commodity group	$r^* = 0.03$		$r^* = 0.05$		$r^* = 0.10$	
	ε	$\dot{\beta}$	ε	$\dot{\beta}$	ε	$\dot{\beta}$
Durables	1.909	0.109	1.864	0.167	1.770	0.209
Food	1.054	0.057	1.050	0.090	1.043	0.117
Clothing	3.990	0.068	3.130	0.084	2.239	0.079
Other nondurables	3.508	0.069	3.220	0.100	2.725	0.111
Housing services	6.968	0.125	6.090	0.172	4.722	0.175
Transportation services	0.851	0.005	0.881	0.009	0.921	0.012
Other services	21.234	0.476	6.974	0.246	3.163	0.146
Leisure	3.821	0.090	3.560	0.132	3.079	0.150

therefore think twice and calculate the future costs of adopting a new consumption pattern.

What is the influence of the (real) rate of interest? Let r^* pass from 3 to, respectively, 5 or 10 percent: the rational correction factors ε_i tend systematically to 1 for all commodity groups. Less weight is given to the cost of future habit formation: the present value of future costs is lower.

When confronted with purchase prices instead of user costs, the rational consumer readjusts the weights in his myopic short-run utility function. For most commodity groups, and especially for "food" and "durables," β_i is larger than $\dot{\beta}_i$ when the real rate of interest is 3 percent. The reverse is true for two groups: "housing" and "other services," for which ε_i is particularly high. For these two groups, the user cost c_i is relatively much higher than the purchase price p_i used in the estimation of the myopic system. The cost of future habit formation is, indeed, important in expenditures on "housing services" and on "other services," which include medical care, cleaning, movies, and higher education. The relative importance of the marginal propensity to consume "other services" of the rational consumer who faces true user costs is impressive. Welfare comparisons made in terms of the vector $\dot{\beta}$ should lead to conclusions that are rather different from those made on the basis of the vector β.

There is a considerable reshuffling of the differences between β_i and $\dot{\beta}_i$, however, when other values of the real rate of interest are considered. As of $r^* = 0.05$, there are five commodity groups for which β_i is smaller than $\dot{\beta}_i$: "clothing," "other nondurables," "housing services," "other services," and "leisure." Given the normalization rule $\Sigma_i \beta_i = 1$, the number of commodities for which the *relative* difference between user cost and purchase price is higher increases when the real rate of interest is higher.

The reader will have noticed that our reasoning starts from a given $\dot{\beta}_i$, which is readjusted to a particular β_i for a given constant real rate of interest and a given historical sequence of purchase prices. As it is β_i that is parametrized, we had to do our computations the other way around, i.e., from estimated β's to alternative $\dot{\beta}$'s.

E. Consistency and Time Preference

Time preference is implied in the postulates set up by Koopmans (1960) to derive the intertemporal utility function, and these postulates do "*not* imply that, after one period has elapsed, the ordering then applicable to the 'then' future will necessarily be the same as that now applicable to the 'present' future" (Koopmans *et al.*, 1964). The rational consumer is "impatient," whether his tastes change or not. But what about consistency?

Consistency is automatically achieved when future behavior is pre-committed, even if utility is maximized instantaneously (as in the case of naive habit formation). And one way to achieve commitment is to have what Blackorby, Nissen, Primont, and Russell (1973) call a preference inheritance mechanism according to which preference of the next generation (or time period) are imposed by the previous generation (or period). Such a mechanism is in fact implied in the state variable approach, as the preferences today are endogenously determined by the consumption decisions made yesterday. One could say that the habit forming consumer is on a track and cannot get off it. The conditions for consistency for a naive consumer as well as for a "sophisticated" (i.e., rational) consumer are simply not applicable, because they refer to consistent planning in the absence of commitment.

Inconsistency can arise in the state variable approach only through the presence of a discount function, in addition to the inheritance mechanism described by the instantaneous utility function. It is only if the discount function changes that inconsistency arises. If we continue to assume an exponential discount function, this implies a change in the rate of time preference γ used in successive planning, given that $\rho = 1/(1 + \gamma)$.

Since Fisher (1930), we know that γ is a decreasing function of total consumption and an increasing function of the riskiness of future events. With a data set spanning a period as long as 1929–1967, in which there was a great depression, a world war and a Korean war, the rate of time preference must have jumped quite significantly. Can we verify this?

Optimal control theory shows (Phlips, 1974, Chapter 10) that the rate of change of the Lagrangian multiplier associated with the wealth constraint is a function of the rate of time preference and of the rate of interest. Given estimates of the multiplier and given the real rate of interest, it should thus be possible to estimate γ.

This multiplier is nothing but our rational λ_t. Remember also that our consumer is maximizing

$$\left(\frac{1}{a}\right) e_t^a + \beta(t) \, \xi_{t+1}^{a-1} \left(\frac{1}{a}\right) w_{t+1}^a$$

with respect to e_t and w_t, subject to the wealth constraint

$$e_t + i_t \, w_{t+1} = w_t$$

as can be seen on replacing y_t and w_{Ft} by e_t and w_t, respectively, in equation (21). In terms of the Lagrange multiplier associated with the wealth constraint, this maximization implies, at any t

$$e_t^{a-1} = \dot{\lambda}_t$$

which leads to Eq. (48) when $a = 0$, and

$$\beta(t)\xi_{t+1}^{a-1} w_{t+1}^{a-1} = i_t \dot{\lambda}_t \tag{50}$$

The current value, at t, of the optimal value of utility is

$$\xi_t^{a-1}\left(\frac{1}{a}\right) w_t^a$$

so that

$$\dot{\lambda}_t = \frac{\partial}{\partial w_t}\left[\left(\frac{1}{a}\right)\xi_t^{a-1} w_t^a\right] = \xi_t^{a-1} w_t^{a-1}$$

and

$$\dot{\lambda}_{t+1} = \xi_{t+1}^{a-1} w_{t+1}^{a-1}$$

Substituting into equation (50) yields

$$\begin{aligned}
\dot{\lambda}_{t+1} &= \frac{1}{\beta(t)} i_t \dot{\lambda}_t \\
&= \rho^{-1}\left[\frac{\pi(c_{t+1})}{\pi(c_t)}\right]^a i_t \dot{\lambda}_t \\
&= \frac{1 + \gamma_t}{1 + r_t}\left[\frac{\pi(c_{t+1})}{\pi(c_t)}\right]^a \dot{\lambda}_t
\end{aligned} \tag{51}$$

In terms of the real rate of interest r^*, and for $a = 0$, this result can be rewritten as

$$\dot{\lambda}_{t+1} = \frac{1 + \gamma_t}{1 + r^*}\left[\frac{\pi(c_t)}{\pi(c_{t+1})}\right]\dot{\lambda}_t \tag{51a}$$

with the implication that

$$\gamma_t = (1 + r^*)\left(\frac{\dot{\lambda}_{t+1}}{\dot{\lambda}_t}\right)\left(\frac{\pi(c_{t+1})}{\pi(c_t)}\right) - 1 \tag{52}$$

We prefer to use (51a) rather than equation (51) because the nominal rate of interest on human and nonhuman wealth (r_t) is very hard to estimate, while the real rate of interest r^* can be assumed constant. Furthermore, we know that the price index is equal to

$$\pi(c_t) = \prod_i c_{it}^{\dot{\beta}_i}$$

when the utility function is Stone–Geary. All we need in addition is a time series $\dot{\lambda}_t$.

For r^*, we choose alternative constant values of 0.03, 0.05, and 0.10 as before. The series $\dot{\lambda}_t$ is proportional to λ_t according to Eq. (48), so that there is no point in computing $\dot{\lambda}_t$ separately, given that the marginal utility of money (here of full income) is defined up to a monotonic transformation. One series λ_t results from the iteration used in the estimation of the parameters in Table 1. This iteration refers to the budget constraint $\tilde{y}_t = \Sigma_i p_{it} x_{it} - p_{\ell t} h_t$, given the absence of date on leisure. (The variable h_t measures the number of hours worked and $p_{\ell t}$ is the observed wage rate.) The λ_t series we are interested in is associated with full income $y_t = \Sigma_i p_{it} x_{it} + p_{\ell t} \ell_t$, where $\ell_t = T - h_t$ represents leisure. This λ_t is defined as

$$\lambda_t = \frac{1}{\tilde{y}_t - \sum_{i=1}^{7} p_{it}\, \gamma_{it} + p_{\ell t}\gamma_{ht}} \tag{53}$$

where $\gamma_{ht} = T - \gamma_{\ell t}$ is the maximum number of hours one is ready to work. The reader will readily check that

$$\tilde{y}_t - \sum_{i=1}^{7} p_{it}\, \gamma_{it} + p_{\ell t}\, \gamma_{ht} = y_t - \sum_{i=1}^{7} p_{it}\, \gamma_{it} - p_{\ell t}\, \gamma_{lt}$$

so that the λ_t series defined by Eq. (53) is identical with the λ_t series obtained in the iterative estimation procedure.

Table 3 reproduces the λ_t series and the corresponding γ_t and ρ_t values for r^* equal to 0.03, 0.05, and 0.10. When r^* is equal to 3 or 5 percent, many rates of time preference are negative. This is incompatible with the axioms of intertemporal consumer choice, which imply "impatience" and therefore $\gamma > 0$. On the contrary, a real rate of interest of 10 percent is compatible with impatience for most of the years in the sample. We interpret this to mean that 10 percent is closer to the true value of the real rate of interest than 3 or 5 percent. In other words, we interpret our computations as an indirect way of estimating both the real rate of interest on human and nonhuman wealth (corrected for habit formation) and the rate of time preference. It should be clear, also, that equation (51) establishes the correct theoretical causal relationship: it is the difference between the rate of time preference and the (nominal) rate of interest that determines the time shape of λ.

With these provisos in mind, we may have a closer look at γ and ρ, given $r^* = 0.10$ and given our λ_t series. Notice first that λ climbed to impressive heights during the Second World War. This is due to the fact that the opportunity cost of leisure is included in our budget constraint and that working hours were pushed to the psychologically admissible upper limit in the war effort: h is practically equal to γ_h in 1943 (see

Table 3

Year	λ_t	$r^* = 0.03$		$r^* = 0.05$		$r^* = 0.10$	
		γ_t	ρ_t	γ_t	ρ_t	γ_t	ρ_t
1929	1.00000	0.42	0.70	0.44	0.70	0.50	0.67
1930	1.40330	0.14	0.87	0.16	0.86	0.21	0.83
1931	1.69213	0.21	0.83	0.22	0.82	0.27	0.78
1932	2.24272	0.22	0.82	0.26	0.80	0.32	0.76
1933	2.85584	0.03	0.97	0.05	0.95	0.10	0.91
1934	2.65407	0.03	0.97	0.05	0.95	0.10	0.91
1935	2.63643	0.02	0.98	0.04	0.96	0.09	0.92
1936	2.57572	0.08	0.93	0.10	0.91	0.15	0.87
1937	2.58247	−0.12	1.13	−0.10	1.12	−0.06	1.07
1938	2.21864	0.00	1.00	0.02	0.98	0.07	0.93
1939	2.17071	0.04	0.96	0.06	0.94	0.12	0.90
1940	2.16617	0.22	0.82	0.25	0.80	0.32	0.76
1941	2.40737	1.29	0.44	1.37	0.42	1.50	0.40
1942	4.86100	1.11	0.47	1.16	0.46	1.26	0.44
1943	9.30103	−0.42	1.73	−0.41	1.70	−0.38	1.62
1944	4.87569	−0.59	2.45	−0.58	2.39	−0.56	2.28
1945	1.87019	−0.53	2.11	−0.52	2.10	−0.50	2.01
1946	0.79195	0.11	0.90	0.12	0.89	0.17	0.85
1947	0.76857	0.10	0.91	0.13	0.89	0.19	0.84
1948	0.76314	−0.04	1.04	−0.03	1.03	0.01	0.99
1949	0.71295	−0.02	1.02	0.00	1.00	0.05	0.95
1950	0.66638	0.28	0.78	0.30	0.77	0.37	0.73
1951	0.77966	0.03	0.97	0.04	0.96	0.09	0.92
1952	0.75297	−0.06	1.07	−0.05	1.05	−0.01	1.01
1953	0.66059	−0.09	1.10	−0.08	1.08	−0.03	1.04
1954	0.57339	−0.02	1.02	−0.01	1.01	0.03	0.97
1955	0.53193	0.06	0.94	0.08	0.93	0.13	0.89
1956	0.53023	−0.01	1.02	0.00	1.00	0.05	0.95
1957	0.48991	−0.04	1.04	−0.02	1.02	0.03	0.97
1958	0.44744	0.03	0.97	0.04	0.96	0.09	0.92
1959	0.43314	0.05	0.95	0.07	0.93	0.12	0.89
1960	0.43359	0.00	1.00	0.02	0.98	0.07	0.94
1961	0.41567	0.01	0.99	0.03	0.97	0.08	0.92
1962	0.40331	−0.01	1.01	0.01	0.99	0.05	0.95
1963	0.38064	−0.01	1.01	0.01	0.99	0.05	0.95
1964	0.35706	0.01	0.99	0.03	0.97	0.07	0.93
1965	0.34360	0.06	0.94	0.08	0.93	0.12	0.89
1966	0.34249	0.06	0.94	0.08	0.93	0.13	0.89
1967	0.34062	—	—	—	—	—	—

Table III in Phlips, 1978). As a result, λ had to come down very sharply at the end of the war.

As for γ, we are glad to report that it is indeed very sensitive to economic conditions, as suggested by Irving Fisher. During the big depression, the rate of time preference was very high. With the recovery, it came down sharply. In 1941, Pearl Harbor made impatience rise again. The years 1943–1945 were years of forced savings, so that γ became negative: the average American consumer was forced to prefer the future to the present. After 4 "back-to-normal" years, the Korean war produced another sharp rise, possibly followed in 1952–1953 by a compensating movement in savings. Since 1954, the rate of time preference stabilized at values somewhere between 0 and 13 percent. The negative value of γ in 1937 seems hard to explain.

The corresponding movements of ρ can be followed in the last column of Table 3. When $\rho = 1$, $1 - \rho$ is no doubt equal to 0. According to equation (40), the rational consumer then reduces $\dot{e}$, his uncommitted expenditures, to 0 and restricts himself to committed expenditures. A higher rate of time preference implies a smaller ρ and therefore a higher level of uncommitted expenditures.

ACKNOWLEDGMENTS

C.O.R.E. (Université Catholique de Louvain) and Katholieke Universiteit Leuven. We are grateful to N. Kiefer for helpful discussions and to D. Van Grunderbeeck for cheerful computational assistance. The second author acknowledges financial assistance by N.F.W.O.

REFERENCES

Abbott, M., and O. Ashenfelter (1976). Labor supply, commodity demand, and the allocation of time, *Review of Economic Studies 43*, 389–411.

Blackorby, C., D. Nissen, D. Primont, and R. R. Russell (1973). Consistent intertemporal decision making, *Review of Economic Studies 40*, 239–248.

Blackorby, C., D. Primont, and R. R. Russell (1975). Budgeting, decentralization, and aggregation, *Annals of Economic and Social Measurement 4*, 23–44.

Brown, J. A. C., and A. Deaton (1972). Surveys in applied economics: models of consumer behaviour, *Economic Journal 82*, 1145–1236.

Chow, G. (1960). Statistical demand functions for automobiles and their use for forecasting, in *The Demand for Durable Goods*, A. C. Harberger (ed.), Chicago: University of Chicago Press.

Eisner, R., and R. H. Strotz (1963). Determinants of business investment. In *Impacts of Monetary Policy*, Commission on Money and Credit, Englewood Cliffs: Prentice-Hall.

Farrell, M. J. (1952). Irreversible demand functions, *Econometrica 20*, 171–186.

Fisher, I. (1930). *The Theory of Interest*, New York: Macmillan.

Gorman, W. (1971). *Two Stage Budgeting*, London School of Economics, mimeo.

Griliches, Z. (1967). Distributed lags: a survey, *Econometrica 35*, 16–49.

Hakansson, W. H. (1970). Optimal investment and consumption strategies under risk for a class of utility functions, *Econometrica 38*, 587–607.

Harberger, A. C. (1960). *The Demand for Durable Goods*, Chicago: University of Chicago Press.

Heckman, J. J., and T. E. MaCurdy (1979). *A Life Cycle Model of Female Labor Supply*, Center for Mathematical Studies in Business and Economics, University of Chicago, mimeo.

Houthakker, H. S., and L. D. Taylor (1970). *Consumer Demand in the United States 1929–1970*, 2nd ed., Cambridge, Mass.: Harvard University Press.

Koopmans, T. C. (1960). Stationary utility and impatience, *Econometrica 28*, 287–309.

Koopmans, T. C., P. A. Diamond, and R. E. Williamson (1964). Stationary utility and time perspective, *Econometrica 32*, 82–100.

Lluch, C. (1973). The extended linear expenditure system, *European Economic Review 4*, 21–32.

Lluch, C. (1974). Expenditures, savings and habit formation, *International Economic Review 15*, 786–797.

Lucas, R. E. (1967). Adjustment costs and the theory of supply, *Journal of Political Economy 75*, 321–334.

Marshall, A. (1920). *Principles of Economics*, 8th ed., London: Macmillan.

Mirrlees, J. (1974). Optimum allocation under uncertainty: the case of stationary returns to investment, In *Allocation Under Uncertainty*, J. Drèze (ed.), The International Economic Association, London: Macmillan.

Miller, B. (1974). Optimal consumption with a stochastic income stream, *Econometrica 42*, 253–266.

Pencavel, J. H. (1977). Constant-utility index numbers of real wages, *American Economic Review 67*, 91–100.

Pencavel, J. H. (1979). Constant-utility index numbers of real wages: revised estimates, *American Economic Review 69*, 240–243.

Phelps, E. (1962). The accumulation of risky capital: a sequential analysis, *Econometrica 30*, 729–743.

Phlips, L. (1974). *Applied Consumption Analysis*, Advanced Textbooks in Economics, Vol. 5, Amsterdam: North–Holland.

Phlips, L. (1975). Comment [on "Budgeting, decentralization, and aggregation"], *Annals of Economic and Social Measurement 4*, 45–48.

Phlips, L. (1978). The demand for leisure and money, *Econometrica 46*, 1025–1043.

Phlips, L., and P. Pieraerts (1979). Substitution versus addiction in the true index of real wages, *American Economic Review 69*, 977–982.

Pollak, R. A. (1975). The intertemporal cost of living index, *Annals of Economic and Social Measurement 4*, 179–195.

Pollak, R. A. (1978). Endogenous tastes in demand and welfare analysis, *American Economic Review 68*, 374–379.

Samuelson, P. A. (1969). Lifetime portfolio selection by dynamic stochastic programming, *Review of Economics and Statistics 51*, 239–246.

Spinnewyn, F. (1979). The cost of consumption and wealth in a model with habit formation, *Economics Letters 2*, 145–148.

Spinnewyn, F. (1981). Rational habit formation, *European Economic Review 15*, 91–110.

Stigler, G. J., and G. S. Becker (1977). De gustibus non est disputandum, *American Economic Review 67*, 76–90.

Taylor, L. D. (1974). On the dynamics of dynamic demand models, *Recherches Economiques de Louvain 40*, 21–31.

Taylor, L. D., and D. Weiserbs (1972). On the estimation of dynamic demand functions, *Review of Economics and Statistics 54*, 459–465.

Weiserbs, D. (1974). More about dynamic demand systems, *Recherches Economiques de Louvain 40*, 33–43.

MODELS FOR THE ANALYSIS OF LABOR FORCE DYNAMICS

C. J. Flinn and J. J. Heckman

ABSTRACT

This article presents new econometric methods for the empirical analysis of individual labor market histories. The techniques developed here extend previous work on continuous time models in four ways: (1) a structural economic interpretation of these models is presented; (2) time varying explanatory variables are introduced into the analysis in a general way; (3) unobserved heterogeneity components are permitted to be correlated across spells; and (4) a flexible model of duration dependence is presented that accommodates many previous models as a special case and that permits tests among competing specifications within a unified framework. In addition, longer range types of state dependence can be introduced into the model and their empirical importance tested with our model.

We contrast our methods with more conventional discrete time and regression procedures. The parameters of continuous time models are invariant to the sampling time unit used to record observations. Parameters of discrete time models defined for one time unit are not in general com-

Advances in Econometrics, volume 1, pages 35–95.
ISBN: 0-89232-138-5

parable to parameters of discrete time models defined for other time units. Two problems that plague the regression approach to analyzing duration data do not plague the likelihood approach advocated in this article. The first problem is that standard regression estimators are ill-equipped to deal with censored spells of events that arise in short panels. The second problem is that the regression approach cannot be readily adopted to accommodate time varying explanatory variables. The functional forms of regression functions depend on the time paths of the explanatory variables. *Ad hoc* solutions to this problem can make exogenous variables endogenous to the model and so can induce simultaneous equations bias. The likelihood approach advocated in this article can readily accommodate time varying explanatory variables.

Two sets of empirical results are presented. The first set is an analysis of employment and nonemployment data using both regression and maximum likelihood procedures. Standard regression methods are shown to perform rather poorly and to produce estimates wildly at variance with the estimates from our maximum likelihood procedure. The maximum likelihood estimates are more in accord with *a priori* theoretical notions. A major conclusion of this analysis is that the discrete time Markov model widely used in labor market analysis is inconsistent with the data.

The second set of empirical results is a test of the hypothesis that "unemployment" and "out of the labor force" are behaviorally different labor market states. Contrary to recent claims, we find that they are separate states for our sample of young men.

This article presents new econometric methods for the empirical analysis of individual labor market histories. Jovanovic's (1979) equilibrium model of worker turnover, the McCall–Mortensen search model, and Holt's (1979) model of labor force dynamics can be estimated, and crucial assumptions can be tested, with our techniques.

Our point of departure is the continuous time Markov model widely utilized in sociology (Coleman, 1964; Singer and Spilerman, 1976; Tuma *et al.*, 1979). The methodology developed here extends this work in four ways.

1. A structural economic interpretation of these models is provided. It is demonstrated that continuous time models naturally arise from optimal stopping rules that are the essence of a variety of economic problems (see Brock *et al.*, 1979, Flinn and Heckman, 1982).
2. The methods developed here admit the introduction of time varying explanatory variables into the analysis in a general way. Previous work either ignores such variables or utilizes special procedures for selected variables (e.g., Tuma *et al.*, 1979). Regression procedures for introducing time varying variables require special as-

sumptions that are unlikely to be realized in empirical work with labor force data.

We present a flexible empirical procedure that can be used to estimate duration models with time varying variables and demonstrate, both theoretically and empirically, the importance of being careful about the way time varying variables are introduced into duration models.

3. We extend previous work by introducing unobserved components ("heterogeneity") that are correlated across spells. Previous work assumes that unobserved components are independently distributed across spells—a strong and (as we demonstrate below for one data set) a counter-factual assumption.

4. We produce a flexible econometric model with general types of "state dependence." Many models commonly used in the analysis of continuous time data can be written as a special case of our model. Our framework can be used to test among competing model specifications.

We present empirical estimates of a two-state model of employment and nonemployment[1] in the youth labor market. We then proceed to test a critical assumption often used in labor market analysis: that "unemployment" and "out of the labor force" are legitimately separate labor market states. We find that this is so and that the behavioral equations that generate movement into and out of these states are fundamentally different.

The structure of the paper is as follows. In Section I we present a continuous time model of worker turnover. We demonstrate that this model can be used as a framework within which it is possible to estimate Jovanovic's model and many other models as well. The model is extended to allow for heterogeneity, time varying variables and general types of dependence of labor market transition rates on the individual's labor market history. The likelihood function for a two-state model is presented and solutions to the problem of correct treatment of the initial conditions of the process (sometimes called the "left censoring" problem) are offered.

Section II presents a discussion of the advantages of continuous time models over discrete time models. Certain limitations of continuous time models are discussed as well.

Section III discusses pitfalls that arise in using regression methods to analyze duration data. Two problems plague the regression approach. First, standard regression estimators are ill-equipped to deal with censored spells of events that arise in short panels. Failure to account for censored spells leads to biased estimates of the parameters of population regression functions. Second, the regression approach cannot be readily adapted to accommodate time varying explanatory variables. The functional forms of population regression functions depend on the time paths of the explanatory variables. *Ad hoc* solutions to this problem can make exogenous variables endogenous to the model and so can induce simultaneous equations bias.

Section IV presents two sets of empirical results. The first set is an analysis of employment and nonemployment data using both regression and maximum likelihood procedures. The second set is a test of the hypothesis that "unemployment" and "out of the labor force" are behaviorally different labor market states.

Appendix A presents a general multiple state, multiple spell likelihood function for a continuous time model. Appendix B presents the Weibull regression model used in some of our empirical work. Appendix C presents a simple economic model in which non-Markovian, long-term dependence between labor market outcomes is generated.

I.   CONTINUOUS TIME ECONOMETRIC MODELS OF TURNOVER AND UNEMPLOYMENT

A.   First Passage Time Distributions as an Economic Construct

We start with the influential model of Jovanovic (1979). A worker and firm together constitute a match. At the start of the match, both are uncertain about the productivity of the match but both learn about this productivity through a Bayesian learning algorithm. Both worker and firm start with the same prior about the productivity of the match. The prior does not depend on the previous labor market history of the worker because each match is unique: the productivity is not inherent in either the worker or the firm alone. The prior is then updated as the two partners continue their relationship.

Jovanovic (1979) demonstrates that a competitive equilibrium wage policy of the firm, which is also a socially optimal wage policy, is to pay all employees their expected marginal productivity where the expectation is computed with respect to the updated prior on the productivity of the worker–firm match. Workers, however, have alternatives. These alternatives include employment in other firms, participation in social transfer programs that subsidize unemployment, or nonmarket activity.

Jovanovic (1979) demonstrates that the worker and firm continue their match until the time when the perceived productivity of the match—$\hat{W}(t)$—falls below the reservation wage—$Q(t)$—defined as the monetary value of the best alternative to the current employment match. From his assumption of a Wiener wage growth process, $\hat{W}(t)$ is normally distributed. The length of the match is the first passage time to the event $\hat{W}(t)$ < $Q(t)$. The first time that this occurs is denoted t^*.

Another way to formulate this model is in terms of the index function model widely used in labor economics. Define

$$I(t) = \hat{W}(t) - Q(t).$$

When $I(t) < 0$, the worker leaves the firm (for a match to exist at all the initial value of the index function—$I(0)$—must be nonnegative). The first time in the match that $I(t)$ becomes negative—T^*—is termed the first passage time. (See Jovanovic, 1979:981, for the explicit formula for T^* in his model.)

Denote the distribution of T^* by $F(t^*)$ with density $f(t^*)$. For the moment, we ignore any dependence of this distribution on observed or unobserved components. The Jovanovic model implies a special functional form for this distribution. Moreover, it implies that the same distribution characterizes all spells of a worker's employment with firms, and that the outcomes of previous matches do not determine the distribution of the first passage time or exit time from a current match.

At this point it is useful to rewrite the Jovanovic model in a more convenient form. To do so requires the introduction of the hazard function, $h(t^*)$. The hazard function is a conditional density of first passage or exit time from a spell given the length of time spent in the spell. For expositional convenience assume that the distribution function is continuous and differentiable.

Let $g(T^*|T^* \geq t^*)$ be the conditional density of the first passage time T^* given that T^* is greater than or equal to t^*. From the definition, $1 - F(t^*)$ is the probability that the first passage occurs after t^*. Thus

$$h(t^*) = g(T^*|T^* \geq t^*) = \frac{f(t^*)}{1 - F(t^*)}$$

A given F implies a given h. Conversely, given h and our assumptions, F is uniquely defined because

$$h(t^*)dt^* = \frac{f(t^*)dt^*}{1 - F(t^*)}$$

so

$$F(t^*) = 1 - \exp[-\int_o^{t^*} h(u)du]$$

and also

$$f(t^*) = h(t^*)\exp[-\int_o^{t^*} h(u)du]. \qquad (1)$$

Duration dependence is said to exist if $[\partial h(t^*)]/\partial t^* \neq 0$. The only (continuous) density of exit times with no duration dependence is the exponential density. Thus if

$$f(t^*) = a\exp(-at^*) \quad a > 0$$
$$h(t^*) = a$$

and

$$\frac{\partial h(t^*)}{\partial t^*} = 0.$$

If $[\partial h(t^*)]/\partial t^* > 0$ there is positive duration dependence. In this case, the longer a worker has been in a job, the more likely he is to escape it in the next "interval" of time $(t^*, t^* + dt^*)$. If $[\partial h(t^*)]/\partial t^* < 0$, there is negative duration dependence, and the longer a worker has been in a job the less likely he is to exit it in the next "small interval" of time. Positive duration dependence during unemployment is associated with a declining reservation wage in search theory (e.g., Lippmann and McCall, 1976). Negative duration dependence during employment is associated with firm specific capital in the theory of turnover.

The hazard function arises as a simple and readily interpreted representation of the *structural conditional distribution of first passage times* in many models of labor market turnover. The Mortensen, Lippman, and McCall (Mortensen, 1970; Lippman and McCall, 1976) search theory also generates a structural distribution of first passage times. In the infinite horizon case with a stationary economic environment, the optimal search strategy is stationary so that there is no duration dependence in unemployment spells. A shrinking horizon (Gronau, 1971), systematic job search over different wage distributions (Salop, 1973), or declining assets in a utility maximizing job search model (with constant relative risk aversion, see Danforth, 1979 or Hall, Lippman, and McCall, 1979) all generate optimal stopping time distributions with positive duration dependence. The precise functional form of the hazard function is determined by the distribution of the random shocks facing the agents. Typically, these specific distributional assumptions are imposed as a matter of mathematical convenience in formulating a theory *and* are not, themselves, justified by an appeal to theory. For this reason, it is important to develop a flexible approach to estimation that does not require special functional forms to secure estimates. The approach to empirical model building that is developed in the following sections permits the analyst to explore the sensitivity of his estimates to special assumptions about functional forms.

Holt's (1970) model of labor market dynamics, while not derived from an explicit optimizing model (but see Toikka, 1976), offers another example of a continuous time labor market model. Holt (1970) works with the probability that an individual will be in one of a set of labor market states at a point in time. For convenience of exposition, we consider only a two-state model and we designate those states by e and u— shorthand notation for employment and unemployment. We assume all workers participate in the labor force at each point in time.

The first passage time or exit time distribution *from* the employment state is $f_e(t_e)$. The first passage time *from* the unemployment state is $f_u(t_u)$. The labor market history of an individual is governed by these two distributions. Given the initial state, labor market histories are generated by realizations of these first passage distributions. By assuming no duration dependence (or constant hazard) in either labor market state, Holt specializes these distributions to

$$f_e(t_e) = a_e\exp(-a_e t_e)$$
$$f_u(t_u) = a_u\exp(-a_u t_u).$$

Holt (1970) does not work with these duration distributions directly. Rather, he works with the probabilities that a person will be in each state at a point in time, $P_e(t)$ and $P_u(t)$ [$= 1 - P_e(t)$]. These probabilities can be derived from the densities of exit times by the following argument.

Suppose that a person is in state e at time t. This probability is $P_e(t)$. The conditional probability of exit from the state in time interval ($t + \Delta t$) is simply the hazard, ($a_e\Delta t$). Thus the probability of exit from the employment state to the unemployment state is ($a_e\Delta t$) and by a parallel argument the probability of exit from the unemployment state to the employment state is ($a_u\Delta t$). The conditional probability of remaining in the unemployment state is $1 - (a_u\Delta t)$. As $\Delta t \to 0$, the probability of remaining in the state becomes unity—a result consistent with fixed costs of changing state. Assuming that a_e and a_u are bounded positive numbers, the probability that a person is employed at time $t + \Delta t$ is

$$P_e(t + \Delta t) = (1 - a_e\Delta t)P_e(t) + (a_u\Delta t)P_u(t)$$

i.e., a person is employed at $t + \Delta t$ either by remaining employed [with probability $(1 - a_e\Delta t)$] or becoming employed from the unemployment state (which occurs with probability $a_u\Delta t$).

Rearranging terms

$$\frac{P_e(t + \Delta t) - P_e(t)}{\Delta t} = -a_e P_e(t) + a_u P_u(t).$$

Passing to the limit as $\Delta t \to 0$

$$\dot{P}_e(t) = -a_e P_e(t) + a_u P_u(t).$$

By a parallel argument

$$\dot{P}_u(t) = a_e P_e(t) - a_u P_u(t).$$

This system of equations generates a continuous time Markov process. Given the probability of being in each initial state, these equations can be solved to yield

$$P_e(t) = \frac{a_u}{a_e + a_u} + \left[P_e(0) - \frac{a_u}{a_e + a_u} \right] \exp[-(a_e + a_u)t]$$

and

$$P_u(t) = \frac{a_e}{a_e + a_u} + \left[P_u(0) - \frac{a_e}{a_e + a_u} \right] \exp[-(a_e + a_u)t].$$

As $t \to \infty$, these probabilities converge to constants irrespective of initial conditions. If the process starts in equilibrium [so $P_e(0) = a_u/(a_e + a_u)$ and $P_u(0) = a_e/(a_e + a_u)$], convergence is immediate.

The equilibrium probabilities have strong intuitive appeal. The larger the exit rate (or hazard) a_u from the unemployment state relative to the exit rate from the employment state a_e, the more likely is the person to be found in the employment state at a point in time. In equilibrium, the odds of finding someone in the employment state are a_u/a_e.

Burdett and Mortensen (1977) present a model of search and labor supply that is developed in terms of state probabilities. It is Markovian conditional on market wages and reservation wages. Knowledge of the hazard function and the initial state of the process is sufficient information to calculate the state probabilities. Thus the methods presented in this paper can be used with some modification (by incorporating wages) to estimate their model. Flinn and Heckman, 1982, present a general discussion of econometric models for analyzing dynamic models of unemployment and labor force turnover and wage growth.

B. Introducing Heterogeneity into the Model

Heterogeneity is defined as unmeasured and measured exogenous variables that differ among individuals and that may differ over time for the same individual. The term is usually reserved for unobservables as perceived by the data analyst. This article considers both types of variables. Uncorrected heterogeneity leads to biased estimates of duration dependence. If individual exit time distributions are exponential but individuals have different exponential parameters, estimated hazard functions exhibit negative duration dependence.

To see this, let the exit time density be $a[\exp(-at)]$. The density of a in the population is $g(a)$. Assuming an ideal data set in which all spells are completed, for a large random sample of individuals the estimated empirical distribution function of exit times $\hat{K}(t)$ converges to the population distribution $K(t)$ defined as

$$K(t) = 1 - \int \exp(-at)g(a)da.$$

The empirical hazard function converges to

$$h(t) = \frac{k(t)}{1 - K(t)} = \frac{\int a\exp(-at)g(a)da}{\int \exp(-at)g(a)da}$$

where

$$\frac{\partial h(t)}{\partial t} < 0$$

by the Cauchy–Schwartz inequality.[2] Intuitively, high a individuals are the first to exit the state, leaving behind the low a individuals. This shows up as negative duration dependence in the fitted distribution.

By a theorem of Barlow and Proschan (1965:37), if each individual exit time distribution exhibits negative duration dependence over the entire range of values of exit time, the fitted hazard function also exhibits negative duration dependence. The only way for the fitted hazard to exhibit positive duration dependence is for some (but not necessarily all) individual exit time distributions to have positive duration dependence over at least some portion of the domain of the distribution of exit times.

This paper controls for heterogeneity in observed and unobserved variables by parameterizing the hazard function in a general way. The strategy adopted here is to write

$$h(t) = \exp[Z(t + \tau)\beta + \gamma_1\frac{t^{\lambda_1} - 1}{\lambda_1} + \gamma_2\frac{t^{\lambda_2} - 1}{\lambda_2} + V(t + \tau)] \qquad (2)$$

given $\lambda_2 > \lambda_1 \geqslant 0$ and where $Z(t + \tau)$ is a $1 \times K$ vector of exogenous variables as of calendar time $t + \tau$; β is a $K \times 1$ vector of coefficients; and τ is the calendar time at which the spell commences. Duration dependence is captured by the two terms $(t^{\lambda_1} - 1)/\lambda_1$ and $(t^{\lambda_2} - 1)/\lambda_2$. This treatment of the duration terms is clearly analogous to the Box–Cox (1964) transformation used in regression analysis. Unobserved variables $V(t + \tau)$ are permitted to be functions of time $(t + \tau)$. By exponentiating the term in brackets, we ensure that $h(t)$ is positive as required since $h(t)$ is a conditional density function.

This formulation of the hazard is more general than any we have seen.

It contains, as special cases, virtually all of the commonly utilized hazard functions. For example, setting all elements of β equal to zero except for the intercept term β_0, and assuming $V(t + \tau) = 0$ for all t and τ, a variety of interesting special cases widely used in the literature on reliability theory can be generated. If we set $\lambda_1 = 0$ and $\gamma_2 = 0$, we obtain the Weibull hazard rate

$$h(t) = \exp(\beta_0)t^{\gamma_1} \qquad \text{(Weibull).} \qquad (3)$$

Duration dependence is monotone in this model and its sign is the same as the sign of γ_1. If we set $\lambda_1 = 1$ and $\gamma_2 = 0$, we obtain the Gompertz hazard rate

$$h(t) = \exp(\beta_0 - \gamma_1)\exp(\gamma_1 t) \qquad \text{(Gompertz).} \qquad (4)$$

By specifying alternative values for λ_1, γ_1, λ_2, and γ_2, a variety of models of duration dependence can be generated. In particular, the essential features of Jovanovic's turnover model can be captured by choosing $\lambda_1 = 1$ and $\lambda_2 = 2$. Jovanovic (1979) predicts that $\gamma_1 > 0$ and $\gamma_2 < 0$, so that initial positive duration dependence is eventually followed by negative duration dependence. We demonstrate below that γ_1, γ_2, λ_1, and λ_2 can be estimated and classical hypothesis testing procedures can be used to test among competing models of duration dependence.

Our model equation (2) extends previous work by permitting the exogenous variables to vary freely within spells.[3] Although time varying variables are a computational nuisance, they are a fact of life. In the empirical work reported later, we demonstrate that this extension makes an important difference in our estimates of the impact of key economic variables on turnover probabilities and enables us to generate sensible parameter estimates.

Finally, our treatment of heterogeneity generalizes previous work by permitting unobserved components to be correlated across spells. Work by Tuma, Hannan, and Groeneveld (1979) assumes that unobserved components are uncorrelated across spells.[4] However, in this article our treatment of heterogeneity components is somewhat restrictive. We assume that within each spell $V(t + \tau) = V$, i.e., that heterogeneity components are constant *within* spells. Heterogeneity components are permitted to vary across spells. There is no particular reason to assume that unobserved components behave the way we assume they do unless unobserved heterogeneity components are immutable person-specific effects. It is likely that unobserved components change within spells. This assumption is made solely to simplify the computational procedure discussed later. Its relaxation is a major goal of our future research.

In order to simplify the exposition we have thus far confined our attention to the formulation of the hazard function for a single spell of an event. The procedure outlined earlier can be extended to multiple episodes of the event. Let j index the episode number. The hazard for the jth episode may be written as

$$h_j(t_j) = \exp[Z(t_j + \tau_j)\beta_j + \gamma_{1j}\frac{(t_j^{\lambda_{1j}} - 1)}{\lambda_{1j}} + \gamma_{2j}\frac{(t_j^{\lambda_{2j}} - 1)}{\lambda_{2j}} + V_j]$$ (5)

given $\lambda_{1j} < \lambda_{2j}$ and where τ_j is the date of the onset of the jth spell; β_j, λ_{1j}, γ_{1j}, γ_{2j}, and λ_{2j} are coefficients for the jth spell and V_j is an unobserved heterogeneity component for the jth spell. This general parameterization permits behavioral coefficients to differ depending on the serial order of the spell. Such shifts in coefficients have been termed "occurrence dependence" by Heckman and Borjas (1980). A simple economic model of "occurrence dependence" or stigma is presented in Appendix C. To simplify the computations, we restrict unobserved heterogeneity across spells to a one-factor error specification where $V_j = C_j V$ and C_j is a parameter of the model.

The extension to a two-state multiepisode model is immediate. Let e and u denote the two states. The hazard function for the jth episode of state ℓ (ℓ = e,u) may be written as

$$h_{j\ell}(t_{j\ell}) = \exp[Z(t_{j\ell} + \tau_{j\ell})\beta_{j\ell} + \gamma_{1j\ell}\frac{(t_{j\ell}^{\lambda_{1j\ell}} - 1)}{\lambda_{1j\ell}} + \gamma_{2j\ell}\frac{(t_{j\ell}^{\lambda_{2j\ell}} - 1)}{\lambda_{2j\ell}} + V_{j\ell}]$$ (6)

where $\lambda_{1j\ell} < \lambda_{2j\ell}$. Again, to simplify the calculations, we restrict heterogeneity to a one-factor specification

$$V_{j\ell} = C_{j\ell} V.$$ (7)

C. The Likelihood Function for a Two-State Model

This section presents the likelihood function for a two-state version of our model. The general likelihood function is presented in Appendix A.

Individuals are observed for a time interval of length T. At the start of the interval, the individual is in one of two states e or u. To commence the analysis we adopt the simplifying assumption that the beginning of the observation interval is also the initial entry date of the individual into the work force. This assumption permits us to postpone discussion of the problem of correct treatment of initial conditions for the process until the next section. The data analyzed in this article are consistent with this assumption.

To simplify the notation, write hazard function (6) with heterogeneity specification (7) as

$$h_{j\ell}(t_{j\ell}|V)$$

where conditioning on the exogenous Z variables and the date of the onset of the spell is left implicit. Recall that $\ell =$ e or u and that j denotes the serial order of the spell. Subscript 3e thus denotes the third spell of employment, which starts at calendar time τ_{3e}. $q(V|\theta)$ is the density of heterogeneity components in the population. θ is a parameter vector that characterizes the distribution. The V component is the same for each individual across spells but is independently distributed across people.

The density function of exit times $t_{j\ell}$ for an individual who has K_e completed spells of employment and K_u completed spells of unemployment and who at the end of interval T is in an uncompleted spell of event ℓ_T of length $\bar{t}_{K_T, \ell_T}$ (where K_T is either $K_e + 1$ or $K_u + 1$ and ℓ_T is either e or u) is, using Eq. (1)

$$\int \left\{ \left[\prod_{j=1}^{K_e} h_{je}(t_{je}|V) \exp\left[-\int_o^{t_{je}} h_{je}(\eta|V)d\eta \right] \right] \right\}$$

$$\times \left\{ \left[\prod_{j=1}^{K_u} h_{ju}(t_{ju}|V) \exp\left[-\int_o^{t_{ju}} h_{ju}(\eta|V)d\eta \right] \right] \right\}$$

$$\times \left\{ \exp\left[-\int_o^{\bar{t}_{K_T,\ell_T}} h_{K_T,\ell_T}(\eta|V)d\eta \right] \right\} q(V)dV,$$

where

$$\sum_{j=1}^{K_e} t_{je} + \sum_{j=1}^{K_u} t_{ju} + \bar{t}_{K_T,\ell_T} = T.$$

K_e and K_u differ by at most one in absolute value because the individual is always in one of the two states.

The first term in brackets is the product of the K_e densities of exit times from employment. Each of these densities is conditioned on V, the heterogeneity component. The second term in brackets is the product of K_u conditional (on V) densities of exit times from unemployment. The third term is the probability that the K_Tth spell of event ℓ_T lasts at least $\bar{t}_{K_T,\ell_T}$. This probability is also conditioned on V, the unobserved heterogeneity component. Integration with respect to V eliminates the conditioning. Integrating out V is formally equivalent to integrating out nuisance parameters. An alternative approach to estimation would be to treat V as a fixed effect for each individual. Except for some very special cases, the latter approach leads to a serious incidental parameters problem (see, for example, Heckman, 1981) and results in inconsistent parameter estimates in short panels. For this reason we adopt a "random effect" approach in our empirical analysis.

Under the assumption that individual event histories are obtained from random samples of individuals, the appropriate log likelihood is the sum of the log of density (8) for each individual in the sample. Maximizing this function with respect to the parameters β, $\gamma_{1j\ell}$, $\gamma_{2j\ell}$, $\lambda_{1j\ell}$, $\lambda_{2j\ell}$, $C_{j\ell}$ (for ℓ = e or u), and θ [the parameters generating the density $q(V|\theta)$] produces maximum likelihood estimators that can be shown to be both consistent and asymptotically normally distributed as the number of event histories becomes large. Valid large sample test statistics for parameter vectors can be based on the estimated information matrix. To implement the model, it is necessary to make some assumption about the functional form of $q(V|\theta)$. In this article, we assume that it is a standard normal density. Since the parameters C_{je} and C_{ju} can be freely chosen, this specification does not restrict the values of variances of $V_{j\ell}$ across spells. In later work, we plan to experiment with a variety of densities for V in order to check the sensitivity of the estimates to alternative specifications of the density of heterogeneity components.

The likelihood function presented in this section generalizes previous work by permitting (1) introduction of time varying explanatory variables, (2) correction for heterogeneity components correlated across spells, and (3) estimation of general forms of duration dependence. By permitting structural coefficients to change across different spells of the event, we can estimate a model of "stigma" or "occurrence dependence" of the sort discussed in Heckman and Borjas (1980) and derived in Appendix C. Lagged values of lengths of previous spells can also be introduced as explanatory variables in the model to capture the notion of "lagged duration dependence" advanced by Heckman and Borjas (1980). Since the likelihood function accounts for each unit of time spent in the sampling interval (O, T), it naturally corrects for incomplete or censored spells of events that are a consequence of the sampling scheme.

Testing for the presence of heterogeneity raises certain delicate statistical problems that arise in testing for values of parameters at the boundaries of parameter spaces (Moran, 1973). A straightforward test for the presence of *serially correlated* unobserved components can be constructed that avoids these problems.

The following test procedure is proposed. Under the null hypothesis that there is no serial correlation in unobservables, future values of duration variables should not be statistically significant determinants of current duration distributions *if heterogeneity is ignored in estimating the parameters of current duration distributions*. Standard (asymptotic) significance tests on the estimated coefficients of future duration variables estimated *without correcting for heterogeneity* can be used to test the hypothesis of no serial correlation in unobservables for any two spells of the event.[5] This test is not informative on the presence or absence of heterogeneity components distributed independently across spells.

It is possible to estimate both $\lambda_{1j\ell}$ and $\lambda_{2j\ell}$ (subject to the restriction that $\lambda_{1j\ell} < \lambda_{2j\ell}$) and the associated coefficients $\gamma_{1j\ell}$ and $\gamma_{2j\ell}$. Using the estimated information matrix, one can construct a joint confidence interval for these coefficients and determine whether or not certain restricted models lie within the confidence interval. If they do, the data are consistent with the restricted models. Thus, for example, if the estimated confidence interval includes $\gamma_{2j\ell} = 0$ and $\lambda_{1j\ell} = 1$, a Gompertz hazard is consistent with the data for spell j of event ℓ. If the confidence interval includes $\gamma_{2j\ell} = 0$ and $\lambda_{1j\ell} = 0$, the data are consistent with a Weibull hazard. By examination of the confidence interval for the general model it may thus be possible to select a more parsimonious model.

D.   Initializing the Process[6]

It is a rare data set for which the beginning of the sample observation interval is also the beginning of the individual's entry into the workforce—the assumption made in the last section. More typically, a sample begins with individuals caught midstream in an employment or unemployment spell. It is commonly the case that we know which state an individual occupies at the beginning of the sample, and possibly the serial order of the spell, but we do not know the length of time spent in the spell before the individual is observed. This section presents methods for adjusting the likelihood function presented in the preceding section to account for this problem.

In order to focus on the essential aspects of the problem, we commence the analysis under the assumption of a strictly stationary economic environment, and under the further assumption that the process is in equilibrium. People can be in only one of two states: employed or unemployed. The density of exit time from employment, $f_e(t_e)$, is the same across people and across time for the same person. The same is true of the density of exit time from unemployment, $f_u(t_u)$. The process is assumed to have been in operation for a long time for each person. Let μ_e and μ_u be the mean time in employment and unemployment, respectively. These means are assumed to be finite. We abstract from occurrence and lagged duration dependence, but permit duration dependence.

Suppose that we first observe the process for each individual at calendar time τ_o. The probability that a randomly selected person will be found to be employed at τ_o is

$$\pi_e = \frac{\mu_e}{\mu_e + \mu_u} .$$

A derivation for this expression can be found in Cox (1962:86). Intuitively, each complete employment and unemployment episode lasts $\mu_e + \mu_u$ on average and each complete employment spell lasts μ_e. Hence

π_e is the proportion of time we expect to find an individual employed over a long observation period.

Given that a person is employed at time τ_o, what is the distribution of a *completed* employment spell sampled at τ_o? The completed spell length includes the portion observed after the start of the observation period at τ_o and the unobserved portion completed prior to τ_o. The distribution of exit times from the sampled spell is *not* the distribution $f_e(t_e)$. This is so because the completed lengths of spells sampled at τ_o are on average longer than the typical spell. Longer spells are more likely to be sampled than shorter spells. Amplifying an heuristic argument due to Cox and Lewis (1966:61–63), the density of the sampled completed spell, denoted t_e^o, can be derived in the following way.[7]

Condition on the event that the individual is employed at the time he is sampled. The number of employment spells of length x that occur in J episodes of total time spent in employment $\Sigma_{j=1}^{J} t_{je}$ is $n^{(J)}(x)$. For a random sampling scheme, random across time for a single person or across people at a point in time, the probability of sampling a spell of length x is

$$\frac{x n^{(J)}(x)}{\sum\limits_{j=1}^{J} t_{je}}.$$

This expression is the ratio of the total length of spells of length x to the total length of the employment process. On average, one will tend to oversample longer spells by the random sampling process. Divide the numerator and denominator by J, the number of spells of employment, and let J grow large, so that total time spent in employment gets large. Then

$$\lim_{J \to \infty} \frac{\sum\limits_{j=1}^{J} t_{je}}{J} = \mu_e$$

by the strong law of large numbers and

$$\lim_{J \to \infty} \frac{n^{(J)}(x)}{J} = f_e(x).$$

Then the density of sampled employment spells of length x is

$$\lim_{J \to \infty} \frac{x \frac{n^{(J)}(x)}{J}}{\sum\limits_{j=1}^{J} t_{je}} = \frac{x f_e(x)}{\mu_e}.$$

The mean of the *sampled* employment distribution exceeds the mean of employment μ_e so long as the variance of $t_e(\sigma_e^2)$ is positive. The mean of the sampled distribution is $\mu_e + \sigma_e^2/\mu_e$ which is clearly greater than μ_e since the mean is always positive. For exponential exit time distributions this mean is twice μ_e, the mean value of an employment interval. By randomly sampling across time for a single person or across people, we overestimate the population mean length of employment (and unemployment) duration.

Collecting results, the density of the completed employment spell sampled at time period τ_o is

$$g(t_e^o) = \frac{t_e^o f_e(t_e^o)}{\mu_e} . \tag{9}$$

We do not observe t_e^o. Instead we observe $\bar{t}_e^o$, the time from the origin of the sample to the completion of the spell.

For any length of completed spell t_e^o, as a consequence of stationarity any value of $\bar{t}_e^o$ is equally likely as long as $0 \leq \bar{t}_e^o \leq t_e^o$. Thus the conditional density of $\bar{t}_e^o$ given t_e^o is

$$k(\bar{t}_e^o|t_e^o) = \frac{1}{t_e^o} \qquad 0 \leq \bar{t}_e^o \leq t_e^o. \tag{10}$$

The joint density of $\bar{t}_e^o$ and t_e^o is the product of Eqs. (9) and (10),

$$m(\bar{t}_e^o, t_e^o) = \frac{1}{t_e^o} \frac{t_e^o f_e(t_e^o)}{\mu_e} .$$

Thus the marginal density of $\bar{t}_e^o$ is

$$\psi_e(\bar{t}_e^o) = \int_{\bar{t}_e}^{x} \frac{1}{\mu_e} f_e(t_e) dt_e$$

$$= \frac{1 - F_e(\bar{t}_e^o)}{\mu_e} . \tag{8}$$

Recall that these derivations depend on the assumption that the sampled spell is an employment spell. The probability that the sampled spell is an employment spell is $\pi_e = \mu_e/(\mu_e + \mu_u)$. Thus the unconditional density of an observed first spell of employment is

$$\psi_e^*(\bar{t}_e^o) = \psi_e(\bar{t}_e^o)\pi_e = \frac{1 - F_e(\bar{t}_e^o)}{\mu_e + \mu_u} .$$

By an entirely parallel argument, the unconditional density of an observed first spell of unemployment is

$$\psi_u^*(\bar{t}_u^o) = \psi_u(\bar{t}_u^o)\pi_u = \frac{1 - F_u(\bar{t}_u^o)}{\mu_e + \mu_u} ,$$

where the new symbols used in this expression are defined in the obvious way replacing e with u.

It is straightforward to modify the analysis by adding exogenous heterogeneity components provided that these components are identical across spells. They may differ across people. Thus, in place of $f_\ell(t_\ell)$ (ℓ = e,u) we may write $f_\ell(t_\ell|Z,V)$ and the derivation may be repeated as before with $\psi_{\ell_o}^*(\bar{t}_{\ell_o}^o|Z,V)$, ℓ_o = e,u, written in place of $\psi_{\ell_o}^*(\bar{t}_{\ell_o}^o)$.

With this modification, the density function for the exit times $\bar{t}_{\ell_o}^o$ (where the subscript denotes the state at sampling time period τ_o) and $t_{j\ell}$ for an individual who has K_e completed spells of employment and K_u completed spells of unemployment and who at the end of interval T is in an incomplete spell of event ℓ_T of length $\bar{t}_{K_T,\ell_T}$ (where K_T is either $K_e + 1$ or $K_u + 1$ and ℓ_T is either e or u) is

$$\int \psi_{\ell_o}^*(\bar{t}_{\ell_o}^o|Z,V)\left\{\prod_{j=1}^{K_e} h_e(t_{je}|V)\exp\left[-\int_o^{t_{je}} h_e(\eta|V)d\eta\right]\right\}$$

$$\times \left\{\prod_{j=1}^{K_u} h_u(t_{ju}|V)\exp\left[-\int_o^{t_{ju}} h_u(\eta|V)d\eta\right]\right\} \quad (11)$$

$$\times \left\{\exp\left[-\int_o^{t_{K_T,\ell_T}} h_{\ell_T}(\eta|V)d\eta\right]\right\}q(V)dV.$$

Under the assumption that individual event histories are obtained from random samples of individuals, the appropriate log likelihood for this sampling scheme is the sum of the log of density (11) for each individual in the sample. Maximizing this function with respect to the parameters of the model produces consistent and asymptotically normally distributed estimators as the number of event histories becomes large.

This procedure produces an exact solution to the problem of initializing the likelihood in a stationary environment if the process is in stationary equilibrium. It is not a general solution. In many cases the two key assumptions—equilibrium and a stationary environment—are unlikely to be even approximately correct. In this case the procedure just presented is not valid.

We postpone a general discussion of this problem to a later occasion. Here we sketch two solutions, both of which are patterned after a discussion by one of us in a previous publication (Heckman, 1981). In a general nonstationary environment, in order to correctly initialize the process, we require the probability distribution of the first spell in our sample. Its derivation depends on the rule used to select the sample being analyzed, the probability that the individual is in a given state at the time he is sampled, and the distribution of the length of time spent in the first spell in the observed sample period given the state that the individual is in when the sampling begins. The density of the first spell duration $\tilde{t}_{\ell_0}^0$ may be written as

$$\lambda\left(\tilde{t}_{\ell_0}^0 \middle| V, \left\{Z(r)\right\}_{-\infty}^{\tilde{t}_{\ell_0}^0}\right) \qquad \ell_0 = \text{e,u.}$$

This density does not, in general, have the same functional form as f_e or f_u. It depends on presample values of the exogenous variables as well as within sample values. In general, we do not know its exact functional form. However, we can approximate it using the flexible functional forms for the hazards given in Eqs. (6) and (7). One strategy for empirical work is to parameterize the first spell in the sample differently from that of subsequent spells and utilize density λ in place of $\psi_{\ell_0}^*$ in Eq. (11).

A practical difficulty with this solution to the problem of initial conditions is that presample values of the exogenous variables are required to form the density of the exit time from the first spell in the sample. While such data may be available for some samples, this is unlikely in most cases.

There are two approaches to this problem. Denote the density function for the exogenous variables by $k(Z|\chi)$ where χ is a vector of parameters of the density generating the data. The first approach estimates this density from data. The exogenous variables within the sample period might be used to estimate the density or else auxiliary data sources might be utilized. Given consistent estimates of the density function of the missing data, denoted $\hat{k}(Z|\chi)$, one can form $\lambda_{\ell_0}^*$ defined as

$$\lambda_{\ell_0}^* = \int \lambda_{\ell_0}\left(\tilde{t}_{\ell_0}^0 \middle| \left\{Z(r)\right\}_{-\infty}^{\tilde{t}_{\ell_0}^0}, V\right)\hat{k}(Z|\chi)dZ. \tag{12}$$

Inserting $\lambda_{\ell_0}^*$ in place of λ_ℓ in density (11) is equivalent to integrating out the missing data and forming an estimated likelihood function. From the exogeneity of Z and the assumed convergence of $\hat{k}(Z|\chi)$ to $k(Z|\chi)$, the estimated likelihood converges to the true likelihood, and maximum likelihood estimators based on the estimated likelihood converge to the true maximum likelihood estimators.[9]

The second approach is to jointly estimate the data density and structural parameters of the model. Given the exogeneity of Z, no advantage accrues to this computationally more demanding approach.

A second solution to the problem of initial conditions proceeds conditionally on V. Substituting λ for ψ^* in density (11) and given $V = v$, the probability density for the sample exit times is

$$
\lambda\left(\tilde{t}_{\ell_o}^o \middle| v, \left\{Z(r)\right\}_{-\infty}^{\tilde{t}_{\ell_o}^o}\right)\left\{\prod_{j=1}^{K_e} h_e(t_{je}|v) \exp\left[-\int_o^{t_{je}} h_e(\eta|v)d\eta\right]\right\}
$$

$$
\times \left\{\prod_{j=1}^{K_u} h_u(t_{ju}|v) \exp\left[-\int_o^{t_{ju}} h_u(\eta|v)d\eta\right]\right\}\left\{\exp\left[-\int_o^{t_{K_T,\ell_T}} h_{\ell_T}(\eta|v)d\eta\right]\right\}. \quad (13)
$$

v is a parameter for each individual. One may further condition on $\tilde{t}_{\ell_o}^o$ to write the density of the sample exit times *given* v *and* $\tilde{t}_{\ell_o}^o$. This conditional density is

$$
\left\{\prod_{j=1}^{K_e} h_e(t_{je}|v) \exp\left[-\int_o^{t_{je}} h_e(\eta|v)d\eta\right]\right\}\left\{\prod_{j=1}^{K_u} h_u(t_{ju}|v) \exp\left[-\int_o^{t_{ju}} h_u(\eta|v)d\eta\right]\right\}
$$

$$
\times \left\{\exp\left[-\int_o^{t_{K_T,\ell_T}} h_{\ell_T}(\eta|v)d\eta\right]\right\} \quad (14)
$$

and does not depend on the parameters of the initial exit time distribution. Maximizing the conditional likelihood function with respect to the parameters of the model (including a value of v for each person in the sample) generates consistent parameter estimates as number of spells per person becomes large ($K_e + K_u \to \infty$). However, in the case of short panels, it is in general not possible to consistently estimate v, and because of the nonlinearity of the model, estimated parameters will not be consistent because the maximum likelihood estimator will involve joint estimation of v and the structural parameters. The inconsistency in the estimator of v will be transmitted to the estimator of the structural parameters (Heckman, 1981).

II. CONTINUOUS TIME VERSUS DISCRETE TIME MODELS

The principal advantage of continuous time models for discrete panel data over more conventional discrete time models for discrete panel data is that the parameters generating the continuous time model are invariant to the time unit used in empirical work. Commonly utilized discrete time models such as logit and probit lack this invariance property. A probit model for the occurrence of an event in a time interval of a specified length does not imply a probit model for the probability of events in time intervals of different length. Dependence of the parameters and functional form of the model on the data used to estimate it is an undesirable feature of discrete time models that is avoided by use of the continuous time approach. Put differently, a continuous time model can always be used to generate a discrete time model, whereas a discrete time model is critically dependent for its parameterization and interpretation on the particular time interval on which it is estimated.

To demonstrate this point, we consider the first passage time associated with a single spell of an event. We do not observe the process continuously but we know in which of a series of discrete, equispaced intervals the first passage occurs. To simplify the exposition, we ignore heterogeneity in unobserved components and initially assume that measured variables stay constant within each spell. The stochastic process starts at time o. We observe the occurrence of the event only in equispaced time intervals of length Δ.

For a continuous time model with hazard function $h(u)$[10], the probability that a first passage occurs in the ith interval is

$$\exp\left[-\int_0^{(j-1)\Delta} h(u)\,du\right] - \exp\left[-\int_0^{j\Delta} h(u)\,du\right]. \tag{15}$$

This is simply the probability that the first passage occurs sometime between $(j-1)\Delta$ and $j\Delta$, i.e., $F(j\Delta) - F[(j-1)\Delta]$. No matter how wide or small the intervals are defined and irrespective of whether or not successive intervals are of equal length, the first passage time probability is generated by the same structural hazard function $h(u)$. Thus if Δ_ℓ is the width of the ℓth interval, the probability of a first passage in the jth interval is simply

$$\exp\left[-\int_0^{\sum_{\ell=1}^{j-1}\Delta_\ell} h(u)\,du\right] - \exp\left[-\int_0^{\sum_{\ell=1}^{j}\Delta_\ell} h(u)\,du\right].$$

The conventional discrete time model (e.g., Kiefer and Neumann, 1979 or Heckman and Willis, 1975) assumes that there is a "true" time interval of length Δ. P_Δ is the probability that an event does not occur in the interval. For example, if the probit model is adopted, it is assumed that

$$P_\Delta = \Phi(\beta Z)$$

where Φ is the cumulative distribution function of the normal distribution, and Z is a vector of explanatory variables with associated coefficient vector β. For this model, the probability of a first passage in the jth interval is

$$P_\Delta^{j-1}(1 - P_\Delta) = [\Phi(\beta Z)]^{j-1}[1 - \Phi(\beta Z)].$$

Suppose that in another data set the interval widths are longer (e.g., quarters and not months). For the continuous time model, this enlargement of the interval creates no problem and the probability of first passage can be expressed as a function of the underlying $h(u)$ function by a straightfoward modification of expression (15).

For the discrete time model to be defined at all on the new time scale, that scale must be a positive integer multiple of the original scale. For the discrete time model, unlike the continuous time model, fractional intervals have no meaning because the discrete time model is silent on the behavior of the process within any interval. If in fact the new time scale is m times the old scale (with m a positive integer), the probability of a first passage in the jth *new interval* is

$$P_\Delta^{(j-1)m}\left[1 - \sum_{\ell=1}^{m} \binom{m}{\ell} P_\Delta^{m-\ell}(1 - P_\Delta)^\ell \right] = P_\Delta^{(j-1)m}[1 - (P_\Delta)^m] \qquad (16)$$

The second term in the expression on the left-hand side is the probability that at least one event occurs in the jth time interval measured on the new scale. Neither the probability of occurrence of at least one event in the new interval $(1 - P_\Delta^m)$ nor the probability of occurrence of exactly one event in the new interval $[1 - \binom{m}{1} P_\Delta^{m-1}(1 - P_\Delta)]$ are probit functions if the probability of occurrence of the event in the old interval is probit. Of course, in this simple example, it is possible to write these probabilities in terms of the underlying probit model for the old intervals. But note that it will be necessary to modify a likelihood function used to compute parameter estimates to account for the modification of the interval width. And, as noted earlier, there is no legitimate procedure available to modify the discrete time model to account for noninteger expansion or shrinkage of the original interval length. It is necessary to postulate a new model—which might be assumed to be probit in the new intervals—with new parameters that cannot be derived from the original parameters of the model defined on the original interval.

Continuous time models can be used to generate discrete time models. Indeed, in light of the discussion in this section, the models consisting of equations (6), (7), and (8) can be interpreted as providing a general algorithm for producing a class of discrete time models for the analysis of discrete panel data. In contrast with conventional approaches in econometrics, the approach offered in this article provides a parameterization of discrete time models that is independent of the time scale in which the occurrence of discrete events is measured.

We do not want to overstate the case for continuous time models. As noted by Singer and Spilerman (1976), Phillips (1976), and others, aggregation of continuous time data into interval data of the sort described in this section may lead to nonidentification of the hazard function $h(u)$. This is clearly the case if the hazard is arbitrarily specified. If sufficient smoothness is imposed on the hazard, as is done for the hazards utilized in this paper [see equations (2), (5), and (6)], this identification problem does not arise. Nonetheless, it is important to note that without imposing information of some sort, time aggregated data may not always be used to recover the underlying hazard. An infinity of hazard functions defined over time intervals within observed sampling periods can produce the same time aggregated data. Unless a smoothness assumption is imposed, it is not possible to utilize the time aggregated data to recover the underlying hazard $h(u)$. Without such an assumption, there is no necessary advantage in using continuous time models in place of a conventional discrete time approach. Put differently, in the absence of such identifying assumptions, and in the presence of time aggregated data, the relative merits of the continuous time approach fade, and the models advanced in this paper must be interpreted as just one of a variety of discrete time models that might be used to analyze discrete panel data.

III. PITFALLS IN USING REGRESSION METHODS TO ANALYZE DURATION DATA

Appendix B presents a derivation of the properties of a Weibull regression model that can be used to analyze duration data and estimate duration dependence parameters. This section considers two important problems that arise in using standard regression analysis to analyze duration data. The first problem is one of sample selection bias.[11] The second problem is the difficulty that arises from introducing time varying explanatory variables into regression models. The first problem arises because most panel samples are short. In the course of a panel, some individuals never complete a single spell of an event whereas others will have multiple spells, and even those individuals will usually have one unfinished spell in the course of the panel. Commonly used procedures, such as utilizing only completed spells of events for regression analysis, impose a sample selection criterion on the sample used to execute the empirical work. Failure to account for such conditioning results in biased parameter estimates. The resulting bias depends on the particular rule chosen and on the length of the panel. The dependence of the bias on the length of the panel makes regression estimates from panel samples of different lengths noncomparable even when the same selection rule is employed for generating data to estimate models.

The second problem—introducing time varying exogenous variables into a regression analysis for duration data—arises because the appropriate *functional form* of the regression equation depends on the time profile of the exogenous variables. Conditioning duration regressions on "exogenous" variables measured after a spell begins may induce simultaneous equations bias in the regression estimators. *Ad hoc* solutions to these problems convert truly exogenous variables into endogenous variables and hence result in biased estimates. This section considers both of these problems, starting with the first one.

To focus on essential ideas, consider a regression analysis of duration data for a particular type of event, e.g., the lengths of time spent in consecutive jobs. To simplify the analysis we assume that no time elapses between consecutive jobs. The density of duration in a given job for an individual with fixed characteristics Z is

$$f(t|Z).$$

Unobserved heterogeneity components are assumed to be absent from the model. The expected length of t given Z is

$$E(t|Z) = \int_o^\infty tf(t|Z)dt = g(Z). \tag{17}$$

From a regression analysis we seek to estimate the parameters of $g(Z)$. For example, if $f(t|Z) = \theta(Z) \exp[-\theta(Z)t]$, $\theta(Z) > 0$

$$E(t|Z) = \frac{1}{\theta(Z)}. \tag{18}$$

Defining $\theta(Z) = (\beta Z)^{-1}$

$$E(t|Z) = \beta Z. \tag{19}$$

Under ideal conditions, a regression of t on Z will estimate β. We now specify those conditions.

Suppose that the data at our disposal come from a panel data set of length T. To avoid inessential detail suppose that at the origin of the sample, 0, everyone begins a spell of the event. This assumption enables us to ignore problems with initial conditions.

We would like to use this data to estimate $E(t|Z)$. But in our panel sample, the expected value of the length of the first spell is *not* $E(t|Z)$ but is rather

$$E(t|Z,T) = \int_o^T tf(t|Z)dt + T\int_T^\infty f(t|Z)dt \leq E(t|Z). \tag{20}$$

Thus, in the exponential example

$$E(t|Z,T) = \beta Z\{1 - \exp(-T/\beta Z)\}. \tag{21}$$

Clearly, a least squares regression of t on Z will *not* estimate β. As T

$\to \infty$, the bias disappears. In the exponential example, as T becomes big relative to the mean duration, $1/\theta(Z)$, the bias becomes small.

One widely used method utilizes only completed first spells. This results in another type of selection bias. The expected value of t given that $t < T$ is

$$E(t|Z,T,t < T) = \frac{\int_o^T tf(t|Z)dt}{\int_o^T f(t|Z)dt}. \tag{22}$$

In our exponential example

$$E(t|Z,T,t < T) = \beta Z\left\{1 - \frac{(T/\beta Z)\exp(-T/\beta Z)}{1 - \exp(-T/\beta Z)}\right\}.$$

Again, a simple least squares regression of t on Z does not estimate β for this sample. As $T \to \infty$, the bias disappears. (Note that the model could be consistently estimated by nonlinear least squares.)

Clearly there is also selection bias when we analyze the expected duration of a completed second spell of the event. Denote the length of spell i by t_i. The expected length of the second spell is

$$E(t_2|Z,T,t_1 + t_2 < T) = \frac{\int_o^T \int_o^{T-t_2} t_2 f(t_2|Z)f(t_1|Z)dt_1 dt_2}{\int_o^T \int_o^{T-t_2} f(t_2|Z)f(t_1|Z)dt_1 dt_2}. \tag{24}$$

Because t_1 and t_2 are conditionally independent, and hence the subscripts 1 and 2 can be interchanged without affecting the validity of the expression, this is also the conditional expectation of the length of the first spell.[12] For a sample of individuals with at least two completed spells of the event

$$E(t_2|Z,T,t_1 + t_2 < T)$$

$$= \beta Z\left[\frac{1 - \exp(-T/\beta Z)(1 + T/\beta Z) - (\beta Z/2)\exp(-T/\beta Z)}{1 - \exp(-T/\beta Z) - (T/\beta Z)\exp(-T/\beta Z)}\right]. \tag{25}$$

Note further that $E(t_1|Z,T,t_1 + t_2 < T) \neq E(t_1|Z,T,t_1 < T)$.

The key point to extract from this discussion is that for short panels in which T is "small," regression estimators do not estimate the parameters of regression function (19). Least squares estimators are critically dependent on both the sample selection rule and the length of the panel.

Two studies that utilize the same sample selection rule for generating "usable" observations will produce different regression coefficients if the studies are based on panels of different length.

It is possible to estimate the true structural parameters of the model. The maximum likelihood estimator discussed in Section I automatically corrects for the panel length bias. Moreover, it is obvious from our exponential examples that by use of nonlinear regression it is possible to retrieve the structural parameters of interest.

The same main conclusions can be obtained if we relax the simplifying assumption that the process starts up at the origin date of the panel. In addition to sample selection bias and panel length bias, in models with duration dependence regression estimators that do not correctly account for the length of time spent in a spell prior to the time the panel begins are subject to a further source of bias. Except for exponential duration distributions, the distribution of a left censored first spell is not the same as the distribution of an uncensored spell [see equation (12)]. The conditional expectation of a left censored distribution is not the same as the conditional expectation of the uncensored distribution. As noted in Section I.D, the maximum likelihood estimator can be used to correct for this source of bias as well.

Regression methods for the analysis of duration data also break down in the presence of time varying explanatory variables. The functional forms of the regression equations depend on the time paths of the explanatory variables. Even if the lengths of consecutive spells of an event are generated by hazard functions of identical functional form, the regression functions for durations of consecutive events will have different functional forms. In the presence of unmeasured heterogeneity components, regression equations fit conditional on the "exogenous variables" measured starting at the onset of a spell may generate biased coefficients. This is so because the particular values assumed by the explanatory variables selected in this fashion may depend on the lengths of the preceding spells. This is certainly the case for time trended explanatory variables like age, and in the empirical work we report later, it is also the case for our national unemployment rate variable. Assuming that unmeasured heterogeneity components are correlated across spells, the initial values of time trended variables in a spell will be correlated with the regression error term and will become endogenous variables. For the usual reasons, least squares estimators will be biased.

To focus on the essential aspects of the problem, suppose that we have access to a very long panel data set ($T \to \infty$) so that we can safely ignore the length of panel bias previously considered. As before, there is only one type of event and we assume that the stochastic process begins at the beginning of our sample. The duration time distribution depends on time varying variables $Z(\tau)$ where τ denotes calendar time measured from the origin of our sample.

A common functional form for the hazard function, $h(\cdot)$, is assumed for all spells. V is a heterogeneity component common across all spells. The density of duration time in the first spell, t_1, is

$$\text{First spell: } h[t_1, Z(t_1), V] \exp\left\{ -\int_0^{t_1} h[u, Z(u), V] du \right\}.$$

The density for the duration time in the second spell t_2 *given that the first spell ends at calendar time t_1* is

Conditional second spell:

$$h[t_2, Z(t_2 + t_1), V] \exp\left\{ -\int_0^{t_2} h[u, Z(u + t_1), V] du \right\}.$$

The marginal second spell density is obtained by integrating out t_1. Thus

$$f^*(t_2, Z, V) = \int_0^\infty \left(h[t_2, Z(t_2 + t_1), V] \exp\left\{ -\int_0^{t_2} h[u, Z(u + t_1), V] du \right\} \right)$$

$$\times \left(h[t_1, Z(t_1), V] \exp\left\{ -\int_0^{t_1} h[u, Z(u), V] du \right\} \right) dt_1.$$

In the case in which the distribution of $Z(t)$ does not depend on time (i.e., time stationarity in the exogenous variables),

$$f^*(t_2, Z, V) = h[t_2, Z(t_2 + t_1), V] \exp\left\{ -\int_0^{t_2} h[u, Z(u + t_1), V] du \right\}.$$

Otherwise the marginal second spell density will be of a different functional form than the marginal first spell density, and the regression function for the second spell will have a functional form different from that of the first spell regression function.

A simple example may serve to clarify the main points. We first demonstrate that the functional form of the regression will depend on the time path of the exogenous variables that drive the model. Consider the following exponential model for the first spell of an event

$$f(t_1 | Z, V) = \theta(Z, V) \exp[-\theta(Z, V) t_1] \qquad 0 < t_1 < \infty$$

where $\theta(Z, V) = 1/(\beta Z + V)$, and Z remains constant over the entire spell. The regression function for duration in the first spell is

$$E(t_1 | Z, V) = \frac{1}{\theta(Z, V)} = \beta Z + V. \tag{26}$$

Suppose we consider another individual who is subject to a different value of Z before and after calendar time τ_1. The density of t_1 for this person is derived most simply from the conditional density before and after τ_1, i.e.,

$$f(t_1|Z,V,t_1 < \tau_1) = \frac{\theta(Z_1,V)\exp[-\theta(Z_1,V)t_1]}{1 - \exp[-\theta(Z_1,V)\tau_1]} \qquad 0 < t_1 < \tau_1$$

and

$$f(t_1|Z,V,t_1 > \tau_1) = \frac{\theta(Z_2,V)\exp[-\theta(Z_2,V)t_1]}{\exp[-\theta(Z_2,V)\tau_1]} \qquad t_1 \geq \tau_1.$$

The conditional expectation of duration in the first spell is

$$E(t_1|Z_1,Z_2,\tau_1,V)$$

$$= \frac{1}{\theta(Z_1,V)} + \exp[-\theta(Z_1,V)\tau_1]\left(\frac{1}{\theta(Z_2,V)} - \frac{1}{\theta(Z_1,V)}\right). \qquad (27)$$

The functional form of the regression equation (27) differs dramatically from that of equation (26), and the problems of inference and parameter estimation differ greatly between the two equations. In general, different time paths for the exogenous variables will result in different functional forms for the regression equations.

A commonly used regression procedure for the analysis of duration data computes regression equations conditional on the values of exogenous variables that occur at or after the starting date of a spell. The intuition that underlies this procedure is that it is only the variables that occur during a spell that can explain the duration of a spell. In the presence of unobserved heterogeneity components correlated across spells, this procedure is inherently dangerous. In the presence of heterogeneity, selection of explanatory variables in this fashion converts exogenous variables into endogenous ones and guarantees simultaneous equations bias in least squares estimators.

To show this, assume the same functional form for the hazard function in all spells of the event. The conditional expectation of duration in the second spell, given values of the exogenous variables that confront the individual *after the end of the first spell*, is, for a case of no time varying variables

$$E(t_2|Z,V) = 1/\theta(Z,V). \qquad (28)$$

For the case of time varying variables, the conditional expectation depends on whether or not $t_1 > \tau_1$. If $t_1 < \tau_1$, the conditional expectation is

$$E(t_2|Z_1,Z_2,t_1,V,t_1 < \tau_1) = \frac{1}{\theta(Z_1,V)}$$

$$+ \exp[-\theta(Z_1,V)(\tau_1 - t_1)]\left[\frac{1}{\theta(Z_2,V)} - \frac{1}{\theta(Z_1,V)}\right] \qquad t_1 \leqslant \tau_1. \qquad (29)$$

For $t_1 > \tau_1$, the conditional expectation is

$$E(t_2|Z_1,Z_2,t_1,V,t_1 > \tau_1) = \frac{1}{\theta(Z_2,V)} \qquad t_1 > \tau_1. \qquad (30)$$

Although equations (29) and (27) are of the same functional form, there is one important difference: in equation (29) t_1 is an explanatory variable. Since unobserved heterogeneity component V is correlated across spells, t_1 is an endogenous variable in a regression model that treats V as a component of the error term of the model (i.e., a model that is not computed conditional on V). Partitioning the data on the basis of $t_1 < \tau_1$ raises further problems. By Bayes theorem, the conditional mean of V in equations (29) and (30) depends on t_1 and the explanatory variables so that the error term (inclusive of V) associated with regression specifications for equations (29) or (30) does not in general have a zero mean. A standard least squares assumption is violated and least squares estimators of duration equations will be biased and inconsistent.

The main point is quite general: whenever there are time trended or nonstationary explanatory variables in the model, conditioning the durations of subsequent spells on explanatory variables measured from the onset of those spells induces correlation between the explanatory variables and the heterogeneity component in the model.[13]

One solution to these problems is to use the marginal second spell density and compute the conditional expectation of t_2 with respect to it. For the case of no time varying variables, and in the more general case of time stationary exogenous variables, the marginal and conditional densities coincide so that the right-hand side of equation (27) is the conditional expectation of t_2 with respect to the marginal second spell density. In the presence of nonstationary explanatory variables, the two distributions differ.

In our example, the conditional expectation of t_2 computed with respect to the marginal distribution of t_2 is

$$E(t_2|Z_1,Z_2,\tau_1,V) = \frac{1}{\theta(Z_1,V)} + \exp[-\theta(Z_1,V)\tau_1]$$

$$\times \left[\frac{\theta(Z_1,V) - \theta(Z_2,V)}{\theta(Z_2,V)}\right]\left[\frac{1}{\theta(Z_1,V)} + \tau_1\right]^{(14)}. \qquad (31)$$

In long panels, estimation of this equation avoids the endogeneity problem induced by selecting explanatory variables on the basis of past realizations of the process. Note, however, from inspection of equations (27) and (31), that successive conditional expectations of duration times taken with respect to the successive marginal distributions have different functional forms. This is so even though the functional form of the hazard function is invariant across spells. This means that in the presence of time varying variables it is not possible to simply pool data across successive spells of the event to estimate the common parameters of a linear regression function. Moreover, due to the nonstationarity of the exogenous variables, simple regression tests of "occurrence dependence" will tend not to reject that hypothesis (comparing differences in regression coefficients across consecutive spells of an event).

Two *ad hoc* procedures for coping with time trended or general nonstationary variables in a regression format are readily discussed and disposed of. The first uses average values of the regression variables *within a spell* in a standard linear regression format.[15] This procedure ignores the change in functional form that results from different paths for regressors. It fails to capture the essential dependence of first passage time densities on the *entire* sequence of exogenous variables, not just those realized in a spell. Exogenous variables that are selected in this fashion become endogenous variables. To demonstrate this point by way of an example, consider a strictly positively trended explanatory variable. The average value of the variable within a spell is simply a multiple of the length of the spell and is clearly endogenous.

A second *ad hoc* procedure for introducing time varying variables into a regression format is to use exogenous variables measured at a start of a spell. Again, this procedure results in a misspecification of the true conditional expectation function and for nonstationary explanatory variables manufactures simultaneous equations bias for models with heterogeneity components by selecting "explanatory" variables on the basis of prior realizations of the process.

The standard regression approach to the analysis of duration data is thus seen to be a rather fragile empirical procedure. Only in the case of long panels in stationary economic environments does it produce valid parameter estimates. These conditions are unlikely to be realized in the analysis of microeconomic labor market data. The likelihood approach corrects for length of panel bias and, suitably modified, corrects for other sampling rules. Time varying explanatory variables can readily be accommodated in the likelihood approach. For both reasons, we strongly prefer the likelihood approach to the regression approach in the analysis of labor market duration data.

IV. EMPIRICAL ANALYSIS

This section reports the results of two empirical analyses. Section IV.A compares empirical results obtained from regression and maximum likelihood procedures used to analyze spells of employment and nonemployment for a sample of young men. Our results from this analysis are of considerable substantive interest and also serve to illustrate the biases inherent in using regression techniques to analyze duration data. Section IV.B presents tests of the proposition that it is legitimate to aggregate the "unemployment" and "out of the labor force" states into one state called nonemployment. This proposition is of interest given recent claims that the distinction between the two nonemployment states is artificial (see, for example, Clark and Summers, 1978). We find that the states are empirically distinct.

The sample used to perform all the empirical work reported here is selected from the National Longitudinal Survey of Young Men and is the same as that previously employed by Heckman and Borjas (1980). We follow 122 young men for 30 consecutive months, from the time they graduate from high school. The small size of our sample is due to the stringent selection criteria imposed. To be included in the sample an individual must (1) be white; (2) have received a high school diploma in the spring or early summer of 1969; and (3) not have returned to school in the period beginning in the fall of 1969 and ending in December of 1971.

The sample was selected in this manner in an attempt to minimize the initial conditions problem discussed in Section I.D. By using individuals who have recently completed schooling, we have selected individuals with little or no previous labor force experience. The vast majority of individuals in our sample have not worked in full-time jobs during high school. We can safely ignore the initial conditions problem in deriving the maximum likelihood estimates presented here.

A.   Comparison of Regression and Maximum Likelihood Estimates of Employment and Nonemployment Spell Duration Models

The regression specification employed here is similar to the Weibull model used by Heckman and Borjas (1980). A more complete discussion of the Weibull regression model and its statistical properties is presented in Appendix B. We assume that duration times conditional on heterogeneity components are Weibull distributed, and consider the first two completed spells of employment and nonemployment. In terms of hazard (6), the specification estimated is obtained by setting $\lambda_{1je} = 0$, $\gamma_{2je} = 0$, and $Z(u + \tau_{je}) = Z_{je}$ for $0 \leq u \leq t_{je}$, $j = 1, 2$, where 1 = employment (e) and 2 = nonemployment (n). (Recall that τ_{je} is the date in calendar time at which the *j*th spell of event ℓ begins.) The last condition imposes the requirement that the values of the exogenous variables are fixed over the duration of a spell. In our empirical analysis the values of the exogenous variables are fixed in two different ways. In the first way, we fix the exogenous variables at their *beginning of spell values,* so that

$$Z_{j\ell}^{(1)} = Z(\tau_{j\ell}).$$

The second way uses *within spell averages* of the Z

$$Z_{j\ell}^{(2)} = \frac{\int_0^{t_{j\ell}} Z(\tau_{j\ell} + k)dk}{t_{j\ell}}$$

to approximate the "true" value of $Z_{j\ell}$ within the *j*th spell of event ℓ.

We adopt the following one factor Weibull regression model specification:

$$\ln t_{j\ell} = Z_{j\ell}\tilde{\beta}_{j\ell} + \tilde{V}_{j\ell} + W_{j\ell}$$

where $\tilde{\beta}_{j\ell} = -\beta_{j\ell}/(1 + \gamma_\ell)$

$$\tilde{V}_{j\ell} = \frac{C_\ell\phi}{1 + \gamma_\ell}.$$

C_ℓ is a factor loading for event ℓ on heterogeneity component ϕ, and

$$E(W_{j\ell}) = 0, \ E(\tilde{V}_{j\ell}) = 0, \ E(\tilde{V}_{j\ell}W_{j\ell}) = 0,$$

and $W_{j\ell}$ is i.i.d. across spells and people. The variance of $W_{j\ell}$ is $\pi^2/6(\gamma_\ell + 1)^2$, a result derived in Appendix B.

Differencing successive *completed* log durations in state ℓ eliminates $\tilde{V}_{j\ell}$ from the regression. Focusing on the first and second completed spells of event ℓ, we may write

$$\ln t_{1\ell} - \ln t_{2\ell} = (Z_{2\ell} - Z_{1\ell})\tilde{\beta}_{2\ell} + Z_{1\ell}(\tilde{\beta}_{2\ell} - \tilde{\beta}_{1\ell}) + W_{2\ell} - W_{1\ell}.$$

The residual variance for this equation has mean zero and variance $\pi^2/[3(\gamma_\ell + 1)^2]$. From the estimated residual variance it is thus possible to consistently estimate the duration dependence parameter γ_ℓ. As noted in Appendix B this estimate is derived under the assumption that there is no error in measuring completed durations. If there is, the estimated duration dependence parameter is downward biased.

As noted in Section III, restricting attention in the empirical analysis to completed spells of events generates sample selection bias. In our empirical work, we lose approximately two-thirds of our sample by imposing this sample selection requirement.

We include only two regressors in the empirical results presented here: the first is a dummy variable set to one if the individual is married with spouse present (MSP) and zero otherwise and the second is the national unemployment rate for prime age white males. The second variable is a proxy for aggregate demand. In addition to the first-differenced specification described earlier, we also present estimates of a two-equation system of first and second spell completed log duration times using generalized least squares.

A topic of considerable interest in estimating the regression equations is the determination of the sensitivity of parameter estimates to the method used to select spell constant values for the time varying exogenous variables. For the regressors used here, the national unemployment rate varies by month, whereas marital status is observed yearly. In our sample period (1969–1971), the within spell variation of the unemployment variable is likely to be far greater than that of marital status. We thus expect to find that the parameters associated with unemployment will show more sensitivity to the method of selecting spell constant exogenous variables.

Because the regression approach has been shown to yield biased parameter estimates (see Section III), it is difficult to isolate the effect of fixing the exogenous variables over spells using the two regression methods examined here. To provide a benchmark we present maximum likelihood estimates of the Weibull duration model using both methods of fixing the exogenous variables. We then incorporate time varying variables. Differences among the estimates are considerable.

Regression results for log employment durations are presented in Table 1. The top panel reports the estimates of the two-spell GLS model, and the lower panel reports estimates from the first difference specification. On the left side of the table, the regressors are defined as the average value over the spell ($Z_{je}^{(2)}$) and on the right side of the table as the values observed in the first month of the spell ($Z_{je}^{(1)}$). As discussed in Section III, the second method of fixing the regressors may also produce biased coefficients because the values of the "exogenous variables" at the start of the second spell of an event will depend on the lengths of previous spells of events if the true exogenous variables are time trended. In our sample the unemployment measure has an extreme positive time trend.

The two methods for fixing the regressors produce large differences in parameter estimates. Although most parameters are not significantly different from zero by conventional standards, the coefficient of the unemployment rate in the first spell GLS equations using $Z_{je}^{(2)}$ is three times as large as the coefficient based on $Z_{je}^{(1)}$. The sign of the estimated second spell coefficient unemployment rate differs depending on the method used to fix time varying variables. The coefficients associated with marital status are statistically insignificant and are much less sensitive to the method of selecting explanatory variables.

The two regression specifications yield very different parameter esti-

Table 1.   Ln Employment Durations (Based on Two
Completed Spells)[a]

	Within spell averages of exogenous variables				Start of spell exogenous variables			
	Spell one	t	Spell two	t	Spell one	t	Spell two	t
Intercept	1.232	(2.16)	−1.052	(1.25)	7.094	(2.1)	−2.048	(3.2)
Marital status (1 if married)	.624	(1.43)	−.449	(.72)	−.409	(.81)	−.490	(.75)
National unemployment	−2.020	(5.40)	−.975	(.21)	−6.523	(2.5)	.531	(1.88)
	Difference specifications							
Intercept	2.502	(1.95)			12.423	(2.5)		
Δ Marital status	−.138	(.17)			0.112	(.01)		
Δ Unemployment	.185	(.56)			.858	(.337)		
Marital status (first spell)	−.570	(.49)			−.496	(1.11)		
National unemployment (first spell)	1.946	(2.41)			8.951	(2.43)		
	$\gamma_e = 1.08$				$\gamma_e = .65$			

[a] t statistics are reported in parentheses.

mates. For the model using $Z_{je}^{(1)}$ the estimate of the coefficient of unemployment for second spell duration is .531 in the GLS system as opposed to .858 from the first difference specification. The coefficients of the unemployment rate on first spell employment duration are 9.81 in the first difference specification and −6.523 in the GLS system. These disparities and the generally poor fits demonstrate the difficulties inherent in the regression approach utilized here.

The estimate of the Weibull parameter γ_e is substantially greater than zero, using either of the two methods for computing $Z_{j\ell}$. A value of γ_e greater than zero indicates positive duration dependence, i.e., the longer an individual is in a state, the more likely he is to leave it. The same results using a different list of variables were also found by Heckman and Borjas (1980).

Regression results for the nonemployment equations are presented in Table 2. Once again estimates based on $Z_{jn}^{(1)}$ and $Z_{jn}^{(2)}$ are very different. When within spell averages are used ($Z_{jn}^{(2)}$), the unemployment measure has a negative estimated effect on employment duration. Because the prime age male unemployment rate is time trended in our sample, using the average value of the employment rate as a regressor causes longer duration times to be associated with higher within spell unemployment rates for purely mechanical reasons. A strong empirical relationship is

Table 2. Ln Nonemployment Durations (Based on Two Completed Spells)[a]

	Within spell averages of exogenous variables				Start of spell exogenous variables			
	Spell one	t	Spell two	t	Spell one	t	Spell two	t
Intercept	−.398	(.97)	.44	(.65)	−1.051	(2.28)	−1.011	(1.61)
Marital status (1 if married, spouse present)	−.117	(.24)	.16	(.44)	−.375	(.764)	−.093	(.25)
National unemployment	−.335	(1.46)	−.53	(1.74)	.057	(.21)	.151	(.51)
	Difference specifications							
Intercept			−.074	(.084)			.950	(1.1)
Δ Marital status			−.342	(.645)			−.656	(1.31)
Δ Unemployment			−.402	(.85)			.544	(1.32)
Marital status (first spell)			.091	(−.13)			.280	(.52)
Unemployment (first spell)			−.252	(.60)			−.653	(1.42)
			$\gamma_n = 1.23$				$\gamma_n = .74$	

[a] *t* statistics are reported in parentheses.

found not because of any causal link, but only because the unemployment measure is a transformation of the dependent variable.

We find evidence of positive duration dependence in the unemployment equations. γ_n is approximately equal to one. The coefficients associated with the unemployment measures switch signs in both the top and bottom panels according to whether $Z_{jn}^{(1)}$ or $Z_{jn}^{(2)}$ is used.

We now discuss estimates obtained from maximum likelihood estimation of the parameters of the hazard function (6). In order to compare these estimates to those from the regressions, we initially adopt a Weibull specification. The coefficient associated with the log of the duration in the state is γ_ℓ. Later on in this section we present results from a more general parameterization of duration dependence and compare results from this model with those from the Weibull.

The maximum likelihood parameter estimates for the employment–nonemployment model are presented in Table 3. Panel A contains estimates from the model using $Z_{je}^{(2)}$, in Panel B are the estimates using regressors $Z_{je}^{(1)}$, and in Panel C are the parameter estimates for the case when the regressors are allowed to vary within the spells. On the left side of the page are the coefficients associated with the employment to nonemployment transition, and on the right side are the coefficients

Table 3. Maximum Likelihood Estimates—Weibull Model[1]

	Employment to Nonemployment	Nonemployment to Employment
Panel A: Regressors Fixed at Average Value Over Spell		
Intercept	.971	−.093
	(1.535)	(.221)
ℓn Duration (γ)	−.137	−.287
	(1.571)	(2.976)
MSP	−1.093	.347
	(2.679)	(1.134)
Unemployment	−1.800	−.577
	(6.286)	(3.119)
£[2] = −711.457		
Panel B: Regressors Fixed at Value for First Month of Spell		
Intercept	−3.743	−1.054
	(12.074)	(3.464)
ℓn Duration (γ)	−.230	−.363
	(2.888)	(4.049)
MSP	−.921	.297
	(2.310)	(.902)
Unemployment	.569	−.130
	(3.951)	(.900)
£ = −740.998		
Panel C: Regressors Free to Vary Over the Spell		
Intercept	−3.078	−.899
	(8.670)	(2.742)
ℓn Duration (γ)	−.341	−.316
	(3.941)	(3.279)
MSP	−.610	.362
	(1.971)	(1.131)
Unemployment	.209	−.204
	(1.194)	(1.321)
£ = −746.515		

[1] Absolute value of asymptotic normal statistics in parentheses.
[2] £ denotes the value of the log likelihood function.

associated with the nonemployment to employment transition. First note that, in contrast to the regression results, the estimates of γ_ℓ indicate negative duration dependence in all states and for all methods of fixing regressors. The duration dependence parameter is highly significant in virtually all transitions. However, spurious negative duration dependence can be generated by not properly accounting for population heterogeneity. In fact, when heterogeneity is introduced in the model there is no evidence of duration dependence in the employment to nonemployment transition (see Table 4).

The coefficient of MSP is significant in all three panels in explaining employment duration, though there are large differences in the absolute

Table 4.   Maximum Likelihood Estimates with Time Varying
Variables and Heterogeneity[1]

	Employment to Nonemployment	Nonemployment to Employment
Intercept	−3.600	−.879
	(8.395)	(2.525)
ℓn duration	.015	−.312
	(.121)	(3.170)
MSP	−.498	.320
	(1.384)	(.961)
Unemployment	−.017	−.172
	(.101)	(1.056)
C_{ij}	1.196	−.133
	(4.651)	(.756)
£ = −740.126		

[1] Absolute value of asymptotic normal statistics in parentheses.

values of the estimates. Allowing the MSP variable to change over the
course of the spell results in a parameter estimate almost one-half as
large in absolute value as the coefficient value that results from using
the average spell value in the employment to nonemployment transition.
In the nonemployment–employment equations, the method of introducing exogenous variables has little effect on the value of the MSP parameter, though in all cases the coefficient is approximately equal to its
standard error. In all three panels the interpretation of the effect of
marital status on exit times is the same: individuals married with spouse
present have lower rates of transition out of employment and higher
rates of transition from nonemployment than others.

The differences in parameter estimates are much more extreme for the
coefficients of the prime age male unemployment variable. Recall that
this variable is strongly time trended. The coefficients of the unemployment variable in both panels A and B are highly significant for the
employment–nonemployment transition, but are of *opposite sign*. Allowing the variables to change over the spell results in an estimate that
is positive but not statistically significant. Use of spell constant regressors
leads to dramatically different interpretations depending on the technique
employed to arrive at a spell constant value. This same remark is true
with regard to the unemployment rate coefficients in the nonemployment–employment transition. Taken as a whole, these results demonstrate the seriousness of the biases introduced into the parameter estimates by restricting the variability of exogenous variables. These findings
cast considerable doubt on the value of regression methods for estimating
duration models.

We next turn to an investigation of the effects of not controlling for heterogeneity on estimates of duration dependence. The specification of the one factor scheme we adopt is given in equation (7) in Section I. The same set of regressors is used as was used in the estimation of the model in Table 3, Panel C, so that all variables are allowed to vary within spells. Table 4 presents the estimates.

It is interesting to note that unobservable heterogeneity is an important determinant of the rate of transition out of the employment state but has no effect on the rate of leaving nonemployment. There has been much attention given to separating the effect of heterogeneity and state dependence in the length of nonemployment spells, but our estimates suggest that for young men estimates of duration dependence are not affected by the inclusion of heterogeneity into the model. However, the duration dependence effect vanishes with the introduction of heterogeneity in the employment–nonemployment transition. The introduction of heterogeneity reduces the magnitude of all the parameters (with the exception of the constant) in the employment equation, whereas the coefficients in the nonemployment equation are barely affected.

These findings indicate that employment–nonemployment transition probabilities are non-Markovian and call into question the standard discrete time Markov assumption widely used in labor market analysis (see, for example, Marston, 1976). The source of departure from the Markov model differs between the employment to nonemployment transition and the nonemployment to employment transition. The former transition is non-Markovian because of uncontrolled heterogeneity that gives rise to the classical mover–stayer problem. The latter transition is non-Markovian because of structural duration dependence.

All the estimation done up to this point has been predicated on the assumption that the exit time distributions are Weibull. We now relax this assumption. We estimate a model that allows for general forms of duration dependence. This specification is obtained by letting $\lambda_{1j\ell} = 1$ and $\lambda_{2j\ell} = 2$ for all values of j and ℓ [see equation (6)]. Empirical results are presented in Table 5 for models estimated with and without heterogeneity corrections. The models estimated without heterogeneity show some evidence of linear duration dependence. The estimates of the coefficients of the explanatory variables do not differ much from the estimates obtained in the Weibull model. When the heterogeneity correction is added, there is no evidence of duration dependence in the rate of leaving employment. Recall that a similar result was found in the Weibull case. For the nonemployment to employment transition, the exit rate to employment also appears to be a linear function of duration. In our data we do not reject the null hypothesis that the squared duration term is insignificant in each of the transition densities. Assuming that this is so,

Table 5. Maximum Likelihood Estimates with Time Varying Variables, Heterogeneity, and General Duration Dependence[1]

	Without heterogeneity		With heterogeneity	
	$E \rightarrow N$	$N \rightarrow E$	$E \rightarrow N$	$N \rightarrow E$
Const.	−3.271	−.762	−3.565	−.748
	(8.901)	(2.425)	(8.537)	(2.247)
Tenure/10	−.806	−1.714	.045	−1.704
	(1.858)	(2.731)	(.085)	(2.685)
Tenure^2/100	.028	.602	−.120	.603
	(.145)	(1.673)	(.607)	(1.666)
MSP	−.568	.349	−.490	.313
	(1.731)	(1.089)	(1.353)	(.956)
Unemployment	.329	−.192	.075	−.164
	(1.865)	(1.271)	(.392)	(1.042)
C_{ij}			1.088	−.118
			(3.572)	(.650)
£		−742.334		−739.177

[1] Absolute value of asymptotic normal statistics in parenthesis.

it then becomes possible to test between the Weibull ($\lambda_{1j\ell} = 0$) and Gompertz ($\lambda_{1j\ell} = 1$) specifications. The difference in log likelihoods between the two models is negligible. (−739.2 versus −740.6.) The evidence suggests a slight preference for the Weibull specification. The estimates of the coefficients of the explanatory variables do not change much between those specifications, and for the sake of brevity we do not report the detailed empirical results from this model.

B.   Tests of a Three-State versus a Two-State Model[16]

The preceding empirical work lumps the "unemployed" and those "out-of-the-labor-force" into a common "nonemployed" category. There is considerable controversy in the literature over the issue of whether or not the categories unemployed and out-of-the-labor-force are behaviorally distinct labor force states. This issue is particularly relevant in the study of the labor market dynamics of youth. Given the range of nonmarket options available to many youths and given practices of many state unemployment compensation agencies that effectively limit the eligibility for unemployment compensation of many youths, it seems especially likely that there is *no* distinction between unemployment and out-of-the-labor-force status for young people. Recent papers by Clark and Summers (1978) and Ellwood (1979) have made this claim. In this section of the article we present a test of this proposition and reject it. We find that distinct behavioral equations govern transitions from out-of-the-labor-force to employment and from unemployment to employment.

Recent theory suggests that being unemployed and out-of-the-labor-force describe different behavior. For example, in search theory (e.g., Burdett and Mortensen, 1977), a key difference between unemployed individuals and those out-of-the-labor-force is that the former are at an interior point with respect to the optimal amount of time they devote to search, whereas the latter are at a corner and spend no time searching. Separate behavioral equations generate observations in these two states.

Even though these theoretical distinctions are widely accepted, many economists claim that the empirical distinction between reported unemployment and reported out-of-the-labor-force is so arbitrary that it is of little or no analytical value. This point would seem to have some merit after examining the official Current Population Survey definition of unemployment, which defines those individuals as unemployed "who had no employment during the survey week, were available for work, and (1) had engaged in any specific job seeking activity within the past four weeks, (2) were waiting to be called back to a job from which they had been laid off, or (3) were waiting to report to a new wage or salary job scheduled to start within the following 30 days." Because there is no stipulation as to the quality or quantity of searches made within the month, the unemployment–out-of-the-labor-force distinction may be of little value in predicting employment probabilities for the nonemployed.

In this section we present a test to determine whether or not the classifications "u" (unemployed) and "o" (out of the labor force) are behaviorally meaningless distinctions. The idea underlying the test is as follows: controlling for heterogeneity if the hazard rate for exit to employment from unemployment (h_{ue}) is the same as the hazard rate for exit to employment out of the labor force (h_{oe}), the origin state ("o" or "u") is irrelevant in determining the rate at which individuals leave nonemployment to go to employment. In a simple 3 state Markov model, this test is equivalent to testing the proposition that the two nonemployment states can be aggregated into a single state and a properly specified two state Markov model can be defined for employment and nonemployment. To simplify the exposition we assume that there is no heterogeneity in observed or unobserved characteristics. This assumption is not essential and is not used in performing the empirical work reported below.

To motivate the test, we consider two cases. The first case assumes that individuals exit employment at a rate governed by density $f_e(t_e)$. The probability that a person terminating employment classifies himself as a "u" or "o" is determined by tossing a coin that comes up "u" fraction π of the time and "o" fraction $1 - \pi$ of the time. Once acquired the person keeps these labels as long as he is nonemployed so there is no switching between "o" and "u" states (a patently counterfactual case).

The density of duration in the nonemployment state is governed by density $f_n(t_n)$. The associated hazard h_n is

$$h_n = \frac{f_n(t_n)}{1 - F_n(t_n)} \, .$$

The joint probability density that an individual is classified as unemployed and leaves nonemployment at t_n is

$$\pi f_n(t_n)$$

with associated hazard

$$h_{ue} = h_n.$$

The joint probability that an individual is classified as out of the labor force and leaves nonemployment at t_n is

$$(1 - \pi)f_n(t_n)$$

with associated hazard

$$h_{oe} = h_n.$$

The hazard rate for entry to employment will be the same whether or not the nonemployed individual is classified as an "o" or an "u".[17]

In the second case considered here, individuals are allowed to switch their reported nonemployment status "randomly". By this we mean that initial nonemployment classification is random (governed as before by a toss of the coin) and that individuals switch randomly between "o" and "u". The continuous time analogue of discrete time independent Bernoulli trials is an exponential waiting time model (Cox, 1962). Write the hazard for durations from "o" to "u" as h_{ou} and the hazard from "u" to "o" as h_{uo}, the density of time spent going from o to e (t_{oe}) is

$$h_{oe} \exp - \{(h_{oe} + h_{ou})t_{oe}\}$$

while the density of time spent going from u to e (t_{ue}) is

$$h_{ue} \exp - \{(h_{ue} + h_{uo})t_{ue}\}.$$

Individuals may change among reported nonemployment states for whatever reason. All that is required for the origin state (o or u) to be irrelevant for characterizing transition rates from nonemployment to employment is for $h_{oe} = h_{ue}$.

The condition $h_{oe} = h_{ue}$ is also the requirement that must be satisfied in a Markov model to aggregate "o" and "u" into a single state n, and for the resulting two state model for e and n to be a properly defined Markov model. To demonstrate this it is most convenient to work with the state probability representation of the three state Markov model.

Define $P_j(t)$ as the probability that state j is occupied at time t and $\dot{P}_j(t)$ as the instantaneous rate of change of this probability. The three state generalization of the two state model presented in Section I.b is

$$\begin{bmatrix} \dot{P}_e(t) \\ \dot{P}_o(t) \\ \dot{P}_u(t) \end{bmatrix} = \begin{bmatrix} -(h_{eu} + h_{eo}) & h_{oe} & h_{ue} \\ h_{eo} & -(h_{oe} + h_{ou}) & h_{uo} \\ h_{eu} & h_{ou} & -(h_{ue} + h_{uo}) \end{bmatrix} \begin{bmatrix} P_e(t) \\ P_o(t) \\ P_u(t) \end{bmatrix}$$

or

$$\dot{P}^{(3)}(t) = AP^{(3)}(t)$$

using matrix notation. Note that the rank of A is at most 2.

In order to aggregate "o" and "u" into a two state model defined in terms of n, we require that we be able to collapse the three state system into

$$\begin{bmatrix} \dot{P}_e(t) \\ \dot{P}_n(t) \end{bmatrix} = \begin{bmatrix} -h_{en} & h_{ne} \\ h_{en} & -h_{ne} \end{bmatrix} \begin{bmatrix} P_e(t) \\ P_n(t) \end{bmatrix}$$

where $P_n(t) = P_o(t) + P_u(t)$. In matrix notation $\dot{P}^{(2)}(t) = BP^{(2)}(t)$. The rank of B is 1. For this to be an equivalent representation of the three state model, a necessary condition is that rank $(A) =$ rank $(B) = 1$. A necessary and sufficient condition is that $h_{oe} = h_{ue} = h_{ne}$. Sufficiency may be checked by direct substitution into A.

This interpretation of the test is also informative in that it makes precise the sense in which o and u are "irrelevant." Aggregating o and u into a single state for the purpose of statistical analysis does not alter the Markov property of the model. The rate at which individuals leave nonemployment to enter employment does not depend on which nonemployment state individuals are in. (This is the key hypothesis and can be satisfied in nonMarkov models as well.)

It is tempting to extend this type of reasoning to consider transitions from employment to the two nonemployment states. Thus is might be argued that if u and o are "irrelevant" distinctions, the rate of transition from e to u (h_{eu}) would be the same as the rate of transition from e to o (h_{eo}). This argument is correct only if $\pi = 1 - \pi = \frac{1}{2}$. If $f_e(t_e)$ is the density of employment length durations with hazard rate $h_e(t_e)$ the hazard rate for transitions from e to u is

$$h_{eu} = \pi h_e$$

while the hazard rate for transitions from e to o is

$$h_{eo} = (1 - \pi)h_e.$$

Obviously $h_{eu} + h_{eo} = h_e$, as is required by the law of conditional probability. But unless $\pi = 1 - \pi = \frac{1}{2}$, $h_{eu} \neq h_{eo}$. We have no theory

Table 6. Parameter Estimates from the Three State Unrestricted
Model

	From employment to		To employment from	
	Unemployment	OLF	Unemployment	OLF
Constant	−3.822	−7.193	−.698	−2.384
	(9.778)[1]	(2.768)	(3.782)	(2.078)
Tenure/10	.482	.700	−1.253	1.441
	(.846)	(.379)	(1.530)	(.365)
Tenure^2/100	−.240	−.019	.481	.208
	(1.004)	(.030)	(.547)	(.084)
MSP	−.355	.086	−.065	1.154
	(.837)	(.068)	(.193)	(.400)
C_{ij}	1.396	2.788	−.342	−1.866
	(3.336)	(1.025)	(1.633)	(1.081)
£ = −784.33				

[1] Absolute value of asymptotic normal statistics in parentheses.

of π. Even if reporting oneself as unemployed is strictly a matter of tossing a coin, nothing requires $\pi = \frac{1}{2}$.

Table 6 presents estimates of the three state model estimated with heterogeneity. The fact that the standard errors are so large relative to the magnitude of the parameters is to be expected given that we are attempting to estimate twenty parameters with so few degrees of freedom. The parameter signs are generally consistent with our earlier results from the employment–nonemployment model. Only the constant terms and the factor loading of the employment to unemployment transition are greater than twice their standard errors.

The estimates from the restricted three state model are given in Table 7. Let $\theta_{ij} \equiv (\beta_{ij}\ c_{ij})$. The restrictions imposed are $\theta_{oe} = \theta_{ue}$, which forces all parameters in the "unemployment" to employment and "out of the labor force" to employment transitions to equality. There are a total of five restrictions. Performing the likelihood ration test on the restricted versus the unrestricted model, the value of the test statistic is 28.72 which is distributed $\chi^2(5)$. The critical value for a 5 percent significance level is 11.07. We are able to reject the null hypothesis of the equality of the parameters governing the two nonemployment states. These empirical results suggest that "out of the labor force" and "unemployment" are not artificial distinctions for this sample of young men.

V.   SUMMARY AND CONCLUSIONS

This article presents new econometric methods for the empirical analysis of individual labor market histories. The techniques developed here ex-

Table 7. Parameter Estimates from the Three State Restricted Model

	From Employment to: Unemployment	OLF	Nonemployment to Employment
Constant	−3.735	−7.718	−.857
	(9.934)[1]	(2.596)	(4.756)
Tenure/10	.400	.782	−1.460
	(.706)	(.528)	(1.790)
Tenure^2/100	−.220	−.004	.683
	(.940)	(.007)	(1.116)
MSP	−.397	.160	.202
	(.966)	(.148)	(.577)
C_{ij}	1.327	3.102	−.421
	(4.195)	(1.078)	(1.894)
£ = −798.69			

[1] Absolute value of asymptotic normal statistics in parentheses.

tend previous work on continuous time models in four ways: (1) a structural economic interpretation of these models is presented; (2) time varying explanatory variables are introduced into the analysis in a general way; (3) unobserved heterogeneity components are permitted to be correlated across spells; and (4) a flexible model of duration dependence is presented that accommodates many previous models as a special case and that permits tests among competing specifications within a unified framework. In addition, longer range types of state dependence can be introduced into the model and their empirical importance tested with our model.

We contrast our methods with more conventional discrete time and regression procedures. The parameters of continuous time models are invariant to the sampling time unit used to record observations. Parameters of discrete time models defined for one time unit are not in general comparable to parameters of discrete time models defined for other time units. Two problems that plague the regression approach to analyzing duration data do not plague the likelihood approach advocated in this article. The first problem is that standard regression estimators are ill-equipped to deal with censored spells of events that arise in short panels. The second problem is that the regression approach cannot be readily adopted to accommodate time varying explanatory variables. The functional forms of regression functions depend on the time paths of the explanatory variables. *Ad hoc* solutions to this problem can make exogenous variables endogenous to the model and so can induce simultaneous equations bias. The likelihood approach advocated in this paper can readily accommodate time varying explanatory variables.

Two sets of empirical results are presented. The first set is an analysis of employment and nonemployment data using both regression and maximum likelihood procedures. Standard regression methods are shown to perform rather poorly and to produce estimates wildly at variance with the estimates from our maximum likelihood procedure. The maximum likelihood estimates are more in accord with *a priori* theoretical notions. A major conclusion of this analysis is that the discrete time Markov model widely used in labor market analysis is inconsistent with the data.

The second set of empirical results is a test of the hypothesis that unemployment and out-of-the-labor-force are behaviorally different labor market states. Contrary to recent claims, we find that they are separate states for our sample of young men.

APPENDIX A

The Likelihood Function for a Multistate-Multiepisode Model

In this appendix we discuss general issues in the estimation of continuous time probability models and the particular features of the likelihood function we employ in the empirical work presented in the text. Because our data start at the beginning of the labor market history of individuals, we can safely ignore the initial conditions problem discussed in the text. We defer a general discussion of this problem to a later article. (See also our discussion in Section I.D).

Let there be N states the individual can occupy at any moment of time. If the individual begins "life" in state i there are $N - 1$ "latent times" with densities

$$f_{ij}(t_{ij}) = h_{ij}(t_{ij}) \exp\left[-\int_o^{t_{ij}} h_{ij}(u)du \right] \quad (j = 1, \ldots, N; j \neq i) \quad \text{(A1)}$$

where $f_{ij}(\cdot)$ is the density function of exit times from state i into state j, and $h_{ij}(\cdot)$ is the associated hazard function. The joint density of the $N - 1$ latent exit times is given by

$$\prod_{\substack{j=1 \\ j \neq i}}^{N} h_{ij}(t_{ij}) \exp\left[-\int_o^{t_{ij}} h_{ij}(u)du \right]. \quad \text{(A2)}$$

An individual exits from state i to state j' if the j'th first passage time is the smallest of the $N - 1$ potential first passage times, i.e., if

$$t_{ij'} < t_{ij} \quad (j = 1, \ldots, N; j \neq j'; j, j' \neq i)$$

Let the probability that the individual leaves state i and enters state j'

be denoted $P_{ij'}$. Then

$$
P_{ij'} = \int_0^\infty \left[\int_{t_{ij'}}^\infty \cdots \int_{t_{ij'}}^\infty \left\{ \prod_{\substack{j=1 \\ j\neq i \\ j\neq j'}}^N h_{ij}(t_{ij}) \exp\left[-\int_0^{t_{ij}} h_{ij}(u)du \right] dt_{ij} \right\} \right.
$$

$$
\left. \times \left\{ h_{ij'}(t_{ij'}) \exp\left[-\int_0^{t_{ij'}} h_{ij'}(u)du \right] \right\} \right] dt_{ij'} \qquad \text{(A3)}
$$

$$
= \int_0^\infty h_{ij'}(t_{ij'}) \exp\left\{ -\int_0^{t_{ij'}} \left[\sum_{\substack{k=1 \\ k\neq i}}^N h_{ik}(u) \right] du \right\} dt_{ij'}.
$$

The conditional density of exit times from state i into state j' given that $t_{ij} < t_{ij}$, $(\forall; j \neq j'; j, j' \neq i)$ is

$$
g(t_{ij'}|t_{ij'} < t_{ij})(\forall j; j \neq j'; j,j' \neq i) \qquad \text{(A4)}
$$

$$
= \frac{h_{ij'}(t_{ij'}) \exp\left\{ -\int_0^{t_{ij'}} \left[\sum_{\substack{k=1 \\ k\neq i}}^N h_{ik}(u) \right] du \right\}}{P_{ij'}}
$$

It follows that the density of exit times from state i into any other state can be written

$$
f_{i.}(t_{i.}) = \sum_{\substack{j'=1 \\ j'\neq i}}^N P_{ij'} g(t_{ij'}|t_{ij'} < t_{ij})(\forall j; j \neq j'; j,j' \neq i)
$$

$$
= \left[\sum_{\substack{k=1 \\ k\neq i}}^N h_{ik}(t_{i.}) \right] \exp\left\{ -\int_0^{t_{i.}} \left[\sum_{\substack{k=1 \\ k\neq i}}^N h_{ik}(u) \right] du \right\}. \qquad \text{(A5)}
$$

The probability that the spell is uncompleted by time T is simply

$$
\text{Prob } (t_{i.} > T) = \int_T^\infty f_{i.}(t)dt
$$

$$
= \exp\left\{ -\int_0^T \left[\sum_{\substack{k=1 \\ k\neq i}}^N h_{ik}(u) \right] du \right\}. \qquad \text{(A6)}
$$

This term enters the likelihood function for spells uncompleted as of the end of sample period T. In this manner all spells, not only completed ones, are used in the estimation of the parameters of the hazard function.

This is not the case in regression analyses of durations in a state (or some transformation of duration) on exogenous variables, where only completed spells can be used in a straightforward fashion.

We now describe in some detail the specific form of the likelihood function used in the analysis performed here. Let $Z_{rm}(u + \tau_{rm})$ be a $K \times 1$ vector of explanatory variables of the rth individual in his mth spell at time $(u + \tau_{rm})$, where u is the duration of time spent in the current spell and τ_{rm} is the date in calendar time at which the individual began his mth spell. Included among the explanatory variables are functions of the spell duration variables. In particular, the form of $Z'_{rm}(u + \tau_{rm})$ is

$$[1 \quad Z_{1rm}(u + \tau_{rm}) \quad \ldots \quad Z_{(K - 2)rm}(u + \tau_{rm}) \quad V_r]$$

The last element is an unobserved heterogeneity term, invariant over time for the individual, which is assumed to have a standard normal distribution, i.e.,

$$V_r \sim N(0,1) \ \forall r.$$

Parameter vectors are indexed by transition. β_{ij} is $K \times 1$ vector of coefficients of explanatory variables in the hazard function. To be specific

$$\beta_{ij} = [\beta_{0ij} \quad \beta_{1ij} \quad \ldots \quad \beta_{(K - 2)ij} \quad C_{ij}] \tag{A7}$$

As discussed in the text [Eq. (7)], we impose a one factor specification, so that C_{ij} is the factor loading associated with the i to j transition.

Now we write the hazard function for the mth spell and rth individual as

$$h_{i_m j_m}(t_{rm}) = \exp\left[Z'_{rm}(t_{rm} + \tau_{rm})\beta_{i_m j_m} \right] \tag{A8}$$

$$= \frac{f_{i_m j_m}(t_{rm})}{1 - F_{i_m j_m}(t_{rm})}.$$

Then the cumulative density for i to j exit times is

$$F_{i_m j_m}(t_{rm}) = 1 - \exp\left\{ -\int_0^{t_{rm}} \left[h_{i_m j_m}(x) \right] dx \right\} \tag{A9}$$

and the probability density is

$$f_{i_m j_m}(t_{rm}) = h_{i_m j_m}(t_{rm})\exp\left\{ -\int_0^{t_{rm}} \left[h_{i_m j_m}(x) \right] dx \right\}. \tag{A10}$$

Now consider one individual's contribution to the likelihood function (we henceforth suppress the individual subscript in the density and distribution function)

$$L_r(\beta, V) = \left[\prod_{m=1}^{M-1} f_{i_m j_m}(t_m) \right] \left\{ \prod_{\substack{k=1 \\ k \neq i_M}}^{N} [1 - F_{i_M k}(t_M)] \right\}, \tag{A11}$$

where t_M is the time spent in the Mth spell, which is censored. Because heterogeneity is modeled as a random effect, it is necessary to obtain the expected value of L_r with respect to the assumed distribution of V. Denote the conditional likelihood by $\bar{L}_r(\beta)$, where

$$\bar{L}_r(\beta) = \int_{-\infty}^{\infty} L_r(\beta, V) \exp(-V^2/2) dV (2\pi)^{-1/2}. \tag{A12}$$

Now define

$$\pounds_r(\beta) \equiv \ln[\bar{L}_r(\beta)].$$

In taking first partials note that

$$\frac{\partial \pounds_r(\beta)}{\partial \beta_{gij}} = \frac{1}{\bar{L}_r(\beta)} \frac{\partial \bar{L}_r(\beta)}{\partial \beta_{gij}}$$

$$= \frac{1}{\bar{L}_r(\beta)} \int_{-\infty}^{\infty} \frac{\partial L_r(\beta, V)}{\partial \beta_{gij}} \exp(-V^2/2) dV (2\pi)^{-1/2} \tag{A13}$$

where g denotes an element of the parameter vector. For notational convenience define the set

$$S_{ij} = \{m | i_m = i, j_m = j\}$$

which consists of all spells that begin in state i and end in state j for the individual. Then

$$\frac{\partial L_r(\beta, V)}{\partial \beta_{gij}} = \left\{ \sum_{\substack{m \in S_{ij} \\ m < M}} \left[\frac{\partial f_{i_m j_m}}{\partial \beta_{gij}} \bigg|_{t_m} \right] \left[\prod_{\substack{b \neq m \\ b < M}} f_{i_b j_b}(t_b) \right] \right\}$$

$$\times \prod_{\substack{h \neq i_M \\ h=1}} \left[1 - F_{i_m h}(t_M) \right] \tag{A14}$$

$$+ \left[\prod_{m=1}^{M-1} f_{i_m j_m}(t_m) \right] \left[-\frac{\partial F_{i_M j}}{\partial \beta_{gij}} \bigg|_{t_M} \right] \left\{ \prod_{\substack{h \neq i_m, j \\ h=1}} [1 - F_{i_M h}(t_M)] \right\}.$$

Now we evaluate the partial derivative of the density with respect to the parameters

$$\frac{\partial f_{i_m j_m}}{\partial \beta_{gij}}\bigg|_{t_m} = \left[\frac{\partial h_{i_m j_m}(t_m)}{\partial \beta_{gij}} - h_{i_m j_m}(t_m)\int_0^{t_m} \frac{\partial h_{i_m j_m}(u)}{\partial \beta_{gij}}\,du\right]$$
$$\times \exp\left(-\int_0^{t_m} h_{i_m j_m}(u)\,du\right). \qquad \text{(A15)}$$

But note that

$$\frac{\partial h_{i_m j_m}(u)}{\partial \beta_{gij}} = Z_g(u + \tau_m)h_{i_m j_m}(u).$$

After making the appropriate substitutions, we have

$$\frac{\partial f_{i_m j_m}}{\partial \beta_{gij}}\bigg|_{t_m} = \left[Z_g(t_m + \tau_m) - \int_0^{t_m} Z_g(u + \tau_m)h_{i_m j_m}(u)\,du\right]f_{i_m j_m}(t_m) \quad \text{(A16)}$$

and

$$\frac{\partial F_{i_M j}}{\partial \beta_{gij}}\bigg|_{t_m} = \int_0^{t_M} \frac{\partial h_{ij}(u)}{\partial \beta_{gij}}\,du \cdot \exp\left[-\int_0^{t_M} h_{ij}(u)\,du\right] \quad \text{for } i = i_m$$
$$= \int_0^{t_M} Z_g(u + \tau_M)h_{ij}(u)\,du[1 - F_{ij}(t_M)] \quad \text{for } i = i_m. \qquad \text{(A17)}$$

Upon making a last round of substitutions, we get that

$$\frac{\partial L_r(\beta, V)}{\partial \beta_{gij}} = \left\{\sum_{\substack{m \varepsilon Sij \\ m < M}}\left[Z_g(t_m + \tau_m) - \int_0^{t_m} Z_g(u + \tau_m)h_{i_m j_m}(u)\,du\right]\right\}$$

$$\cdot L_r(\beta, V) - \left[\int_0^{t_m} Z_g(u + \tau_m)h_{ij}(u)\,du\right]L_r(\beta, V)$$

$$= L_r(\beta, V)\left\{\sum_{\substack{m \varepsilon Sij \\ m < M}}\left[Z_g(t_m + \tau_m) - \int_0^{t_m} Z_g(u + \tau_m)h_{i_m j_m}(u)\,du\right]\right. \qquad \text{(A18)}$$

$$\left. - \int_0^{t_M} Z_g(u + \tau_m)h_{i_m j}(u)\,du\right\}$$

$$= A_{gij}L_r(\beta, V),$$

where A_{gij} is defined to be the expression in braces in the second to last line above.

$$\frac{\partial^2 \mathfrak{L}_r(\beta)}{\partial \beta_{gij} \partial \beta_{g'i'j'}} = -\frac{1}{[\bar{L}_r(\beta)]^2} \frac{\partial \bar{L}_r(\beta)}{\partial \beta_{gij}} \frac{\partial \bar{L}_r(\beta)}{\partial \beta_{g'i'j'}} + \frac{1}{\bar{L}_r(\beta)} \frac{\partial^2 \bar{L}_r(\beta)}{\partial \beta_{gij} \partial \beta_{g'i'j'}} \quad \text{(A19)}$$

$$\frac{\partial^2 \bar{L}_r(\beta)}{\partial \beta_{gij} \partial \beta_{g'i'j'}} = \int_{-\infty}^{\infty} \frac{\partial^2 L_r(\beta, V)}{\partial \beta_{gij} \partial \beta_{g'i'j'}} \exp(-V^2/2) \, dV (2\pi)^{-1/2}. \quad \text{(A20)}$$

If $i \neq i'$ or $j \neq j'$, then this last term is

$$\int_{-\infty}^{\infty} A_{g'i'j'} A_{gij} L_r(\beta, V) \exp(-V^2/2) dV (2\pi)^{-1/2} \quad \text{(A21)}$$

and if $i = i'$ and $j = j'$, then it is

$$\left\{ A_{g'i'j'} A_{gij} - \sum_{\substack{m \varepsilon Sij \\ m < M}} \left[\int_0^{t_m} Z_g(u + \tau_m) Z_{g'}(u + \tau_m) h_{i_m j_m}(u) du \right] \right.$$
$$\left. - \int_0^{t_M} Z_g(u + \tau_M) Z_{g'}(u + \tau_M) h_{i_M j}(u) du \right\} L_r(\beta, V)$$

where the last term in the braces enters only if $i_M = i = i'$.

To derive the sample likelihood, simply sum the individual contributions, i.e.,

$$\mathfrak{L}(\beta) = \sum_{r=1}^{R} \mathfrak{L}_r(\beta)$$

where R is the number of individuals in the sample. First and second partials are similarly computed for the sample by the summation of each individual's contribution. In computing the matrix of second partials, we can employ the well-known approximation based on the summed outer product of the vector of first partials for each observation based on a suggestion of Anderson (1959) or the exact second partials presented above.

APPENDIX B

The Weibull Regression Model

This appendix presents a brief derivation and discussion of the Weibull regression model utilized by Heckman and Borjas (1980) and employed in this article as well. We derive the conditional regression function of the log of duration in the jth spell of state ℓ, $\ln t_{j\ell}$, discuss the distribution of the regression errors, and demonstrate how it is possible to estimate duration dependence parameters using regression analysis. The efficiency of least squares estimators relative to maximum likelihood is derived for a special case.

The regression model derived here is the conditional regression function computed with respect to the density generated by hazard function (6) in the text with exogenous variables assumed to be fixed within each spell at value $Z_{j\ell}$ and with $\lambda_{1j\ell} = 0$ and $\gamma_{2j\ell} = 0$. To simplify notation we define $\gamma_{j\ell}$ in place of $\gamma_{1j\ell}$ in the more general model. The hazard function that generates the density of duration times is

$$h_{j\ell}(t_{j\ell}) = \exp[Z_{j\ell}\beta_{j\ell} + (\ln t_{j\ell})\gamma_{j\ell} + V_{j\ell}].$$ (B1)

Define $M_{j\ell} = \exp(Z_{j\ell}\beta_{j\ell} + V_{j\ell})$. The expectation of $\ln t_{j\ell}$ given $Z_{j\ell}$ and $V_{j\ell}$ and assuming a long panel (so there is no panel length bias as discussed in the text) is

$$E(\ln t_{j\ell}|Z_{j\ell}, V_{j\ell}) = \int_0^\infty (\ln t_{j\ell})M_{j\ell}(t_{j\ell})^{\gamma_{j\ell}} \exp\left(-\left(\frac{M_{j\ell}}{\gamma_{j\ell} + 1}\right)t_{j\ell}^{\gamma_{o\ell}+1}\right) dt_{j\ell}.$$

Define

$$\phi_{j\ell} = \left(\frac{M_{j\ell}}{\gamma_{j\ell} + 1}\right)t_{j\ell}^{\gamma_{j\ell}+1}.$$

Then

$$d\phi_{j\ell} = (M_{j\ell})t_{j\ell}^{\gamma_{j\ell}}dt_{j\ell}.$$

Substituting $\phi_{j\ell}$ for $t_{j\ell}$ and using standard LaPlace transforms

$$E(\ln t_{j\ell}|Z_{j\ell}, V_{j\ell}) = \int_0^\infty \left(\ln \phi_{j\ell} - \ln\left(\frac{M_{j\ell}}{\gamma_{j\ell} + 1}\right)\right)\frac{1}{\gamma_{j\ell} + 1}\exp(-\phi_{j\ell})d\phi_{j\ell}$$

$$= \left(\frac{1}{\gamma_{j\ell} + 1}\right)[\Gamma'(1) + \ln(\gamma_{j\ell} + 1) - Z_{j\ell}\beta_{j\ell} - V_{j\ell}]$$ (B2)

where $\Gamma'(1)$ is the derivative of the gamma function evaluated at one $(= -.5772)$.

The full regression model may be written as

$$\ln t_{j\ell} = E(\ln t_{j\ell}|Z_{j\ell}, V_{j\ell}) + W_{j\ell}$$

where

$$E(W_{j\ell}) = 0 \qquad E(W_{j\ell}^2) = \frac{B}{(\gamma_{j\ell} + 1)^2}$$ (B3)

where $B = [d\ln \Gamma(\theta)]/d\theta$ evaluated at $\theta = 1$ ($B = \pi^2/6$).

Note that the variance of error term $W_{j\ell}$ does *not* depend on $\beta_{j\ell}$.

To prove these results most directly it is helpful to derive the characteristic function of $W_{j\ell}$. Let $E(\ln t_{j\ell}) = \mu_{j\ell}$ so $W_{j\ell} = \ln t_{j\ell} - \mu_{j\ell}$. Then

$$E[\exp(i\theta W_{j\ell})] = E\{\exp[i\theta(\ln t_{j\ell} - \mu_{j\ell})]\}$$

$$= \exp(-i\theta\mu_{j\ell})\int_0^\infty M_{j\ell}t^{i\theta}t^{\gamma_{j\ell}} \exp\left[-\frac{M_{j\ell}}{(\gamma_{j\ell} + 1)}t^{\gamma_{j\ell}+1}\right]dt_{j\ell} \quad (B4)$$

$$= \exp(-i\theta\mu_{j\ell})(M_{j\ell}^{-i\theta/(\gamma_{j\ell}+1)})\Gamma\left(\frac{i\theta}{\gamma_{j\ell} + 1} + 1\right)(\gamma_{j\ell} + 1)^{i\theta/(\gamma_{j\ell}+1)}.$$

Since

$$\mu_{j\ell} = \frac{\Gamma'(1) - \ln M_{j\ell} + \ln(\gamma_{j\ell} + 1)}{\gamma_{j\ell} + 1},$$

then

$$E[\exp(i\theta W_{j\ell})] = \Gamma\left(\frac{i\theta}{\gamma_{j\ell} + 1} + 1\right)\exp\left(-\frac{i\theta\Gamma'(1)}{\gamma_{j\ell} + 1}\right).$$

Thus the characteristic function does not depend on $\beta_{j\ell}$ as asserted and the moments of $W_{j\ell}$ are not functions of $Z_{j\ell}$, $\beta_{j\ell}$, or $V_{j\ell}$. Differentiating the characteristic function produces the moments stated above.

The density of $W_{j\ell}$ can be obtained by a direct application of the inversion theorem or by direct substitution. In our notation, the density of $W_{j\ell}$ is

$$k(W_{j\ell}) = \frac{M_{j\ell}}{(1 + \gamma_{j\ell})} \exp[(\gamma_{j\ell} + 1)(W_{j\ell} + \mu_{j\ell})]$$

$$\times \exp\left\{-\frac{M_{j\ell}}{1 + \gamma_{j\ell}} \exp[(1 + \gamma_{j\ell})(\mu_{j\ell} + W_{j\ell})]\right\}. \quad (B5)$$

If there is no duration dependence ($\gamma_{j\ell} = 0$), the density simplifies to

$$k(W_{j\ell}) = M_{j\ell} \exp(W_{j\ell} + \mu_{j\ell}) \exp\{-M_{j\ell}[\exp(W_{j\ell} + \mu_{j\ell})]\}.$$

Because of the conditional independence of the $t_{j\ell}$, $j = 1, \ldots, J$; $\ell = 1, \ldots, L$ (given $Z_{j\ell}$ and $V_{j\ell}$), the $W_{j\ell}$ terms are independently distributed, and $E(W_{j\ell}W_{j'\ell'}) = 0$ for $j \neq j'$ or $\ell \neq \ell'$ or both.

Collecting results and redefining the intercept term in $\beta_{j\ell}$ to include $\Gamma'(1) + \ln(\gamma_{j\ell} + 1)$, the new coefficients may be defined as $\vec{\beta}_{j\ell}$. Collecting the unobservables into a composite error term $[-1/(\gamma_{j\ell} + 1)]V_{j\ell} + W_{j\ell}$, we may write the conditional expectation of $\ln t_{j\ell}$ given $Z_{j\ell}$ as

$$E(\ln t_{j\ell}|Z_{j\ell}) = \frac{-1}{\gamma_{j\ell} + 1}Z_{j\ell}\vec{\beta}_{j\ell} \quad (B6)$$

with associated disturbance term $U_{j\ell}$ defined by

$$U_{j\ell} = \frac{-1}{\gamma_{j\ell} + 1} V_{j\ell} + W_{j\ell} \tag{B7}$$

with zero mean and variance

$$\left(\frac{1}{\gamma_{j\ell} + 1}\right)^2 [\sigma^2_{j\ell} + B]$$

where $E(V^2_{j\ell}) = \sigma^2_{j\ell}.$ Heterogeneity components are independent of the $W_{j\ell}$ [see Eq. (B4)] but are freely correlated across states and spells. Thus $E(V_{j\ell}V_{j'\ell'}) = \sigma_{j\ell,j'\ell'} \neq 0$ in general for $j \neq j'$ and/or $\ell \neq \ell'$.

Estimation and Identification in the Weibull Model

Under standard assumptions, least squares estimators of $\beta_{j\ell}/(1 + \gamma_{j\ell})$ derived from samples of durations of the jth spell of event ℓ are unbiased, consistent but not efficient. Consistency is achieved in the usual cross-sectional sense: by letting the number of individuals in the sample become large. The lack of efficiency is due to the highly nonnormal skewed distribution of $W_{j\ell}$ and is proved in the next section for an instructive special case.

Provided that the intercept term in $\beta_{j\ell}$ is zero, it is possible under certain conditions to estimate $1 + \gamma_{j\ell}$. The intercept term in the reparameterized model is

$$\frac{\Gamma'(1) + \ln(\gamma_{j\ell} + 1)}{\gamma_{j\ell} + 1}.$$

If the estimated intercept is negative, it is possible to solve for $\gamma_{j\ell}$ uniquely from the estimated intercept in the reparameterized model. If the estimated intercept is positive and less than or equal to $\exp[\Gamma'(1) - 1]$, a solution exists but is not unique unless it equals $\exp[\Gamma'(1) - 1]$.

In the general case, it is not possible to consistently estimate $\beta_{j\ell}$ or $\gamma_{j\ell}$ from the estimated regression coefficients. Provided that further structure is imposed on the distribution of the heterogeneity components $V_{j\ell}$, it is possible to consistently estimate $\beta_{j\ell}$ and $\gamma_{j\ell}$ provided that we have access to panel data in which more than one spell of an event is observed.

Consider the following one-factor structure

$$V_{j\ell} = C_\ell \phi \tag{B8}$$

where $E(\phi) = 0$, $E(\phi^2) = \sigma^2_\phi$, and the C_ℓ are parameters $\ell = 1, \ldots,$ L. As is customary in factor analysis, we normalize $C_1 = 1$. $E(V_{j\ell}V_{j'\ell'}) = C_\ell C_{\ell'}\sigma^2_\phi$.

Provided that there are data on two or more spells, we can consistently estimate $\gamma_{j\ell}$, $\beta_{j\ell}$, and C_ℓ. To see how, note that the residual variance of the regression equation for log duration of the jth spell of event ℓ is

$$\frac{C^2_\ell \sigma^2_\phi}{(\gamma_{j\ell} + 1)^2} + \frac{B}{(\gamma_{j\ell} + 1)^2} . \tag{B9}$$

The covariance between the residual in the jth duration equation and that in the j'th duration equation for event ℓ is

$$\frac{C^2_\ell \sigma^2_\phi}{(\gamma_{j\ell} + 1)(\gamma_{j'\ell} + 1)} . \tag{B10}$$

From the two residual variances (for spells j and j') and the covariance, it is possible to solve for $\gamma_{j\ell}$ and $\gamma_{j'\ell}$. Replacing population moments by estimated sample moments, we derive unique consistent estimators for these parameters.

Define S_{jj} as the estimated residual variance from the jth duration interval. $S_{j'j'}$ is defined in a similar fashion. $S_{jj'}$ is the estimated interspell residual covariance. The interspell residual correlation is $r_{jj'}$. From these sample moments, which are consistently estimated, it is possible to estimate $C^2_\ell \sigma^2_\phi$, $\gamma_{j'\ell}$, and $\gamma_{j\ell}$. Let $\hat{\ }$ denote estimate. Then

$$\widehat{C^2_\ell \sigma^2_\phi} = \frac{B r_{jj'}}{1 - r_{jj'}}$$

$$\hat{\gamma}_{j\ell} = \frac{B}{S_{jj}} \left(\frac{1}{1 - r_{jj'}} \right)^{1/2} - 1 \tag{B11}$$

$$\hat{\gamma}_{j'\ell} = \frac{B}{S_{jj'}} \left(\frac{1}{1 - r_{jj'}} \right)^{1/2} - 1$$

where positive values of square roots are used to evaluate these expressions. From consistency of the sample moments we have consistency of the estimators. Note that a negative $r_{jj'}$ is evidence against the one-factor structure. Given consistent estimators of these parameters, it is clearly possible to estimate $\beta_{j\ell}$ and $\beta_{j'\ell}$.

These estimators of the duration dependence parameters are sensitive to measurement error in the dependent variable that is independently distributed across spells. Such measurement error generates downward biased estimators of duration dependence parameters. Permanent measurement error components are absorbed in ϕ leading to an upward bias in the estimate of $C^2_\ell \sigma^2_\phi$ but no bias in the other coefficients.

Other covariance restrictions could be imposed to secure estimates of model parameters but we do not pursue the matter further here. For additional discussion of the regression approach, see Heckman and Borjas (1980).

The Relative Inefficiency of the Least Squares Estimator[18]

We consider only a single episode of an event. Further assume that the heterogeneity component is zero for everyone in our sample, $V_{je} = 0$. To simplify the notation, we suppress all subscripts for events and spells. The panel is assumed to be of sufficient length that there is no censoring. We further assume that γ is known, in order to simplify the analysis.

The regression model may be written for individual i as

$$\ln t_i = \left(\frac{1}{\gamma + 1}\right)[\Gamma'(1) + \ln(\gamma + 1) - Z_i\beta] + W_i \quad i = 1, \ldots, I.$$

$$E(W_i) = 0; \ E(W_i^2) = (\pi^2/6)\left(\frac{1}{\gamma + 1}\right)^2.$$

Given γ, the least squares estimators of $\beta, \hat{\beta}$ has the sampling variance

$$\text{var}(\hat{\beta}) = \frac{\pi^2}{6}(\Sigma Z'_i Z_i)^{-1}. \tag{B12}$$

The likelihood for the sample is

$$\pounds = \prod_{i=1}^{I} t_i^{\gamma} \exp(Z_i\beta) \exp -\{[\exp(Z_i\beta)] \frac{1}{\gamma + 1} t_i^{\gamma+1}\}.$$

The log likelihood is

$$\ln \pounds = \gamma \sum_{i=1}^{I} \ln t_i + \sum_{i=1}^{I} Z_i\beta - \frac{1}{\gamma + 1} \sum_{i=1}^{I} [\exp(Z_i\beta)] t_i^{\gamma+1}.$$

Given γ, the maximum likelihood estimator of β is obtained by solving

$$\frac{\partial \ln \pounds}{\partial \beta} = \sum_{i=1}^{I} Z_i - \sum_{i=1}^{I} [\exp(Z_i\beta)] \frac{t_i^{\gamma+1}}{\gamma + 1} Z_i = 0.$$

Note further that

$$\frac{\partial^2 \ln \pounds}{\partial \beta' \partial \beta} = -\sum_{i=1}^{I} \exp(Z_i\beta) \frac{t_i^{\gamma+1}}{\gamma + 1} Z'_i Z_i$$

and

$$E\left(-\frac{\partial^2 \ln \pounds}{\partial \beta' \partial \beta}\right) = \sum_{i=1}^{I} Z'_i Z_i.$$

Therefore the asymptotic variance–covariance matrix of the maximum likelihood estimator is

$$(\Sigma Z'_i Z_i)^{-1} \tag{B13}$$

Thus the asymptotic relative efficiency of the maximum likelihood estimator compared to the least squares estimator is $\pi^2/6$.

APPENDIX C

A Model of "Stigma" or "Occurrence Dependence"

Workers differ in turnover propensities and productivity characteristics. These attributes cannot be directly observed. Because of fixed costs of hiring, firm specific capital investments, or costs of monitoring worker output, some information—albeit imperfect—about unobserved attributes may be valued by firms in making wage offers to potential employees.

One source of information about a worker is his employment record. Information about the number of previous jobs held, their duration, circumstances under which these jobs were terminated, and what the worker did after his termination is useful in estimating the productivity of a potential match. It is not obvious that this information is of any market value. This is so because (1) workers have an incentive to misrepresent their work history or, more generally, accurate work histories are hard to come by; and (2) contingent contracts [c.f. Becker and Stigler (1974) and Salop and Salop (1976)] might be written that select workers out by their productivity characteristics and turnover propensities, so that the past record of an employee is irrelevant.

Here we sketch an idealized model of "stigma" and focus only on one piece of information: the *number* of jobs held by a worker of a given age. We assume that each job terminates with a spell of unemployment and that there is no recall. (Becker, 1980, considers a model of stigma in the marriage market).

Jobs terminate for many reasons. We assume that termination probabilities are determined in part by worker "quit" or "mismatch" characteristics as well as by micro demand shocks experienced by firms. To capture this notion most simply we suppose that $1 - P$ is the per period probability of termination of a match. This probability is exogenously determined. P varies across workers but we assume it stays constant across unemployment spells for the worker. In a more general model, P would be influenced by firm wage policy.

Firms know the number of jobs held by workers. They adjust to this information by offering them wages contingent on their age and on their job history. For the moment, abstract further and suppose that the wage offer distributions are indexed only by the number of employment spells. Suppose that after n jobs, the worker falls into a terminal state and is "marked" as a loser for life. We assume n is finite but this assumption is inessential.

Let $F^{(j)}(X)$ denote the wage offer distribution available to a worker with a history of j jobs. $F^{(j)}$ is stochastically dominated by $F^{(j-1)}$ and dominates $F^{(j+1)}$. For a risk neutral worker with n jobs, the optimal job search strategy for an unemployed worker is trivial to establish. Let $W_n(X)$ be the value function for a worker who receives a wage offer of

X from distribution $F^{(n)}$. The job terminates with probability $1 - P$ and the discount factor is β. W_n is defined as the expected value of $W_n(X)$ with respect to $F^{(n)}$. There is a fixed cost of search C with one offer per "period."[19]

Thus

$$W_n(X) = \max\left\{\frac{X}{1 - P\beta} + \frac{\beta(1 - P)}{1 - P\beta} W_n; W_n\right\}$$

and

$$W_n = -C + \beta \operatorname*{E}_{x} \max\left\{\frac{X}{1 - \beta P} + \frac{(1 - P)\beta}{1 - \beta P} W_n; W_n\right\}$$

The reservation wage, ε_n, is $(1 - \beta)W_n$.

It is obvious that the greater the values of β and P, the greater the reservation wage and the longer the expected length of search. It is also well known (see, for example, Kiefer and Neumann, 1979) that if the mean of the wage offer distribution increases (a pure translation of the distribution), the reservation wage increases by less than the increase in the mean so that the expected length of time in search decreases with increases in the mean of the distribution. Defining θ_n as a translation parameter,

$$\frac{\partial \varepsilon_n}{\partial \theta_n} = \frac{\dfrac{\beta}{1 - \beta P}[1 - F(\varepsilon_n)]}{1 + \dfrac{\beta}{1 - \beta P}[1 - F(\varepsilon_n)]} \leq 1 \quad (= 1 \text{ if } P = \beta = 1).$$

We next consider a worker who has $n - 1$ spells of employment. The value of a wage offer of X obtained from distribution $F^{(n-1)}$ is

$$W_{n-1}(X) = \max\left\{\frac{X}{1 - P\beta} + \frac{(1 - P)\beta}{1 - P\beta} W_n; W_{n-1}\right\}$$

The first term in the braces is the expected value of accepting a wage offer of X. It is the sum of two terms: the discounted value of the wage offer (inclusive of the termination probability) and the discounted expected value of search from distribution $F^{(n)}$. The second term in braces is the discounted expected value of search from distribution $F^{(n-1)}$.

It is obvious that $W_n < W_{n-1}$. Further, it is easy to see that the reservation wage for the worker is

$$\varepsilon_{n-1} = (1 - P\beta)W_{n-1} - (1 - P)\beta W_n.$$

Alternatively

$$\varepsilon_{n-1} - \varepsilon_n = (1 - \beta P)(W_{n-1} - W_n),$$

so that the reservation wage for a worker with $n - 1$ spells of employment exceeds that for a worker with n spells. This does not necessarily imply that workers with $n - 1$ jobs search longer on average than workers with n jobs. Although the mean of distribution $F^{(n-1)}$ necessarily exceeds the mean of distribution $F^{(n)}$ by the assumed stochastic dominance relations, the variance of $F^{(n-1)}$ may or may not be smaller, hence the expected search time in spell $n - 1$ may be shorter or longer than for spell n. However, if it is assumed that the distributions differ only in the mean, then workers with $n - 1$ jobs necessarily search less on the average than workers with n or more jobs.

To show this in a direct way note that the equation for W_{n-1} may be written as

$$W_{n-1}(1 - P\beta)(1 - \beta)$$
$$= -C(1 - P\beta) + \beta \int_{\varepsilon_{n-1}}^{\infty} (X - \varepsilon_{n-1})dF^{(n-1)}(X - \theta_{n-1})$$

where $\theta_{(n-1)}$ is a translation parameter for distribution $n - 1$. If $\theta_{n-1} = \theta_n = 0$, $F^{(n)} = F^{(n-1)}$, $W_n = W_{n-1}$, and $\varepsilon_n = \varepsilon_{n-1}$. Note that

$$\frac{\partial \varepsilon_{n-1}}{\partial \theta_{n-1}} = (1 - \beta P)\frac{\partial W_{n-1}}{\partial \theta_{n-1}}.$$

In a neighborhood of $\theta_{(n-1)} = \theta_{(n)} = 0$

$$\frac{\partial \varepsilon_{n-1}}{\partial \theta_{n-1}} = \frac{\beta(1 - F)}{1 - \beta F} \leq 1 \quad (= 1 \text{ for } \beta = 1).$$

Thus, for the case of a negative translation in wage distributions across successive spells, on average individuals with $n - 1$ spells of employment will spend less time in search than individuals with n spells of employment. By recursion, this argument can be extended to demonstrate that geometric exit time distributions have successively greater means for individuals who have held more jobs. Thus the exit time distribution for the jth spell of unemployment is stochastically dominated by the exit time distribution for spell $j + 1$ and stochastically dominates the exit time distribution for spell $j - 1$. This generates structural occurrence dependence.

This model can be extended to account for age, although it is not especially illuminating to do so. However, it is obvious that employers would utilize age to estimate mismatch and turnover propensities. Holding P fixed, older workers will hold more jobs than younger workers. Moreover, it is also clear that the length of previous employment spells may also provide information about expected worker productivity. This gives rise to lagged duration dependence as defined by Heckman and Borjas (1980).

ACKNOWLEDGMENT

This research is supported by NSF grant SOC 77-27136 and grant 10-P-90748/9-01 from the Social Security Administration. We are grateful to Takeshi Amemiya, Marjorie McElroy, George Neumann, Guilherme Sedlacek, George Yates, and especially Gary Chamberlain and Burton Singer for comments on this article. George Yates provided extremely competent programming assistance. Portions of this article were presented at the Summer Meetings of the Econometric Society, Montreal, June, 1979.

NOTES

1.   The nonemployment state comprises the states unemployment and out-of-the-labor-force.

2.

$$
\frac{\partial h(t)}{\partial t} = \frac{\left[\int a \exp(-at) g(a) da\right]^2 - \left[\int a^2 \exp(-at)\, g(a) da\right] \cdot \left[\int \exp(-at)\, g(a) da\right]}{\left[\int \exp(-at)\, g(a) da\right]^2}
$$

The numerator of the expression on the right-hand side is nonpositive by the Cauchy–Schwartz inequality for integrals (Buck, 1968, p. 123). It is strictly negative so long as $g(a)$ is nondegenerate.

3.   Tuma, Hannan, and Groeneveld (1979) permit one variable in a set of variables to change within spells.

4.   Heckman and Borjas (1980) introduce heterogeneity correlated across spells.

5.   We advocate use of future values rather than lagged values in constructing the test because of the possibility that lagged duration variables may be present in the structural model. See Heckman and Borjas (1980).

6.   Discussions with Marjorie McElroy and Burton Singer clarified our thinking on the problems discussed in this section.

7.   For discussion of this point in the analysis of unemployment spells see Salant (1977, p. 56).

8.   This density is also the density for time in the spell prior to τ_o, Δ_e^o. (See Cox, 1962, p. 61.) Replacing $\bar{t}_e^o$ by Δ_e^o in $\psi_e(\bar{t}_e^o)$ produces the density for Δ_e^o.

9.   Due to the nonlinearity of the model, integrating out the missing data with respect to its distribution is *not*, in general, equivalent to replacing the missing values with estimated mean values as is customary in standard linear regression models.

10.   For simplicity we do not explicitly note the dependence of the hazard function on exogenous variables.

11.   This problem is discussed in Tuma and Hannan (1979).

12.   Thus in testing for "mean occurrence dependence" (i.e., different regression functions for consecutive spells), the sample selection bias discussed in the text does not bias the test based on regression mehods. This result is critically dependent on the assumption that the Z variables remain constant both within and across spells, and of course, that the same rule is used to generate first and second spells.

13.   Gary Chamberlain (1982) has also discussed this problem.

14.   This expectation is computed from the joint density of t_1, t_2, which is

$$\theta(Z_1, V) \exp[-\theta(Z_1, V)t_1]\theta(Z_1, V) \exp[-\theta(Z_1, V)t_2] \quad 0 < t_2 < \tau_1 - t_1$$
$$0 < t_1 < \tau_1$$

$$\theta(Z_2, V) \exp[-\theta(Z_2, V)t_2]\theta(Z_1, V) \exp[-\theta(Z_1, V)t_1]$$

$$\exp\{[\theta(Z_2, V) - \theta(Z_1, V)](\tau_1 - t_1)\} \quad 0 < t_1 < \tau_1$$
$$\tau_1 - t_1 < t_2$$

$$\theta(Z_2, V) \exp[-\theta(Z_2, V)t_2]\theta(Z_2, V) \exp[-\theta(Z_2, V)t_1] \exp\{[\theta(Z_2, V) - \theta(Z_1, V)]\tau_1\} \quad 0 < t_2$$
$$\tau_1 < t_1$$

15.   Cox and Lewis (1966) suggest this approach but only for explanatory variables that are not strongly time trended.

16.   We are indebted to Gary Chamberlain for clarifying our thinking on the test proposed in this section.

17.   The proof is trivial. Assume $f_n(t_n)$ is not defective so that $\int_0^\infty f_n(t_n)dt_n = 1$. The hazard rate for exit from unemployment to employment is

$$h_{ue} = \frac{\pi f_n(t_n)}{\pi - \pi F_n(t_n)} = h_n.$$

The term in the denominator is the probability that the exit occurs from u to e after time t_n. A parallel argument demonstrates that $h_{oe} = h_n$.

18.   Takeshi Amemiya suggested the line of proof used in this section.

19.   Our analysis of the terminal state is similar to that of Lippman and McCall (1979). They do not, however, discuss "stigma" or "occurrence dependence."

REFERENCES

Anderson, T. W. (1959). Some scaling models and estimation procedures in the latent class model, In *Probability and Statistics,* U. Grenander (ed.), Uppsala.

Barlow, R. E. and F. Proschan (1965). *Mathematical Theory of Reliability,* New York: Wiley.

Becker, G. (1980). Imperfect information, marriage and divorce, In "A treatise on the family," Chapter 12, Unpublished manuscript, University of Chicago.

Becker, G. and G. Stigler (1974). Law enforcement, malfeasance and compensation of enforcers, *Journal of Legal Studies 3,* 1–18.

Box, G. and D. R. Cox (1964). The analysis of transformations, *Journal of the Royal Statistical Society, Series B, 26,* 211–252.

Brock, W., M. Rothschild, and J. Stiglitz (1979). Notes on stochastic capital theory, University of Wisconsin.

Buck, G. (1968). *Advanced Calculus,* 2d ed., New York: Macmillan.

Burdett, K. and D. Mortensen (1977). Labor supply under uncertainty, Discussion paper 297, Northwestern University.

Chamberlain, G., "On the Use of Panel Data," In Heckman, J. and B. Singer, *The Analysis of Longitudinal Labor Market Data,* Academic Press, 1982.

Clark, K. and L. Summers (1978). The dynamics of youth unemployment, N.B.E.R. Working Paper No. 274.

Coleman, J. S. (1964). *Introduction to Mathematical Sociology,* Glencoe, Ill.: Free Press of Glencoe.

Cox, D. R. (1962). *Renewal Theory,* London: Butler and Tanner.

Cox, D. R. and P. A. W. Lewis (1966). *The Statistical Analysis of Series of Events,* London: Methuen.

Danforth, J. (1979). On the role of consumption and decreasing absolute risk aversion in the theory of job search, In *Studies in the Economics of Search,* S. Lippman and J. McCall (eds.), Amsterdam: North Holland, pp. 109–132.

Ellwood, D. (1979). Teenage unemployment: temporary scar or permanent blemish, N.B.E.R. Working Paper No. 399.

Flinn, C. and J. Heckman, Econometric Methods for Analyzing Labor Force Dynamics, forthcoming, *Journal of Econometrics, 1982.*

Gronau, R. (1971). Information and frictional unemployment, *American Economic Review* 60, 290–301.

Hall, J., S. Lippman, and J. McCall (1979). Expected utility maximizing job search, In *Studies in the Economics of Search,* S. Lippman and J. McCall (eds.), Amsterdam: North Holland, pp. 133–156.

Heckman, J. (1981). The incidental parameters problem and the problem of initial conditions in estimating discrete time—discrete data stochastic process and some Monte Carlo evidence, In *Structural Analysis of Discrete Data with Econometric Applications,* C. Manski and D. McFadden (eds.), Cambridge: MIT Press.

Heckman, J. and G. Borjas, (1980). Does unemployment cause future unemployment? Definitions, questions and answers from a continuous time model of heterogeneity and state dependence. Forthcoming in a special issue on the economics of unemployment, *Economica,* Vol. 47, May, 1980, pp. 247–283.

Heckman, J. and R. Willis (1975). Estimation of a stochastic model of reproduction: an econometric approach. In *Household Production and Consumption,* N. Terleckyj (ed.), Stanford, Calif.: National Bureau of Economic Research.

Holt, C. (1970). Job search, Phillips wage resolutions and union influence: theory and evidence, In *Microeconomic Foundations,* E. Phelps *et al.* (eds.), New York: Norton, pp. 53–123.

Jovanovic, B. (1979). Job matching and the theory of turnover, *Journal of Political Economy 87,* 972–990.

Kiefer, N. and G. Neumann (1979). An empirical job search model with a test of the constant resolution wage hypothesis. *Journal of Political Economy 87,* 89–108.

Lippmann, S. and J. J. McCall (1976). The economics of job search: a survey, Part I. *Economic Inquiry 14,* 155–189.

——— (1979). Search unemployment: mismatches, layoffs and unemployment insurance. Western Management Science Institute, UCLA.

Marston, S. (1976). Employment instability and high unemployment rates, *Brookings Papers on Economic Activity 7,* 169–203.

McCall, John J. "Economics of Information and Job Search," *Quarterly Journal of Economics,* 84, 1970, pp. 113–126.

Moran, P. A. P. (1971). Maximum likelihood estimation in non-standard conditions, *Proceedings Cambridge Philosophical Society 70,* 441–450.

Mortensen, D. (1970). Job search, the duration of unemployment and the Phillips curve, *American Economic Review 60,* 847–862.

Phillips, P. C. B. (1976). The problem of identification in finite parameter continuous time models, In *Statistical Inference in Continuous Time Economic Models,* A. R. Bergstrom (ed.), Amsterdam: North Holland, pp. 123–134.

Salant, S. (1977). Search theory and duration data, *The Quarterly Journal of Economics 91,* 39–57.

Salop, S. (1973). Systematic job search and unemployment, *Review of Economic Studies 40*, 191–201.

Salop, S. and J. Salop (1976). Self selection and turnover in the labor market, *Quarterly Journal of Economics 90*, 629–649.

Singer, B. and S. Spilerman (1976). Some methodological issues in the analysis of longitudinal surveys, *Annals of Economic and Social Measurement 4*, 447–474.

Toikka, R. S. (1976). A Markovian model of labor market decisions by workers, *American Economic Review 66*, 821–834.

Tuma, N., M. Hannan, and L. Groeneveld (1979). Dynamic analysis of event histories, *American Journal of Sociology 84*, 820–854.

Tuma, N. and M. Hannan (1979). Approaches to the censoring problem in analysis of event histories, In *Sociological Methodology*, K. Schuessler (ed.), San Francisco: Jossey Bass, pp. 209–240.

THE TRANSCENDENTAL
LOGARITHMIC MODEL OF
AGGREGATE CONSUMER
BEHAVIOR

Dale W. Jorgenson, Lawrence J. Lau and
Thomas M. Stoker

I.   INTRODUCTION

The objective of this article is to present a new econometric model of aggregate consumer behavior and to implement this model for the United States for the period 1958–1974. The model incorporates aggregate time series data on quantities consumed, prices, the level and distribution of total expenditures, and demographic characteristics of the population. It also incorporates individual cross section data on the allocation of consumer expenditures among commodities for households with different demographic characteristics.

Advances in Econometrics, volume 1, pages 97–238.

Our econometric model can be applied to the generation of projections of aggregate consumer demand in the United States. Projected future prices, the future level and distribution of total expenditures, and the future demographic development of the population are required for projections. The model can also be used to make projections for groups of individuals within the United States, classified by total expenditure and by demographic characteristics. Finally, it can be employed in assessing the impacts of alternative economic policies on the welfare of individuals with common demographic characteristics.

Our model of aggregate consumer behavior unifies two distinct lines of empirical research on consumer behavior. The first line of research, issuing from the seminal contributions of Schultz (1938), Stone (1954b), and Wold (1953), has focused on the role of prices and total expenditure as determinants of the pattern of consumer expenditures. The theory of consumer behavior is used to derive a model of the representative consumer. This model is implemented on the basis of aggregate time series data on prices, per capita quantities consumed, and per capita total expenditure.

A second line of research, represented by the classic studies of family budgets by Leser (1963), Prais and Houthakker (1955), and Working (1942), has focused on the role of demographic characteristics and total expenditures of individual households as determinants of the pattern of consumer expenditures. The theory of consumer behavior is used to derive a model of the individual consumer. This model is implemented on the basis of cross section data on quantities consumed, total expenditure, and demographic characteristics of individual households.

Time series and cross section data have been combined by Stone (1954b) and Wold (1953) in aggregate models of consumer behavior based on a model of the representative consumer. Cross section data are used to estimate the impact of per capita total expenditure and time series data are used to estimate the impact of prices within a model that determines per capita quantities consumed. This pioneering research omits an important link between individual and aggregate consumer behavior arising from the fact that aggregate demand functions can be represented as the sum of individual demand functions.

Aggregate demand functions depend on prices and total expenditures, as in the theory of individual consumer behavior. However, aggregate demand functions depend on individual total expenditures rather than aggregate expenditure. If individual expenditures are allowed to vary independently, models of aggregate consumer behavior based on aggregate expenditure or per capita expenditure imply restrictions that severely limit the dependence of individual demand functions on individual expenditure. Alternatively, if individual expenditures are functions of aggregate expenditure, for example, if each individual expenditure is a fixed proportion of aggregate expenditure so that the expenditure distribution is fixed, the implications of the theory of consumer behavior for aggregate demand functions are extremely limited.

One consequence of the theory of individual consumer behavior is that the weighted sum of aggregate demand functions with each function multiplied by the price of the corresponding commodity is equal to aggregate expenditure. A second consequence is that aggregate demand functions are homogeneous of degree zero in prices and individual expenditures. For a fixed expenditure distribution aggregate demand functions are homogeneous of degree zero in prices and aggregate expenditure. Diewert (1977) and Sonnenschein (1974) have shown that any system of aggregate demand functions that satisfies these two conditions, but is otherwise arbitrary, can be rationalized as the sum of systems of individual demand functions with a fixed expenditure distribution.

A.   Representative Consumer

We now turn to the implication of models of aggregate consumer behavior based on per capita expenditure and quantities consumed. Before proceeding with the presentation, we first set down some notation. There are K consumers, indexed by $k = 1, 2, \ldots, K$. There are N commodities in the economy, indexed by $n = 1, 2, \ldots, N$; p_n is the price of the nth commodity, assumed to be the same for all consumers. We denote by $p = (p_1, p_2, \ldots, p_N)$ the vector of prices of all commodities. The quantity of the nth commodity demanded by the kth consumer is x_{nk}, and total expenditure of the kth consumer is $M_k = \sum_{n=1}^{N} p_n x_{nk}$. Finally, A_k is a vector of individual attributes of the kth consumer.[1]

We assume that the demand for the nth commodity by the kth consumer x_{nk} can be expressed as a function f_{nk} of the price vector p, total expenditure M_k and the vector of attributes A_k

$$x_{nk} = f_{nk}(p, M_k, A_k). \tag{1}$$

Aggregate demand for the nth commodity is given by:

$$\sum_{k=1}^{K} x_{nk} = \sum_{k=1}^{K} f_{nk}(p, M_k, A_k)$$

In models of consumer behavior based on aggregate quantities consumed, the aggregate demand function depends on the price vector p, aggregate expenditure $\Sigma_{k=1}^{K} M_k$, and possibly some index of aggregate attributes, say $\Sigma_{k=1}^{K} A_k$. Thus, we may write:

$$\sum_{k=1}^{K} f_k (p, M_k, A_k) = F (p, \sum_{k=1}^{K} M_k, \sum_{k=1}^{K} A_k) \qquad (2)$$

where f_k is a vector-valued function:

$$f_k = \begin{bmatrix} f_{1k} \\ f_{2k} \\ \vdots \\ f_{Nk} \end{bmatrix}, \qquad (k = 1, 2, \ldots, K),$$

giving the vector of demands for all N commodities by the kth consumer, and F is a vector-valued aggregate demand function giving the vector of demands for all N commodities by all K consumers.

The conditions under which equation (2) holds for all expenditures M_k $(k = 1, 2, \ldots, K)$, all prices, and all possible attributes, have been derived by Gorman (1953) under the assumption of utility maximization by individual consumers. Gorman's conditions imply

(1) $f_k(p, M_k, A_k) = h_1(p)M_k + h_2(p)A_k + C_k(p)$
       $(k = 1, 2, \ldots, K)$

(2) $F(p, \sum_{k=1}^{K} M_k, \sum_{k=1}^{K} A_k) = h_1(p) \sum_{k=1}^{K} M_k + h_2(p) \sum_{k=1}^{K} A_k$

$$+ \sum_{k=1}^{K} C_k(p)$$

where the vector-valued function $h_1(p)$ is homogeneous of degree minus one and the vector-valued functions $h_2(p)$ and $C_k(p)$ $(k = 1, 2, \ldots, K)$ are homogeneous of degree zero. In other words, the individual demand functions are linear in expenditure and attributes. They are identical up to the addition of a function that is independent of expenditure and attributes. Furthermore, if aggregate demands are equal to zero when aggregate expenditure is equal to zero, individuals must have identical homothetic preferences.

We can illustrate Gorman's results by considering the case of two individuals. The aggregate demand function F is the sum of two individual demand functions

$$f_1(p, M_1, A_1) + f_2(p, M_2, A_2) = F(p, M_1 + M_2, A_1 + A_2)$$

Since interchanging M_1 and M_2 and interchanging A_1 and A_2 leaves the right-hand side unaffected, it must also leave the left-hand side unaffected. Thus:

$$f_1(p,M_1,A_1) + f_2(p,M_2,A_2) = f_1(p,M_2,A_2) + f_2(p,M_1,A_1)$$

which upon rearrangement becomes:

$$f_1(p,M_1,A_1) - f_2(p,M_1,A_1) = f_1(p,M_2,A_2) - f_2(p,M_2,A_2)$$

The left-hand side is independent of M_2 and A_2; the right-hand side is independent of M_1 and A_1. In order for the two sides to be equal, they must both depend only on prices. Therefore

$$f_1(p,M_k,A_k) - f_2(p,M_k,A_k) = C(p)$$

or:

$$f_k(p,M_k,A_k) = f(p,M_k,A_k) + C_k(p) \qquad (k = 1, 2)$$

This shows that $f_1 (p, M_1, A_1)$ and $f_2 (p, M_2, A_2)$ are identical up to the addition of a vector-valued function $C_k (p)$ independent of expenditure.
Next we consider

$$f(p,M_1,A_1) + C_1(p) + f(p,M_2,A_2) + C_2(p) = F(p,M_1 + M_2, A_1 + A_2)$$

Under the assumption of differentiability of the aggregate demand function we can differentiate this equation with respect to one of the individual expenditures, so that:

$$\frac{\partial f}{\partial M_1} (p,M_1,A_1) = \frac{\partial F}{\partial M_1} (p,M_1 + M_2,A_1 + A_2)$$

(We will see later that it is not essential to assume differentiability.) In order for this equation to hold for all M_1 and M_2 and all A_1 and A_2, the function $\partial F/\partial M$ must be independent of its second and third arguments, so that:

$$\frac{\partial f}{\partial M_1} (p,M_1,A_1) = h_1(p)$$

Similarly,

$$\frac{\partial f}{\partial A_1} (p,M_1,A_1) = h_2(p)$$

so that the aggregate demand function is linear in expenditure and attributes:

$$F(p, M_1 + M_2, A_1 + A_2) = h_1 (p) [M_1 + M_2] + h_2(p)[A_1 + A_2] + C (p)$$

as Gorman has shown under the assumption that the individual attributes are fixed. If aggregate demands are zero when aggregate expenditure is equal to zero, then

$$C(p) = 0$$

individuals must have identical homothetic preferences.[2]

Homothetic preferences are inconsistent with well-established empirical regularities in the behavior of individual consumers, such as Engel's law, which states that the proportion of expenditure devoted to food is a decreasing function of total expenditure.[3] Identical preferences for individual households are inconsistent with empirical findings that expenditure patterns depend on demographic characteristics of individual households.[4] Even the weaker form of Gorman's results, that quantities consumed are linear functions of expenditure with identical slopes for all individuals, is inconsistent with empirical evidence from budget studies.[5]

Despite the conflict between Gorman's characterization of individual consumer behavior and the empirical evidence from cross section data, this characterization has provided an important stimulus to empirical research based on aggregate time series data. The linear expenditure system, proposed by Klein and Rubin (1947) and implemented by Stone (1954a), has the property that individual demand functions are linear in total expenditure. The resulting system of aggregate demand functions has been used widely as the basis for econometric models of aggregate consumer behavior. Generalizations of the linear expenditure system that retain the critical property of linearity of individual demand functions in total expenditure have also been employed in empirical research.[6]

Muellbauer (1975, 1976a) has substantially generalized Gorman's characterization of the representative consumer model. Aggregate expenditure shares, interpreted as the expenditure shares of a representative consumer, may depend on prices and on a function of individual expenditures not restricted to aggregate or per capita expenditure. In Muellbauer's model of the representative consumer individual preferences are identical but not necessarily homothetic. Furthermore, quantities consumed may be nonlinear functions of expenditure rather than linear functions, as in Gorman's characterization. An important consequence of this nonlinearity is that aggregate demand functions depend on the distribution of expenditure among individuals. Berndt, Darrough, and Diewert (1977) and Deaton and Muellbauer (1980a) have implemented aggregate models of consumer behavior that conform to Muellbauer's characterization of the representative consumer model, retaining the assumption that preferences are identical among individuals.

B. Exact Aggregation

Lau (1977b) has developed a theory of exact aggregation that makes it possible to incorporate differences in individual preferences. One of the most remarkable implications of Lau's theory of exact aggregation is that systems of demand functions for individuals with common demographic characteristics can be recovered uniquely from the system of aggregate demand functions. This feature makes it possible to exploit all of the implications of the theory of the individual consumer in specifying a model of aggregate consumer behavior. The corresponding feature of the model of a representative consumer accounts for the widespread utilization of this model in previous empirical research.

We first generalize the concept of an aggregate demand function to that of a function that depends on general symmetric functions of individual expenditures and attributes

$$\sum_{k=1}^{K} f_k(p, M_k, A_k) = F[p, g_1(M_1, M_2, \ldots, M_K, A_1, A_2, \ldots, A_K),$$

$$g_2(M_1, M_2, \ldots M_K, A_1, A_2 \ldots A_K), \ldots, \qquad (3)$$

$$g_L(M_1, M_2 \ldots, M_K, A_1, A_2, \ldots, A_K)]$$

where each function g_ℓ ($\ell = 1, 2, \ldots, L$) is symmetric in individual expenditures and attributes, so that the value of this function is independent of the ordering of the individuals. For example, g_1 may be $\sum_{k=1}^{K} M_k$, g_2 may be $\sum_{k=1}^{K} [M_k - \sum_{j=1}^{K} M_j/K]^2$, and g_3 may be $\sum_{k=1}^{K} M_k A_k$.

We refer to the functions g_ℓ ($\ell = 1, 2, \ldots, L$) as index functions. These functions can be interpreted as statistics describing the population. To avoid triviality we assume also that the set of functions g_ℓ ($\ell = 1, 2, \ldots, L$) is functionally independent; there is no nonconstant function G such that

$$G[g_1(M_1, M_2, \ldots, M_K, A_1, A_2, \ldots, A_K), g_2(M_1, M_2, \ldots, M_K, A_1, A_2,$$

$$\ldots, A_K), \ldots, g_L(M_1, M_2, \ldots, M_K, A_1, A_2, \ldots, A_K)] = 0$$

for all $\{M_k, A_k\}$. We note that the representation in equation (3) is not unique. Given any function F and a set of L functions g_ℓ ($\ell = 1, 2, \ldots, L$), we can represent the same aggregate demand function by

$$\sum_{k=1}^{K} f_k(p, M_k, A_k) = F^*[p, g_1^*(M_1, M_2, \ldots, M_K, A_1, A_2, \ldots, A_K),$$

$$g_2^*(M_1, M_2, \ldots, M_K, A_1, A_2, \ldots, A_K), \ldots,$$

$$g_L^*(M_1, M_2, \ldots, M_K, A_1, A_2, \ldots, A_K)]$$

where the functions g_ℓ^* ($\ell = 1, 2, \ldots, L$) are obtained by a nonsingular transformation of the original L functions g_ℓ ($\ell = 1, 2, \ldots, L$) and F^* is chosen so that

$$F^* = F$$

for all prices, expenditures, and attributes $\{p, M_k, A_k\}$

The first result we discuss provides the foundation for the theory of exact aggregation. We consider the conditions under which the sum of individual demand functions can be represented in the form of equation (3). The Fundamental Theorem of Exact Aggregation establishes conditions for equation (3) to hold for all prices, individual expenditures and individual attributes. In our notation, this theorem can be stated as

Theorem 1. An aggregate demand function can be written in the form

$$\sum_{k=1}^K f_k(p, M_k, A_k) = F[p, g_1(M_1, M_2, \ldots, M_K, A_1, A_2, \ldots, A_K),$$

$$g_2(M_1, M_2, \ldots, M_K, A_1, A_2, \ldots, A_K), \ldots,$$

$$g_L(M_1, M_2, \ldots, M_K, A_1, A_2, \ldots, A_K)],$$

where:

(1) Each function g_ℓ ($\ell = 1, 2, \ldots, L$) is nonconstant and symmetric with respect to the individuals $\{1, 2, \ldots, K\}$;

(2) There exists no functional relationship among the functions g_ℓ ($\ell = 1, 2, \ldots, L$), that is, there exists no nonconstant function G such that $G(g_1, g_2, \ldots, g_L) = O$;

(3) There exist price vectors $p^1, p^2, \ldots, p^L$ such that the system of functions $F(p^\ell, g_1, g_2, \ldots, g_L)$, ($\ell = 1, 2, \ldots, L$), is invertible in $g_1, g_2, \ldots, g_L$ and the range of each $F(p^\ell, g_1, g_2, \ldots, g_L)$ is an interval of the nonnegative real line ($\ell = 1, 2, \ldots, L$);

(4) The function $F(p, g_1, g_2, \ldots, g_L)$ is nonnegative; if and only if

(a)

$$f_k(p, M_k, A_k) = \sum_{\ell=1}^L h_\ell(p) g_\ell^*(M_k, A_k) + C_k^*(p)$$

$$(k = 1, 2, \ldots, K) \quad (4)$$

(b)

$$g_\ell(M_1, M_2, \ldots, M_K, A_1, A_2, \ldots, A_K) = \sum_{k=1}^K g_\ell^*(M_k, A_k)$$

$$(\ell = 1, 2, \ldots, L) \quad (5)$$

(c)

$$F[p, g_1(M_1,M_2, \ldots ,M_K,A_1,A_2, \ldots , A_K), g_2(M_1,M_2, \ldots , M_K, A_1,A_2,$$
$$\ldots , A_K), \ldots , g_L(M_1,M_2, \ldots , M_K, A_1,A_2, \ldots , A_K)] \tag{6}$$

$$= \sum_{\ell=1}^{L} h_\ell(p) \sum_{k=1}^{K} g_\ell^*(M_k, A_k) + \sum_{k=1}^{K} C_k^*(p)$$

where the functions h_ℓ and g_ℓ^* ($\ell = 1,2, \ldots , L$) are two sets of linearly independent functions.

If, in addition, it is assumed that:

$$F[p,g_1(M_1,M_2, \ldots , M_K,A_1,A_2, \ldots , A_K), g_2 (M_1, M_2, \ldots , M_K,$$
$$A_1, A_2, \ldots , A_K), \ldots , g_L(M_1,M_2, \ldots , M_K,A_1,A_2, \ldots , A_K)] \tag{7}$$
$$= 0$$

if $\Sigma_{k=1}^{K} M_k = 0$, we have

$$F[p,g_1(M_1, M_2, \ldots , M_K, A_1, A_2, \ldots , A_K), g_2 (M_1, M_2, \ldots M_K,$$
$$A_1, A_2, \ldots , A_K), \ldots , g_L(M_1,M_2, \ldots , M_K, A_1,A_2, \ldots , A_K)] \tag{8}$$

$$= \sum_{\ell=1}^{L} h_\ell(p) \sum_{k=1}^{K} g_\ell^{**}(M_k, A_k)$$

where

$$g_\ell^{**}(M_k,A_k) = g_\ell^*(M_k,A_k) - g_\ell^*(0,A_k) \qquad (\ell = 1,2, \ldots , L)$$

Finally, if we add the assumption that

$$f_k(p,M_k,A_k) \geqq 0 \qquad (k = 1,2, \ldots , K) \qquad \cdot \tag{9}$$

then we have[7]

$$f_k(p,M_k,A_k) = \sum_{\ell=1}^{L} h_\ell(p)g_\ell^{**}(M_k,A_k) \qquad (k = 1, 2, \ldots , K) \tag{10}$$

From an economic point of view, Theorem 1 has the following very striking implications:

1. All the individual demand functions for the same commodity are identical up to the addition of a function independent of individual expenditure and attributes.
2. All the individual demand functions must be sums of products of separate functions of the prices and of the individual expenditure and attributes.

3. The aggregate demand functions depend on certain index functions of individual expenditures and attributes. The only admissible index functions are additive in functions of individual expenditures and attributes.
4. The aggregate demand functions can be written as linear functions of the index functions.

Our results imply that an index function such as the Gini coefficient is not admissible as an argument in an aggregate demand function since it is not additive in individual expenditures. Our results also apply to cases in which one or more of the index functions depend only on the individual attributes. An index function of the age distribution, such as the average age of the population in the highest quantile, is not admissible as an index in the aggregate demand function, since it is not additive in the individual ages. On the other hand, the proportion of population above age 65 is admissible because it is the sum of the following functions:

$$g(A) = \begin{cases} 1, A \geqq 65 \\ 0, A < 65 \end{cases}$$

$$g(A_1, A_2, \ldots, A_K) = \sum_{k=1}^{K} g(A_K)$$

The proportion of the population that is above age 65 is $\sum_{k=1}^{K} g(A_k)/K$.

We note that these very strong conclusions follow from relatively weak restrictions on the individual demand functions. The only restrictions that have been placed on the individual demand functions are that they exist and are well defined. We have not assumed that the individual demand functions are generated by utility maximization. The invertibility assumption rules out the possibility that the aggregate demand function $F(p, g_1, g_2, \ldots, g_L)$ can be written in terms of a smaller number of functions g_ℓ, $(\ell = 1, 2, \ldots, L)$, even though there is no relationship among these functions. For example, consider the aggregate demand function $F[p, G(g_1, g_2), g_3, \ldots, g_L]$; then there exists no set of L price vectors such that the corresponding values of the aggregate demand function F_n $(n = 1, 2, \ldots, N)$ are invertible in the functions $\{g_1, g_2, \ldots, g_L\}$. The difficulty is with g_1 and g_2; the two of them are effectively only a single index function, namely, the function G.

Specializations of Theorem 1 have appeared earlier in the literature. For example, if there is only one index function and we take $g_1 = \sum_{k=1}^{K} M_k$, aggregate expenditure for the economy, then Theorem 1 implies that for given prices, all consumers must have parallel linear Engel curves. Restricting demands to be nonnegative for all prices and expenditures implies that for given prices, all consumers have identical linear Engel curves. These are the results of Gorman (1953). Lau (1977b) has shown that if there is only one index function g_1 and the individual demand functions satisfy individual budget constraints, then g_1 must be aggregate expenditure $\Sigma_{k=1}^K M_k$, weakening the assumptions required for the validity of Gorman's results.

Our approach can be clearly distinguished from that of Muellbauer (1975, 1976a,b) in that we do not require the notion of a representative consumer. Muellbauer's condition for the existence of a representative consumer

$$\sum_{k=1}^K f_{nk}(p,M_k) = F_n[g_2(M_1,M_2, \ldots , M_K),p]\left(\sum_{k=1}^K M_k \right)$$

$$(n = 1,2, \ldots , N)$$

can be viewed as a special case of equation (3) with the number of indexes L equal to two and the first index function $g_1(M_1,M_2, \ldots , M_K)$ $= \Sigma_{k=1}^K M_k$, equal to aggregate expenditure. The representative consumer interpretation fails for the case of more than two index functions. We show in Section II that summability of the individual demand functions implies that for two index functions one can always choose $g_1(M_1,M_2, \ldots , M_k) = \Sigma_{k=1}^K M_k$ in equation (3). For two indexes our approach coincides with the approach of Muellbauer with identical implications under the assumption of individual utility maximization. However, our approach encompasses more than two indexes and can be applied to individual consumers with different preferences.

C. Integrability

In this article we develop an econometric model of aggregate consumer behavior based on the theory of exact aggregation. In this theory the assumption that the impact of individual expenditures on aggregate demand can be represented by a single function of individual expenditures, such as aggregate or per capita expenditure, is replaced by the assumption that there may be a number of such functions. These functions may depend not only on individual expenditures but also on attributes of individuals, such as demographic characteristics, that give rise to differences in preferences.

By permitting aggregate quantities demanded to depend on a number of functions of individual expenditures and by allowing explicitly for differences in preferences among individuals we are able to overcome the limitations of the model of a representative consumer. At the same time we can test the model of a representative consumer as a special case within the framework provided by the theory of exact aggregation. Eliminating differences in preferences among individuals and suitably restricting the dependence of aggregate demands on individual expenditures, our model of aggregate consumer behavior can be reduced to the model of a representative consumer.

To specify a model of aggregate consumer behavior based on the theory of exact aggregation, we must first specify a model of the individual consumer. A complete characterization of the behavior of an individual consumer can be given in terms of the properties of the corresponding system of individual demand functions. If the system of individual demand functions can be generated by maximization of a utility function, subject to a budget constraint, the system is said to be *integrable*. If the individual demand functions are continuously differentiable, integrability implies the following restrictions:

1.   *Homogeneity*. The individual demand functions are homogeneous of degree zero in prices and expenditure

$$x_{nk} = f_{nk} (\lambda p, \lambda M_k, A_k) = f_{nk} (p, M_k, A_k)$$

$$(k = 1, 2, \ldots, K; n = 1, 2, \ldots, N)$$

for all prices p, expenditure M_k, and positive λ.

2.   *Summability*. A weighted sum of the individual demand functions with each function multiplied by the price of the corresponding commodity is equal to expenditure

$$\sum_{n=1}^{N} p_n f_{nk} (p, M_k, A_k) = M_k \qquad (k = 1, 2, \ldots, K)$$

for all prices p and expenditure M_k.

3.   *Symmetry*. The matrix of compensated own- and cross-price effects must be symmetric

$$\frac{\partial f_{nk}}{\partial p_m} - x_{nk} \sum_{\ell=1}^{N} \frac{\partial f_{nk}}{\partial p_\ell} \cdot \frac{p_\ell}{M_k} = \frac{\partial f_{mk}}{\partial p_n} - x_{mk} \sum_{\ell=1}^{N} \frac{\partial f_{mk}}{\partial p_\ell} \cdot \frac{p_\ell}{M_k}$$

$$(k = 1, 2, \ldots, K; \qquad m, n = 1, 2, \ldots, N)$$

for all prices p and all expenditure M_k.

4.   *Nonnegativity*. The individual quantities demanded are nonnegative:

$$x_{nk} = f_{nk} (p, M_k, A_k) \geqq 0, (k = 1, 2, \ldots, K; \qquad n = 1, 2, \ldots, N)$$

for all prices p and all expenditure M_k.

5.   *Monotonicity*. The matrix of compensated own- and cross-price effects must be nonpositive definite for all prices p and all expenditure M_k.

A useful interpretation of the monotonicity condition is provided by composite demand functions. First, we consider proportional variations in prices:

$$dp_n = \lambda_n \, dp \qquad (n = 1, 2, \ldots, N)$$

We can define a composite demand function, say c_k, as a weighted sum of the demand functions

$$c_k(p, M_k, A_k; \qquad \lambda_1, \lambda_2, \ldots, \lambda_N) = \Sigma \, \lambda_n f_{nk} \, (p, M_k, A_k)$$

The compensated own-price substitution effect for the composite demand function is nonpositive

$$\Sigma \, \Sigma \, \lambda_n \, \lambda_m \left(\frac{\partial x_{nk}}{\partial p_m} - x_{nk} \, \Sigma \, \frac{\partial x_{nk}}{\partial p_\ell} \cdot \frac{p_\ell}{M_k} \right) \leq 0$$

for all λ_n $(n = 1, 2, \ldots, N)$ and all expenditure M_k.

Given homogeneity, summability, and symmetry, the system of individual demand functions can be generated as the solutions of the system of partial differential equations:

$$\frac{\partial \, \ell n \, V_k}{\partial \, \ell n \, p_n} = \frac{p_n \, x_{nk}}{M_k} \, \Sigma \, \frac{\partial \, \ell n \, V_k}{\partial \, \ell n \, p_\ell}$$

$$(k = 1, 2, \ldots, K; \qquad n = 1, 2, \ldots, N)$$

defining a family of indirect utility functions V_k. Given nonnegativity and monotonicity these indirect utility functions can be obtained from one another by means of monotonically increasing transformations. An alternative and equivalent characterization of the behavior of an individual consumer can be given in terms of the following properties of the indirect utility function:

1. *Homogeneity.* The indirect utility function is homogeneous of degree zero in prices and expenditure

$$V_k = V_k(\lambda p, \lambda M_k, A_k) = V_k(p, M_k, A_k) \qquad (k = 1, 2, \ldots, K)$$

for all prices p, expenditure M_k, and positive λ.

2. *Monotonicity.* The indirect utility function is nonincreasing in prices and nondecreasing in expenditure

$$\frac{\partial \, V_k}{\partial \, p} \leq 0, \frac{\partial \, V_k}{\partial \, M_k} \geq 0 \qquad (k = 1, 2, \ldots, K)$$

for all prices p and expenditure M_k.

3. *Quasiconvexity.* The indirect utility function is quasiconvex in prices and expenditure for all prices p and expenditure M_k.

D. Overview

The theory of exact aggregation can be employed to derive restrictions on individual demand functions that allow aggregate demand functions to be expressed in terms of index functions that depend on individual expenditures and attributes. We first derive the conditions under which an aggregate demand function can be obtained as the sum of individual demand functions. We then impose the restrictions implied by utility maximization by individual consumers on the individual demand functions.

A system of individual demand functions that conforms to the theory of exact aggregation must be linear in a number of functions of total expenditure and attributes of the individual. If the individual demand functions are summable, one of the functions of individual expenditure and attributes must be independent of attributes and must reduce to expenditure itself. If there is only a single function of individual expenditure and attributes, this characterization of individual preferences reduces to Gorman's model of a representative consumer. Demand functions are linear in expenditure with identical slopes for all individuals.

In Section II we consider the dependence of individual and aggregate demand functions on individual expenditures. We first assume that preferences are identical for all individuals, but allow the system of individual demand functions to depend on two linearly independent functions of expenditure. The first function must reduce to expenditure itself, but the second must be nonlinear in expenditure. If the individual demand functions are summable and homogeneous of degree zero, the nonlinear function of individual expenditure must be the product of expenditure and either the logarithm of expenditure or a power function of expenditure. This characterization of individual demand functions reduces to Muellbauer's model of a representative consumer. Although the system of demand functions is identical for all individuals, the system of aggregate demand functions depends on the distribution of expenditures among individuals as well as the level of per capita expenditure.

In Section III we dispense with the model of a representative consumer in order to incorporate differences in preferences among individuals. If we allow individual demand functions to depend on two linearly independent functions of the attributes and expenditure of individuals, one of these functions is independent of attributes and reduces to expenditure itself, while the second function involves an arbitrary function of the individual attributes and a logarithmic or power function of individual expenditure. While this specification is consistent with evidence from budget studies that individual preferences depend on demographic characteristics and Engel curves are nonlinear, the impact of differences in demographic characteristics and the impact of differences in functions of expenditure are related to each other.

We conclude our discussion of the theory of exact aggregation by considering a representation of individual demand functions that depends on attributes as well as expenditures of individuals and does not require Engel curves to be linear. In this representation we allow the system of individual demand functions to depend on three linearly independent functions of the expenditures and attributes of individuals. One of these functions is independent of attributes and reduces to expenditure itself. A second function is nonlinear in expenditure and does not depend on attributes. A third function depends on both expenditure and attributes. This specification does not impose restrictions on the impact of differences in attributes and the impact of differences in expenditure.

Under summability and homogeneity the nonlinear function of expenditure that occurs in the system of individual demand functions must be the product of expenditure and either the logarithm of expenditure or a power function of expenditure. The individual demand functions also depend on attributes of individuals, such as demographic characteristics. By representing aggregate demand functions as the sum of these individual demand functions, the aggregate demand functions depend on the distribution of expenditures among individuals as well as the level of aggregate expenditure and prices. The aggregate demand functions also depend on the joint distribution of demographic characteristics and expenditures over the population.

The theory of exact aggregation enables us to specify the dependence of systems of individual demand functions on expenditure and attributes. To incorporate the implications of the theory of the individual consumer we must also specify the dependence of systems of individual demand functions on prices. In Section IV we show that only the transcendental logarithmic or translog indirect utility functions is capable of combining flexibility in the representation of preferences with parsimony in the number of parameters that must be estimated.[8]

To incorporate differences in individual preferences into a model of aggregate consumer behavior we allow the indirect translog utility function for each individual to depend on attributes, such as demographic characteristics, that vary among individuals. The theory of exact aggregation requires that the individual demand functions must be linear in a number of functions of the expenditure and attributes of the individual. We impose the resulting parametric restrictions on the indirect translog utility function for each individual.

Integrability of systems of individual demand functions requires that the indirect utility function for each individual must be homogeneous, monotone, and quasiconvex. In Section V we impose the corresponding restrictions on the indirect translog utility functions for all individuals. To construct a system of individual demand functions we apply Roy's (1943) Identity to the indirect translog utility function.[9] The resulting models of individual consumer behavior consist of systems of demand functions giving the shares of total expenditure allocated to each commodity group. For given values of prices the expenditure shares are linear in the logarithm of expenditure and the attributes of individuals.

To construct a model of aggregate consumer behavior we first multiply the expenditure shares for each individual by expenditure for that individual and divide by expenditure for the population as a whole. We then sum the resulting weighted individual demand functions across the whole population. The resulting model of aggregate consumer behavior gives the share of aggregate expenditure allocated to each commodity group as a function of prices. The aggregate expenditure shares also depend on averages of the logarithms of individual expenditures and the attributes, weighted by the share of expenditure for each individual in expenditure for the population.

We find it convenient to represent the attributes of individuals, such as demographic characteristics, by variables equal to unity for an individual with the corresponding attribute and zero otherwise. For this representation the appropriate weighted average for each attribute is simply the share of all individuals with that attribute in aggregate expenditure. To incorporate the impact of changes in the demographic characteristics of the population on the allocation of aggregate expenditure among commodity groups, we include the shares of aggregate expenditure for all demographic groups as explanatory variables. Similarly, the weighted average of the logarithm of individual expenditures has weights equal to the shares of all individuals in expenditure for the population as a whole. To incorporate the impact of the distribution of expenditure on the allocation of aggregate expenditure, we include the weighted average of the logarithm of expenditure for the population as an explanatory variable.

A model of aggregate consumer behavior based on the theory of exact aggregation can be implemented from individual cross section data on expenditure shares, prices, total expenditure, and demographic characteristics. Alternatively, since the system of demand functions for an individual with given demographic characteristics can be recovered uniquely from the system of aggregate demand functions, a model of aggregate consumer behavior can be implemented from time series data on aggregate expenditure shares, prices, shares of demographic groups in aggregate expenditure, and a weighted average of the logarithms of expenditure. If cross section data are limited to individual expenditure shares and total expenditure, with prices taking the same values for all individuals, a model of aggregate consumer behavior can be implemented by pooling aggregate time series data with individual cross section data along the lines discussed in Section VI.

In Section VII we present a transcendental logarithmic model of aggregate consumer behavior for the United States for the period 1958–1974. We analyze the allocation of aggregate consumer expenditures among five categories of goods and services—energy, food and clothing, consumer services, capital services, and other nondurable goods. We employ a breakdown of individual consumer units by family size, age of head of household, region, race, and urban versus rural residence. We implement this model from a cross-section survey of individual consumer expenditures for the United States for the year 1972 and annual time series observations on aggregate consumer expenditure for the period 1958–1974.

We find that as total expenditure increases, the share of the consumer budget allocated to capital services increases substantially, while the shares allocated to the other four groups of goods and services decline. Demographic effects are very important for all categories of consumer expenditures. The impact of changes in total expenditures on the allocation of the consumer budget depends strongly on demographic characteristics. These characteristics also have a substantial effect on the impact of changes in relative prices on budget allocation.

II. EXACT AGGREGATION FOR CONSUMERS WITH IDENTICAL PREFERENCES

In Section I we have stated the Fundamental Theorem of Exact Aggregation. Under this Theorem all the individual demand functions for the same commodity are identical up to the addition of a function that is independent of individual attributes and expenditure. The individual demand functions must be sums of products of separate functions of prices and of individual expenditure and attributes. The aggregate demand functions depend on index functions that are additive in functions of expenditure and attributes for individuals. Finally, the aggregate demand functions can be written as linear functions of the index functions.

In this Section we combine the theory of exact aggregation with restrictions on individual consumer behavior implied by maximization of a utility function, subject to a budget constraint. We first consider consumers with identical preferences, so that individual expenditures on all commodity groups depend on total expenditure, but not on attributes of the individual consumer such as demographic characteristics. We impose the restrictions on individual demand functions implied by utility maximization and derive the resulting restrictions on aggregate demand functions. For systems of individual demand functions that are integrable, we can summarize these restrictions in terms of an indirect utility function for each consumer.

We begin with the case of two index functions of individual expenditures. Under exact aggregation the individual demand functions take the form

$$f_k(p, M_k) = h_1(p)g_1^*(M_k) + h_2(p)g_2^*(M_k) + C_k(p)$$

$$(k = 1, 2, \ldots, K) \quad (11)$$

where without loss of generality we take $g_1^*(0) = g_2^*(0) = 0$. The index functions of individual expenditures take the form

$$g_\ell(M_1, M_2, \ldots, M_K) = \sum_{k=1}^{K} g_\ell^*(M_k) \quad (\ell = 1,2) \quad (12)$$

and the aggregate demand function takes the form

$$F[p, g_1(M_1, M_2, \ldots, M_K), g_2(M_1, M_2, \ldots, M_K)]$$

$$= h_1(p) \sum_{k=1}^{K} g_1^*(M_k) + h_2(p) \sum_{k=1}^{K} g_2^*(M_k) + \sum_{k=1}^{K} C_k(p) \quad (13)$$

A.   Summability

We assume that the individual demand functions are summable, that is

$$\sum_{n=1}^{N} p_n f_{nk}(p, M_k) = M_k \quad (14)$$

or

$$\sum_{n=1}^{N} p_n h_{n1}(p)g_1^*(M_k) + \sum_{n=1}^{N} p_n h_{n2}(p)g_2^*(M_k) + \sum_{n=1}^{N} p_n C_{nk}(p) = M_k \quad (15)$$

Let $M_k = 0$, then $\Sigma_{n=1}^{N} p_n C_{nk}(p) = 0$. Let $h_1^*(p) \equiv \Sigma_{j=1}^{N} p_n h_{n1}(p)$ and $h_2^*(p) \equiv \Sigma_{n=1}^{N} p_n h_{n2}(p)$; then equation (15) may be rewritten as

$$h_1^*(p)g_1^*(M_k) + h_2^*(p)g_2^*(M_k) = M_k \quad (16)$$

By Theorem 1 above $g_1^*(M_k)$ and $g_2^*(M_k)$ are linearly independent functions.

Now consider any two price vectors, say p^1 and p^2; by equation (16), we have

$$h_1^*(p^1)g_1^*(M_k) + h_2^*(p^1)g_2^*(M_k) = M_k \quad (17)$$

and

$$h_1^*(p^2)g_1^*(M_k) + h_2^*(p^2)g_2^*(M_k) = M_k \tag{18}$$

so that

$$[h_1^*(p^1) - h_1^*(p^2)]g_1^*(M_k) + [h_2^*(p^1) - h_2^*(p^2)]g_2^*(M_k) = 0$$

for all p^1 and p^2. But $g_1^*(M_k)$ and $g_2^*(M_k)$ are linearly independent functions, which implies that

$$h_1^*(p^1) - h_1^*(p^2) = 0$$

and

$$h_2^*(p^1) - h_2^*(p^2) = 0$$

for all p^1 and p^2, so that

$$h_1^*(p) = \bar{h}_1^*, \ h_2^*(p) = \bar{h}_2^*$$

both constants.

Substituting the constants $\bar{h}_1^*$ and $\bar{h}_2^*$ into equation (16) we have

$$\bar{h}_1^* g_1^*(M_k) + \bar{h}_2^* g_2^*(M_k) = M_k$$

We cannot have both $\bar{h}_1^* = 0$ and $\bar{h}_2^* = 0$, otherwise any positive M_k leads to a contradiction. Suppose $\bar{h}_1^* \neq 0$; then we can solve for $g_1^*(M_k)$ as follows

$$g_1^*(M_k) = \frac{1}{\bar{h}_1^*} M_k - \frac{\bar{h}_2^*}{\bar{h}_1^*} g_2^*(M_k)$$

By defining

$$h_{n1}^*(p) \equiv h_{n1}(p)\frac{1}{\bar{h}_1^*}$$

$$h_{n2}^*(p) \equiv -h_{n1}(p)\frac{\bar{h}_2^*}{\bar{h}_1^*} + h_{n2}(p) \qquad (n = 1, 2, \ldots, N)$$

each individual demand function may be written as

$$f_{nk}(p,M_k) = h_{n1}^*(p)M_k + h_{n2}^*(p)g_2^*(M_k) + C_{nk}(p)$$

$$(n = 1, 2, \ldots, N; k = 1, 2, \ldots, K)$$

with the restrictions that

$$\sum_{n=1}^{N} p_n h_{n1}^*(p) = 1; \ \sum_{n=1}^{N} p_n h_{n2}^*(p) = 0; \ \sum_{n=1}^{N} p_n C_{nk}(p) = 0$$

The argument used here is perfectly general and can be easily extended to the case of an arbitrary finite number of index functions of expenditures. Thus, we have proved:

Theorem 2. Under the assumption that the individual demand functions are summable, a system of aggregate demand functions can be written in the form:

$$\sum_{k=1}^{K} f_{nk}(p,M_k) = F_n[p,g_1(M_1,M_2', \ldots, M_K),$$

$$g_2(M_1,M_2, \ldots, M_K), \ldots, g_L(M_1, M_2, \ldots, M_K)]$$

$$(n = 1,2, \ldots, N)$$

where the functions g_ℓ ($\ell = 1,2, \ldots, L$) and F_n ($n = 1,2, \ldots, N$) satisfy assumptions (1) through (4) in Theorem 1, if and only if

$$(1) \qquad f_{nk}(p,M_k) = h_{n1}(p)M_k + \sum_{\ell=2}^{L} h_{n\ell}(p)g_\ell^*(M_k) + C_{nk}(p)$$

$$(n = 1,2, \ldots, N; k = 1,2, \ldots, K)$$

where $h_{n\ell}(p)$ and $C_{nk}(p)$ are arbitrary functions of p satisfying

$$\sum_{n=1}^{N} p_n h_{n1}(p) = 1 \qquad \sum_{n=1}^{N} p_n h_{n\ell}(p) = 0 \qquad (\ell = 2, 3, \ldots, L)$$

$$\sum_{n=1}^{N} p_n C_{nk}(p) = 0 \qquad\qquad (k = 1, 2, \ldots, K)$$

and

$$(2) \qquad g_1(M_1,M_2, \ldots, M_K) = \sum_{k=1}^{K} M_k$$

$$g_\ell(M_1,M_2, \ldots, M_K) = \sum_{k=1}^{K} g_\ell^*(M_k) \qquad (\ell = 2,3, \ldots, L)$$

$$(3) \qquad F_n(p,g_1(M_1,M_2, \ldots, M_K), g_2(M_1,M_2, \ldots, M_K), \ldots,$$

$$g_L(M_1, \ldots, M_K)] = h_{n1}(p) \sum_{k=1}^{K} M_k + \sum_{\ell=2}^{L} h_{n\ell}(p) \sum_{k=1}^{K} g_\ell^*(M_k)$$

$$+ \sum_{k=1}^{K} C_{nk}(p) \qquad (n = 1, 2, \ldots, N)$$

Theorem 2 implies that the individual demand function for at least one commodity must have a term that is linear in expenditure. If there is only one demand function with a term that is linear in expenditure, then the corresponding function $h_{n1}(p)$ must be equal to one. All other such functions must be equal to zero. We note further that index functions that are not linear in expenditures must appear in the demand functions of more than one commodity; otherwise, $\sum_{n=1}^{N} p_n h_{n\ell}(p) \neq 0$ for some

$\ell \neq 1$. It is possible that the individual demand functions for some commodities do not have the linear expenditure term.

B. Homogeneity

Next, we consider the implications of zero degree homogeneity, given summability, for the individual demand functions. Under summability, Theorem 2 implies for two index functions that the individual demand function has the form

$$f(p,M) = h_1(p)M + h_2(p)g(M) + C(p) \qquad (19)$$

where $g(0) = 0$. Homogeneity of degree zero of the individual demand function implies that:

$$h_1(\lambda p)\lambda M + h_2(\lambda p)g(\lambda M) + C(\lambda p) = h_1(p)M + h_2(p)g(M) + C(p) \quad (20)$$

Let $M = 0$ and equation (20) becomes

$$C(\lambda p) = C(p),$$

so that $C(p)$ is homogeneous of degree zero in p.

Subtracting $C(p)$ from both sides of equation (20) we obtain

$$h_1(\lambda p)\lambda M + h_2(\lambda p)g(\lambda M) = h_1(p)M + h_2(p)g(M) \qquad (21)$$

Dividing both sides by M, we obtain

$$h_1(\lambda p)\lambda + h_2(\lambda p)\lambda \frac{g(\lambda M)}{\lambda M} = h_1(p) + h_2(p)\frac{g(M)}{M} \qquad (22)$$

By a change of the dependent variable $g^*(M) \equiv g(M)/M$ with the requirement that $\lim_{M \to 0} M \cdot g^*(M) = 0$, equation (22) becomes

$$h_2(\lambda p)\lambda g^*(\lambda M) - h_2(p)g^*(M) = h_1(p) - h_1(\lambda p)\lambda \qquad (23)$$

Equation (23) holds for all M, and in particular one can choose $M = M_1$ and M_2, so that

$$h_2(\lambda p)\lambda g^*(\lambda M_1) - h_2(p)g^*(M_1) = h_2(\lambda p)\lambda g^*(\lambda M_2) - h_2(p)g^*(M_2)$$

which upon rearrangement becomes

$$\frac{h_2(\lambda p)\lambda}{h_2(p)} [g^*(\lambda M_1) - g^*(\lambda M_2)] = g^*(M_1) - g^*(M_2). \qquad (24)$$

Equation (24), which must hold for all p, M_1, M_2 and λ, implies that $h_2(\lambda p)\lambda/h_2(p)$ is at most a function of λ, say $k(\lambda)$

$$\frac{h_2(\lambda p)\lambda}{h_2(p)} = k(\lambda)$$

or

$$h_2(\lambda p) = k^*(\lambda)h_2(p) \tag{25}$$

where $k^*(\lambda) \equiv k(\lambda)/\lambda$. This is the generalized Euler's equation for a homogeneous function with the solution

$$h_2(\lambda p) = \lambda^{-\sigma} h_2(p) \tag{26}$$

In other words, $h_2(p)$ is a homogeneous of degree $-\sigma$ function. It follows that

$$k(\lambda) = \lambda^{-\sigma+1}$$

Substituting equation (26) and $k(\lambda)$ into equation (23) we obtain

$$\lambda^{-\sigma+1} g^*(\lambda M) - g^*(M) = \frac{h_1(p) - h_1(\lambda p)\lambda}{h_2(p)} \tag{27}$$

Each side of equation (27) must be a function of λ only, say $\ell(\lambda)$. Thus we have

$$\lambda^{-\sigma+1}g^*(\lambda M) - g^*(M) = \ell(\lambda) \tag{28}$$

with $\ell(1) = 0$. By setting $M = 1$, we have

$$\lambda^{-\sigma+1}g^*(\lambda) - g^*(1) = \ell(\lambda) \tag{29}$$

Substituting equation (29) into equation (28), we obtain

$$\lambda^{-\sigma+1}g^*(\lambda M) - g^*(M) = \lambda^{-\sigma+1}g^*(\lambda) - g^*(1) \tag{30}$$

By interchanging the roles of λ and M in equation (30), we obtain

$$M^{-\sigma+1}g^*(\lambda M) - g^*(\lambda) = M^{-\sigma+1}g^*(M) - g^*(1) \tag{31}$$

By equating the values of $g^*(\lambda M)$ in equations (30) and (31), we obtain

$$\lambda^{\sigma-1}g^*(M) + g^*(\lambda) - \lambda^{\sigma-1}g^*(1) = M^{\sigma-1}g^*(\lambda) + g^*(M) - M^{\sigma-1}g^*(1)$$

which may be rearranged as

$$\lambda^{\sigma-1}g^*(M) - g^*(M) - \lambda^{\sigma-1}g^*(1) + g^*(1)$$
$$= M^{\sigma-1}g^*(\lambda) - g^*(\lambda) - M^{\sigma-1}g^*(1) + g^*(1)$$

which, if $\sigma \neq 1$ may be factorized as

$$(\lambda^{\sigma-1} - 1)[g^*(M) - g^*(1)] = (M^{\sigma-1} - 1)[g^*(\lambda) - g^*(1)]$$

so that

$$g^*(M) - g^*(1) = D[M^{\sigma-1} - 1] \tag{32}$$

where D is a constant.

If $\sigma = 1$, then by equation (28) we have

$$g^*(\lambda M) = g^*(M) + \ell(\lambda)$$

a functional equation with the well known general solution:

$$g^*(M) = D_1 \ln M + D_2 \tag{33}$$

where D_1, D_2 are constants. Since $g(M) = g^*(M) M$, we have, either

$$g(M) = D_1 M^\sigma + D_2 M \tag{34}$$

where D_1, D_2 are constants. The condition that $g(0) = 0$ requires that $\sigma \geqq 0$. Or

$$g(M) = D_1 M \ln M + D_2 M, \tag{35}$$

where D_1, D_2 are constants.

If we substitute equation (34) into equation (22) and make use of the homogeneity of degree $-\sigma$ of $h_2(p)$, we obtain

$$h_1(\lambda p)\lambda + h_2(p)\lambda^{-\sigma}(D_1\lambda^\sigma M^{\sigma-1} + D_2\lambda)$$

$$= h_1(p) + h_2(p)(D_1 M^{\sigma-1} + D_2), \tag{36}$$

which results in

$$h_1(\lambda p)\lambda + D_2 h_2(p)\lambda^{1-\sigma} = h_1(p) + D_2 h_2(p) \tag{37}$$

or

$$h_1(\lambda p)\lambda + D_2 h_2(\lambda p)\lambda = h_1(p) + D_2 h_2(p) \tag{38}$$

or $h_1(p) + D_2 h_2(p)$ is homogeneous of degree minus one.

By defining $h_1^*(p) \equiv h_1(p) + D_2 h_2(p)$, $h_2^*(p) \equiv D_1 h_2(p)$ we can write the individual demand function as

$$f(p,M) = h_1^*(p)M + h_2^*(p)M^\sigma + C(p) \tag{39}$$

where $h_1^*(p)$ is homogeneous of degree minus one, $h_2^*(p)$ is homogeneous of degree $-\sigma$ and $C(p)$ is homogeneous of degree zero and $\sigma > 0$.

If we substitute equation (35) into equation (22) we obtain

$$h_1(\lambda p)\lambda + h_2(p)\lambda^{-1}[D_1\lambda(\ln M + \ln \lambda) + D_2\lambda]$$

$$= h_1(p) + h_2(p)[D_1 \ln M + D_2], \tag{40}$$

which simplifies into

$$\lambda h_1(\lambda p) + D_1 h_2(p) \ln \lambda = h_1(p)$$

or

$$\lambda h_1(\lambda p) - h_1(p) + D_1 h_2(p) \ln \lambda = 0 \tag{41}$$

or

$$\frac{h_1(\lambda p)}{D_1 h_2(\lambda p)} - \frac{h_1(p)}{D_1 h_2(p)} + \ln \lambda = 0 \tag{42}$$

Exponentiating equation (42) we obtain

$$\exp[h_1(\lambda p)/D_1 h_2(\lambda p)] = \lambda^{-1} \exp[h_1(p)/D_1 h_2(p)]$$

so that $h_1^*(p) \equiv \exp[h_1(p)/D_1 h_2(p)]$ is homogeneous of degree minus one in p. Let $h_2^*(p) \equiv D_1 h_2(p)$. Thus, we can write the individual demand function as

$$f(p,M) = h_1(p)M + h_2^*(p)[M \ln M + (D_2/D_1)M] + C(p) \tag{43}$$

$$= h_2^*(p) \ln h_1^{**}(p)M + h_2^*(p)M \ln M + C(p)$$

where $h_1^{**}(p) \equiv \exp(D_2/D_1) \, h_1^*(p)$ and $h_2^*(p)$ are homogeneous of degree minus one and $C(p)$ is homogeneous of degree zero.

If an aggregate demand function exists with two index functions that depend on individual expenditures alone, equations (39) and (43) are the only possible forms for the individual demand function under the assumptions of summability and zero degree homogeneity. Equations (39) and (43) are precisely the forms proposed by Muellbauer (1975, 1976a,b). We have shown that these forms are necessary within a much more general framework.[10] Thus, we have proved

Theorem 3. Under the assumption that the individual demand functions are summable and zero degree homogeneous in prices and expenditure, a system of aggregate demand functions can be written in the form:

$$\sum_{k=1}^{K} f_{nk}(p, M_k) = F_n[p, g_1(M_1, M_2, \ldots, M_K), g_2(M_1, M_2, \ldots, M_K)]$$

$$(n = 1, 2, \ldots, N)$$

where g_ℓ ($\ell = 1,2$) and F satisfy assumptions (1) through (4) in Theorem 1, if and only if

$$(1) \quad f_{nk}(p, M_k) = \begin{cases} h_{n1}(p)M_k + h_{n2}(p)M_k^\sigma + C_{nk}(p) & (n = 1,2, \ldots, N) \\ h_{n2}^*(p) \ln h_{n1}^*(p)M_k + h_{n2}^*(p)M_k \ln M_k + C_{nk}(p) \\ (n = 1,2, \ldots, N) \end{cases}$$

where $h_{n1}(p)$, $h_{n2}^*(p)$ and $h_{n1}^*(p)$ are homogeneous of degree minus one, $h_{n2}(p)$ is homogeneous of degree $-\sigma$, $\sigma > 0$, $\sigma \neq 1$, and $C_{nk}(p)$ is homogeneous of degree zero, $(n = 1,2, \ldots, N)$; furthermore

$$\sum_{n=1}^{N} p_n h_{n1}(p) = \sum_{n=1}^{N} p_n h_{n2}^*(p) \ln h_{n1}^*(p) = 1$$

$$\sum_{n=1}^{N} p_n h_{n2}(p) = \sum_{n=1}^{N} p_n h_{n2}^*(p) = 0$$

$$\sum_{n=1}^{N} p_n C_{nk}(p) = 0$$

(2) $$g_1(M_1, M_2, \ldots, M_K) = \sum_{k=1}^{K} M_k$$

(3) $$F_n[p, g_1(M_1, M_2, \ldots, M_K), g_2(M_1, M_2, \ldots, M_K)]$$

$$= \begin{cases} h_{n1}(p) \sum_{k=1}^{K} M_k + h_{n2}(p) \sum_{k=1}^{K} M_k^\sigma + \sum_{k=1}^{K} C_{nk}(p), \quad (n = 1,2, \ldots, N) \\[2em] h_{n2}^*(p) \ln h_{n1}^*(p) \sum_{k=1}^{K} M_k + h_{n2}^*(p) \sum_{k=1}^{K} M_k \ln M_k + \sum_{k=1}^{K} C_{nk}(p) \\[1em] (n = 1,2, \ldots, N) \end{cases}$$

We also have

Corollary 3.1. If, in addition to the assumption of the theorem, $\Sigma_{k=1}^{K} M_k = 0$ implies that

(5) $$F_n[p, g_1(M_1, M_2, \ldots, M_K), g_2(M_1, M_2, \ldots, M_K)] = 0$$

$$(n = 1,2, \ldots, N)$$

then $\Sigma_{k=1}^{K} C_{nk}(p) \equiv 0$. The proof of this corollary is obvious.

Corollary 3.2. If in addition to the assumptions of the theorem and Corollary 3.1 we have

(6) $$f_{nk}(p, M_k) \geq 0 \quad (k = 1,2, \ldots, K; n = 1,2, \ldots, N)$$

then

$$f_{nk}(p, M_k) = \begin{cases} h_{n1}(p)M_k + h_{n2}(p)M_k^\sigma \quad (n = 1,2, \ldots, N) \\ h_{n2}^*(p) \ln h_{n1}^*(p)M_k + h_{n2}^*(p)M_k \ln M_k \\ (k = 1,2, \ldots, K; n = 1,2, \ldots, N) \end{cases}$$

where $h_{n1}(p) \geq 0$, $h_{n2}(p) \geq 0$, $h_{n2}^*(p) \ln h_{n1}^*(p) \geq 0$

Proof: It is obvious that

$$C_{nk}(p) = 0 \qquad (k = 1,2, \ldots, K; n = 1,2, \ldots, N)$$

To see that $h_{n1}(p) \geqq 0$ and $h_{n2}(p) \geqq 0$ are necessary for the nonnegativity of $h_{n1}(p)M_k + h_{n2}(p)M_k^\sigma$, suppose $\sigma > 1$. Then for large M_k, the second term dominates, which implies $h_{n2}(p) \geqq 0$; and for $M_k < 1$, the first term dominates, which implies $h_{n1}(p) \geqq 0$. The same argument works in reverse if $\sigma < 1$.[11] To see that $h_{n2}^*(p) \ln h_{n1}^*(p) \geqq 0$ is necessary and sufficient for the nonnegativity of $h_{n2}^*(p) \ln h_{n1}^*(p)M_k + h_{n2}^*(p)M_k \ln M_k$, rewrite the individual demand function as

$$f_{nk}(p,M_k) = h_{n2}^*(p) \ln h_{n1}^*(p/M_k)M_k$$

$$(k = 1,2, \ldots, K; n = 1,2, \ldots, N)$$

where we have made use of the fact that $h_{n1}^*(p)$ is homogeneous of degree minus one. The condition we have stated is necessary as well as sufficient.[12]

C. Symmetry

If a system of aggregate demand functions with two index functions of expenditures exists, Theorem 2 implies that under summability, zero degree homogeneity, and nonnegativity, the systems of individual demand functions must have one of the two following forms

$$f_{nk}(p,M_k) = h_{n1}(p)M_k + h_{n2}(p)M_k^\sigma$$

$$(k = 1,2, \ldots, K; n = 1,2, \ldots, N) \quad (44)$$

or

$$f_{nk}(p,M_k) = h_{n2}^*(p) \ln h_{n1}^*(p)M_k + h_{n2}^*(p)M_k \ln M_k$$

$$(k = 1,2, \ldots, K; n = 1,2, \ldots, N) \quad (45)$$

where $h_{n1}(p)$, $h_{n2}^*(p)$ and $h_{n1}^*(p)$ are homogeneous of degree minus one and $h_{n2}(p)$ is homogeneous of degree $-\sigma$, $\sigma > 0$.

We first take up the case of equation (44). Symmetry of the Slutsky substitution matrix, under the additional assumption of continuous differentiability of the individual demand functions, implies

$$\frac{\partial f_{jk}(p,M_k)}{\partial p_n} + f_{nk}(p,M_k)\frac{\partial f_{jk}(p,M_k)}{\partial M_k} = \frac{\partial f_{nk}(p,M_k)}{\partial p_j}$$

$$+ f_{jk}(p,M_k)\frac{\partial f_{nk}(p,M_k)}{\partial M_k}.$$

When applied to equation (44), this yields

$$\frac{\partial}{\partial p_n} h_{j1}(p)M_k + \frac{\partial}{\partial p_n} h_{j2}(p)M_k^\sigma + [h_{n1}(p)M_k + h_{n2}(p)M_k^\sigma][h_{j1}(p) +$$

$$\sigma h_{j2}(p)M_k^{\sigma-1}] = \frac{\partial}{\partial p_j} h_{n1}(p)M_k + \frac{\partial}{\partial p_j} h_{n2}(p)M_k^\sigma + [h_{j1}(p)M_k + h_{j2}(p)M_k^\sigma]$$

$$[h_{n1}(p) + \sigma h_{n2}(p)M_k^{\sigma-1}]$$

which simplifies into

$$h_{j1n}(p)M_k + h_{j2n}(p)M_k^\sigma + \sigma h_{n1}(p)h_{j2}(p)M_k^\sigma + h_{n2}(p)h_{j1}(p)M_k^\sigma$$

$$= h_{n1j}(p)M_k + h_{n2j}(p)M_k^\sigma + \sigma h_{j1}(p)h_{n2}(p)M_k^\sigma + h_{j2}(p)h_{n1}(p)M_k^\sigma$$

or

$$h_{j1n}(p)M_k + [h_{j2n}(p) - (1 - \sigma)h_{j2}(p)h_{n1}(p)]M_k^\sigma \qquad (46)$$

$$= h_{n1j}(p)M_k + [h_{n2j}(p) - (1 - \sigma)h_{n2}(p)h_{j1}(p)]M_k^\sigma$$

Equation (46) must hold for all M_k, and thus

$$h_{j1n}(p) - h_{n1j}(p) = 0 \qquad (j,n = 1,2, \ldots, N)$$

This implies that

$$h_{n1}(p) = \frac{\partial \ln H^*(p)}{\partial p_n} \qquad (n = 1,2, \ldots, N)$$

where $\ln H^*(p)$ is a function of p. By the summability condition, $\Sigma_{n=1}^N p_n h_{n1}(p) = 1$, so that $H^*(p)$ is homogeneous of degree one. Similarly:

$$h_{j2n}(p) - (1 - \sigma)h_{j2}(p)h_{n1}(p) = h_{n2j}(p) - (1 - \sigma)h_{n2}(p)h_{j1}(p) \qquad (47)$$

Multiplying equation (47) through by $H^*(p)^{-(1-\sigma)}$ we obtain

$$\frac{\partial}{\partial p_n} [H^*(p)^{-(1-\sigma)}h_{j2}(p)] = \frac{\partial}{\partial p_j} [H^*(p)^{-(1-\sigma)}h_{n2}(p)]$$

so that

$$H^*(p)^{-(1-\sigma)}h_{n2}(p) = \frac{\partial H^{**}(p)}{\partial p_n}$$

where $H^{**}(p)$ is another function of p. By the summability condition, $\Sigma_{n=1}^N p_n h_{n2}(p) = 0$, so that $H^{**}(p)$ is homogeneous of degree zero.

Let the indirect utility function of the kth consumer be given by:

$$V_k(p,M_k) = \frac{1}{(\sigma - 1)} H^*(p)^{(\sigma-1)}M_k^{-(\sigma-1)} + H^{**}(p) \qquad (48)$$

where $H^*(p)$ is homogeneous of degree one and $H^{**}(p)$ is homogeneous of degree zero. Application of Roy's Identity then yields

$$
\begin{aligned}
f_{nk}(p,M_k) &= \frac{-\partial V_k(p,M_k)/\partial p_n}{\partial V_k(p,M_k)/\partial M_k} \\[2mm]
&= \frac{-\left\{ H^*(p)^{(\sigma-2)} \dfrac{\partial H^*(p)}{\partial p_n} M_k^{-(\sigma-1)} + \dfrac{\partial H^{**}(p)}{\partial p_n} \right\}}{-H^*(p)^{(\sigma-1)}M_k^{-\sigma}} \\[2mm]
&= \frac{\partial \ln H^*(p)}{\partial p_n} M_k + H^*(p)^{-(\sigma-1)} \frac{\partial H^{**}(p)}{\partial p_n} M_k^\sigma
\end{aligned}
$$

which is precisely the same form as equation (44) after taking into account symmetry of the Slutsky substitution matrix.

We next take up the case of equation (45).

$$
f_{nk}(p,M_k) = h_{n2}^*(p) \ln h_{n1}^*(p)M_k + h_{n2}^*(p)M_k \ln M_k
$$

$$
(k = 1,2, \ldots, K; \ n = 1,2, \ldots, N). \quad (49)
$$

Symmetry of the Slutsky substitution matrix, under the additional assumption of continuous differentiability of the individual demand functions implies

$$
h_{j2n}^*(p)[\ln h_{j1}^*(p)M_k + M_k \ln M_k] + \frac{h_{j2}^*(p)h_{j1n}^*(p)}{h_{j1}^*(p)} M_k + h_{n2}^*(p)
$$

$$
[\ln h_{n1}^*(p)M_k + M_k \ln M_k]h_{j2}^*(p)[\ln h_{j1}^*(p) + \ln M_k + 1]
$$

$$
= h_{n2j}^*(p)[\ln h_{n1}^*(p)M_k + M_k \ln M_k] + \frac{h_{n2}^*(p)h_{n1j}^*(p)}{h_{n1}^*(p)} M_k + h_{j2}^*(p)
$$

$$
[\ln h_{j1}^*(p)M_k + M_k \ln M_k]h_{n2}^*(p)[\ln h_{n1}^*(p) + \ln M_k + 1]
$$

$$
(j, n = 1,2, \ldots, N)
$$

which simplifies into

$$
h_{j2n}^*(p)[\ln h_{j1}^*(p) + \ln M_k] + \frac{h_{j2}^*(p)h_{j1n}^*(p)}{h_{j1}^*(p)} + h_{n2}^*(p) \ln h_{n1}^*(p)h_{j2}^*(p)
$$

$$
(50)
$$

$$
= h_{n2j}^*(p)[\ln h_{n1}^*(p) + \ln M_k] + \frac{h_{n2}^*(p)h_{n1j}^*(p)}{h_{n1}^*(p)} + h_{j2}^*(p) \ln h_{j1}^*(p)h_{n2}^*(p)
$$

Equation (50) must hold for all M_k, implying that the coefficients for the $\ln M_k$ term and the constant term must be identically zero. Thus, we have

$$
h_{j2n}^*(p) = h_{n2j}^*(p) \qquad (j, n = 1,2, \ldots, N), \quad (51)
$$

and:

$$h_{j2n}^*(p) \ln h_{j1}^*(p) + \frac{h_{j2}^*(p)h_{j1n}^*(p)}{h_{j1}^*(p)} + h_{n2}^*(p) \ln h_{n1}^*(p)h_{j2}^*(p)$$

$$= h_{n2j}^*(p) \ln h_{n1}^*(p) + \frac{h_{n2}^*(p)h_{n1j}^*(p)}{h_{n1}^*(p)} + h_{j2}^*(p) \ln h_{j1}^*(p)h_{n2}^*(p) \qquad (52)$$

$$(j, n = 1,2, \ldots, N)$$

Equation (51) implies that

$$h_{n2}^*(p) = \frac{-\partial \ln H^*(p)}{\partial p_n} \qquad (n = 1,2, \ldots, N) \qquad (53)$$

where $-\ln H^*(p)$ is a function of p. By the summability condition

$$\sum_{n=1}^{N} p_n h_{n2}^*(p) = 0$$

Thus, $-\ln H^*(p)$ and, equivalently, $H^*(p)$ must be homogeneous of degree zero. Zero degree homogeneity of $-\ln H^*(p)$ or, equivalently, $H^*(p)$ is sufficient to imply that $h_{n2}^*(p)$ is homogeneous of degree minus one as required. Given equation (53), equation (52) may be rewritten as

$$\frac{\partial}{\partial p_n} [H^*(p) \frac{\partial \ln H^*(p)}{\partial p_j} \ln h_{j1}^*(p)] = \frac{\partial}{\partial p_j} [H^*(p) \frac{\partial \ln H^*(p)}{\partial p_n} \ln h_{n1}^*(p)]$$

$$(j, n = 1,2, \ldots, N)$$

so that

$$\frac{\partial H^*(p)}{\partial p_n} \ln h_{n1}^*(p) = \frac{\partial \ln H^{**}(p)}{\partial p_n} \qquad (n = 1,2, \ldots, N) \qquad (54)$$

where $\ln H^{**}(p)$ is another function of p.
   By the summability condition,

$$\sum_{n=1}^{N} p_n h_{n2}^*(p) \ln h_{n1}^*(p) = 1$$

Thus

$$\sum_{n=1}^{N} p_n \left(\frac{-\partial \ln H^*(p)}{\partial p_n} \right) \ln h_{n1}^*(p) = \frac{-1}{H^*(p)} \sum_{n=1}^{N} \frac{\partial \ln H^{**}(p)}{\partial \ln p_n} = 1$$

or:

$$H^*(p) = - \sum_{n=1}^{N} \frac{\partial \ln H^{**}(p)}{\partial \ln p_n} \qquad (55)$$

Given any $H^{**}(p)$, $H^*(p)$ is uniquely determined by equation (55). Since $H^*(p)$ is homogeneous of degree zero, it follows that $\sum_{n=1}^{N} (\partial \ln H^{**}(p)/\partial \ln p_n)$ is a homogeneous function of degree zero, which implies that:

$$\sum_{j=1}^{N} \sum_{n=1}^{N} \frac{\partial^2 \ln H^{**}(p)}{\partial \ln p_j \, \partial \ln p_n} = 0 \tag{56}$$

If $H^{**}(p)$ were a homogeneous function, then $H^*(p)$ would be constant. This also implies, by equation (53), that

$$h_{n2}^*(p) = \frac{-\sum_{j=1}^{N} \dfrac{\partial^2 \ln H^{**}(p)}{\partial p_n \, \partial \ln p_j}}{\sum_{j=1}^{N} \dfrac{\partial \ln H^{**}(p)}{\partial \ln p_j}} \qquad (n = 1, 2, \ldots, N)$$

which is identically zero under homogeneity of $H^{**}(p)$.

Further, by equations (53), (54) and (55)

$$h_{n2}^*(p) \ln h_{n1}^*(p) = - \frac{\partial \ln H^*(p)}{\partial p_n} \cdot \frac{\partial \ln H^{**}(p)}{\partial p_n} \Big/ \frac{\partial H^*(p)}{\partial p_n}$$

$$= - \frac{1}{H^*(p)} \cdot \frac{\partial \ln H^{**}(p)}{\partial p_n}$$

$$= \frac{\partial \ln H^{**}(p)}{\partial p_n} \Big/ \sum_{j=1}^{N} \frac{\partial \ln H^{**}(p)}{\partial \ln p_j} \tag{57}$$

and

$$\ln h_{n1}^*(p) = \left\{ \frac{\partial \ln H^{**}(p)}{\partial p_n} \Big/ \sum_{j=1}^{N} \frac{\partial \ln H^{**}(p)}{\partial \ln p_j} \right\} \Big/$$

$$- \frac{\partial \ln H^*(p)}{\partial p_n}$$

$$= \left\{ \frac{\partial \ln H^{**}(p)}{\partial p_n} \Big/ \sum_{j=1}^{N} \frac{\partial \ln H^{**}(p)}{\partial \ln p_j} \right\} \Big/$$

$$\left\{ \sum_{j=1}^{N} \frac{\partial^2 \ln H^{**}(p)}{\partial p_n \partial \ln p_j} \Big/ - \sum_{j=1}^{N} \frac{\partial \ln H^{**}(p)}{\partial \ln p_j} \right\}$$

$$= - \frac{\partial \ln H^{**}(p)}{\partial \ln p_n} \Big/ \sum_{j=1}^{N} \frac{\partial^2 \ln H^{**}(p)}{\partial \ln p_n \, \partial \ln p_j} \tag{58}$$

assuming that $h_{n2}^*(p) \neq 0$.

But then $h_{n1}^*(p)$ must be homogeneous of degree minus one, which implies and is implied by

$$\sum_{j=1}^{N} \frac{\partial \ln h_{n1}^*(p)}{\partial \ln p_j} = -1$$

But

$$\sum_{j=1}^{N} \frac{\partial \ln h_{n1}^*(p)}{\partial \ln p_j} = \sum_{j=1}^{N} \frac{\partial^2 \ln H^{**}(p)}{\partial \ln p_j \partial \ln p_n} \bigg/ - \sum_{j=1}^{N} \frac{\partial^2 \ln H^{**}(p)}{\partial \ln p_n \partial \ln p_j} \tag{59}$$

$$- \frac{\partial \ln H^{**}(p)}{\partial \ln p_n} \cdot \sum_{j=1}^{N} \frac{\partial}{\partial \ln p_j} \left[- \sum_{j=1}^{N} \frac{\partial^2 \ln H^{**}(p)}{\partial \ln p_n \partial \ln p_j} \right] \bigg/ \left[- \sum_{j=1}^{N} \frac{\partial^2 \ln H^{**}(p)}{\partial \ln p_n \partial \ln p_j} \right]^2$$

The first term is equal to minus one. The second term is identically zero because of equation (56). Thus, by Euler's equation, $h_{n1}^*(p)$ is homogeneous of degree minus one. We conclude that there are no additional conditions on $H^{**}(p)$ other than that $\sum_{j=1}^{N} \partial \ln H^{**}(p)/\partial \ln p_j$ must be homogeneous of degree zero.

We note that the individual demand function may be rewritten as

$$f_{nk}(p,M_k) = h_{n2}^*(p) \ln h_{n1}^*(p) M_k + h_{n2}^*(p) M_k \ln M_k$$

$$= \frac{\partial \ln H^{**}(p)/\partial p_n}{\sum_{j=1}^{N} \partial \ln H^{**}(p)/\partial \ln p_j} M_k \tag{60}$$

$$- \frac{\sum_{j=1}^{N} \partial^2 \ln H^{**}(p)/\partial p_n \partial \ln p_j}{\sum_{j=1}^{N} \partial \ln H^{**}(p)/\partial \ln p_j} M_k \ln M_k$$

Consider now an indirect utility function of the form

$$V_k(p,M_k) = \ln H^{**}(p/M_k) \tag{61}$$

where $\sum_{j=1}^{N} \partial \ln H^{**}(p)/\partial \ln p_j$ is homogeneous of degree zero. The individual demand function may be derived by using Roy's Identity as

$$f_{nk}(p,M_k) = \frac{-\partial V_k(p,M_k)/\partial p_n}{\partial V_k(p,M_k)/\partial M_k}$$

$$= \frac{\partial \ln H^{**}(p/M_k)/\partial(p_n/M_k)}{\sum_{j=1}^{N} \partial \ln H^{**}(p/M_k)/\partial \ln (p_j/M_k)}$$

$$= \left[\frac{\sum_{j=1}^{N} \dfrac{\partial^2 \ln H^{**}(p/M_k)}{\partial(p_n/M_k)\partial \ln (p_j/M_k)}}{\sum_{j=1}^{N} \dfrac{\partial \ln H^{**}(p/M_k)}{\partial \ln (p_j/M_k)}} \right] \left[\frac{\dfrac{\partial \ln H^{**}(p/M_k)}{\partial(p_n/M_k)}}{\sum_{j=1}^{N} \dfrac{\partial^2 \ln H^{**}(p/M_k)}{\partial(p_n/M_k)\partial \ln (p_j/M_k)}} \right]$$

assuming that $H^{**}(p)$ is not homogeneous. The term in the first square bracket is homogeneous of degree minus one. By equation (58) the exponential of the term in the second square bracket with adjustment of sign if necessary is also homogeneous of degree minus one. Thus

$$f_{nk}(p,M_k) = \frac{\partial \ln H^{**}(p)/\partial p_n}{\sum\limits_{j=1}^{N} \partial \ln H^{**}(p)/\partial \ln p_j} M_k$$

$$- \frac{\sum\limits_{j=1}^{N} \partial^2 \ln H^{**}(p)/\partial p_n \partial \ln p_j}{\sum\limits_{j=1}^{N} \partial \ln H^{**}(p)/\partial \ln p_j} M_k \ln M_k$$

which is identical to equation (60).

We conclude that any system of individual demand functions which satisfies summability, zero degree homogeneity, nonnegativity and symmetry must be derivable from an indirect utility function of the form in equation (61) where $\Sigma_{j=1}^{N} \partial \ln H^{**}(p)/\partial \ln p_j$ is homogeneous of degree zero.

We wish to characterize the class of functions $H^{**}(p)$ further; the sums of the partial logarithmic derivatives of these functions are zero degree homogeneous but not constant. We thus seek the general solution of the partial differential equation:

$$\sum_{n=1}^{N} \frac{\partial \ln H^{**}(\ln p_1, \ln p_2, \ldots, \ln p_N)}{\partial \ln p_n} = f(\ln p_1, \ln p_2, \ldots, \ln p_N) \quad (62)$$

where the function f is nonconstant and zero degree homogeneous in p, that is

$$f(\ln p_1 + \ln \lambda, \ln p_2 + \ln \lambda, \ldots, \ln p_N + \ln \lambda)$$

$$= f(\ln p_1, \ln p_2, \ldots, \ln p_N)$$

We note, first, that any homogeneous of degree zero function can be rewritten as $f^{*}(\ln p_2 - \ln p_1, \ln p_3 - \ln p_1, \ldots, \ln p_N - \ln p_1)$. We can transform both the dependent and independent variables by the nonsingular transformation

$$z_1 = \ln p_1$$

$$z_2 = \ln p_2 - \ln p_1$$

$$\cdot \quad \cdot \quad \cdot \quad \cdot \quad \cdot$$

$$z_N = \ln p_N - \ln p_1,$$

$$G(z_1, z_2, \ldots, z_N) = \ln H^{**}(\ln p_1, \ln p_2, \ldots, \ln p_N)$$

The partial differential equation then becomes

$$\sum_{n=1}^{N} \frac{\partial \ln H^{**}(\ln p_1, \ldots, \ln p_N)}{\partial \ln p_n} = \sum_{n=1}^{N} \sum_{j=1}^{N} \frac{\partial G}{\partial z_j} \cdot \frac{\partial z_j}{\partial \ln p_n}$$

$$= \frac{\partial G}{\partial z_1} - \sum_{j=2}^{N} \frac{\partial G}{\partial z_j} + \sum_{n=2}^{N} \frac{\partial G}{\partial z_n}$$

$$= f(\ln p_1, \ln p_2, \ldots, \ln p_N)$$

$$= f^*(z_2, z_3, \ldots, z_N)$$

Thus, we have

$$\frac{\partial G}{\partial z_1}(z_1, \ldots, z_N) = f^*(z_2, \ldots, z_N)$$

which can be immediately integrated to yield

$$G(z_1, z_2, \ldots, z_n) = f^*(z_2, z_3, \ldots, z_N) z_1 + f_0^*(z_2, z_3, \ldots, z_N)$$

We conclude that the general solution to the partial differential equation (62) is

$$\ln H^{**}(\ln p_1, \ln p_2, \ldots, \ln p_N) = H_1^{**}(p) \ln p_1 + H_2^{**}(p)$$

where $H_1^{**}(p)$ and $H_2^{**}(p)$ are both homogeneous of degree zero. Any function $H^{**}(p)$ satisfying equation (62) can be written in this form. We can verify by direct computation that

$$\sum_{j=1}^{N} \frac{\partial \ln H^{**}(p)}{\partial \ln p_j} = \ln p_1 \sum_{j=1}^{N} \frac{\partial H_1^{**}(p)}{\partial \ln p_j} + H_1^{**}(p)$$

$$+ \sum_{j=1}^{N} \frac{\partial H_2^{**}(p)}{\partial \ln p_j}$$

$$= H_1^{**}(p)$$

by zero degree homogeneity of $H_1^{**}(p)$ and $H_2^{**}(p)$. We can therefore rewrite the indirect utility function as

$$V_k(p, M_k) = H_1^{**}(p) \ln (p_1/M_k) + H_2^{**}(p)$$

We note further that the indirect utility function can be rewritten in a more symmetric form

$$V_k(p, M_k) = -H_1^{**}(p) \ln M_k + H_1^{**}(p) \ln p_1 + H_2^{**}(p)$$

$$= -H_1^{**}(p) \ln M_k + \ln [p_1^{H_1^{**}(p)} e^{H_2^{**}(p)}]$$

The term in the square brackets satisfies:

$$(\lambda p_1)^{H_1^{**}(\lambda p)} e^{H_2^{**}(\lambda p)} = \lambda^{H_1^{**}(p)} p_1^{H_1^{**}(p)} e^{H_2^{**}(p)}$$

and is homogeneous of degree $H_1^{**}(p)$. Moreover, any such function can be written as $H^*(p)^{H_1^{**}(p)}$, where $H^*(p)$ is homogeneous of degree one. Thus, we can write

$$V_k(p,M_k) = -H_1^{**}(p) \ln M_k + H_1^{**}(p) \ln H^*(p) \qquad (k = 1, 2, \ldots, K)$$

where $H^*(p)$ is homogeneous of degree one and $H_1^{**}(p)$ is homogeneous of degree zero.

We conclude that the individual demand functions can be written as

$$f_{nk} = \frac{-\partial V_k(p,M_k)/\partial p_n}{\partial V_k(p,M_k)/\partial M_k}$$

$$= \frac{[\partial H_1^{**}(p)/\partial p_n] \ln H^*(p) + H_1^{**}(p)\, \partial \ln H^*(p)/\partial p_n}{H_1^{**}(p)} M_k$$

$$- \frac{\dfrac{\partial H_1^{**}(p)}{\partial p_n}}{H_1^{**}(p)} M_k \ln M_k \qquad (n = 1, 2, \ldots, N; k = 1, 2, \ldots, K)$$

Given the existence of an indirect utility function from which the system of individual demand functions may be derived, nonpositive definiteness of the Slutsky substitution matrix implies and is implied by quasiconvexity of the indirect utility function. It is clear that these curvature conditions will imply restrictions on the aggregate demand functions. Thus, we have proved:

Theorem 4. Under the assumption that the individual demand functions are continuously differentiable and integrable, a system of aggregate demand functions can be written in the form

$$\sum_{k=1}^{K} f_{nk}(p,M_k) = F_n(p, g_1(M_1, M_2, \ldots, M_K), g_2(M_1, M_2, \ldots, M_K)]$$

$$(n = 1, 2, \ldots, N)$$

where the functions g_ℓ $(\ell = 1,2)$ and F_n $(n = 1, 2, \ldots, N)$ satisfy assumptions (1) through (4) of Theorem (1), and the assumption of zero aggregate demand for zero aggregate expenditure, if and only if

$$(1) \quad f_{nk}(p,M_k) = \begin{cases} \dfrac{\partial \ln H^*(p)}{\partial p_n} M_k + H^*(p)^{-(\sigma-1)} \dfrac{\partial H_1^{**}(p)}{\partial p_n} M_k^\sigma \\[4pt] (n = 1, 2, \ldots, N) \\[8pt] \left[\dfrac{\partial \ln H_1^{**}(p)}{\partial p_n} \ln H^*(p) + \dfrac{\partial \ln H^*(p)}{\partial p_n} \right] M_k \\[4pt] \quad - \dfrac{\partial \ln H_1^{**}(p)}{\partial p_n} M_k \ln M_k \\[4pt] (n = 1, 2, \ldots, N) \end{cases}$$

where $H^*(p)$ is positive and homogeneous of degree one and $H_1^{**}(p)$ is homogeneous of degree zero.

(2) $\quad g_1(M_1, M_2, \ldots, M_K) = \displaystyle\sum_{k=1}^{K} M_k$

$$g_2(M_1, M_2, \ldots, M_K) = \begin{cases} \displaystyle\sum_{k=1}^{K} M_k^{\sigma} & \sigma > 0, \sigma \neq 1 \\[2em] \displaystyle\sum_{k=1}^{K} M_k \ln M_k \end{cases}$$

(3) $\quad F_n[p, g_1(M_1, M_2, \ldots, M_K), g_2(M_1, M_2, \ldots, M_K)]$

$$= \begin{cases} \dfrac{\partial \ln H^*(p)}{\partial p_n} \displaystyle\sum_{k=1}^{K} M_k + H^*(p)^{-(\sigma-1)} \dfrac{\partial H_1^{**}(p)}{\partial p_n} \displaystyle\sum_{k=1}^{K} M_k^{\sigma} \\[2em] \left[\dfrac{\partial \ln H_1^{**}(p)}{\partial p_n} \ln H^*(p) + \dfrac{\partial \ln H^*(p)}{\partial p_n} \right] \displaystyle\sum_{k=1}^{K} M_k \\[1em] \quad - \dfrac{\partial \ln H_1^{**}(p)}{\partial p_n} \displaystyle\sum_{k=1}^{K} M_k \ln M_k \\[1em] (n = 1, 2, \ldots, N) \end{cases}$$

(4)   The indirect utility function is defined as

$$V_k(p, M_k) = \begin{cases} \dfrac{1}{(\sigma - 1)} H^* \left(\dfrac{p}{M_k} \right)^{\sigma-1} + H_1^{**} \left(\dfrac{p}{M_k} \right) \\[2em] H_1^{**} \left(\dfrac{p}{M_k} \right) \ln H^* \left(\dfrac{p}{M_k} \right) \end{cases}$$

This function is nonincreasing in prices, nondecreasing in expenditures, and quasiconvex in prices and expenditure.

D.   Summary and Conclusion

In this Section we have considered the implications of the theory of exact aggregation under further restrictions implied by the theory of individual consumer behavior. First, if we assume that systems of individual demand functions are summable, one of the functions of individual expenditure must be individual expenditure itself and one of the index functions for aggregate demand functions must be aggregate expenditure. These conclusions hold for any number of index functions.

We next consider individual demand functions that depend on only two functions of individual expenditure. If we assume that the individual demand functions are summable and homogeneous of degree zero in prices and expenditure, one of the functions must be expenditure itself and the other must be either a power function of expenditure or the product of expenditure and the logarithm of expenditure. The corresponding aggregate demand functions depend on two index functions. One of these functions must be aggregate expenditure and the other must be either a sum of power functions of individual expenditures with the same power for all individuals or the sum of products of expenditure and the logarithm of expenditure for all individuals.

Finally, we consider individual demand functions that are integrable, that is, summable, homogeneous of degree zero in prices and expenditure, and nonnegative, with a Slutsky substitution matrix that is symmetric and nonpositive definite. These conditions imply that the individual demand functions can be derived from an indirect utility function that is nonincreasing in prices, nondecreasing in expenditure, and quasiconvex in prices and expenditure. The indirect utility function for each consumer can be represented in one of two possible ways. In either case the indirect utility function depends on a function that is positive and homogeneous of degree one in ratios of prices to expenditure and another function that is homogeneous of degree zero in these ratios.

Our overall conclusion is that the theory of exact aggregation and the theory of individual consumer behavior imply strong restrictions on systems of individual and aggregate demand functions. These restrictions can be used to simplify the specifications of individual and aggregate models of consumer behavior. Up to this point we have not admitted index functions that depend on both individual attributes and individual expenditures. In the following Section we derive the implications of the theory of exact aggregation for individual demand functions that incorporate differences in individual preferences.

III. EXACT AGGREGATION WITH DIFFERENCES IN INDIVIDUAL PREFERENCES

In Section 2 we have shown that exact aggregation and integrability impose restrictions on the dependence of demand functions on individual expenditures. However, we have limited consideration to consumers with identical preferences. In this Section we derive the implications of the theory of exact aggregation for index functions that depend on individual attributes and expenditures, so that preferences may differ among individuals. We begin by stating a theorem that if an index function incorporating individual attributes has a nontrivial effect on aggregate demand, the index function must depend nontrivially on individual expenditures.

Theorem 5. Under the assumptions (1) through (4) of Theorem 1 and the assumptions of zero aggregate demand for zero aggregate expenditure and nonnegativity of the individual demand functions, an aggregate demand function can be written in the form

$$\sum_{k=1}^{K} f_k(p, M_k, A_k)$$

$$= F[p, g_1(M_1, M_2, \ldots, M_K, A_1, A_2, \ldots, A_K), g_2(M_1, M_2, \ldots, M_K,$$

$$A_1, A_2, \ldots, A_K), \ldots, g_{L^*}(M_1, M_2, \ldots, M_K, A_1, A_2, \ldots, A_K),$$

$$g_{L^*+1}(A_1, A_2, \ldots, A_K), \ldots, g_L(A_1, A_2, \ldots, A_K)]$$

so that the last $(L - L^*)$ index functions g_ℓ $(\ell = 1, 2, \ldots, L)$ do not depend on individual expenditures if and only if

(1) $$f_k(p, M_k, A_k) = \sum_{\ell=1}^{L^*} h_\ell(p) g_\ell^*(M_k, A_k) \qquad (k = 1, 2, \ldots, K)$$

(2) $$F[p, g_1(M_1, M_2, \ldots, M_K, A_1, A_2, \ldots, A_K), g_2(M_1, M_2,$$

$$\ldots, M_K, A_1, A_2, \ldots, A_K), \ldots, g_L(A_1, A_2, \ldots, A_K)]$$

$$= \sum_{\ell=1}^{L^*} h_\ell(p) \sum_{k=1}^{K} g_\ell^*(M_k, A_k)$$

where $g_\ell^*(0, A_k) = 0$, $(\ell = 1, 2, \ldots, L^*)$ and the functions h_ℓ and $g_\ell^*(M_k, A_k)$ $(\ell = 1, 2, \ldots, L^*)$ are linearly independent functions.

In other words, an index function with nontrivial effects on aggregate demand must depend on individual expenditures. For example, an index function which depends only on the age distribution is not an admissible index function under our assumptions. In order for a change in the distribution of individual attributes to affect aggregate demand, it must affect the distribution of individual expenditures.

A. Two Index Functions

We now specialize to the case of two index functions that depend on individual expenditures and attributes. We consider the restrictions implied by utility maximization by individual consumers. By Theorem 1, the individual demand functions take the form:

$$f_{nk}(p, M_k, A_k) = h_{n1}(p) g_1^{**}(M_k, A_k) + h_{n2}(p) g_2^{**}(M_k, A_k)$$

$$(n = 1, 2, \ldots, N; k = 1, 2, \ldots, K)$$

where $g_\ell^{**}(0, A_k) = 0$, $(\ell = 1, 2)$.

Under the additional assumption of summability the individual demand functions must sum to M_k, so that

$$\sum_{n=1}^{N} p_n h_{n1}(p) \, g_1^{**}(M_k,A_k) + \sum_{n=1}^{N} p_n h_{n2}(p) g_2^{**}(M_k,A_k) = M_k$$

As in Section II we can show that

$$\sum_{n=1}^{N} p_n h_{n1}(p) = \bar{h}_1^*, \qquad \sum_{n=1}^{N} p_n h_{n2}(p) = \bar{h}_2^*$$

This implies that

$$g_1^{**}(M_k,A_k) = \frac{M_k}{\bar{h}_1^*} - \frac{\bar{h}_2^*}{\bar{h}_1^*} g_2^{**}(M_k,A_k)$$

so that

$$f_{nk}(p,M_k,A_k) = h_{n1}^*(p)M_k + h_{n2}^*(p)g_2^{**}(M_k,A_k)$$

$$\sum_{n=1}^{N} p_n h_{n1}^*(p) = 1; \qquad \sum_{n=1}^{N} p_n h_{n2}^*(p) = 0$$

Under the additional assumption of zero degree homogeneity, we have

$$h_{n1}^*(\lambda p)\lambda M_k + h_{n2}^*(\lambda p)g_2^{**}(\lambda M_k,A_k) = h_{n1}^*(p)M_k + h_{n2}^*(p)g_2^{**}(M_k,A_k)$$

The implications of zero degree homogeneity can be analyzed by using an argument strictly analogous to that presented in Section II.B.

First, we show, as in equation (26), that

$$h_2(\lambda p) = \lambda^{-\sigma}h_2(p)$$

Then, from equation (28), we have

$$\lambda^{-\sigma+1} \frac{g_2^{**}(\lambda M_k,A_k)}{\lambda M_k} - \frac{g_2^{**}(M_k,A_k)}{M_k} = \ell(\lambda) \qquad (63)$$

Equation (63) must hold for all A_k and in particular for $A_k = 0$ or, equivalently, some reference level. Thus:

$$\lambda^{-\sigma+1} \left[\frac{g_2^{**}(\lambda M_k,A_k)}{\lambda M_k} - \frac{g_2^{**}(\lambda M_k,0)}{\lambda M_k} \right] = \frac{g_2^{**}(M_k,A_k)}{M_k} - \frac{g_2^{**}(M_k,0)}{M_k}$$

We conclude that $\dfrac{g_2^{**}(M_k,A_k)}{M_k} - \dfrac{g_2^{**}(M_k,0)}{M_k}$ is homogeneous of degree $\sigma - 1$ in M_k for all values of A_k. Thus, $g_2^{**}(M_k,A_k)$ must have the form

$$g_2^{**}(M_k,A_k) = g_2^{**}(M_k,0) + \ell^*(A_k)M_k^{\sigma}$$

Substituting the function $g_2^{**}(M_k, A_k)$ into equation (63), we obtain

$$\lambda^{-\sigma+1} \left[\frac{g_2^{**}(\lambda M_k, 0)}{\lambda M_k} + \frac{\ell^*(A_k)\lambda^\sigma M_k^\sigma}{\lambda M_k} \right] - \left[\frac{g_2^{**}(M_k, 0)}{M_k} + \frac{\ell^*(A_k)M_k^\sigma}{M_k} \right] = \ell(\lambda)$$

which reduces to:

$$\lambda^{-\sigma+1} \frac{g_2^{**}(\lambda M_k, 0)}{\lambda M_k} - \frac{g_2^{**}(M_k, 0)}{M_k} = \ell(\lambda) \tag{64}$$

Equation (64) has the same form as equation (28), with solution given by

$$g_2^{**}(M_k, 0) = \begin{cases} D_1 M_k^\sigma + D_2 M_k & \sigma \neq 1, \sigma > 0 \\ D_1 M_k \ln M_k + D_2 M_k & \sigma = 1 \end{cases}$$

where D_1 and D_2 are constants. This implies

$$g_2^{**}(M_k, A_k) = \begin{cases} [D_1 + \ell^*(A_k)] M_k^\sigma + D_2 M_k, & \sigma \neq 1, \sigma > 0 \\ D_1 M_k \ln M_k + [D_2 + \ell^*(A_k)]M_k & \sigma = 1 \end{cases}$$

We conclude that under the additional assumption of zero degree homogeneity, the individual demand functions must take the form either

$$f_{nk}(p, M_k, A_k) = h_{n1}^*(p)M_k + h_{n2}^*(p)\,\ell^{**}(A_k)M_k^\sigma \tag{65}$$

$$\sum_{n=1}^N p_n h_{n1}^*(p) = 1; \qquad \sum_{n=1}^N p_n h_{n2}^*(p) = 0$$

or

$$f_{nk}(p, M_k, A_k) = h_{n1}^*(p)M_k + h_{n2}^*(p)\,[\ell^{**}(A_k)M_k + M_k \ln M_k] \tag{66}$$

$$\sum_{n=1}^N p_n h_{n1}^*(p) = 1; \qquad \sum_{n=1}^N p_n h_{n2}^*(p) = 0$$

The aggregate demand functions are given by either

$$F_n[p, g_1(M_1, M_2, \ldots, M_K, A_1, A_2, \ldots, A_K), g_2(M_1, M_2, \ldots, M_K,$$

$$A_1, A_2, \ldots, A_K)] = h_{n1}^*(p) \sum_{k=1}^K M_k + h_{n2}^*(p) \sum_{k=1}^K \ell^{**}(A_k)M_k^\sigma$$

$$(n = 1, 2, \ldots, N)$$

or

$$F_n[p, g_1(M_1, M_2, \ldots, M_K, A_1, A_2, \ldots, A_K), g_2(M_1, M_2, \ldots, M_K,$$

$$A_1, A_2, \ldots, A_K] = h_{n1}^*(p) \sum_{k=1}^K M_k + h_{n2}^*(p) \sum_{k=1}^K [\ell^{**}(A_k)M_k + M_k \ln M_k]$$

$$(n = 1, 2, \ldots, N)$$

where the appropriate homogeneity conditions must be satisfied by the functions $h_{n\ell}^*(p)(\ell = 1, 2)$.

Finally, we consider the implications of symmetry of the Slutsky substitution matrix of the system of individual demand functions. Using the results of Section II.C, symmetry implies for equation (65) that the individual demand functions take the form

$$f_{nk}(p,M_k,A_k) = \frac{\partial \ln H^*(p)}{\partial p_n} M_k + H^*(p)^{-(\sigma-1)} \frac{\partial H_1^{**}(p)}{\partial p_n} \ell^{**}(A_k)M_k^{\sigma}$$

where $H^*(p)$ is homogeneous of degree one and $H_1^{**}(p)$ is homogeneous of degree zero.

For equation (66), we can write the individual demand functions as

$$f_{nk}(p,M_k,A_k) = [h_{n1}^*(p) + h_{n2}^*(p)\ell^{**}(0)]M_k + h_{n2}^*(p)M_k \ln M_k$$
$$+ h_{n2}^*(p)[\ell^{**}(A_k) - \ell^{**}(0)]M_k$$

Let $A_k = 0$. By the results of Section II.C, symmetry implies that the individual demand functions take the form

$$f_{nk}(p,M_k,0) = \left[\frac{\partial \ln H_1^{**}(p)}{\partial p_n} \ln H^*(p) + \frac{\partial \ln H^*(p)}{\partial p_n}\right]M_k$$
$$- \frac{\partial \ln H_1^{**}(p)}{\partial p_n} M_k \ln M_k \qquad (n = 1, 2, \ldots, N)$$

where $H^*(p)$ is homogeneous of degree one and $H_1^{**}(p)$ is homogeneous of degree zero. This implies that

$$f_{nk}(p,M_k,A_k) = \left[\frac{\partial \ln H_1^{**}(p)}{\partial p_n} \ln H^*(p) + \frac{\partial \ln H^*(p)}{\partial p_n}\right]M_k$$
$$- \frac{\partial \ln H_1^{**}(p)}{\partial p_n} M_k \ln M_k + \frac{\partial \ln H_1^{**}(p)}{\partial p_n} \ell^{***}(A_k)M_k$$
$$(n = 1, 2, \ldots, N; k = 1, 2, \ldots, K)$$

For both forms of the individual demand functions the total expenditure effect and the attribute effect on the expenditure shares are related; for the power form:

$$\frac{\partial}{\partial M_k} \cdot \frac{p_n f_{nk}(p,M_k,A_k)}{M_k} = (\sigma - 1)H^*(p)^{-(\sigma-1)} \frac{\partial H_1^{**}(p)}{\partial p_n} \ell^{**}(A_k)M_k^{(\sigma-2)} p_n$$

and

$$\frac{\partial}{\partial \ell^{**}(A_k)} \cdot \frac{p_n f_{nk}(p,M_k,A_k)}{M_k} = H^*(p)^{-(\sigma-1)} \frac{\partial H_1^{**}(p)}{\partial p_n} M_k^{(\sigma-1)} p_n$$

so that

$$\frac{\dfrac{\partial}{\partial M_k} \cdot \dfrac{p_n f_{nk}(p,M_k,A_k)}{M_k}}{\dfrac{\partial}{\partial \ell^{**}(A_k)} \cdot \dfrac{p_n f_{nk}(p,M_k,A_k)}{M_k}} = (\sigma - 1)M_k^{-1} \qquad (n = 1, 2, \ldots, N)$$

for the logarithmic form

$$\frac{\partial}{\partial M_k} \cdot \frac{p_n f_{nk}(p,M_k,A_k)}{M_k} = -\frac{\partial \ln H_1^{**}(p)}{\partial p_n} M_k^{-1} p_n$$

and

$$\frac{\partial}{\partial \ell^{***}(A_k)} \cdot \frac{p_n f_{nk}(p,M_k,A_k)}{M_k} = \frac{\partial \ln H_1^{**}(p)}{\partial p_n} p_n$$

so that

$$\frac{\dfrac{\partial}{\partial M_k} \cdot \dfrac{p_n f_{nk}(p,M_k,A_k)}{M_k}}{\dfrac{\partial}{\partial \ell^{***}(A_k)} \cdot \dfrac{p_n f_{nk}(p,M_k,A_k)}{M_k}} = -M_k^{-1} \qquad (n = 1,2, \ldots, N)$$

Restrictions on the expenditure and attribute effects limit the degree of generality of the systems of individual demand functions with different attributes. If the expenditure term enters as a power function and if $\ell^{**}(A_k)$ is equal to zero for some A_k, the Engel curves for all individual consumers with attributes equal to A_k will be linear and homogeneous in expenditure for all commodities. Empirical evidence on Engel curves is inconsistent with this restriction. Note that this restriction does not apply if the expenditure term enters as expenditure times the natural logarithm of expenditure. We conclude that the case of two index functions does not provide an adequate representation of individual and aggregate demand functions when there are consumers with different expenditures and attributes. We therefore consider the case of three index functions in order to obtain a more satisfactory representation.

B. Three Index Functions

An aggregate demand function with two index functions of individual expenditures alone and one index function of individual expenditures and attributes takes the form:

$$\sum_{k=1}^{K} f_k(p,M_k,A_k) = F[p,g_1(M_1 M_2, \ldots, M_K),g_2(M_1,M_2, \ldots, M_K),$$

$$g_3(M_1,M_2, \ldots, M_K,A_1,A_2, \ldots, A_K)]$$

where we can assume without loss of generality that

$$g_1(0, 0, \ldots, 0) = 0$$

$$g_2(0, 0, \ldots, 0) = 0$$

$$g_3(0, 0, \ldots, 0; A_1, A_2, \ldots, A_K) = 0$$

and

$$g_3(M_1, M_2, \ldots, M_K; 0, 0, \ldots, 0) = 0$$

This aggregate demand function implies that the individual demand functions have the form

$$f_{nk}(p, M_k, A_k) = h_{n1}(p)g_1^*(M_k) + h_{n2}(p)g_2^*(M_k) + h_{n3}(p)g_3^*(M_k, A_k) + C_{nk}(p)$$

$$(n = 1, 2, \ldots, N; k = 1, 2, \ldots, K)$$

where without loss of generality, $g_1^*(0) = g_2^*(0) = g_3^*(0, A_k) = g_3^*(M_k, 0) = 0$.

Under the assumption of zero aggregate demand for zero aggregate expenditure and nonnegativity

$$C_{nk}(p) = 0 \quad (n = 1, 2, \ldots, N; k = 1, 2, \ldots, K)$$

Under the assumption of summability the individual demand functions must sum to M_k, so that

$$f_{nk}(p, M_k, A_k) = h_{n1}(p)M_k + h_{n2}(p)g_2^*(M_k) + h_{n3}(p)g_3^*(M_k, A_k)$$

where

$$\sum_{n=1}^{N} p_n h_{n1}(p) = 1; \quad \sum_{n=1}^{N} p_n h_{n\ell}(p) = 0; \quad (\ell = 2, 3)$$

Under the additional assumption of zero degree homogeneity, we have

$$h_{n1}(\lambda p)\lambda M_k + h_{n2}(\lambda p)g_2^*(\lambda M_k) + h_{n3}(\lambda p)g_3^*(\lambda M_k, A_k) \tag{67}$$

$$= h_{n1}(p)M_k + h_{n2}(p)g_2^*(M_k) + h_{n3}(p)g_3^*(M_k, A_k)$$

Letting $A_k = 0$, equation (67) reduces to equation (21) with the solutions given by Theorem 4. Subtracting both sides of equation (21) from equation (67) we obtain

$$h_{n3}(\lambda p)g_3^*(\lambda M_k, A_k) = h_{n3}(p)g_3^*(M_k, A_k)$$

or

$$\frac{h_{n3}(\lambda p)}{h_{n3}(p)} = \ell(\lambda)$$

In other words, $h_{n3}(p)$ must be a homogeneous of degree $-\sigma_2$ function. It follows that $g_3^*(M_k, A_k)$ must be homogeneous of degree σ_2 in M_k, and

$g_3^*(0,A_k) = 0$ implies that $\sigma_2 \geqq 0$. Hence

$$g_3^*(M_k,A_k) = \ell^*(A_k)M_k^{\sigma_2}$$

The individual demand functions take the form:

$$f_{nk}(p,M_k,A_k) = \begin{cases} h_{n1}(p)M_k + h_{n2}(p)M_k^{\sigma_1} + h_{n3}(p)\ell^*(A_k)M_k^{\sigma_2} \\ \\ \quad (k = 1, 2, \ldots, K; n = 1, 2, \ldots, N) \\ \\ h_{n2}^*(p) \ln h_{n1}^*(p)M_k + h_{n2}^*(p)M_k \ln M_k + h_{n3}^*(p)\ell^*(A_k)M_k^{\sigma_2} \\ \\ \quad (k = 1, 2, \ldots, K; n = 1, 2, \ldots, N) \end{cases}$$

where $h_{n1}(p)$, $h_{n2}^*(p)$ and $h_{n1}^*(p)$ are homogeneous of degree -1, $h_{n2}(p)$ is homogeneous of degree $-\sigma_1$. The functions $h_{n3}(p)$ and $h_{n3}^*(p)$ are homogeneous of degree $-\sigma_2$, $\sigma_1, \sigma_2 \geqq 0$, $\sigma_1 \neq 1$, and $\ell^*(0) = 0$.

The assumption of symmetry implies additional restrictions on the form of the individual demand functions. First, let $A_k = 0$, then the results of Section II.D apply. Now suppose A_k is arbitrary. Symmetry of the Slutsky substitution matrix, under the additional assumption of once continuous differentiability of the individual demand functions, implies for the first case considered above

$$h_{j1n}(p)M_k + h_{j2n}(p)M_k^{\sigma_1} + h_{j3n}(p)\ell^*(A_k)M_k^{\sigma_2}$$
$$+ [h_{n1}(p)M_k + h_{n2}(p)M_k^{\sigma_1} + h_{n3}(p)\ell^*(A_k)M_k^{\sigma_2}]$$
$$[h_{j1}(p) + \sigma_1 h_{j2}(p)M_k^{\sigma_1-1} + \sigma_2 h_{j3}(p)\ell^*(A_k)M_k^{\sigma_2-1}]$$
$$= h_{n1j}(p)M_k + h_{n2j}(p)M_k^{\sigma_1} + h_{n3j}(p)\ell^*(A_k)M_k^{\sigma_2}$$
$$+ [h_{j1}(p)M_k + h_{j2}(p)M_k^{\sigma_1} + h_{j3}(p)\ell^*(A_k)M_k^{\sigma_2}]$$
$$[h_{n1}(p) + \sigma_1 h_{n2}(p)M_k^{\sigma_1-1} + \sigma_2 h_{n3}(p)\ell^*(A_k)M_k^{\sigma_2-1}]$$

which simplifies into

$$h_{j1n}(p)M_k + h_{j2n}(p)M_k^{\sigma_1} + h_{j3n}(p)\ell^*(A_k)M_k^{\sigma_2}$$
$$+ \sigma_1 h_{n1}(p)h_{j2}(p)M_k^{\sigma_1} + \sigma_2 h_{n1}(p)h_{j3}(p)\ell^*(A_k)M_k^{\sigma_2}$$
$$+ h_{n2}(p)h_{j1}(p)M_k^{\sigma_1} + \sigma_2 h_{n2}(p)h_{j3}(p)\ell^*(A_k)M_k^{\sigma_1+\sigma_2-1}$$
$$+ h_{n3}(p)h_{j1}(p)\ell^*(A_k)M_k^{\sigma_2} + \sigma_1 h_{n3}(p)h_{j2}(p)\ell^*(A_k)M_k^{\sigma_1+\sigma_2-1}$$
$$= h_{n1j}(p)M_k + h_{n2j}(p)M_k^{\sigma_1} + h_{n3j}(p)\ell^*(A_k)M_k^{\sigma_2}$$
$$+ \sigma_1 h_{j1}(p)h_{n2}(p)M_k^{\sigma_1} + \sigma_2 h_{j1}(p)h_{n3}(p)\ell^*(A_k)M_k^{\sigma_2}$$
$$+ h_{j2}(p)h_{n1}(p)M_k^{\sigma_1} + \sigma_2 h_{j2}(p)h_{n3}(p)\ell^*(A_k)M_k^{\sigma_1+\sigma_2-1}$$
$$+ h_{j3}(p)h_{n1}(p)\ell^*(A_k)M_k^{\sigma_2} + \sigma_1 h_{j3}(p)h_{n2}(p)\ell^*(A_k)M_k^{\sigma_1+\sigma_2-1}$$

By setting $A_k = 0$, the above equation reduces to equation (46), which has been solved. By subtracting equation (46) from the above equation we obtain

$$
\begin{aligned}
[(\sigma_2 - 1)h_{j3}(p)h_{n1}(p) &+ h_{j3n}(p)]\ell^*(A_k)M_k^{\sigma_2} \\
&+ (\sigma_2 - \sigma_1)h_{j3}(p)h_{n2}(p)\ell^*(A_k)M_k^{\sigma_1+\sigma_2-1} \\
= [(\sigma_2 - 1)h_{n3}(p)h_{j1}(p) &+ h_{n3j}(p)]\ell^*(A_k)M_k^{\sigma_2} \\
&+ (\sigma_2 - \sigma_1)h_{n3}(p)h_{j2}(p)\ell^*(A_k)M_k^{\sigma_1+\sigma_2-1}
\end{aligned}
\tag{68}
$$

Equation (68) must hold identically in M_k. Note that $\sigma_2 \neq \sigma_1 + \sigma_2 - 1$, for otherwise $\sigma_1 = 1$, which is ruled out. Thus:

$$
(\sigma_2 - 1)h_{j3}(p)h_{n1}(p) + h_{j3n}(p) = (\sigma_2 - 1)h_{n3}(p)h_{j1}(p) + h_{n3j}(p) \tag{69}
$$

and

$$
(\sigma_2 - \sigma_1)h_{j3}(p)h_{n2}(p) = (\sigma_2 - \sigma_1)h_{n3}(p)h_{j2}(p) \tag{70}
$$

Now from Section II.C

$$
h_{n1}(p) = \frac{\partial \ln H^*(p)}{\partial p_n}
$$

so that equation (69) becomes

$$
\frac{\partial}{\partial p_n} H^*(p)^{\sigma_2-1} h_{j3}(p) = \frac{\partial}{\partial p_j} H^*(p)^{\sigma_2-1} h_{n3}(p)
$$

which implies that

$$
H^*(p)^{\sigma_2-1} h_{n3}(p) = \frac{\partial}{\partial p_n} H^{***}(p) \tag{71}
$$

By summability

$$
\sum_{n=1}^{N} p_n h_{n3}(p) = \sum_{n=1}^{N} \frac{\partial H^{***}(p)}{\partial \ln p_n} H^*(p)^{1-\sigma_2} = 0
$$

Thus, $H^{***}(p)$ is homogeneous of degree zero in p.

If $\sigma_2 - \sigma_1 = 0$, equation (70) is trivially satisfied, so that the individual demand functions must take the form

$$
\begin{aligned}
f_{nk}(p,M_k,A_k) = \frac{\partial \ln H^*(p)}{\partial p_n} M_k &+ H^*(p)^{-(\sigma_1-1)} \frac{\partial H^{**}(p)}{\partial p_n} M_k^{\sigma_1} \\
&+ H^*(p)^{-(\sigma_1-1)} \frac{\partial H^{***}(p)}{\partial p_n} \ell^*(A_k)M_k^{\sigma_1}
\end{aligned}
\tag{72}
$$

$$
(n = 1, 2, \ldots, N; k = 1, 2, \ldots, K)
$$

where $H^*(p)$ is homogeneous of degree one, $H^{**}(p)$ and $H^{***}(p)$ are homogeneous of degree zero.

Suppose $\sigma_2 - \sigma_1 \neq 0$. Then by making use of the fact from Section II.C that

$$h_{n2}(p) = \frac{\partial H^{**}(p)}{\partial p_n} \cdot H^*(p)^{-(\sigma_1-1)}$$

equation (70) becomes

$$h_{j3}(p) \frac{\partial H^{**}(p)}{\partial p_n} = h_{n3}(p) \frac{\partial H^{**}(p)}{\partial p_j}$$

which by using equation (71) leads to

$$\frac{\partial H^{**}(p)}{\partial p_n} \bigg/ \frac{\partial H^{***}(p)}{\partial p_n} = \frac{\partial H^{**}(p)}{\partial p_j} \bigg/ \frac{\partial H^{***}(p)}{\partial p_j} \qquad (n,j = 1, 2, \ldots, N)$$

This implies that

$$H^{***}(p) = t[H^{**}(p)]$$

where $t(\cdot)$ is a function of a single variable.

We conclude that the individual demand functions must take the form

$$f_{nk}(p,M_k,A_k) = \frac{\partial \ln H^*(p)}{\partial p_n} M_k + H^*(p)^{-(\sigma_1-1)} \frac{\partial H^{**}(p)}{\partial p_n} M_k^{\sigma_1}$$

$$+ H^*(p)^{-(\sigma_2-1)} \frac{\partial}{\partial p_n} t(H^{**}(p))\ell^*(A_k)M_k^{\sigma_2} \qquad (73)$$

$$(n = 1, 2, \ldots, N; k = 1, 2, \ldots, K)$$

where $H^*(p)$ is homogeneous of degree one, $H^{**}(p)$ is homogeneous of degree zero and $t(\cdot)$ is a function of a single variable. This form implies that

$$\frac{h_{n2}(p)}{h_{n3}(p)} = \frac{H^*(p)^{-(\sigma_1-\sigma_2)}}{t'[H^{**}(p)]} \qquad (n = 1, 2, \ldots, N)$$

In other words, the ratio of the nonlinear expenditure effect to the attribute expenditure effect is the same for all commodities.

Symmetry of the Slutsky substitution matrix implies for the second case considered above:

$$h_{j2n}^*(p)[\ln h_{ji}^*(p)M_k + M_k \ln M_k] + \frac{h_{j2}^*(p)h_{j1n}^*(p)}{h_{ji}^*(p)} \cdot M_k + h_{j3n}^*(p)\ell^*(A_k)M_k^{\sigma_2}$$

$$+ \{h_{n2}^*(p)[\ln h_{ni}^*(p)M_k + M_k \ln M_k] + h_{n3}^*(p)\ell^*(A_k)M_k^{\sigma_2}\} \qquad (74)$$

$$\{h_{j2}^*(p)[\ln h_{ji}^*(p) + \ln M_k + 1] + \sigma_2 h_{j3}^*(p)\ell^*(A_k)M_k^{\sigma_2-1}\}$$

$$= h_{n2j}^*(p)[\ln h_{n1}^*(p)M_k + M_k \ln M_k] + \frac{h_{n2}^*(p)h_{n1j}^*(p)}{h_{n1}^*(p)} \cdot M_k + h_{n3j}^*(p)\ell^*(A_k)M_k^{\sigma_2}$$

$$+ \{h_{j2}^*(p)[\ln h_{ji}^*(p)M_k + M_k \ln M_k] + h_{j3}^*(p)\ell^*(A_k)M_k^{\sigma_2}\}$$

$$\{h_{n2}^*(p)[\ln h_{n1}^*(p) + \ln M_k + 1] + \sigma_2 h_{n3}^*(p)\ell^*(A_k)M_k^{\sigma_2-1}\}$$

By setting $A_k = O$ the equation given above reduces to equation (50), which has been solved. Subtracting M_k times equation (50) from equation (74), we obtain

$$h_{j3n}^*(p)\ell^*(A_k)M_k^{\sigma_2} + (\sigma_2 - 1)h_{j3}^*(p)\ell^*(A_k)h_{n2}^*(p)M_k^{\sigma_2}[\ln h_{n1}^*(p) + \ln M_k]$$

$$- h_{j3}^*(p)h_{n2}^*(p)\ell^*(A_k)M_k^{\sigma_2}$$

$$= h_{n3j}^*(p)\ell^*(A_k)M_k^{\sigma_2} + (\sigma_2 - 1)h_{n3}^*(p)\ell^*(A_k)h_{j2}^*(p)M_k^{\sigma_2}[\ln h_{ji}^*(p) + \ln M_k]$$

$$- h_{n3}^*(p)h_{j2}^*(p)\ell^*(A_k)M_k^{\sigma_2}$$

To hold identically, this implies for $\sigma_2 = 1$

$$h_{j3n}^*(p) - h_{j3}^*(p)h_{n2}^*(p) = h_{n3j}^*(p) - h_{n3}^*(p)h_{j2}^*(p)$$

which, by making use of equation (53), can be written as

$$\frac{\partial}{\partial p_n} h_{j3}^*(p) H_1^*(p) = \frac{\partial}{\partial p_j} h_{n3}^*(p)H_1^*(p)$$

where $H_i^*(p)$ is homogenous of degree zero, so that

$$h_{n3}^*(p)H_1^*(p) = \frac{\partial}{\partial p_n} H^{***}(p)$$

By summability, $\Sigma_{n=1}^N p_n h_{n3}^*(p) = 0$, which implies that $H^{***}(p)$ is homogeneous of degree zero. We conclude that

$$h_{n3}^*(p) = \frac{\partial H^{***}(p)}{\partial p_n} \bigg/ H_1^*(p),$$

which is homogeneous of degree minus one as required.

For $\sigma_2 \neq 1$, symmetry implies

$$h_{j3}^*(p)h_{n2}^*(p) = h_{n3}^*(p)h_{j2}^*(p), \tag{75}$$

and

$$h_{j3n}^*(p) + (\sigma_2 - 1)h_{j3}^*(p)h_{n2}^*(p) \ln h_{n1}^*(p)$$

$$= h_{n3j}^*(p) + (\sigma_2 - 1)h_{n3}^*(p)h_{j2}^*(p) \ln h_{ji}^*(p) \tag{76}$$

From equation (53):

$$h_{n2}^*(p) = \frac{\partial H_1^*(p)}{\partial p_n}$$

From equation (75):

$$h_{n3}^*(p) = \frac{\partial t[H_1^*(p)]}{\partial p_n}$$

where $t(.)$ is a function of a single variable.

By summability,

$$\sum_{n=1}^{N} p_n h_{n3}^*(p) = t'[H_1^*(p)] \sum_{n=1}^{N} p_n \frac{\partial H_1^*(p)}{\partial p_n} = 0$$

which is identically satisfied by zero degree homogeneity of $H_1^*(p)$. Moreover, $h_{n3}^*(p)$ is homogeneous of degree $-\sigma_2$ which implies that $t[H_1^*(p)] + D$, D a constant, must be homogeneous of degree $-\sigma_2 + 1$ so that

$$t'[H_1^*(p)] \sum_{n=1}^{N} p_n \frac{\partial H_1^*(p)}{\partial p_n} = (-\sigma_2 + 1)(t + D)$$

But the left-hand-side is equal to zero. Hence the right-hand-side must also equal zero. Since $h_{n3}^*(p) \neq 0$, for all n and all p, $\sigma_2 = 1$.

We conclude that the individual demand functions must take the form:

$$f_{nk}(p, M_k, A_k) = \left[\frac{\partial \ln H_1^{**}(p)}{\partial p_n} \ln H^*(p) + \frac{\partial \ln H^*(p)}{\partial p_n} \right] M_k$$

$$- \frac{\partial \ln H_1^{**}(p)}{\partial p_n} M_k \ln M_k + \left[\frac{\partial H_2^{**}(p)}{\partial p_n} \bigg/ H_1^{**}(p) \right] \ell^*(A_k) M_k \quad (77)$$

$$(n = 1, 2, \ldots, N; k = 1, 2, \ldots, K)$$

where $H^*(p)$ is homogeneous of degree one, the functions $H_\ell^{**}(p)$ ($\ell = 1, 2$) are homogeneous of degree zero, and $\ell^*(0) = 0$. We note that in this case the ratio of the nonlinear expenditure effect to the attribute expenditure effect need not be the same for all commodities. Thus, for the second of the two cases considered above, the only admissible mixed index of expenditures and attributes is of the form

$$\sum_{k=1}^{K} g_3^*(M_k, A_k) = \sum_{k=1}^{K} \ell^*(A_k) M_k$$

The individual demand function of the form in equation (77) may be derived from an indirect utility function of the form:

$$V_k(p,M_k,A_k) = H_1^{**}(p) \ln H^*(p/M_k) + H_2^{**}(p)\ell^*(A_k)$$

$$(k = 1, 2, \ldots, K) \quad (78)$$

where $H^*(p)$ is homogeneous of degree one and the functions $H_\ell^{**}(p)$ ($\ell = 1, 2$) are homogeneous of degree zero and $\ell^*(0) = 0$.

Equations (72) and (77) are superior to equation (73) in that they allow the attribute expenditure effect to be different from the expenditure effect for different commodities. By contrast equation (73) requires that the two effects be proportional. We therefore remove equation (73) from further consideration as the basis for the selection of a functional form for our empirical application.

D.   Summary and Conclusion

In this Section we have considered the implications of the theory of exact aggregation under restrictions implied by the theory of individual consumer behavior. In order to allow for differences in preferences among individuals we have admitted index functions that depend on individual attributes as well as individual expenditures. We first observe that if an index function has a nontrivial effect on aggregate demand functions, the index function must depend on individual expenditures and not on individual attributes alone. This conclusion holds for any number of index functions.

We next consider individual demand functions that depend on only two functions of individual attributes and expenditure. If we assume that the individual demand functions are summable, one of the functions must depend on individual expenditure alone and must be individual expenditure itself. As before, one of the index functions for aggregate demand functions must be aggregate expenditure. These conclusions hold for index functions that depend on both individual attributes and expenditures as well as index functions that depend on individual expenditures alone.

If we assume that the individual demand functions are summable and homogeneous of degree zero in prices and expenditure, one of the two functions of individual expenditure and attributes must be expenditure itself. The other function must take one of two possible forms. First, the function may be equal to the product of a function of individual attributes alone and a power function of expenditure. Second, the function may be the product of expenditure and the sum of a function of individual attributes alone and the logarithm of expenditure. The aggregate demand functions depend on two index functions—aggregate expenditure and the sum of the corresponding functions of individual attributes and expenditures for all individuals.

Finally, we consider individual demand functions that are integrable. As before, integrability implies that the individual demand functions can be derived from an indirect utility function that is nonincreasing in prices, nondecreasing in expenditure, and quasiconvex in prices and expenditure. The indirect utility function for each consumer can be represented in one of two possible ways. In either case the indirect utility function depends on a function that is positive and homogeneous of degree one in ratios of prices to expenditure and another function that is homogeneous of degree zero in these ratios. In both cases the indirect utility function also depends on a function of individual attributes alone.

Examination of the form of the individual demand functions under the assumption that these functions are integrable reveals a relationship between the impact of changes in expenditure and the impact of changes in attributes. The ratio of these effects on individual expenditure shares depends only on expenditure and not on prices or individual attributes. We conclude that it is necessary to consider the case of three functions of individual attributes and expenditure in order to obtain a satisfactory representation of individual and aggregate demand functions.

In considering individual demand functions that depend on two functions of individual attributes and expenditure, we have found that summability implies that one of the two functions is equal to expenditure. Under homogeneity of degree zero in prices and expenditure, the second function must take one of two possible forms, but may depend on both individual attributes and expenditure. In considering individual demand functions that depend on three functions, we add a third function that depends on expenditure alone in order to simplify the specification of individual and aggregate demand functions. As before, summability implies that one of the three functions must be equal to expenditure.

If we assume that individual demand functions are homogeneous of degree zero in prices and expenditure, we find that the function of attributes and expenditure must be equal to the product of a function of attributes alone and a power function of individual expenditure. The second function of expenditure alone must take one of two possible forms. First, the function may be a power function of individual expenditure. Second, the function may be the product of expenditure and the logarithm of expenditure. The corresponding aggregate demand functions depend on index functions that are sums of these functions for all individuals.

Finally, if we assume that individual demand functions are integrable, these functions can be derived from an indirect utility function, as before. Considering the second functions of expenditure alone, we find either that the power function of expenditure must be the same as in the function of attributes and expenditure or the power function in the function of attributes and expenditure must be equal to expenditure itself. Otherwise, the impact of changes in expenditure and the impact of changes in attributes are related.

Consideration of index functions that depend on individual attributes and expenditure reinforces the conclusion we reached in Section II, namely, that the theory of exact aggregation and the theory of individual consumer behavior can be employed to simplify the specifications of individual and aggregate models of consumer behavior. In this Section we have derived restrictions on the ways in which functions of individual attributes and individual expenditures can enter individual and aggregate models. We turn next to the dependence of individual and aggregate demand functions on prices.

IV. DEMANDS AS FUNCTIONS OF PRICES

In Sections II and III we have shown that exact aggregation and integrability impose severe restrictions on the dependence of demand functions on individual attributes and expenditures. These restrictions can be used to simplify the specifications of models of individual and aggregate consumer behavior. Complete models of consumer behavior also require the specification of the role of prices in determining the allocation of consumer expenditures. In this Section we consider the dependence of the individual demand functions on prices.

For three index functions—two index functions of individual expenditures alone and one index function of individual attributes and expenditure—we have shown that only two forms can be considered for individual demand functions. The first is the power form

$$f_{nk}(p,M_k,A_k) = \frac{\partial \ln H^*(p)}{\partial p_n} M_k + H^*(p)^{-(\sigma-1)} \frac{\partial H_1^{**}(p)}{\partial p_n} M_k^\sigma$$

$$+ H^*(p)^{-(\sigma-1)} \frac{\partial H_2^{**}(p)}{\partial p_n} \ell^*(A)M_k^\sigma \qquad (79)$$

$$(n = 1, 2, \ldots, N; k = 1, 2, \ldots, K)$$

where $H^*(p)$ is homogeneous of degree one and the functions $H_\ell^{**}(p)$ ($\ell = 1, 2$) are homogeneous of degree zero, $\ell^*(0) = 0$, and $\sigma \neq 1$, since $\sigma = 1$ is equivalent to homothetic preferences for all individuals.

Equation (79) can be derived from an indirect utility function of the form

$$V_k(p,M_k,A_k) = \frac{H^*(p)^{\sigma-1}}{(\sigma - 1)} M_k^{-(\sigma-1)} + H_1^{**}(p)$$

$$+ H_2^{**}(p)\ell^*(A_k) \qquad (k = 1, 2, \ldots, K) \quad (80)$$

An indirect utility function of this form can be characterized as the solution to the partial differential equation

$$\sum_{n=1}^{N} \frac{\partial V_k(p/M_k, A_k)}{\partial \ln (p_n/M_k)} = f(p/M_k, A_k) \quad (81)$$

where $f(p/M_k, A_k)$ is a homogeneous of degree $(\sigma - 1)$ function in p/M_k.

The second functional form for individual demand functions is the logarithmic form:

$$f_{nk}(p, M_k, A_k) = \left[\frac{\partial \ln H_1^{**}(p)}{\partial p_n} \ln H^*(p) + \frac{\partial \ln H^*(p)}{\partial p_n} \right] M_k$$

$$- \frac{\partial \ln H_1^{**}(p)}{\partial p_n} M_k \ln M_k + \frac{\dfrac{\partial H_2^{**}(p)}{\partial p_n}}{H_1^{**}(p)} \ell^*(A_k) M_k \quad (82)$$

$$(n = 1, 2, \ldots, N; k = 1, 2, \ldots, K)$$

where $H^*(p)$ is homogeneous of degree one and the functions $H_\ell^{**}(p)$ ($\ell = 1, 2$) are homogeneous of degree zero and $\ell^*(0) = 0$.

Equation (82) can be derived from an indirect utility function of the form

$$V_k(p, M_k, A_k) = - H_1^{**}(p) \ln M_k + H_1^{**}(p) \ln H^*(p) + H_2^{**}(p)\ell^*(A_k)$$

$$(k = 1, 2, \ldots, K) \quad (83)$$

An indirect utility function of this form can be characterized as the solution to the partial differential equation

$$\sum_{n=1}^{N} \frac{\partial V_k(p/M_k, A_k)}{\partial \ln (p_n/M_k)} = f(p/M_k, A_k) \quad (84)$$

where $f(p/M_k, A_k)$ is a homogeneous of degree zero function in p/M_k.

To estimate the unknown parameters of a system of individual demand functions given by equations (79) or (82), it is necessary to specify the algebraic form of the demand functions. There are at least three possible approaches. First, we can specify a class of indirect utility functions $V_k(p, M_k, A_k)$ and select from it a member which satisfies equation (81) or equation (84). Second, we can specify a class of homogeneous functions and select from it the functions $H^*(p)$ and $H_\ell^{**}(p)$ ($\ell = 1, 2$). Third, we can specify a class of systems of demand functions directly and select from it a system which has the form of equation (79) or equation (82). We discuss each of these approaches in turn. To simplify the notation we set the vector of individual attributes equal to zero. Our conclusions hold for arbitrary individual attributes.

A. Polynomial Specification of the Indirect Utility Function

First, we consider the specification of the indirect utility function of $V_k(p, M_k)$, subject to the conditions given by equation (81) or equation (84). It is desirable to restrict the choice of $V_k(p, M_k)$ to a parametric class of functions that can provide an adequate approximation to arbitrary functions satisfying these equations. We confine our choices of $V_k(p, M_k)$ to the class of second-order generalized polynomials, that is:

$$V_k(p,1) = \alpha_0 + \sum_{i=1}^{N} \alpha_i t_i (\ln p_i) + \tfrac{1}{2} \sum_{i=1}^{N} \sum_{i=1}^{N} \beta_{ij} t_i (\ln p_i) t_j (\ln p_j) \qquad (85)$$

where the functions t_n ($n = 1, 2, \ldots, N$) are monotonic and the parameters (α_i, β_{ij}) are arbitrary constants, possibly depending on the vector of individual attributes A_k. We assume further that the functions t_n ($n = 1, 2, \ldots, N$) are at least three times continuously differentiable.

From equation (85)

$$\sum_{n=1}^{N} \frac{\partial V_k}{\partial \ln p_n} = \sum_{n=1}^{N} (\alpha_n + \sum_{j=1}^{N} \beta_{nj} t_j (\ln p_j)) t_n'(\ln p_n)$$

Differentiating $\sum_{n=1}^{N} \partial V_k / \partial \ln p_n$ with respect to $\ln p_m$, we obtain

$$\left[\alpha_m + \sum_{j=1}^{N} \beta_{mj} t_j (\ln p_j) \right] t_m''(\ln p_m) + \sum_{n=1}^{N} \beta_{mn} t_m'(\ln p_m) t_n'(\ln p_n) \qquad (86)$$

Summing equation (86) over m ($m = 1, 2, \ldots, N$), we obtain

$$\sum_{m=1}^{N} \left[\alpha_m + \sum_{j=1}^{N} \beta_{mj} t_j (\ln p_j) \right] t_m''(\ln p_m) + \sum_{m=1}^{N} \sum_{n=1}^{N} \beta_{mn} t_m'(\ln p_m) t_n'(\ln p_n)$$

If $\sum_{n=1}^{N} \partial V_k / \partial \ln p_n$ is homogeneous of degree $(\sigma - 1)$, $\sigma \neq 1$, then the above expression must be equal to

$$(\sigma - 1) \sum_{n=1}^{N} \left[\alpha_n + \sum_{j=1}^{N} \beta_{nj} t_j (\ln p_j) \right] t_n'(\ln p_n)$$

or

$$\sum_{n=1}^{N} \left[\alpha_n + \sum_{j=1}^{N} \beta_{nj} t_j (\ln p_j) \right] [t_n''(\ln p_n) - (\sigma - 1) t_n'(\ln p_n)]$$

$$+ \sum_{m=1}^{N} \sum_{n=1}^{N} \beta_{mn} t_m'(\ln p_m) t_n'(\ln p_n) = 0 \qquad (87)$$

Differentiating equation (87) with respect to $\ln p_k$, we obtain

$$\left[\alpha_k + \sum_{j=1}^{N} \beta_{kj}t_j(\ln p_j)\right][t_k'''(\ln p_k) - (\sigma - 1)t_k''(\ln p_k)]$$

$$+ \sum_{n=1}^{N} \beta_{nk}t'_k(\ln p_k)[t_n''(\ln p_n) - (\sigma - 1)t_n'(\ln p_n)] \qquad (88)$$

$$+ 2\sum_{n=1}^{N} \beta_{kn}t_n'(\ln p_n)\, t_k''(\ln p_k) = 0$$

Differentiating equation (88) with respect to $\ln p_\ell$, $\ell \neq k$, we obtain

$$\beta_{k\ell}t_\ell'(\ln p_\ell)[t_k'''(\ln p_k) - (\sigma - 1)t_k''(\ln p_k)]$$

$$+ \beta_{\ell k}t_k'(\ln p_k)[t_\ell''(\ln p_\ell) - (\sigma - 1)t_\ell''(\ln p_\ell)] \qquad (89)$$

$$+ 2\beta_{k\ell}t_\ell''(\ln p_\ell)t_k''(\ln p_k) = 0$$

Either $\beta_{k\ell} = 0$, for all ℓ, $\ell \neq k$, in which case we obtain from equation (87)

$$[\alpha_k + \beta_{kk}t_k(\ln p_k)][t_k''(\ln p_k) - (\sigma - 1)t_k'(\ln p_k)] \qquad (90)$$
$$+ \beta_{kk}t_k'(\ln p_k)^2 = C_k$$

a constant, or $\beta_{k\ell} \neq 0$ for some ℓ, $\ell \neq k$, which implies

$$t_\ell'(\ln p_\ell)[t_k'''(\ln p_k) - (\sigma - 1)t_k''(\ln p_k)]$$

$$+ t_k'(\ln p_k)[t_\ell'''(\ln p_\ell) - (\sigma - 1)t_\ell''(\ln p_\ell)] \qquad (91)$$

$$+ 2t_\ell''(\ln p_\ell)t_k''(\ln p_k) = 0$$

If $\beta_{k\ell} = 0$, for all ℓ, $\ell \neq k$, and $\beta_{kk} \neq 0$, then by the transformation

$$t_k^*(\ln p_k) \equiv \alpha_k + \beta_{kk}t_k(\ln p_k)$$

so that

$$t_k^{*\prime}(\ln p_k) = \beta_{kk}t_k'(\ln p_k)$$

$$t_k^{*\prime\prime}(\ln p_k) = \beta_{kk}t_k''(\ln p_k)$$

equation (90) may be rewritten as

$$t_k^*(\ln p_k)t_k^{*\prime\prime}(\ln p_k) + t_k^{*\prime}(\ln p_k)^2 - (\sigma - 1)t_k^*(\ln p_k)t_k^{*\prime}(\ln p_k) = C_k \qquad (92)$$

or:

$$\frac{d}{d \ln p_k}[t_k^*(\ln p_k)t_k^{*\prime}(\ln p_k)] - (\sigma - 1)t_k^*(\ln p_k)t_k^{*\prime}(\ln p_k) = C_k$$

This implies

$$t_k^*(\ln p_k) t_k^{*\prime}(\ln p_k) = C_{k1} e[(\sigma - 1) \ln p_k] + C_{k2}$$

where C_{k1} and C_{k2} are constants, or

$$\frac{d}{d \ln p_k} \tfrac{1}{2} t_k^*(\ln p_k)^2 = C_{k1} e[(\sigma - 1) \ln p_k] + C_{k2}$$

Hence

$$t_k^*(\ln p_k) = \{C_{k1}^* e[(\sigma - 1) \ln p_k] + C_{k2}^* \ln p_k + C_{k3}^*\}^{\frac{1}{2}}$$

where C_{k1}^*, C_{k2}^*, and C_{k3}^* are constants.

We conclude that

$$t_k(\ln p_k) = \frac{\{C_{k1}^* e[(\sigma - 1) \ln p_k] + C_{k2}^* \ln p_k + C_{k3}^*\}^{\frac{1}{2}} - \alpha_k}{\beta_{kk}}$$

which implies that

$$\frac{\partial V_k}{\partial \ln p_k} = [\alpha_k + \beta_{kk} t_k(\ln p_k)] t_k'(\ln p_k)$$

$$= \{C_{k1}^* e[(\sigma - 1) \ln p_k] + C_{k2}^* \ln p_k + C_{k3}^*\}^{\frac{1}{2}}$$

$$\frac{1}{2\beta_{kk}} \{C_{k1}^* e[(\sigma - 1) \ln p_k] + C_{k2}^* \ln p_k + C_{k3}^*\}^{-\frac{1}{2}} \cdot$$

$$\{(\sigma - 1) C_{k1}^* e[(\sigma - 1) \ln p_k] + C_{k2}^*\}$$

$$= \frac{1}{2\beta_{kk}} \{(\sigma - 1) C_{k1}^* e[(\sigma - 1) \ln p_k] + C_{k2}^*\}$$

Hence, $\Sigma_{n=1}^N \partial V_k / \partial \ln p_n$ is homogeneous of degree $(\sigma - 1)$ if and only if $\Sigma_{n=1}^N C_{n2}^* / \beta_{nn} = 0$. Thus

$$V_k(p, 1) = \alpha_0 + \sum_{i=1}^N \alpha_i \frac{(\{C_{ii}^* e[(\sigma - 1) \ln p_i] + C_{i2}^* \ln p_i + C_{i3}^*\}^{\frac{1}{2}} - \alpha_i)}{\beta_{ii}}$$

$$+ \tfrac{1}{2} \sum_{i=1}^N \beta_{ii} \frac{(\{C_{ii}^* e[(\sigma - 1) \ln p_i] + C_{i2}^* \ln p_i + C_{i3}^*\}^{\frac{1}{2}} - \alpha_i)^2}{\beta_{ii}^2}$$

$$= \alpha_0^* + \tfrac{1}{2} \sum_{i=1}^N \frac{1}{\beta_{ii}} \{C_{ii}^* e[(\sigma - 1) \ln p_i] + C_{i2}^* \ln p_i\}$$

$$= \alpha_0^* + \sum_{i=1}^N \alpha_i^* (p_i^{(\sigma - 1)} + \beta_i^* \ln p_i)$$

where $\sum_{i=1}^{N} \alpha_i^* \beta_i^* = 0$. If $\beta_{kk} = 0$, then by equation (90)

$$t_k'(\ln p_k) = C_{k1} e[(\sigma - 1) \ln p_k]$$

and

$$t_k(\ln p_k) = C_{k1}^* e[(\sigma - 1) \ln p_k] + C_{k2}^*$$

a case that we shall consider later.

Equation (91) may be rewritten as

$$t_k'''(\ln p_k) + \left[\frac{2 t_\ell''(\ln p_\ell)}{t_\ell'(\ln p_\ell)} - (\sigma - 1) \right] t_k''(\ln p_k)$$

$$+ \left[\frac{t_\ell'''(\ln p_\ell)}{t_\ell'(\ln p_\ell)} - (\sigma - 1) \frac{t_\ell''(\ln p_\ell)}{t_\ell'(\ln p_\ell)} \right] t_k'(\ln p_k) = 0$$

this may be regarded as a second-order ordinary differential equation in the function $t_k'(\ln p_k)$. In order that the solution of this differential equation is independent of $\ln p_\ell$, it is necessary that the coefficients be constants. Thus

$$\frac{2 t_\ell''(\ln p_\ell)}{t_\ell'(\ln p_\ell)} - (\sigma - 1) = k_1$$

and

$$t_\ell'''(\ln p_\ell) - (\sigma - 1) t_\ell''(\ln p_\ell) = k_2$$

which, to be consistent, require

$$\frac{(\sigma - 1) + k_1}{2} = (\sigma - 1)$$

and

$$k_2 = 0$$

Hence, the constant

$$k_1 = (\sigma - 1)$$

and

$$t_\ell'(\ln p_\ell) = C_{\ell 1} e[(\sigma - 1) \ln p_\ell]$$

$$t_\ell(\ln p_\ell) = C_{\ell 1}^* e[(\sigma - 1) \ln p_\ell] + C_{\ell 2}^*$$

the same as in the case $\beta_{k\ell} = 0$, for all k, ℓ. By symmetry, $t_k(\ln p_k)$ must have the same form.

Substituting the results given above into equation (85), we obtain:

$$V_k(p,1) = \alpha_0^* + \sum_{i=1}^{N} \alpha_i^* e[(\sigma - 1) \ln p_i]$$

$$+ \frac{1}{2} \sum_{i=1}^{N} \sum_{j=1}^{N} \beta_{ij}^* \exp[(\sigma - 1)(\ln p_i + \ln p_j)]$$

By differentiating this expression with respect to $\ln p_n$ and summing over n, we obtain

$$\sum_{n=1}^{N} \frac{\partial V_k}{\partial \ln p_n} = (\sigma - 1)\left\{ \sum_{n=1}^{N} \alpha_n^* e[(\sigma - 1) \ln p_n] \right.$$

$$\left. + \sum_{n=1}^{N} \sum_{j=1}^{N} \beta_{nj}^* \exp[(\sigma - 1)(\ln p_n + \ln p_j)] \right\}$$

Differentiating this expression with respect to $\ln p_m$ we obtain

$$\sum_{n=1}^{N} \frac{\partial^2 V_k}{\partial \ln p_m \, \partial \ln p_n} = (\sigma - 1)^2 \left[\alpha_m^* e[(\sigma - 1) \ln p_m] \right.$$

$$\left. + 2 \sum_{n=1}^{N} \beta_{nm}^* e[(\sigma - 1)(\ln p_n + \ln p_m)] \right]$$

Summing over m, we obtain

$$\sum_{m=1}^{N} \sum_{n=1}^{N} \frac{\partial^2 V_k}{\partial \ln p_m \, \partial \ln p_n}$$

$$= (\sigma - 1)^2 \left\{ \sum_{n=1}^{N} \alpha_n^* \exp[(\sigma - 1) \ln p_n] \right.$$

$$\left. + 2 \sum_{n=1}^{N} \sum_{m=1}^{N} \beta_{nm}^* \exp[(\sigma - 1)(\ln p_n + \ln p_m)] \right\}$$

We see that homogeneity of degree $(\sigma - 1)$ of $\Sigma_{n=1}^{N} \partial V_k / \partial \ln p_n$, which implies

$$\sum_{m=1}^{N} \frac{\partial}{\partial \ln p_m} \left(\sum_{n=1}^{N} \frac{\partial V_k}{\partial \ln p_n} \right) = (\sigma - 1) \left(\sum_{n=1}^{N} \frac{\partial V_k}{\partial \ln p_n} \right)$$

requires that

$$\beta_{nm}^* = 0$$

for all n, m, so that

$$V_k(p,1) = \alpha_0^* + \sum_{i=1}^{N} \alpha_i^* \exp[(\sigma - 1) \ln p_i]$$

We conclude that the only second-order generalized polynomial form that satisfies equation (81) is the following:

$$V_k(p,1) = \alpha_0 + \sum_{i=1}^{N} \alpha_i(p_i^{\sigma-1} + \beta_i \ln p_i) \tag{93}$$

where $\sum_{i=1}^{N} \alpha_i\beta_i = 0$

If $\sum_{n=1}^{N} \partial V_k/\partial \ln p_n$ is homogeneous of degree zero, then the counterpart to equation (89) becomes

$$\beta_{k\ell}t'_\ell(\ln p_\ell)t'''_k(\ln p_k) + 2\beta_{k\ell}t''_\ell(\ln p_\ell)t''_k(\ln p_k)$$

$$+ \beta_{\ell k}t'''_\ell(\ln p_\ell)t'_k(\ln p_k) = 0$$

Either $\beta_{k\ell} = 0$, for all ℓ, $\ell \neq k$, in which case we obtain from equation (87)

$$[\alpha_k + \beta_{kk}t_k(\ln p_k)]t''_k(\ln p_k) + \beta_{kk}t'_k(\ln p_k)^2 = C_k \tag{94}$$

a constant, or $\beta_{k\ell} \neq 0$ for some ℓ, $\ell \neq k$, which implies

$$t'''_k(\ln p_k) + \frac{2t''_\ell(\ln p_\ell)}{t'_\ell(\ln p_\ell)} t''_k(\ln p_k) + \frac{t'''_\ell(\ln p_\ell)}{t'_\ell(\ln p_\ell)} t'_k(\ln p_k) = 0 \tag{95}$$

Equation (94) may be rewritten, using the same transformation as before

$$t^*_k(\ln p_k)t^{*''}_k(\ln p_k) + [t^{*'}_k(\ln p_k)]^2 = C_k$$

or

$$\frac{d}{d \ln p_k} [t^*_k(\ln p_k)t^{*'}_k(\ln p_k)] = C_k$$

or

$$\frac{d^2}{d^2 \ln p_k} \tfrac{1}{2}[t^*_k(\ln p_k)]^2 = C_k$$

so that

$$\frac{d}{d \ln p_k} \tfrac{1}{2}[t^*_k(\ln p_k)]^2 = C_{k1} \ln p_k + C_{k2}$$

and:

$$\tfrac{1}{2}[t^*_k(\ln p_k)]^2 = C_{k1}\frac{(\ln p_k)^2}{2} + C_{k2} \ln p_k + C_{k3}$$

Thus

$$t^*_k(\ln p_k) = [C^*_{k1}(\ln p_k)^2 + C^*_{k2} \ln p_k + C^*_{k3}]^{\frac{1}{2}}$$

where C^*_{k1}, C^*_{k2} and C^*_{k3} are constants.

We conclude that:

$$t_k(\ln p_k) = \frac{[C_{k1}^*(\ln p_k)^2 + C_{k2}^* \ln p_k + C_{k3}^*]^{\frac{1}{2}} - \alpha_k}{\beta_{kk}}$$

and

$$V_k(p,1) = \alpha_0^* + \tfrac{1}{2} \sum_{i=1}^{N} \frac{1}{\beta_{ii}} [C_{i1}^*(\ln p_i)^2 + C_{i2}^* \ln p_i]$$

$$= \alpha_0^* + \sum_{i=1}^{N} \alpha_i^* \ln p_i + \tfrac{1}{2} \sum_{i=1}^{N} \beta_{ii}^*(\ln p_i)^2$$

where $\Sigma_i \beta_{ii}^* = 0$.

Now suppose $\beta_{k\ell} \neq 0$. Equation (95) may be regarded as a second-order ordinary differential equation in the function $t_k'(\ln p_k)$. In order that the solution of this differential equation is independent of $\ln p_\ell$, it is necessary that the coefficients are constants. Thus

$$\frac{2t_\ell''(\ln p_\ell)}{t_\ell'(\ln p_\ell)} = k_1$$

$$\frac{t_\ell'''(\ln p_\ell)}{t_k'(\ln p_\ell)} = k_2$$

Thus, for $k_1 \neq 0$

$$t_\ell'(\ln p_\ell) = C_1 \exp[(k_1/2) \ln p_\ell]$$

$$t_\ell''(\ln p_\ell) = \frac{k_1 C_1}{2} \exp[(k_1/2) \ln p_\ell]$$

$$t_\ell'''(\ln p_\ell) = \frac{k_1^2}{4} C_1 \exp[(k_1/2) \ln p_\ell]$$

or

$$k_2 = \frac{k_1^2}{4}$$

This implies that

$$t_\ell(\ln p_\ell) = C_{1\ell} \exp[(k_1/2) \ln p_\ell] + C_{2\ell} \tag{96}$$

For $k_1 = 0$

$$t_\ell(\ln p_\ell) = C_{1\ell} \ln p_\ell + C_{2\ell} \tag{97}$$

For equation (96), $\Sigma_{n=1}^{N} \partial V_k / \partial \ln p_k$ being homogeneous of degree zero implies that $V_k(p,1)$ must be a homogeneous of degree zero polynomial but this implies that $V_k(p,1)$ is a constant. For equation (97)

$$V_k(p,1) = \alpha_0 + \sum_{i=1}^{N} \alpha_i^* \ln p_i + \tfrac{1}{2} \sum_{i=1}^{N} \sum_{j=1}^{N} \beta_{ij}^* \ln p_i \ln p_j$$

which satisfies equation (84) if and only if $\Sigma_{i=1}^{N} \Sigma_{j=1}^{N} \beta_{ij}^* = 0$.
We have therefore proved

Theorem 6. The only nonhomothetic second-order generalized polynomial functional form that satisfies the exact aggregation condition for
an indirect utility function in equation (81) is

$$V_k(p,1) = \alpha_0 + \sum_{i=1}^{N} \alpha_i(p_i^{\sigma} + \beta_i \ln p_i)$$

where $\Sigma_{i=1}^{N} \alpha_i\beta_i = 0$

Theorem 7. The only nonhomothetic second-order generalized polynomial functional form which satisfies the exact aggregation condition
for an indirect utility function in equation (84) is

$$V_k(p,1) = \alpha_0 + \sum_{i=1}^{N} \alpha_i \ln p_i + \tfrac{1}{2} \sum_{i=1}^{N} \sum_{j=1}^{N} \beta_{ij} \ln p_i \ln p_j$$

where $\Sigma_{i=1}^{N} \Sigma_{j=1}^{N} \beta_{ij} = 0$.
Thus, if we restrict our choice of functional forms for the indirect
utility functions satisfying equation (81) or (84) to second-order generalized polynomial functions that are not themselves homothetic, the only
admissible functional forms are the sum of a constant-elasticity of substitution function and a linear logarithmic function and the transcendental
logarithmic function.

B.   Polynomial Specification of the Functions $H^*(p)$ and $H_\ell^{**}(p)$.

Second, we consider the specification of the functions $H^*(p)$ and
$H_\ell^{**}(p)$ in equations (80) and (83). The individual demand functions can
then be derived by applying Roy's Identity to equations (80) or (83); the
aggregate demand function can be obtained by summing over the individual demand functions. The functions $H^*(p)$ and $H_\ell^{**}(p)$ must satisfy
homogeneity restrictions; it is desirable to choose forms for these functions that can provide an adequate approximation to an arbitrary function.
As before, we restrict consideration to second-order generalized
polynomials

$$H^*(p) = T[\alpha_0 + \sum_{i=1}^{N} \alpha_i t_i(p_i) + \tfrac{1}{2} \sum_{i=1}^{N} \sum_{j=1}^{N} \beta_{ij} t_i(p_i) \, t_j(p_j)] \qquad (98)$$

where the functions T and t_n, ($n = 1, 2, \ldots, N$), are three times continuously differentiable monotonic functions and the parameters $\{\alpha_i, \beta_{ij}\}$ are arbitrary constants.

We state first the following lemma due to Jorgenson and Lau (1979):

Lemma 1 All homogeneous functions with the generalized polynomial form in equation (98) can be written as

$$H^*(p) = T\{P[t_1(p_1), \ldots, t_N(p_N)]\}$$

with either

(1) $\qquad T(Z) = Z^{\sigma_1}; \; t_n(p_n) = p_n^{\sigma_2} \qquad (n = 1, 2, \ldots, N)$

where $P\;(\cdot)$ is a generalized bilinear form with each term consisting of a constant coefficient times the product of two functions $t_n(p_n)$; alternatively

(2) $\qquad T(Z) = e^Z; \; t_n(p_n) = \ln p_n \qquad (n = 1, 2, \ldots, N)$

and P is a second-order polynomial in $t_n(p_n)$ whose coefficients satisfy

$$\sum_{j=1}^{N} \beta_{ij} = 0$$

for all i. In the special case of homogeneity of degree zero, $\Sigma_{i=1}^{N} \alpha_i = 0$, but $T(Z)$ can be arbitrary. We shall not prove this lemma here.

It is obvious that the form (1) cannot be homogeneous of degree zero without being constant, so that the functions $H_\ell^{**}(p)$ have the form

$$\ln H_\ell^{**}(p) = \alpha_0 + \sum_{i=1}^{N} \alpha_i \ln p_i + \tfrac{1}{2} \sum_{i=1}^{N} \sum_{j=1}^{N} \beta_{ij} \ln p_i \ln p_j \qquad (99)$$

where in addition to the restrictions given above the parameter must satisfy $\Sigma_{i=1}^{N} \alpha_i = 0$. This is precisely the form of the transcendental logarithmic indirect utility function.

We now present the forms of $f_{nk}(p, M_k)$ based on alternative specifications of the functions $H^*(p)$ and $H_\ell^{**}(p)$ ($\ell = 1, 2$). By Lemma 1, if we restrict our choices of these functions to second-order generalized polynomial forms, $H^*(p)$ can take only one of the two forms

$$H^*(p) = \begin{cases} \left(\tfrac{1}{2} \sum_{i=1}^{N} \sum_{j=1}^{N} \beta_{ij} \, p_i^{r/2} p_j^{r/2} \right)^{1/r} \\[2em] \exp\left(\alpha_0 + \sum_{i=1}^{N} \alpha_i \ln p_i + \tfrac{1}{2} \sum_{i=1}^{N} \sum_{j=1}^{N} \beta_{ij} \ln p_i \ln p_j \right) \end{cases}$$

where

$$\sum_{i=1}^{N} \alpha_i = 1$$

and

$$\sum_{j=1}^{N} \beta_{ij} = 0$$

for all i; we refer to the first of the generalized polynomial forms as the power form and the second as the logarithmic form.

The functions $H_\ell^{**}(p)$ are homogeneous of degree zero and can take only the logarithmic form:

$$\ln H_\ell^{**}(p) = \alpha_0^\ell + \sum_{i=1}^{N} \alpha_i^\ell \ln p_i + \frac{1}{2} \sum_{i=1}^{N} \sum_{j=1}^{N} \beta_{ij}^\ell \ln p_i \ln p_j$$

where

$$\sum_{i=1}^{N} \alpha_i^\ell = 0$$

and

$$\sum_{j=1}^{N} \beta_{ij}^\ell = 0$$

for all i.

Starting with equation (79), the form of $f_{nk}(p, M_k)$, corresponding to the power form of the generalized polynomial $H^*(p)$ is

$$f_{nk}(p, M_k) = \frac{1}{2} \frac{\sum\limits_{j=1}^{N} \beta_{nj} p_j^{r/2} p_n^{r/2-1}}{\frac{1}{2} \sum\limits_{i=1}^{N} \sum\limits_{j=1}^{N} \beta_{ij} p_i^{r/2} p_j^{r/2}} M_k$$

$$+ \left(\frac{1}{2} \sum_{i=1}^{N} \sum_{j=1}^{N} \beta_{ij} p_i^{r/2} p_j^{r/2} \right)^{-(\sigma-1)/r} \cdot \left(\alpha_n^\ell + \sum_{j=1}^{N} \beta_{nj}^\ell \ln p_j \right) \frac{M_k^\sigma}{p_n} \tag{100}$$

or

$$\frac{p_n f_{nk}(p, M_k)}{M_k} = \frac{\frac{1}{2} \sum\limits_{j=1}^{N} \beta_{nj} p_j^{r/2} p_n^{r/2}}{\frac{1}{2} \sum\limits_{i=1}^{N} \sum\limits_{j=1}^{N} \beta_{ij} p_i^{r/2} p_j^{r/2}}$$

$$+ \left(\frac{1}{2} \sum_{i=1}^{N} \sum_{j=1}^{N} \beta_{ij} p_i^{r/2} p_j^{r/2} \right)^{-(\sigma-1)/r} \left(\alpha_n^\ell + \sum_{j=1}^{N} \beta_{nj}^\ell \ln p_j \right) M_k^{\sigma-1}$$

Even if r and σ were known *a priori*, this equation would be highly nonlinear. A further simplification is possible if it is assumed that $\sigma - 1 = r$. In that case

$$\frac{p_n f_{nk}(p,M_k)}{M_k} = \frac{\frac{1}{2}\sum_{j=1}^{N} \beta_{nj} p_j^{r/2} p_n^{r/2} + \left(\alpha_n^\ell + \sum_{j=1}^{N} \beta_{nj}^\ell \ln p_j\right) M_k^r}{\frac{1}{2}\sum_{i=1}^{N}\sum_{j=1}^{N} \beta_{ij} p_i^{r/2} p_j^{r/2}}$$

For given r, this equation is the ratio of two forms which are linear in parameters and can be readily estimated. However, in general, σ and r will be unknown; if $(\sigma - 1) \neq r$, estimation will be very difficult.

If we let $H^*(p)$ be a first-order homogeneous generalized polynomial, then equation (99) becomes

$$f_{nk}(p,M_k) = \frac{\alpha_n p_n^{r-1} M_k}{\sum_{i=1}^{N} \alpha_i p_i^r} + \left(\sum_{i=1}^{N} \alpha_i p_i^r\right)^{-(\sigma-1)/r} \left(\alpha_n^\ell + \sum_{j=1}^{N} \beta_{nj}^\ell \ln p_j\right) \frac{M_k^\sigma}{p_n} \quad (101)$$

which under the assumption of $\sigma - 1 = r$ simplifies to

$$\frac{p_n f_{nk}(p,M_k)}{M_k} = \frac{\alpha_n p_n^r + \left(\alpha_n^\ell + \sum_{j=1}^{N} \beta_{nj}^\ell \ln p_j\right) M_k^r}{\sum_{i=1}^{N} \alpha_i p_i^r}$$

For given r, this equation is the ratio of two forms that are linear in parameters and can easily be estimated. In general, this will not be the case and estimation will be difficult.

Again starting from Equation (79), the form of $f_{nk}(p,M_k)$ corresponding to the logarithmic form of the generalized polynomial $H^*(p)$ is

$$f_{nk}(p,M_k) = \left(\alpha_n + \sum_{j=1}^{N} \beta_{nj} \ln p_j\right) \frac{M_k}{p_n}$$

$$+ \left[\exp\left(\alpha_0 + \sum_{i=1}^{N} \alpha_i \ln p_i \right.\right. \quad (102)$$

$$\left.\left. + \frac{1}{2}\sum_{i=1}^{N}\sum_{j=1}^{N} \beta_{ij} \ln p_i \ln p_j\right)\right]^{-(\sigma-1)}$$

$$\cdot \left(\alpha_n^\ell + \sum_{j=1}^{N} \beta_{nj}^\ell \ln p_j\right) \frac{M_k^\sigma}{p_n}$$

or

$$\frac{p_n f_{nk}(p,M_k)}{M_k} = \left(\alpha_n + \sum_{j=1}^{N} \beta_{nj} \ln p_j\right)$$

$$+ \exp\left[-(\sigma - 1)\left(\alpha_0 + \sum_{i=1}^{N} \ln p_i + \tfrac{1}{2}\sum_{i=1}^{N}\sum_{j=1}^{N} \beta_{ij} \ln p_i \ln p_j\right)\right]$$

$$\cdot \left(\alpha_n^\ell + \sum_{j=1}^{N} \beta_{nj}^\ell \ln p_j\right) M_k^{\sigma-1}$$

Even if σ were known *a priori*, this equation would be highly nonlinear and is likely to be intractable from the point of view of estimation.

If we let $H^*(p)$ be a first-order homogeneous generalized polynomial, then equation (101) becomes

$$f_{nk}(p,M_k) = \alpha_n \frac{M_k}{p_n} + \left(\prod_{i=1}^{N} p_i^{\alpha_i}\right)^{-(\sigma-1)}\left(\alpha_n^\ell + \sum_{j=1}^{N} \beta_{nj}^\ell \ln p_j\right)\frac{M_k^\sigma}{p_n} \quad (103)$$

which may be rewritten as

$$\frac{p_n f_{nk}(p,M_k)}{M_k} = \alpha_n + \left(\prod_{i=1}^{N} p_i^{\alpha_i}\right)^{-(\sigma-1)}\left(\alpha_n^\ell + \sum_{j=1}^{N} \beta_{nj}^\ell \ln p_j\right) M_k^{\sigma-1}$$

This equation is slightly more tractable than equation (101) although estimation of the parameters $\{\alpha_i\}$ is likely to be difficult.

Starting with equation (82), the form of $f_{nk}(p,M_k)$, corresponding to the power form of the generalized polynomial $H^*(p)$ is

$$f_{nk}(p,M_k) = \left\{\frac{1}{r}\left(\alpha_n^\ell + \sum_{j=1}^{N} \beta_{nj}^\ell \ln p_j\right)\left(\ln\left[\tfrac{1}{2}\sum_{i=1}^{N}\sum_{j=1}^{N} \beta_{ij} p_i^{r/2} p_j^{r/2}\right]\right)\right.$$

$$\left.+ \frac{\left(\sum_{j=1}^{N} \beta_{nj} p_j^{r/2}\right)\beta_{nn} p_n^{r/2}}{\sum_{i=1}^{N}\sum_{j=1}^{N} p_i^{r/2} p_j^{r/2}}\right\}\frac{M_k}{p_n} \quad (104)$$

$$- \left(\alpha_n^\ell + \sum_{j=1}^{N} \beta_{nj}^\ell \ln p_j\right)\frac{M_k \ln M_k}{p_n}$$

If we let $H^*(p)$ be a first-order homogeneous generalized polynomial, then equation (104) becomes

$$
f_{nk}(p,M_k) = \left\{ \frac{1}{r}\left(\alpha_n^\ell + \sum_{j=1}^{N} \beta_{nj}^\ell \ln p_j\right)\left[\ln \sum_{i=1}^{N} \alpha_i p_i^r\right] + \frac{\alpha_n p_n^r}{\sum\limits_{i=1}^{N} \alpha_i p_i^r}\right\}\frac{M_k}{p_n}
$$

$$
- \left(\alpha_n^\ell + \sum_{j=1}^{N} \beta_{nj}^\ell \ln p_j\right)\frac{M_k \ln M_k}{p_n}
$$

(105)

Even if r were known, estimation of equations (104) and (105) is likely to be difficult because the term $\sum_{i=1}^{N} \alpha_i p_i^r$ occurs as both a logarithm and a reciprocal.

The form of $f_{nk}(p,M_k)$ corresponding to the logarithmic form of the generalized polynomial $H^*(p)$ is

$$
f_{nk}(p,M_k) = \left[\left(\alpha_n^\ell + \sum_{j=1}^{N} \beta_{nj}^\ell \ln p_j\right)\left(\alpha_0 + \sum_{i=1}^{N} \alpha_i \ln p_i\right.\right.
$$

$$
+ \sum_{i=1}^{N}\sum_{j=1}^{N} \beta_{ij} \ln p_i \ln p_j\right) + \left(\alpha_n + \sum_{j=1}^{N} \beta_{nj} \ln p_j\right)\left.\right]\frac{M_k}{p_n}
$$

$$
- \left(\alpha_n^\ell + \sum_{j=1}^{N} \beta_{nj}^\ell \ln p_j\right)\frac{M_k \ln M_k}{p_n}
$$

(106)

$$
= \left(\alpha_n^\ell + \sum_{j=1}^{N} \beta_{nj}^\ell \ln p_j\right)\left[\alpha_0 + \sum_{i=1}^{N} \alpha_i \ln p_i\right.
$$

$$
+ \tfrac{1}{2}\sum_{i=1}^{N}\sum_{j=1}^{N} \beta_{ij} \ln p_i \ln p_j - \ln M_k\left.\right]\frac{M_k}{p_n}
$$

$$
+ \left(\alpha_n + \sum_{j=1}^{N} \beta_{nj} \ln p_j\right)\frac{M_k}{p_n}
$$

which can be written as

$$
\frac{p_n f_{nk}(p,M_k)}{M_k} = (\alpha_n^\ell + \alpha_n) + \sum_{j=1}^{N} (\beta_{nj}^\ell + \beta_{nj}) \ln p_j
$$

$$
+ \left(\alpha_n^\ell + \sum_{j=1}^{N} \beta_{nj}^\ell \ln p_j\right)\left(\sum_{i=1}^{N} \alpha_i \ln p_i\right.
$$

$$
+ \tfrac{1}{2}\sum_{i=1}^{N}\sum_{j=1}^{N} \beta_{ij} \ln p_i \ln p_j - \ln M_k\left.\right)
$$

where

$$\alpha_0 = 1, \sum_{i=1}^{N} \alpha_i = 1, \sum_{i=1}^{N} \alpha_i^\ell = 0, \sum_{j=1}^{N} \beta_{ij} = 0, \sum_{j=1}^{N} \beta_{ij}^\ell = 0$$

for all i. If we let $\beta_{nj}^\ell = 0$, for all n,j, then this system of individual demand reduces to the AIDS system of Deaton and Muellbauer (1980a, 1980b).

If we let $H^*(p)$ be a first-order homogeneous generalized polynomial, then equation (106) becomes

$$f_{nk}(p,M_k) = \left(\alpha_n^\ell + \sum_{j=1}^{N} \beta_{nj}^\ell \ln p_j \right)$$

$$\left(\alpha_0 + \sum_{i=1}^{N} \alpha_i \ln p_i - \ln M_k \right) \frac{M_k}{p_n} \qquad (107)$$

$$+ \alpha_n \frac{M_k}{p_n}$$

which can be written as

$$\frac{p_n f_{nk}(p,M_k)}{M_k} = \alpha_n + \left(\alpha_n^\ell + \sum_{j=1}^{N} \beta_{nj}^\ell \ln p_j \right)$$

$$\left(1 + \sum_{i=1}^{N} \alpha_i \ln p_i - \ln M_k \right)$$

To recapitulate, we note that equation (100) is intractable as far as estimation is concerned. For each equation the number of parameters is on the order of $N(N + 1)/2 + N$. The total number of parameters in the system is of the order of $N(N + 1)$. Equation (101) is somewhat more tractable although there are still some unavoidable nonlinearities involving the unknown parameters r and σ. The number of parameters in the system is on the order of $N(N + 1)/2 + N$. Equation (102) is just as intractable as equation (100). Equation (103) is much simpler, although there are still some unavoidable nonlinearities.

Equation (104) is quite intractable with equation (105) somewhat better. Equation (106) has the remarkable property that it is linear in polynomials of the logarithms of prices p_n and expenditures M_k. Unless we impose cross equation constraints, there will be a large number of unknown parameters in each equation, on the order of $N(N + 1)/2 + N$. In addition, there are nonlinear constraints among the parameters within the same equation. These nonlinear constraints remain even under the specialization to the AIDS system. Equation (107) is a simplified version of equation (106) and has each expenditure share equal to a transcendental logarithmic function of special structure.

We next consider the choices of the functions $H^*(p)$ and $H_\ell^{**}(p)$ that give rise to an indirect utility function $V_k(p,M_k)$ of the transcendental logarithmic form. Let

$$\ln H^*(p) = \frac{\alpha_0 + \sum_{i=1}^{N} \alpha_i \ln p_i + \frac{1}{2} \sum_{i=1}^{N} \sum_{j=1}^{N} \beta_{ij} \ln p_i \ln p_j}{\sum_{i=1}^{N} \alpha_i + \sum_{j=1}^{N} \sum_{i=1}^{N} \beta_{ij} \ln p_j}$$

It can be verified directly that

$$\ln H^*(\lambda p) = \ln H^*(p) + \ln \lambda$$

that is, $H^*(p)$ is homogeneous of degree one. Let

$$H_1^{**}(p) \equiv \sum_{i=1}^{N} \alpha_i + \sum_{j=1}^{N} \sum_{i=1}^{N} \beta_{ij} \ln p_j$$

with $\sum_{i=1}^{N} \sum_{j=1}^{N} \beta_{ij} = 0$. It can be verified directly that $H_1^{**}(p)$ is homogeneous of degree zero. The product $H_1^{**}(p) \ln H^*(p)$ has precisely the transcendental logarithmic form.

C. Rational Specification of Individual Demand Functions

Third, we consider the specifications of $f_{nk}(p,M_k)$ in equations (79) and (82) directly. We shall restrict our choices of the expenditure share functions to the ratio of two first-order generalized polynomials in ratios of prices to expenditure, that is

$$\frac{p_n f_{nk}(p,M_k)}{M_k} = \frac{\alpha_n + \sum_j \beta_{nj} g(p_j/M_k)}{-1 + \sum_j \beta_{Mj} g(p_j/M_k)} \qquad (n = 1, 2, \ldots, N) \quad (108)$$

where the function g is monotonic in a single variable. We consider this form since expenditure share functions that are linear in the unknown parameters have been shown by Jorgenson and Lau (1977) and Lau (1977a) to satisfy the conditions of summability and nonnegativity if and only if the expenditure shares are constants. The systems of equations (107) with the restrictions:

$$\sum_{n=1}^{N} \alpha_n = 1, \ \sum_{n=1}^{N} \beta_{nj} = \beta_{Mj}$$

for all j satisfies summability identically.

The implications of symmetry for a system of individual demand functions of the form in equation (108) have been analyzed by Jorgenson and Lau (1977). They imply that either:

(1)   the expenditure shares are constant

or

(2) $g(Z) = Z^{-(\sigma-1)}$

or

(3) $g(Z) = Z \ln Z$

Constant expenditure shares are not an interesting specification. For a power function (2)

$$\frac{p_n f_{nk}(p, M_k)}{M_k} = \frac{\alpha_n + \sum\limits_{j=1}^{N} \beta_{nj} p_j^{-(\sigma-1)} M_k^{\sigma-1}}{-1 + \sum\limits_{j=1}^{N} \beta_{Mj} p_j^{-(\sigma-1)} M_k^{(\sigma-1)}} \tag{109}$$

Equation (109) takes the form of equation (79) only if

$$\beta_{Mj} = 0$$

for all j. This restriction implies, under symmetry of the Slutsky substitution matrix, that[13]

$$\beta_{nj} = \alpha_n \beta_j \qquad n \neq j$$

$$\beta_{nn} = (1 + \alpha_n)\beta_n$$

for all n, j. Equation (109) then takes the form:

$$\frac{p_n f_{nk}(p, M_k)}{M_k} = -\alpha_n - \left[\alpha_n \sum\limits_{j=1}^{N} \beta_j p_j^{-(\sigma-1)} + \beta_n p_n^{-(\sigma-1)} \right] M_k^{(\sigma-1)} \tag{110}$$

This system of individual demand functions can be derived from an indirect utility function of the form

$$\ln V_k(p, M_k) = \alpha_0 + \sum\limits_{n=1}^{N} \alpha_n \ln (p_n/M_k) + \frac{1}{\sigma} \ln \left[\sum\limits_{n=1}^{N} \beta_n (p_n/M_k)^\sigma + 1 \right]$$

This system of individual demand equation has only 2N parameters and lacks the second-order interpolation property. It is obvious that equation (109) cannot take the form of equation (82).

For the logarithmic case (3), we have

$$\frac{p_n f_{nk}(p, M_k)}{M_k} = \frac{\alpha_n + \sum\limits_{j=1}^{N} \beta_{nj} \ln p_j - \sum\limits_{j=1}^{N} \beta_{nj} \ln M_k}{-1 + \sum\limits_{j=1}^{N}\sum\limits_{n=1}^{N} \beta_{nj} \ln p_j + \sum\limits_{j=1}^{N}\sum\limits_{n=1}^{N} \beta_{nj} \ln M_k}. \tag{111}$$

Equation (110) cannot take the form of equation (79). It takes the form of equation (82) only if

$$\sum_{j=1}^{N} \sum_{n=1}^{N} \beta_{nj} = 0$$

A transcendental logarithmic indirect utility function satisfying this restriction will give rise to equation (81). Other possible indirect utility functions lack the second-order interpolation property.[14]

D.   Summary and Conclusion

In this section we have analyzed systems of individual demand functions that can be generated from an indirect utility function and that satisfy the restrictions implied by the theory of exact aggregation. For three index functions of individual attributes and expenditures, where two of these functions depend on expenditures alone, only two forms can be considered for the individual demand functions. The first of these involves a power function of individual expenditures. We refer to this as the power form of the system of individual demand functions. The second involves a logarithmic function of individual expenditures; we refer to this as the logarithmic form.

We have considered three alternative approaches to specification of the dependence of the individual demand functions on prices. First, we specify a class of indirect utility functions that can be used to generate power and logarithmic forms of systems of individual demand functions. We restrict consideration to indirect utility functions that are second-order generalized polynomials. Second, we consider alternative specifications of certain homogeneous functions that occur in the representation of the indirect utility functions. Again, we restrict consideration to homogeneous functions that are first-order and second-order generalized polynomials. Third, we consider specifications of the power and logarithmic forms of a system of individual demand functions that are ratios of first-order generalized polynomials.

We find that the indirect utility function that generates the power form of the system of individual demand functions, restricting consideration to second-order generalized polynomials, can be written

$$V_k(p,1) = \alpha_0 + \sum_{i=1}^{N} \alpha_i \, (p_i^{\sigma} + \beta_i \ln p_i)$$

where $\sum_{i=1}^{N} \alpha_i \beta_i = 0$. This indirect utility function lacks the second-order interpolation property. Similarly, we find that the indirect utility function that generates the logarithmic form of the system of individual demand function can be written

$$V_k(p,1) = \alpha_0 + \sum_{i=1}^{N} \alpha_i \ln p_i + \tfrac{1}{2} \sum_{i=1}^{N} \sum_{j=1}^{N} \beta_{ij} \ln p_i \ln p_j$$

where $\sum_{i=1}^{N} \sum_{j=1}^{N} \beta_{ij} = 0$. This is the transcendental logarithmic indirect utility function and has the second-order interpolation property.

Our second approach to specifying systems of individual demand functions is to specify the homogeneous functions $H^*(p)$ and $H_\ell^{**}(p)$ that occur in the representation of the indirect utility functions that generate the power and logarithm forms of the system of individual demand functions. As before, we restrict consideration to representations of these homogeneous functions as first-order and second-order generalized polynomials. We find that the functional forms involving a power function of individual expenditures are intractable. The functional forms involving a logarithmic function of individual expenditures, including the AIDS system of Deaton and Muellbauer, are more tractable.

Finally, our third approach to specifying systems of individual demand functions is to consider power and logarithmic forms that can be represented as ratios of first-order generalized polynomials. The indirect utility function that generates the power form of the individual demand functions can be written

$$V_k(p,1) = \alpha_0 + \sum_{n=1}^{N} \alpha_n \ln p_n + \frac{1}{\sigma} \ln \left(\sum_{n=1}^{N} \beta_n p_n^{\sigma} + 1 \right)$$

This indirect utility function lacks the second-order interpolation property. The indirect utility function that generates the logarithmic form is the transcendental logarithmic indirect utility function.

Both the transcendental logarithmic demand system and equation (106) are nonlinear in the unknown parameters. In the absence of additional constraints equation (106) has many more parameters than the transcendental logarithmic system. The number of constraints that must be imposed for equation (106) is on the order of N^3, even under the restrictions required for the AIDS system, while the number of constraints that must be imposed is on the order of N^2 for the transcendental logarithmic system. We therefore use the transcendental logarithmic indirect utility function as a point of departure for our empirical application of the theory of exact aggregation.

V. TRANSLOG MODEL OF CONSUMER BEHAVIOR

In this section we present individual and aggregate models of consumer behavior based on the theory of exact aggregation. The theory of exact aggregation requires that the individual demand functions must be linear in a number of functions of individual attributes and expenditure. Representing aggregate demand functions as the sum of individual demand functions, we find that the aggregate demand functions depend on the distribution of expenditure among individuals as well as the level of per capita expenditure and prices. The aggregate demand functions also depend on the joint distribution of expenditures and demographic characteristics among individuals.

In our model of consumer behavior the individual consuming units are households. We assume that household expenditures on commodity groups are allocated so as to maximize a household welfare function. As a consequence, the household behaves in the same way as an individual maximizing a utility function.[15] We require that the individual demand functions are integrable, so that these demand functions can be generated by Roy's Identity from an indirect utility function for each consuming unit. We assume that these indirect utility functions are homogeneous of degree zero in prices and expenditure, nonincreasing in prices and nondecreasing in expenditure, and quasiconvex in prices and expenditure.

To allow for differences in preferences among consuming units, we allow the indirect utility functions for the kth unit to depend on a vector of attributes A_k; each attribute is represented by a dummy variable equal to unity when the consuming unit has the corresponding characteristic and zero otherwise. In our model of consumer behavior there are several groups of attributes. Each consuming unit is assigned one of the attributes in each of the groups.

A.   Exact Aggregation

To represent our model of consumer behavior we require the following additional notation:

$$w_{nk} = p_n x_{nk}/M_k$$

Expenditure share of the nth commodity group in the budget of the kth consuming unit ($k = 1, 2, \ldots, K$)

$$w_k = (w_{1k}, w_{2k} \ldots w_{Nk})$$

Vector of expenditure shares for the kth consuming unit ($k = 1, 2, \ldots, K$)

$$\ln \frac{p}{M_k} = \left(\ln \frac{p_1}{M_k}, \ln \frac{p_2}{M_k}, \ldots, \ln \frac{p_N}{M_k} \right)$$

Vector of logarithms of ratios of prices to expenditure by the kth consuming unit ($k = 1, 2, \ldots, K$)

$$\ln p = (\ln p_1, \ln p_2, \ldots, \ln p_N)$$

Vector of logarithms of prices.

We assume that the kth consuming unit allocates its expenditures in accord with the transcendental logarithmic or translog indirect utility function, say V_k, where

$$\ln V_k = F(A_k) + \ln\frac{p}{M_k}' \alpha_p + \tfrac{1}{2} \ln\frac{p}{M_k}' B_{pp} \ln \frac{p}{M_k}$$

$$+ \ln \frac{p'}{M_k} B_{pA} A_k \qquad (k = 1, 2, \ldots, K) \quad (112)$$

In this representation the function F depends on the attribute vector A_k but is independent of the prices p and expenditure M_k. The vector α_p and the matrices B_{pp} and B_{pA} are constant parameters that are the same for all consuming units.

The expenditure shares of the kth consuming unit can be derived by the logarithmic form of Roy's Identity:

$$w_{nk} = \frac{\partial \ln V_k}{\partial \ln (p_n/M_k)} \bigg/ \sum \frac{\partial \ln V_k}{\partial \ln (p_n/M_k)}$$

$$(n = 1, 2, \ldots, N; k = 1, 2, \ldots, K) \quad (113)$$

Applying this Identity to the translog indirect utility function, we obtain the system of individual expenditure shares:

$$w_k = \frac{1}{D_k}\left(\alpha_p + B_{pp} \ln \frac{p}{M_k} + B_{pA} A_k\right) \qquad (k = 1, 2, \ldots, K) \quad (114)$$

where the denominators $\{D_k\}$ take the form:

$$D_k = \iota' \alpha_p + \iota' B_{pp} \ln \frac{p}{M_k} + \iota' B_{pA} A_k \qquad (k = 1, 2, \ldots, K) \quad (115)$$

and ι is a vector of ones.

We first observe that the function F that appears in the translog indirect utility function does not enter into the determination of the individual expenditure shares. This function is not identifiable from observed patterns of individual expenditure allocation. Second, since the individual expenditure shares can be expressed as ratios of functions that are homogeneous and linear in the unknown parameters α_p, B_{pp}, B_{pA} these shares are homogeneous of degree zero in the parameters. By multiplying a given set of the unknown parameters by a constant we obtain another set of parameters that generates the same system of individual budget shares. Accordingly, we can choose a normalization for the parameters without affecting observed patterns of individual expenditure allocation. We find it convenient to employ the normalization:

$$\iota'\alpha_p = -1$$

Under this restriction any change in the set of unknown parameters will be reflected in changes in individual expenditure patterns.

The conditions for exact aggregation are that the individual expenditure shares are linear in functions of the attributes $\{A_k\}$ and total expenditures $\{M_k\}$ for all consuming units.[16] These conditions will be satisfied if and only if the terms involving the attributes and expenditures do not appear in the denominators of the expressions given above for the individual expenditure shares, so that:

$$\iota' B_{pp} \iota = 0$$

$$\iota' B_{pA} = 0$$

These restrictions imply that the denominators $\{D_k\}$ reduce to

$$D = -1 + \iota' B_{pp} \ln p$$

where the subscript k is no longer required, since the denominator is the same for all consuming units. Under these restrictions the individual expenditure shares can be written

$$w_k = \frac{1}{D} (\alpha_p + B_{pp} \ln p - B_{pp} \iota \cdot \ln M_k + B_{pA} A_k)$$

$$(k = 1, 2, \ldots, K) \quad (116)$$

The individual expenditure shares are linear in the logarithms of expenditures $\{\ln M_k\}$ and the attributes $\{A_k\}$, as required by exact aggregation.

Under the exact aggregation condition the indirect utility function for each consuming unit takes the form:

$$\ln V_k = \ln p'(\alpha_p + \tfrac{1}{2} B_{pp} \ln p + B_{pA} A_k) - \ln M_k \cdot D$$

$$(k = 1, 2, \ldots, K) \quad (117)$$

The indirect utility function is additive in functions of the attributes and total expenditure of the individual consuming unit. This property is invariant with respect to affine transformations of the indirect utility function, but is not preserved by arbitrary monotonic transformations. We conclude that the translog indirect utility function provides a cardinal measure of individual welfare as well as an ordinal measure. Given the indirect utility function for each unit, we can solve explicitly for the expenditure function:

$$\ln M_k = \frac{1}{D} [\ln p'(\alpha_p + \tfrac{1}{2} B_{pp} \ln p + B_{pA} A_k) - \ln V_k]$$

$$(k = 1, 2, \ldots, K) \quad (118)$$

The expenditure function gives the minimum expenditure required for the consuming unit to achieve the utility level V_k, given prices p.

The expenditure function and the indirect utility function can be employed in assessing the impacts of alternative economic policies on the welfare of consuming units with common demographic characteristics. For this purpose we can employ the equivalent variation in total expenditure required for each consuming unit to achieve the level of utility after a change in economic policy at prices prevailing before the policy change. To analyze the impact of a change in economic policy on the welfare of the kth household, we first evaluate the indirect utility function after the change in policy has taken place. Suppose that prices are p^1 and expenditure for the kth household is M_k^1. The level of individual welfare for the kth consuming unit after the policy change V_k^1 is given by

$$\ln V_k^1 = \ln p^{1'} (\alpha_p + \tfrac{1}{2} B_{pp} \ln p^1 + B_{pA} A_k) - \ln M_k^1 \cdot D(p^1)$$

$$(k = 1, 2, \ldots, K) \quad (119)$$

Next, we suppose that the prices prevailing before the change in policy are p^0. We can define the equivalent variation in total expenditure for the kth household, say E_k, as the additional expenditure required to achieve the level of utility after the change in policy V_k^1 at the old prices p^0

$$E_k = M_k^1 - M_k(p^0, V_k^1, A_k) \quad (k = 1, 2, \ldots, K) \quad (120)$$

The equivalent variation depends on the attributes A_k of the kth consuming unit, on the final expenditure and prices, which enter through the indirect utility function of the kth consuming unit $V_k^1(p^1, A_k, M_k^1)$, on the prices p^0 prevailing before the policy change, and on expenditure M_k^1 after the policy change. If the equivalent variation is positive, the total expenditure of the consuming unit must be increased in order to compensate for the policy change. If the equivalent variation is negative, the total expenditure of the consuming unit must be decreased to compensate for the change.

Alternative economic policies result in differences in the prices facing the individual consuming units. They also result in differences in total expenditures for the individual units. Differences in equivalent variations among consuming units reflect the fact that preferences and economic circumstances differ among units. To evaluate the impact of alternative policies on individual welfare, we must compare the equivalent variation in total expenditure required to achieve the level of utility resulting from each policy with the change in total expenditure that actually takes place. For this purpose we define the net equivalent variation in total expenditure for the kth household, say N_k^E, as the difference between the equivalent variation and the change in total expenditure:

$$N_k^E = E_k - (M_k^1 - M_k^0) = M_k^0 - M_k(p^0, V_k^1, A_k)$$

$$(k = 1, 2, \ldots, K) \quad (121)$$

where M_k^0 is total expenditure before the policy change. If the net equivalent variation is negative, the welfare of the consuming unit is increased by the policy change; if the net equivalent variation is positive, the welfare of the consuming unit is decreased.

Alternatively, we can assess the impacts of economic policies on the welfare of individual consuming units by means of the compensating variation in total expenditure. This is the change in expenditure required for each consuming unit to achieve the level of utility before a change in economic policy at prices prevailing after the policy change. To analyze the impact of a change in economic policy on the welfare of the kth household, we first evaluate the indirect utility function before the change in policy has taken place. The level of individual welfare for the kth consuming unit before the policy change V_k^0 is given by

$$\ln V_k^0 = \ln p^{0'} (\alpha_p + \tfrac{1}{2} B_{pp} \ln p^0 + B_{pA} A_k) - \ln M_k^0 \cdot D (p^0)$$

$$(k = 1, 2, \ldots, K) \quad (122)$$

We can define the compensating variation in total expenditure for the kth household, say C_k, as the additional expenditure required to achieve the level of utility before the change in policy V_k^0 at the new prices p^1

$$C_k = M_k (p^1, V_k^0, A_k) - M_k^0 \quad (k = 1, 2, \ldots, K) \quad (123)$$

The compensating variation depends on the attributes A_k of the kth consuming unit, on the initial expenditure and prices, which enter through the indirect utility function of the kth consuming unit $V_k^0(p^0, A_k, M_k^0)$, on the prices p^1 prevailing after the policy change, and on expenditure M_k^0 before the policy change. If the compensating variation is positive, the total expenditure of the consuming unit must be increased in order to compensate for the policy change. If the compensating variation is negative, the total expenditure of the consuming unit must be decreased to compensate for the change.

To evaluate the impact of alternative economic policies on individual welfare, we must compare the compensating variation in total expenditure required to achieve the level of utility resulting from each policy with the change in total expenditure that actually takes place. For this purpose we define the net compensating variation in total expenditure for the kth household, say N_k^C, as the difference between the compensating variation and the change in total expenditure:

$$N_k^C = C_k - (M_k^1 - M_k^0) = M_k (p^1, V_k^0, A_k) - M_k^1$$

$$(k = 1, 2, \ldots, K) \quad (124)$$

If the net compensating variation is negative, the welfare of the consuming unit is increased by the policy change; if the net compensating variation is positive, the welfare of the consuming unit is decreased.[17]

Given the initial prices p^0 and initial expenditure M_k^0 for the kth consuming unit, determining the initial welfare for this unit V_k^0, the net equivalent variation provides a monotonic transformation of the final value of the indirect utility function V_k^1. However, this transformation is not invariant with respect to changes in the initial prices and initial expenditure and does not provide a cardinal measure of individual welfare. Similarly, given the final prices p^1 and the final expenditure M_k^1 for the kth consuming unit, determining the final welfare V_k^1, the net compensating variation provides a monotonic transformation of the final value of the indirect utility function V_k^1. This transformation also fails to provide a cardinal measure of individual welfare. Net equivalent variations based on a given initial policy can be used to provide a unique ordering among a number of alternative economic policies, while net compensating variations can be used only for binary ordering of each policy relative to the initial policy.[18]

Aggregate expenditure shares, say w, are obtained by multiplying individual expenditure shares by expenditure for each consuming unit, adding over all consuming units, and dividing by aggregate expenditure:

$$w = \frac{\Sigma \, M_k \, w_k}{\Sigma M_k} \tag{125}$$

The aggregate expenditure shares can be written

$$w = \frac{1}{D} \left(\alpha_p + B_{pp} \ln p - B_{pp} \, \iota \frac{\Sigma \, M_k \ln M_k}{\Sigma \, M_k} + B_{pA} \frac{\Sigma \, M_k \, A_k}{\Sigma \, M_k} \right) \tag{126}$$

Aggregate expenditure shares depend on prices p. They also depend on the distribution of expenditures over all consuming units through the function $\Sigma \, M_k \ln M_k / \Sigma \, M_k$, which may be regarded as a statistic of the distribution. This single statistic summarizes the impact of changes in the distribution of expenditures among individual consuming units on aggregate expenditure allocation. Finally, aggregate expenditure shares depend on the distribution of expenditures among demographic groups through the functions $\{\Sigma \, M_k A_k / \Sigma \, M_k\}$, which may be regarded as statistics of the joint distribution of expenditures and attributes. Since the attributes are represented as dummy variables, equal to one for a consuming unit with that characteristic and zero otherwise, these functions are equal to the shares of the corresponding demographic groups in aggregate expenditure. We conclude that aggregate expenditure patterns depend on the distribution of expenditure over all consuming units through the statistic $\Sigma \, M_k \ln M_k / \Sigma \, M_k$ and the distribution among demographic groups through the statistics $\{\Sigma \, M_k \, A_k / \Sigma \, M_k\}$.

B.   Integrability

Under exact aggregation systems of individual expenditure shares for consuming units with identical demographic characteristics can be recovered in one and only one way from the system of aggregate expenditure shares. This makes it possible to employ all of the implications of the theory of individual consumer behavior in specifying an econometric model of aggregate expenditure allocation. If a system of individual expenditure shares can be generated from an indirect utility function by means of the logarithmic form of Roy's Identity, we say that the system is *integrable*. A complete set of conditions for integrability, expressed in terms of the system of individual expenditure shares, is the following:

1. *Homogeneity.* The individual expenditure shares are homogeneous of degree zero in prices and expenditure.

We can write the individual expenditure shares in the form

$$w_k = \frac{1}{D} (\alpha_p + B_{pp} \ln p - \beta_{pM} \ln M_k + B_{pA} A_k) \qquad (k = 1, 2, \ldots, K)$$

where the parameter vector β_{pM} is constant and the same for all consuming units. Homogeneity implies that this vector must satisfy the restrictions:

$$\beta_{pM} = B_{pp} \, \iota \tag{127}$$

Given the exact aggregation restriction there are *N-1* restrictions implied by homogeneity.

2. *Summability.* The sum of the individual expenditure shares over all commodity groups is equal to unity

$$\Sigma \, w_{nk} = 1 \qquad (k = 1, 2, \ldots, K)$$

We can write the denominator D in the form

$$D = -1 + \beta_{Mp} \ln p$$

where the parameters $\{\beta_{Mp}\}$ are constant and the same for all commodity groups and all consuming units. Summability implies that these parameters must satisfy the restrictions

$$\beta_{Mp} = \iota' \, B_{pp} \tag{128}$$

Given the exact aggregation restrictions, there are *N-1* restrictions implied by summability.

3. *Symmetry.* The matrix of compensated own- and cross-price effects must be symmetric.

Imposing homogeneity and summability restrictions, we can write the individual expenditure shares in the form

$$w_k = \frac{1}{D}\left(\alpha_p + B_{pp} \ln \frac{p}{M_k} + B_{pA} A_k\right) \qquad (k = 1, 2, \ldots, K)$$

where the denominator D can be written

$$D = -1 + \iota' B_{pp} \ln p \cdot$$

The typical element of the matrix of uncompensated own- and cross-price effects takes the form

$$\frac{\partial x_{nk}}{\partial (p_m/M_k)} = \frac{1}{(p_n/M_k)(p_m/M_k)}\left[\frac{1}{D}\left(\beta_{nm} - w_{nk}\beta_{Mm}\right) - \delta_{nm} w_{nk}\right]$$

$$(n,m = 1,2,\ldots, N; k = 1, 2, \ldots, K)$$

where

$$\beta_{Mm} = \Sigma \beta_{nm} \qquad (m = 1, 2, \ldots, N)$$

and

$$\delta_{nm} = \begin{cases} 0 & \text{if} \quad n \neq m \\ 1 & \text{if} \quad n = m \end{cases} \qquad (n,m = 1, 2, \ldots, N)$$

The corresponding element of the matrix of compensated own- and cross-price effects takes the form

$$\frac{\partial x_{nk}}{\partial (p_m/M_k)} - x_{mk} \Sigma \frac{\partial x_{nk}}{\partial (p_\ell/M_k)} \cdot \frac{p_\ell}{M_k}$$

$$= \frac{1}{(p_n/M_k)(p_m/M_k)}\left[\frac{1}{D}(\beta_{nm} - w_{nk}\beta_{Mm}) - \delta_{nm} w_{nk}\right]$$

$$- x_{mk} \Sigma \frac{1}{(p_n/M_k)(p_\ell/M_k)}\left[\frac{1}{D}(\beta_{n\ell} - w_{nk}\beta_{M\ell}) - \delta_{n\ell} w_{nk}\right]\frac{p_\ell}{M_k}$$

$$(n, m = 1, 2, \ldots, N; k = 1, 2, \ldots, K)$$

The full matrix of compensated own- and cross-price effects, say S_k, becomes

$$S_k = P_k^{-1}\left[\frac{1}{D}(B_{pp} - w_k \iota' B_{pp} - B_{pp} \iota w_k' + w_k \iota' B_{pp} \iota w_k')\right.$$

$$\left. + w_k w_k' - W_k\right] P_k^{-1} (k = 1, 2, \ldots, K) \quad (129)$$

where:

$$
P_k^{-1} = \begin{bmatrix} \dfrac{1}{p_1/M_k} & 0 & \cdots & 0 \\ 0 & \dfrac{1}{p_2/M_k} & \cdots & 0 \\ \vdots & \vdots & & \vdots \\ 0 & 0 & \cdots & \dfrac{1}{p_N/M_k} \end{bmatrix}, \quad W_k = \begin{bmatrix} w_{1k} & 0 & \cdots & 0 \\ 0 & w_{2k} & \cdots & 0 \\ \vdots & \vdots & & \vdots \\ 0 & 0 & \cdots & w_{Nk} \end{bmatrix}
$$

$$(k = 1, 2, \ldots, K)$$

The matrix S_k, $(k = 1, 2, \ldots, K)$, must be symmetric for all consuming units.

If the system of individual expenditure shares is to be generated from a translog indirect utility function, a necessary and sufficient condition for symmetry is that the matrix B_{pp} must be symmetric. Without imposing the condition that this matrix is symmetric we can write the individual expenditure shares in the form:

$$
w_k = \frac{1}{D}\left(\alpha_p + B_{pp} \ln \frac{p}{M_k} + B_{pA} A_k\right) \qquad (k = 1, 2, \ldots, K)
$$

Symmetry implies that the matrix of parameters B_{pp} must satisfy the restrictions:

$$
B_{pp} = B'_{pp} \tag{130}
$$

The total number of symmetry restrictions is $\frac{1}{2} N(N - 1)$.

4. *Nonnegativity.* The individual expenditure shares must be nonnegative

$$
w_{nk} \geqq 0 \qquad (n = 1, 2, \ldots, N; k = 1, 2, \ldots, K)
$$

By summability the individual expenditure shares sum to unity, so that we can write

$$
w_k \geqslant 0 \qquad (k = 1, 2, \ldots, K)
$$

where $w_k \geqslant 0$ implies $w_{nk} \geqq 0$, $(n = 1, 2, \ldots, N)$, and $w_k \neq 0$.

Nonnegativity of the individual expenditure shares is implied by monotonicity of the indirect utility function

$$
\frac{\partial \ln V_k}{\partial \ln (p/M_k)} \leqq 0 \qquad (k = 1, 2, \ldots, K)
$$

For the translog indirect utility function the conditions for monotonicity take the form

$$\frac{\partial \ln V_k}{\partial \ln (p/M_k)} = \alpha_p + B_{pp} \ln \frac{p}{M_k} + B_{pA} A_k \leqq 0$$

$$(k = 1, 2, \ldots, K) \quad (131)$$

Summability implies that not all the expenditure shares are zero, so that:

$$D = -1 + \iota' \beta_{pp} \ln p < 0 \qquad (132)$$

Since the translog indirect utility function is quadratic in the logarithms of prices $\ln p$, we can always choose the prices so that the individual expenditure shares violate the nonnegativity conditions. Alternatively, we can say that it is possible to choose the prices so the monotonicity of the indirect utility function is violated. Accordingly, we cannot impose restrictions on the parameters of the translog indirect utility function that would imply nonnegativity of the individual expenditure shares or monotonicity of the indirect utility function for all prices and expenditure. Instead we consider restrictions on the parameters that imply quasi-convexity of the indirect utility function or monotonicity of the system of individual demand functions for all nonnegative expenditure shares.

5. *Monotonicity.* The matrix of compensated own- and cross-price effects must be nonpositive definite.

We first impose homogeneity, summability, and symmetry restrictions on the expenditure shares. We restrict consideration to values of the prices p, expenditure M_k, $(k = 1, 2, \ldots, K)$, and attributes A_k, $(k = 1, 2, \ldots, K)$ for which the individual expenditure shares satisfy the nonnegativity restrictions, so that $w_k \geqq 0$, $(k = 1, 2, \ldots, K)$. The summability restrictions imply that $\iota' w_k = 1$, $(k = 1, 2, \ldots, K)$. We can write the matrix of price effects in the form

$$S_k = P_k^{-1} \left[\frac{1}{D} (I - \iota w_k')' B_{pp} (I - \iota w_k') + w_k w_k' - W_k \right] P_k^{-1},$$

$$(k = 1, 2, \ldots, K)$$

A necessary and sufficient condition for monotonicity of the system of individual expenditure shares is that the matrix $D^{-1} (I - \iota w_k') B_{pp} (I - \iota w_k') + w_k w_k' - W_k$ $(k = 1, 2, \ldots, K)$, is nonpositive definite for all expenditure shares satisfying the nonnegativity and summability conditions.

C.   Restrictions Implied by Monotonicity

We next consider restrictions on the parameters of the translog indirect utility function implied by monotonicity of the individual expenditure shares. If $\iota' B_{pp} = 0$, the denominator D is independent of prices and the translog indirect utility function is homothetic; otherwise, for a given value of the individual expenditure shares we can make the denominator D as large or as small as we wish by a suitable choice of prices p and expenditure M_k $(k = 1, 2, \ldots, K)$. A necessary and sufficient condition for monotonicity of the system of individual expenditure shares is that the matrices $D^{-1} (I - \iota w_k')' B_{pp} (I - \iota w_k')$ and $w_k w_k' - W_k$, $(k = 1, 2, \ldots, K)$, are both nonpositive definite.

The matrix $w_k w_k' - W_k$, $(k = 1, 2, \ldots, K)$, is nonpositive definite for all expenditure shares satisfying the nonnegativity and summability restrictions. A sufficient condition for nonpositive definiteness of the matrix $D^{-1} (I - \iota w_k')' B_{pp} (I - \iota w_k')$ is that the matrix B_{pp} is nonnegative definite. However, if the quadratic form $z' B_{pp} z$ achieves the value zero, which must be a minimum, for any vector z not equal to zero, then z is a characteristic vector of B_{pp} corresponding to a zero characteristic value. Since $\iota' B_{pp} \iota = 0$ by exact aggregation, ι is a characteristic vector of B_{pp} corresponding to a zero characteristic value if B_{pp} is nonnegative definite. Hence, $B_{pp} \iota = 0$ and the translog indirect utility function is homothetic. If B_{pp} is not nonnegative definite, then there is a vector z such that

$$z' B_{pp} z < 0$$

where z cannot be written in the form:

$$z = (I - \iota w_k') x \qquad (k = 1, 2, \ldots, K)$$

for some x and for individual expenditure shares such that $w_k \geqq 0$, $\iota' w_k = 1$, $(k = 1, 2, \ldots, K)$.

To characterize all vectors z that can be represented in the form given above, we first observe that these vectors can be written:

$$z = x - (w_k' x) \iota \qquad (k = 1, 2, \ldots, K)$$

so that the vector z is equal to a vector x less a vector with elements equal to a weighted average of the elements x. Unless all the elements of x are the same, so that $z = 0$ or unless $w_k' x = 0$, $(k = 1, 2, \ldots, K)$, so that $z = x$, the vector z has at least one positive element and one negative element. Furthermore, if $w_k' x = 0$, $(k = 1, 2, \ldots, K)$, then the vector x has at least one positive and one negative element or complementary slackness obtains:

$$\left. \begin{array}{l} x_n > 0 \text{ implies } w_{nk} = 0 \\ w_{nk} > 0 \text{ implies } x_n = 0 \end{array} \right\} \qquad (n = 1, 2, \ldots, N; k = 1, 2, \ldots, K)$$

We conclude that either the vector z will have at least one positive and one negative element or the vector $z \geqq 0$ or $z \leqq 0$ with at least one zero element. These conditions rule the possibilities that $z > 0$ or $z < 0$, so that if B_{pp} is not nonnegative definite, then

$$z' \, B_{pp}z < 0$$

implies $z > 0$ or $z < 0$. We next consider the class of all matrices B_{pp} that satisfy this condition.

First, we introduce the definition due to Martos (1969) of a *merely positive subdefinite matrix*. A merely positive subdefinite matrix, say M, is a real symmetric matrix such that

$$x' \, Mx < 0$$

implies $Mx \geqslant 0$ or $Mx \leqslant 0$ and M is not nonnegative definite. Similarly, a *strictly merely positive subdefinite* matrix is a real symmetric matrix such that:

$$x' \, Mx < 0$$

implies $Mx > 0$ or $Mx < 0$. A complete characterization of merely positive subdefinite matrices has been provided by Cottle and Ferland (1972), who have shown that such matrices must satisfy the conditions:

1. M consists of only nonpositive elements.
2. M has exactly one negative characteristic value.

A complete characterization of strictly merely positive subdefinite matrices has been provided by Martos (1969), who has shown that a strictly merely positive subdefinite matrix must satisfy the additional condition:

3. M does not contain a row (or column) of zeroes.

We observe that this condition does not imply in itself that a strictly merely positive subdefinite matrix is nonsingular.

We are now in a position to characterize completely the class of matrices B_{pp} such that

$$z' \, B_{pp}z < 0$$

implies $z > 0$ or $z < 0$. A necessary and sufficient condition is that B_{pp}^{-1} exists and is strictly merely positive subdefinite. First, if B_{pp}^{-1} exists and is strictly merely positive subdefinite, then

$$x'B_{pp}^{-1}x < 0$$

implies $B_{pp}^{-1}x > 0$ or $B_{pp}^{-1}x < 0$. But then

$$x'B_{pp}^{-1} \, B_{pp} \, B_{pp}^{-1}x = z' \, B_{pp}z < 0$$

implies $z > 0$ or $z < 0$, where $z = B_{pp}^{-1}x$

Conversely, if the condition on the matrix B_{pp} given above is satisfied, then B_{pp} has exactly one negative characteristic value. This matrix has at least one negative characteristic value, otherwise it would be non-negative definite. If there were two negative characteristic values with characteristic vectors, say z_1 and z_2, then $z_1' B_{pp} z_1 < 0$ and $z_2' B_{pp} z_2 < 0$, so that $z_1 > 0$, $z_2 > 0$, and $z_1' z_2 > 0$, contradicting the orthogonality of the characteristic vectors of a real, symmetric matrix. Second, the matrix B_{pp} has no zero characteristic values; otherwise:

$$(z_- + \alpha z_0)' B_{pp} (z_- + \alpha z_0) = z_-' B_{pp} z_- < 0$$

where z_- is a characteristic vector corresponding to the negative characteristic value, z_0 is a characteristic vector corresponding to a zero characteristic value, and α is a scalar. The scalar α can be chosen so as to make $z_- + \alpha z_0$ violate the conditions that $z_- + \alpha z_0 > 0$ or $z_- + \alpha z_0 < 0$. We conclude that the matrix B_{pp} has no zero characteristic values and is nonsingular.

Since the matrix B_{pp} is nonsingular, the inverse matrix B_{pp}^{-1} exists and we can write:

$$x' B_{pp}^{-1} x = x' B_{pp}^{-1} B_{pp} B_{pp}^{-1} x = z' B_{pp} z < 0$$

implies $z > 0$ or $z < 0$, where $z = B_{pp}^{-1} x$, so that $B_{pp}^{-1} x > 0$ or $B_{pp}^{-1} x < 0$ and B_{pp}^{-1} is strictly merely positive subdefinite. We conclude that the inverse matrix B_{pp}^{-1} consists of only nonpositive elements, has exactly one negative characteristic value, and does not contain a row (or column) of zeros.

To impose restrictions on the matrix B_{pp} implied by monotonicity of the systems of individual expenditure shares, we first provide a Cholesky factorization of this matrix

$$B_{pp} = LDL'$$

where L is a unit lower triangular matrix and D is a diagonal matrix. As an illustration, we can write the matrix B_{pp} in terms of its Cholesky factorization for a model of consumer behavior with five commodity groups as follows

$$B_{pp} = \begin{bmatrix} \delta_1 & \delta_1\lambda_{21} & \delta_1\lambda_{31} \\ \delta_1\lambda_{21} & \delta_1\lambda_{21}^2 + \delta_2 & \delta_1\lambda_{31}\lambda_{21} + \delta_2\lambda_{32} \\ \delta_1\lambda_{31} & \delta_1\lambda_{21}\lambda_{31} + \delta_2\lambda_{32} & \delta_1\lambda_{31}^2 + \delta_2\lambda_{32}^2 + \delta_3 \\ \delta_1\lambda_{41} & \delta_1\lambda_{21}\lambda_{41} + \delta_2\lambda_{42} & \delta_1\lambda_{31}\lambda_{41} + \delta_2\lambda_{32}\lambda_{42} + \delta_3\lambda_{43} \\ \delta_1\lambda_{51} & \delta_1\lambda_{21}\lambda_{51} + \delta_2\lambda_{52} & \delta_1\lambda_{31}\lambda_{51} + \delta_2\lambda_{32}\lambda_{52} + \delta_3\lambda_{53} \end{bmatrix}$$

$$\delta_1\lambda_{41}$$

$$\delta_1\lambda_{41}\lambda_{21} + \delta_2\lambda_{42}$$

$$\delta_1\lambda_{41}\lambda_{31} + \delta_2\lambda_{42}\lambda_{32} + \delta_3\lambda_{43}$$

$$\delta_1\lambda_{41}^2 + \delta_2\lambda_{42}^2 + \delta_3\lambda_{43}^2 + \delta_4$$

$$\delta_1\lambda_{41}\lambda_{51} + \delta_2\lambda_{42}\lambda_{52} + \delta_3\lambda_{43}\lambda_{53} + \delta_4\lambda_{54}$$

$$\delta_1\lambda_{51}$$

$$\delta_1\lambda_{51}\lambda_{21} + \delta_2\lambda_{52}$$

$$\delta_1\lambda_{51}\lambda_{31} + \delta_2\lambda_{52}\lambda_{32} + \delta_3\lambda_{53}$$

$$\delta_1\lambda_{51}\lambda_{41} + \delta_2\lambda_{52}\lambda_{42} + \delta_3\lambda_{53}\lambda_{43} + \delta_4\lambda_{54}$$

$$\delta_1\lambda_{51}^2 + \delta_2\lambda_{52}^2 + \delta_3\lambda_{53}^2 + \delta_4\lambda_{54}^2 + \delta_5$$

where

$$L = \begin{bmatrix} 1 & 0 & 0 & 0 & 0 \\ \lambda_{21} & 1 & 0 & 0 & 0 \\ \lambda_{31} & \lambda_{32} & 1 & 0 & 0 \\ \lambda_{41} & \lambda_{42} & \lambda_{43} & 1 & 0 \\ \lambda_{51} & \lambda_{52} & \lambda_{53} & \lambda_{54} & 1 \end{bmatrix}, \ D = \begin{bmatrix} \delta_1 & 0 & 0 & 0 & 0 \\ 0 & \delta_2 & 0 & 0 & 0 \\ 0 & 0 & \delta_3 & 0 & 0 \\ 0 & 0 & 0 & \delta_4 & 0 \\ 0 & 0 & 0 & 0 & \delta_5 \end{bmatrix}$$

It is important to note that not every matrix with an inverse that is strictly merely positive subdefinite is Cholesky factorizable. For example, if the matrix B_{pp} for a model of consumer behavior with two commodity groups were to take the form:

$$B_{pp} = \begin{bmatrix} 0 & -1 \\ -1 & 0 \end{bmatrix}$$

then the inverse matrix B_{pp}^{-1} would take the form

$$B_{pp}^{-1} = \begin{bmatrix} 0 & -1 \\ -1 & 0 \end{bmatrix}$$

which is strictly merely positive subdefinite with a negative characteristic value -1 and a positive characteristic value $+1$. The formulas for the Cholesky factorization

$$B_{pp} = \begin{bmatrix} \delta_1 & \delta_1\lambda_{21} \\ \delta_1\lambda_{21} & \delta_1\lambda_{21}^2 + \delta_2 \end{bmatrix}$$

reveal that the condition $\delta_1 = 0$ contradicts the condition $\delta_1\lambda_{21} = -1$.

However, the set of real symmetric matrices that are not Cholesky factorizable has measure zero in the set of all real symmetric matrices.

Next for a model of consumer behavior with five commodity groups we can derive an appropriate expression for B_{pp}^{-1}

$$B_{pp}^{-1} = (L')^{-1} D^{-1} L^{-1}$$

where

$$
L^{-1} =
\begin{bmatrix}
1 & 0 & 0 & 0 & 0 \\
-\lambda_{21} & 1 & 0 & 0 & 0 \\
-\lambda_{31} + \lambda_{32}\lambda_{21} & -\lambda_{32} & 1 & 0 & 0 \\
-\lambda_{41} + \lambda_{42}\lambda_{21} + \lambda_{43}\lambda_{31} - \lambda_{43}\lambda_{32}\lambda_{21} & -\lambda_{42} + \lambda_{43}\lambda_{32} & -\lambda_{43} & 1 & 0 \\
-\lambda_{51} + \lambda_{52}\lambda_{21} + \lambda_{53}\lambda_{31} + \lambda_{54}\lambda_{41} - \lambda_{53}\lambda_{32}\lambda_{21} - \lambda_{54}\lambda_{42}\lambda_{21} - \lambda_{54}\lambda_{43}\lambda_{31} + \lambda_{54}\lambda_{43}\lambda_{32}\lambda_{21} & -\lambda_{52} + \lambda_{53}\lambda_{32} + \lambda_{54}\lambda_{42} - \lambda_{54}\lambda_{43}\lambda_{32} & -\lambda_{53} + \lambda_{54}\lambda_{43} & -\lambda_{54} & 1
\end{bmatrix}
$$

and

$$
D^{-1} =
\begin{bmatrix}
\dfrac{1}{\delta_1} & 0 & 0 & 0 & 0 \\[2mm]
0 & \dfrac{1}{\delta_2} & 0 & 0 & 0 \\[2mm]
0 & 0 & \dfrac{1}{\delta_3} & 0 & 0 \\[2mm]
0 & 0 & 0 & \dfrac{1}{\delta_4} & 0 \\[2mm]
0 & 0 & 0 & 0 & \dfrac{1}{\delta_5}
\end{bmatrix}
$$

Representing B_{pp}^{-1} in the form (β_{pp}^{ij}) where β_{pp}^{ij} is the element of the ith row and jth column of B_{pp}^{-1}, we obtain the expressions for these elements in Table 1 for a model of consumer behavior with five commodity groups.

Since the matrix B_{pp}^{-1} is strictly merely positive subdefinite, all the elements of this matrix are nonpositive. Expressing the nonpositivity constraints on these elements in terms of the elements of the Cholesky factorization of the matrix B_{pp}, where:

$$B_{pp} = LDL'$$

we obtain the restrictions given in Table 2 for a model of consumer behavior with five commodity groups. In deriving these restrictions we make use of the fact that B_{pp} has exactly one negative Cholesky value, δ_5, and four positive Cholesky values δ_1, δ_2, δ_3, δ_4.

The exact aggregation condition

$$\iota' B_{pp} \iota = 0$$

implies that

$$\delta_1 (1 + \lambda_{21} + \lambda_{31} + \lambda_{41} + \lambda_{51})^2 + \delta_2 (1 + \lambda_{32} + \lambda_{42} + \lambda_{52})^2$$
$$+ \delta_3 (1 + \lambda_{43} + \lambda_{53})^2 \quad + \delta_4 (1 + \lambda_{54})^2 + \delta_5 = 0$$

so that we can use this restriction to eliminate the parameter δ_1 from the expression for β_{pp}^{11}, obtaining the inequality:

$$\delta_2\delta_3\delta_4\delta_5 (1 + \lambda_{21} + \lambda_{31} + \lambda_{41} + \lambda_{51})^2$$

$$- [\delta_2(1 + \lambda_{32} + \lambda_{42} + \lambda_{52})^2 + \delta_3 (1 + \lambda_{43} + \lambda_{53})^2 + \delta_4 (1 + \lambda_{54})^2 + \delta_5]$$

$$[\delta_3\delta_4\delta_5(-\lambda_{21})^2 + \delta_2\delta_4\delta_5 (-\lambda_{31} + \lambda_{32}\lambda_{21})^2 \tag{133}$$

$$+ \delta_2\delta_3\delta_5(-\lambda_{41} + \lambda_{42}\lambda_{21} + \lambda_{43}\lambda_{31} - \lambda_{43}\lambda_{32}\lambda_{21})^2$$

$$+ \delta_2\delta_3\delta_4(-\lambda_{31} + \lambda_{52}\lambda_{21} + \lambda_{53}\lambda_{31} + \lambda_{54}\lambda_{42} - \lambda_{53}\lambda_{32}\lambda_{21}$$

$$- \lambda_{54}\lambda_{42}\lambda_{21} - \lambda_{54}\lambda_{43}\lambda_{31} + \lambda_{54}\lambda_{43}\lambda_{32}\lambda_{21})] \geqq 0.$$

Finally, we must include restrictions on the Cholesky values; for a model of consumer behavior with five commodity groups these take the form:

$$\delta_5 \leqq 0$$

$$\delta_4 \geqq 0$$

$$\delta_3 \geqq 0 \tag{134}$$

$$\delta_2 \geqq 0$$

$$\delta_1 \geqq 0$$

Table 1.   Elements of B_{pp}^{-1}

$$\beta_{pp}^{11}\;\frac{1}{\delta_1}+\frac{1}{\delta_2}(-\lambda_{21})^2+\frac{1}{\delta_3}(-\lambda_{31}+\lambda_{32}\lambda_{21})^2+\frac{1}{\delta_4}(-\lambda_{41}+\lambda_{42}\lambda_{21}+\lambda_{43}\lambda_{31}-\lambda_{43}\lambda_{32}\lambda_{21})^2+\frac{1}{\delta_5}(-\lambda_{51}+\lambda_{52}\lambda_{21}+\lambda_{53}\lambda_{31}+\lambda_{54}\lambda_{41}$$
$$-\lambda_{53}\lambda_{32}\lambda_{21}-\lambda_{54}\lambda_{42}\lambda_{21}-\lambda_{54}\lambda_{43}\lambda_{31}$$
$$+\lambda_{54}\lambda_{43}\lambda_{32}\lambda_{21})^2$$

$$\beta_{pp}^{12}\;\frac{1}{\delta_2}(-\lambda_{21})+\frac{1}{\delta_3}(-\lambda_{32})(-\lambda_{31}+\lambda_{32}\lambda_{21})+\frac{1}{\delta_4}(-\lambda_{42}+\lambda_{43}\lambda_{32})(-\lambda_{41}+\lambda_{42}\lambda_{21}+\lambda_{43}\lambda_{31}+\frac{1}{\delta_5}(-\lambda_{52}+\lambda_{53}\lambda_{32}+\lambda_{54}\lambda_{42}(-\lambda_{51}+\lambda_{52}\lambda_{21}+\lambda_{53}\lambda_{31}+\lambda_{54}\lambda_{41}$$
$$-\lambda_{43}\lambda_{32}\lambda_{21})\qquad -\lambda_{54}\lambda_{43}\lambda_{32})\qquad -\lambda_{53}\lambda_{32}\lambda_{21}-\lambda_{54}\lambda_{42}\lambda_{21}-\lambda_{54}\lambda_{43}\lambda_{31}$$
$$+\lambda_{54}\lambda_{43}\lambda_{32}\lambda_{21})$$

$$\beta_{pp}^{13}\;\frac{1}{\delta_3}(-\lambda_{31}+\lambda_{32}\lambda_{21})+\frac{1}{\delta_4}(-\lambda_{43})(-\lambda_{41}+\lambda_{42}\lambda_{21}+\lambda_{43}\lambda_{31}+\frac{1}{\delta_5}(-\lambda_{53}+\lambda_{54}\lambda_{43})(-\lambda_{51}+\lambda_{52}\lambda_{21}+\lambda_{53}\lambda_{31}+\lambda_{54}\lambda_{41}$$
$$-\lambda_{43}\lambda_{32}\lambda_{21})\qquad -\lambda_{53}\lambda_{32}\lambda_{21}-\lambda_{54}\lambda_{43}\lambda_{31}-\lambda_{54}\lambda_{43}\lambda_{31}$$
$$+\lambda_{54}\lambda_{43}\lambda_{32}\lambda_{21})$$

$$\beta_{pp}^{14}\;\frac{1}{\delta_4}(-\lambda_{41}+\lambda_{42}\lambda_{21}+\lambda_{43}\lambda_{31}+\frac{1}{\delta_5}(-\lambda_{54})(-\lambda_{51}+\lambda_{52}\lambda_{21}+\lambda_{53}\lambda_{31}+\lambda_{54}\lambda_{41}$$
$$-\lambda_{43}\lambda_{32}\lambda_{21})\qquad -\lambda_{53}\lambda_{32}\lambda_{21}-\lambda_{54}\lambda_{42}\lambda_{21}-\lambda_{54}\lambda_{43}\lambda_{31}$$
$$+\lambda_{54}\lambda_{43}\lambda_{32}\lambda_{21})$$

$$\beta_{pp}^{15}\;\frac{1}{\delta_5}(-\lambda_{51}+\lambda_{52}\lambda_{21}+\lambda_{53}\lambda_{31}+\lambda_{54}\lambda_{41}$$
$$-\lambda_{53}\lambda_{32}\lambda_{21}-\lambda_{54}\lambda_{43}\lambda_{31}$$
$$+\lambda_{54}\lambda_{43}\lambda_{32}\lambda_{21})$$

$$\beta_{pp}^{22} = \frac{1}{\delta_2} + \frac{1}{\delta_3}(-\lambda_{32})^2 + \frac{1}{\delta_4}(-\lambda_{42}+\lambda_{43}\lambda_{32})^2 + \frac{1}{\delta_5}(-\lambda_{52}+\lambda_{53}\lambda_{32}+\lambda_{54}\lambda_{42} \\ -\lambda_{54}\lambda_{43}\lambda_{32})^2$$

$$\beta_{pp}^{23} = \frac{1}{\delta_3}(-\lambda_{32}) + \frac{1}{\delta_4}(-\lambda_{43})(-\lambda_{42}+\lambda_{43}\lambda_{32}) + \frac{1}{\delta_5}(-\lambda_{53}+\lambda_{54}\lambda_{43})(-\lambda_{52}+\lambda_{53}\lambda_{32}+\lambda_{54}\lambda_{42} \\ -\lambda_{54}\lambda_{43}\lambda_{32})$$

$$\beta_{pp}^{24} = \frac{1}{\delta_4}(-\lambda_{42}+\lambda_{43}\lambda_{32}) + \frac{1}{\delta_5}(-\lambda_{54})(-\lambda_{52}+\lambda_{53}\lambda_{32}+\lambda_{54}\lambda_{42} \\ -\lambda_{54}\lambda_{43}\lambda_{32})$$

$$\beta_{pp}^{25} = \frac{1}{\delta_5}(-\lambda_{52}+\lambda_{53}\lambda_{32}+\lambda_{54}\lambda_{42} \\ -\lambda_{54}\lambda_{43}\lambda_{32})$$

$$\beta_{pp}^{33} = \frac{1}{\delta_3} + \frac{1}{\delta_4}(-\lambda_{43})^2 + \frac{1}{\delta_5}(-\lambda_{53}+\lambda_{54}\lambda_{43})^2$$

$$\beta_{pp}^{34} = \frac{1}{\delta_4}(-\lambda_{43}) + \frac{1}{\delta_5}(-\lambda_{54})(-\lambda_{53}+\lambda_{54}\lambda_{43})$$

$$\beta_{pp}^{35} = \frac{1}{\delta_5}(-\lambda_{53}+\lambda_{54}\lambda_{43})$$

$$\beta_{pp}^{44} = \frac{1}{\delta_4} + \frac{1}{\delta_5}(-\lambda_{54})^2$$

$$\beta_{pp}^{45} = \frac{1}{\delta_5}(-\lambda_{54})$$

$$\beta_{pp}^{55} = \frac{1}{\delta_5}$$

Table 2.   Restrictions on the Elements of $B_{pp} = LDL'$.

$\beta^{55}_{pp} \leqq 0 \qquad -\delta_5 \geqq 0$

$\beta^{45}_{pp} \leqq 0 \qquad -\lambda_{54} \geqq 0$

$\beta^{44}_{pp} \leqq 0 \qquad \delta_5 + \delta_4(-\lambda_{54})^2 \geqq 0$

$\beta^{35}_{pp} \leqq 0 \qquad -\lambda_{53} + \lambda_{54}\lambda_{43} \geqq 0$

$\beta^{34}_{pp} \leqq 0 \qquad \delta_5(-\lambda_{43}) + \delta_4(-\lambda_{54})(-\lambda_{53}+\lambda_{54}\lambda_{43}) \geqq 0$

$\beta^{33}_{pp} \leqq 0 \qquad \delta_5\delta_4 + \delta_3\delta_5(-\lambda_{43}) + \delta_3\delta_4(-\lambda_{53}+\lambda_{54}\lambda_{43})^2 \geqq 0$

$\beta^{25}_{pp} \leqq 0 \qquad -\lambda_{52} + \lambda_{53}\lambda_{32} + \lambda_{54}\lambda_{42} - \lambda_{54}\lambda_{43}\lambda_{32} \geqq 0$

$\beta^{24}_{pp} \leqq 0 \qquad \delta_5(-\lambda_{42}+\lambda_{43}\lambda_{32}) + \delta_4(-\lambda_{54})(-\lambda_{52}+\lambda_{53}\lambda_{32}+\lambda_{54}\lambda_{42}$
$\qquad\qquad\qquad -\lambda_{54}\lambda_{43}\lambda_{32}) \geqq 0$

$\beta^{23}_{pp} \leqq 0 \qquad \delta_4\delta_5(-\lambda_{32}) + \delta_3\delta_5(-\lambda_{43})(-\lambda_{42}+\lambda_{34}\lambda_{32}) + \delta_3\delta_4(-\lambda_{53}+\lambda_{54}\lambda_{43})(-\lambda_{52}+\lambda_{53}\lambda_{32}+\lambda_{54}\lambda_{42}$
$\qquad\qquad\qquad -\lambda_{54}\lambda_{43}\lambda_{42}) \geqq 0$

$\beta^{22}_{pp} \leqq 0 \qquad \delta_3\delta_4\delta_5 + \delta_2\delta_4\delta_5(-\lambda_{32})^2 + \delta_2\delta_3\delta_5(-\lambda_{42}+\lambda_{43}\lambda_{32})^2 + \delta_2\delta_3\delta_4(-\lambda_{52}+\lambda_{53}\lambda_{32}+\lambda_{54}\lambda_{42}$
$\qquad\qquad\qquad -\lambda_{54}\lambda_{43}\lambda_{32})^2 \geqq 0$

$$\beta^{15}_{pp} \leqq 0 \quad -\lambda_{51}+\lambda_{52}\lambda_{21}+\lambda_{53}\lambda_{31}+\lambda_{54}\lambda_{41}$$
$$-\lambda_{53}\lambda_{32}\lambda_{21}-\lambda_{54}\lambda_{42}\lambda_{21}-\lambda_{54}\lambda_{43}\lambda_{31}$$
$$+\lambda_{54}\lambda_{43}\lambda_{32}\lambda_{21} \geqq 0$$

$$\beta^{14}_{pp} \leqq 0 \quad \delta_5(-\lambda_{41}+\lambda_{42}\lambda_{21}+\lambda_{43}\lambda_{31}+\delta_4(-\lambda_{54})(-\lambda_{51}+\lambda_{52}\lambda_{21}+\lambda_{53}\lambda_{31}+\lambda_{54}\lambda_{41}$$
$$-\lambda_{43}\lambda_{32}\lambda_{21}) \qquad -\lambda_{53}\lambda_{32}\lambda_{21}-\lambda_{54}\lambda_{42}\lambda_{21}-\lambda_{54}\lambda_{43}\lambda_{31}$$
$$+\lambda_{54}\lambda_{43}\lambda_{32}\lambda_{21}) \geqq 0$$

$$\beta^{13}_{pp} \leqq 0 \quad \delta_4\delta_5(-\lambda_{31}+\lambda_{32}\lambda_{21})+\delta_3\delta_5(-\lambda_{43})(-\lambda_{41}+\lambda_{42}\lambda_{21}+\lambda_{43}\lambda_{31}+\delta_3\delta_4(-\lambda_{53}+\lambda_{54}\lambda_{43})(-\lambda_{51}+\lambda_{52}\lambda_{21}+\lambda_{53}\lambda_{31}+\lambda_{54}\lambda_{41}$$
$$-\lambda_{43}\lambda_{32}\lambda_{21}) \qquad -\lambda_{53}\lambda_{32}\lambda_{21}-\lambda_{54}\lambda_{42}\lambda_{21}-\lambda_{54}\lambda_{43}\lambda_{31}$$
$$+\lambda_{54}\lambda_{43}\lambda_{32}\lambda_{21}) \geqq 0$$

$$\beta^{12}_{pp} \leqq 0 \quad \delta_3\delta_4\delta_5(-\lambda_{21})+\delta_2\delta_4\delta_5(-\lambda_{32})(-\lambda_{31}+\lambda_{32}\lambda_{21})+\delta_2\delta_3\delta_5(-\lambda_{42}+\lambda_{43}\lambda_{32})(-\lambda_{41}+\lambda_{42}\lambda_{21}+\lambda_{43}\lambda_{31}$$
$$-\lambda_{43}\lambda_{32}\lambda_{21})$$
$$+\delta_2\delta_3\delta_4(-\lambda_{52}+\lambda_{53}\lambda_{32}+\lambda_{54}\lambda_{42}(-\lambda_{51}+\lambda_{52}\lambda_{21}+\lambda_{54}\lambda_{41}$$
$$-\lambda_{54}\lambda_{43}\lambda_{32}) \qquad -\lambda_{53}\lambda_{32}\lambda_{21}-\lambda_{54}\lambda_{42}\lambda_{21}-\lambda_{54}\lambda_{43}\lambda_{31}$$
$$+\lambda_{54}\lambda_{43}\lambda_{32}\lambda_{21}) \geqq 0$$

$$\beta^{11}_{pp} \leqq 0 \quad \delta_2\delta_3\delta_4\delta_5+\delta_1\delta_3\delta_4\delta_5(-\lambda_{21})^2+\delta_1\delta_2\delta_4\delta_5(-\lambda_{31}+\lambda_{32}\lambda_{21})^2+\delta_1\delta_2\delta_3\delta_5(-\lambda_{41}+\lambda_{42}\lambda_{21}+\lambda_{43}\lambda_{31}$$
$$-\lambda_{43}\lambda_{32}\lambda_{21})^2$$
$$+\delta_1\delta_2\delta_3\delta_4(-\lambda_{51}+\lambda_{52}\lambda_{21}+\lambda_{53}\lambda_{31}+\lambda_{54}\lambda_{41}$$
$$-\lambda_{53}\lambda_{32}\lambda_{21}-\lambda_{54}\lambda_{43}\lambda_{31}$$
$$+\lambda_{54}\lambda_{43}\lambda_{32}\lambda_{21}) \geqq 0$$

Combining these restrictions with the restrictions on the elements of B_{pp}^{-1} given in Table 2, we obtain a complete set of restrictions implied by the monotonicity of the systems of individual expenditure shares.

D.   Summary and Conclusion

In this Section we have presented a model of aggregate consumer behavior based on transcendental logarithmic or translog indirect utility functions for all consuming units. These indirect utility functions incorporate restrictions on individual behavior that result from maximization of a utility function subject to a budget constraint. Each consuming unit has an indirect utility function that is homogeneous of degree zero in prices and expenditure, nonincreasing in prices and nondecreasing in expenditure, and quasiconvex in prices and expenditure.

To incorporate differences in individual preferences into our model of aggregate consumer behavior we allow the indirect utility functions for all consuming units to depend on attributes, such as demographic characteristics, that vary among individuals. Each attribute is represented by a dummy variable equal to unity when the consuming unit has the corresponding characteristic and zero otherwise.

Given a translog indirect utility function for each consuming unit, we derive the expenditure shares for that unit by means of Roy's Identity. This results in expenditure shares that can be expressed as ratios of two functions that are linear in the logarithms of ratios of prices for all commodities to total expenditure and in attributes. The denominators of these ratios are functions that are the same for all commodity groups. Under exact aggregation the individual expenditure shares are linear in functions of attributes and total expenditure, so that the denominators are independent of total expenditure and attributes and are the same for all individuals.

Under the exact aggregation condition the translog indirect utility function is additive in functions of the attributes and total expenditure of the individual consuming unit and provides a cardinal measure of individual welfare as well as an ordinal measure. Given the indirect utility function for each unit, we can solve explicitly for the expenditure function, giving the minimum expenditure required to achieve a stipulated level of individual welfare for given prices.

The expenditure function and indirect utility function can be employed in assessing the impacts of alternative economic policies on the welfare of individual consuming units. For this purpose we introduce equivalent and compensating variations in expenditure. The equivalent variation gives the additional expenditure required to achieve the level of utility after the change in policy. The compensating variation gives the additional expenditure required to achieve the level of utility before the change in policy.

To derive aggregate expenditure shares we multiply the individual expenditure shares by total expenditure for each consuming unit, sum over all consuming units, and divide by aggregate expenditure. The aggregate expenditure shares, like the individual shares, can be expressed as ratios of two functions. The denominators are the same as for individual expenditure shares. The numerators are linear in the logarithms of prices, in a statistic of the distribution of expenditure over all consuming units $\Sigma \ M_k \ \ln M_k / \Sigma \ M_k$, and in the shares of all demographic groups in aggregate expenditure $\{\Sigma \ M_k \ A_k / \Sigma \ M_k\}$.

The individual expenditure shares are homogeneous of degree zero in prices and expenditure. Given the restrictions implied by exact aggregation, this implies an additional $N - 1$ restrictions on the parameters of the translog indirect utility functions, where N is the number of commodities. Second, the sum of individual expenditure shares over all commodity groups is equal to unity. Again, given the exact aggregation restrictions, there are N additional restrictions implied by summability. Third, the matrix of compensated own- and cross-price effects must be symmetric. This implies $\frac{1}{2} N (N - 1)$ restrictions on the parameters of the translog indirect utility functions.

Monotonicity of the indirect utility functions implies that the individual expenditure shares must be nonnegative. Similarly, quasiconvexity of the indirect utility functions implies that the individual expenditure shares must be monotonic or, equivalently, that the matrix of compensated own- and cross-price substitution effects must be nonpositive definite. It is always possible to choose prices so that monotonicity of the indirect utility functions or nonnegativity of the individual expenditure shares is violated. Accordingly, we consider restrictions that imply monotonicity of the expenditure shares wherever they are nonnegative.

To impose monotonicity of the system of individual expenditure shares we represent the matrix of price coefficients B_{pp} in terms of its Cholesky factorization. There is a one-to-one transformation between the elements of this matrix and the parameters of the Cholesky factorization. To impose the restrictions implied by monotonicity we can fit the parameters of the Cholesky factorization with the constraints on these parameters implied by strict mere positive subdefiniteness of the inverse matrix B_{pp}^{-1}; there are $\frac{1}{2} (N^2 + 3N) - 1$ such restrictions. This completes our discussion of the specification of a model of consumer behavior based on the theory of exact aggregation.

VI. ECONOMETRICS OF THE TRANSLOG MODEL

In this Section we outline the econometric implementation of the translog model of aggregate consumer behavior presented in Section V. Our observations on individual expenditure patterns are limited to a single cross section, providing data on expenditure shares, total expenditure, and demographic characteristics for individual consuming units at a given point of time. We assume that prices are the same for all consuming units, while expenditures and demographic characteristics vary among units. By analyzing individual cross section data we can obtain estimates of expenditure and demographic effects on individual expenditure patterns.

Our observations on aggregate expenditure patterns include time series data on expenditure shares, the level of aggregate expenditure, a weighted average of the logarithms of expenditures for individual consuming units, shares of demographic groups in aggregate expenditure, and prices. It is important to note that our econometric model can be implemented from aggregate time series data alone, provided that the number of demographic groups is small by comparison with the number of observations. By combining time series and cross section data we can obtain more precise estimates of the effects of variations in expenditures and demographic characteristics on patterns of aggregate expenditure allocation.

We begin our discussion of econometrics of the translog model by presenting the stochastic structure employed for cross section and time series data. We next discuss the identification and estimation of unknown parameters for a single cross section, assuming that prices are the same for all consuming units. We then discuss identification and estimation for aggregate time series and the pooling of time series and cross section data. This section provides the link between the theoretical model described in Section V above and the empirical results to be presented in Section VII.

A.　Stochastic Structure

The model of consumer behavior presented in Section V is generated from a translog indirect utility function for each consuming unit. To formulate an econometric model of consumer behavior we add a stochastic component to the equations for the individual expenditure shares. We associate this component with unobservable random disturbances at the level of the individual consuming unit. The consuming unit maximizes utility, but the expenditure shares are chosen with a random disturbance. This disturbance may result from errors in implementation of consumption plans, random elements in the determination of consumer preferences not reflected in our list of attributes of consuming units, or errors of measurement of the individual expenditure shares. We assume that each of the equations for the individual shares has two additive components. The first is a nonrandom function of prices, expenditure and demographic characteristics. The second is an unobservable random disturbance that is functionally independent of these variables.

To represent our econometric model of consumer behavior we introduce some additional notation. We consider observations on expenditure patterns by K consuming units, indexed by $k = 1, 2, \ldots, K$, for T time periods, indexed by $t = 1, 2, \ldots, T$. The vector of expenditure shares for the kth consuming unit in the tth time period is denoted w_{kt} $(k = 1, 2, \ldots, K; t = 1, 2, \ldots, T)$. Similarly, expenditure for the kth unit on all commodity groups in the tth time period is denoted M_{kt} $(k = 1, 2, \ldots, K; t = 1, 2, \ldots, T)$. The vector of prices faced by all consuming units in the tth time period is denoted p_t $(t = 1, 2, \ldots, T)$. Similarly, the vector of logarithms of prices in the tth time period is denoted in $\ln p_t$ $(t = 1, 2, \ldots, T)$. The vector of logarithms of ratios of prices to expenditure for the kth consuming unit in the tth time period is denoted $\ln p_t/M_{kt}$ $(k = 1, 2, \ldots, K; t = 1, 2, \ldots, T)$.

Using our new notation, the individual expenditure shares can be written

$$w_{kt} = \frac{1}{D_t}\left(\alpha_p + B_{pp} \ln \frac{p_t}{M_{kt}} + B_{pA} A_k\right) + \varepsilon_{kt}$$

$$(k = 1, 2, \ldots, K; t = 1, 2, \ldots, T) \quad (135)$$

where:

$$D_t = -1 + \iota' B_{pp} \ln p_t \quad (t = 1, 2, \ldots, T)$$

and ε_{kt} $(k = 1, 2, \ldots, K; t = 1, 2, \ldots, T)$ is the vector of unobservable random disturbances for the kth consuming unit and the tth time period. Since the individual expenditure shares for all commodities sum to unity for each consuming unit in each time period, the unobservable random disturbances for all commodities sum to zero for each unit in each time period

$$\iota' \varepsilon_{kt} = 0 \quad (k = 1, 2, \ldots, K; t = 1, 2, \ldots, T) \quad (136)$$

These disturbances are not distributed independently.

We assume that the unobservable random disturbances for all commodities have expected value equal to zero for all observations:

$$E(\varepsilon_{kt}) = 0 \quad (k = 1, 2, \ldots, K; t = 1, 2, \ldots, T) \quad (137)$$

We also assume that these disturbances have the same covariance matrix for all observations

$$V(\varepsilon_{kt}) = \Omega_\varepsilon \quad (k = 1, 2, \ldots, K; t = 1, 2, \ldots, T)$$

Since the disturbances sum to zero for each observation, this matrix is nonnegative definite with rank at most equal to $N - 1$, where N is the number of commodities. We assume that the covariance matrix has rank equal to $N - 1$.

Finally, we assume that disturbances corresponding to distinct observations are uncorrelated. Under this assumption the covariance matrix of the disturbances for all consuming units at a given point of time has the Kronecker product form

$$
V \begin{pmatrix} \varepsilon_{1t} \\ \varepsilon_{2t} \\ \vdots \\ \varepsilon_{Kt} \end{pmatrix} = \Omega_\varepsilon \otimes I \tag{138}
$$

The covariance matrix of the disturbances for all time periods for a given individual has an analogous form. The unknown parameters of the system of equations determining the individual expenditure shares can be estimated from time series data on individual expenditure shares, prices, total expenditure, and demographic characteristics.

At any point of time the aggregate expenditure shares are equal to the individual expenditure shares multiplied by the ratios of individual expenditure to aggregate expenditure and summed over all individual consuming units. Although the data for individual consuming units and for the aggregate of all consuming units are based on the same definitions, the aggregate data are not obtained by summing over the data for individuals. Observations on individual consuming units are based on a random sample from the population of all consuming units. Observations for the aggregate of all consuming units are constructed from data on production of commodities and on consumption of these commodities by households and by other consuming units such as businesses, governments, and the rest of the world. Accordingly, we must introduce an additional source of random error in the equations for the aggregate expenditure shares, corresponding to unobservable errors of measurement in the observations that underly the aggregate expenditure shares.

We assume that each of the equations for the aggregate expenditure shares has three additive components. The first is a weighted average of the nonrandom functions of prices, expenditure and demographic characteristics that determine the individual expenditure shares. The second is a weighted average of the unobservable random disturbances in equations for the individual expenditure shares. The third is a weighted average of the unobservable random errors of measurement in the observations on the aggregate expenditure shares.

Denoting the vector of aggregate expenditure shares at time t by w_t $(t = 1, 2, \ldots, T)$, we can express these shares in the form:

$$
w_t = \frac{1}{D_t} (\alpha_p + B_{pp} \ln p_t) - \frac{1}{D_t} B_{pp} \iota \frac{\sum_{k=1}^{K} M_{kt} \ln M_{kt}}{\sum_{k=1}^{K} M_{kt}}
$$

$$+ \frac{1}{D_t} B_{pA} \frac{\sum_{k=1}^{K} M_{kt} A_k}{\sum_{k=1}^{K} M_{kt}} + \varepsilon_t \qquad (t = 1, 2, \ldots, T) \quad (139)$$

where

$$D_t = -1 + \iota' B_{pp} \ln p_t \qquad (t = 1, 2, \ldots, T)$$

as before, and ε_t $(t = 1, 2, \ldots, T)$ is the vector of unobservable random disturbances for the *t*th time period.

The aggregate disturbances ε_t can be expressed in the form:

$$\varepsilon_t = \frac{\sum_{k=1}^{K} M_{kt} \varepsilon_{kt}}{\sum_{k=1}^{K} M_{kt}} + \frac{\sum_{k=1}^{K} M_{kt} v_{kt}}{\sum_{k=1}^{K} M_{kt}} \qquad (t = 1, 2, \ldots, T) \quad (140)$$

where $v_{kt}(k = 1, 2, \ldots, K; t = 1, 2, \ldots, T)$ is the vector of errors of measurement that underly the data on the aggregate expenditure shares. Since the random disturbances for all commodities sum to zero in each time period

$$\iota' \varepsilon_t = 0 \qquad (k = 1, 2, \ldots, K; t = 1, 2, \ldots, T) \quad (141)$$

these disturbances are not distributed independently.

We assume that the errors of measurement that underly the data on the aggregate expenditure shares have expected value equal to zero for all observations:

$$E(v_{kt}) = 0 \qquad (k = 1, 2, \ldots, K; t = 1, 2, \ldots, T)$$

We also assume that these errors have the same covariance matrix for all observations:

$$V(v_{kt}) = \Omega_v \qquad (k = 1, 2, \ldots, K; t = 1, 2, \ldots, T)$$

and that the rank of this matrix is equal to $N - 1$.

If the errors of measurement are distributed independently of expenditure and of the disturbances in the equations for the individual expenditure shares, the aggregate disturbances have expected value equal to zero for all time periods:

$$E(\varepsilon_t) = 0 \qquad (t = 1, 2, \ldots, T) \quad (142)$$

and have a covariance matrix given by:

$$V(\varepsilon_t) = \frac{\sum_{k=1}^{K} M_{kt}^2}{\left(\sum_{k=1}^{K} M_{kt}\right)^2} \Omega_\varepsilon + \frac{\sum_{k=1}^{K} M_{kt}^2}{\left(\sum_{k=1}^{K} M_{kt}\right)^2} \Omega_v \qquad (t = 1, 2, \ldots, T)$$

so that the aggregate disturbances for different time periods are heteroscedastic.

We can correct for heteroscedasticity of the aggregate disturbances by transforming the observations on the aggregate expenditure shares as follows

$$\rho_t \, w_t = \frac{\rho_t}{D_t} (\alpha_p + B_{pp} \ln p_t) - \frac{\rho_t}{D_t} B_{pp} \, \iota \, \frac{\sum_{k=1}^{K} M_{kt} \ln M_{kt}}{\sum_{k=1}^{K} M_{kt}}$$

$$+ \frac{\rho_t}{D_t} B_{pA} \frac{\sum_{k=1}^{K} M_{kt} A_k}{\sum_{k=1}^{K} M_{kt}} + \rho_t \, \varepsilon_t, \, (t = 1, 2, \ldots, T)$$

where

$$\rho_t^2 = \frac{\left(\sum_{k=1}^{K} M_{kt} \right)^2}{\sum_{k=1}^{K} M_{kt}^2} \quad (t = 1, 2, \ldots, T)$$

The covariance matrix of the transformed disturbances, say Ω, becomes:

$$V(\rho_t \varepsilon_t) = \Omega_\varepsilon + \Omega_\nu = \Omega$$

This matrix is nonnegative definite with rank equal to $N - 1$. Finally, we assume that the errors of measurement corresponding to distinct observations are uncorrelated. Under this assumption the covariance matrix of the transformed disturbances at all points of time has the Kronecker product form:

$$V \begin{pmatrix} \rho_1 \varepsilon_1 \\ \rho_2 \varepsilon_2 \\ \vdots \\ \rho_T \varepsilon_T \end{pmatrix} = \Omega \otimes I \qquad (143)$$

B. Identification and Estimation

We next discuss the estimation of the translog model of aggregate consumer behavior, combining a single cross section of observations on individual expenditure patterns with several time series observations on aggregate expenditure patterns. We first discuss application of the translog model to cross section data only. We then present methods for pooling individual cross section and aggregate time series data.

Suppose first that we have a random sample of observations on individual expenditure patterns at a given point of time. Prices for all consumers are the same. The translog model (134) takes the form

$$w_k = \gamma_1 + \gamma_2 \ln M_k + \Gamma_3 A_k + \varepsilon_k \qquad (k = 1, 2, \ldots, K) \qquad (144)$$

where we drop the time subscript. In this model γ_1 and γ_2 are vectors of unknown parameters and Γ_3 is a matrix of unknown parameters. Random sampling implies that disturbances for different individuals are uncorrelated. We assume that the data matrix with $(1, \ln M_k, A_k)$ as its kth row is of full rank.

The parameters of γ_1, γ_2 and Γ_3 are identified in the cross section. Moreover, the model (144) is a multivariate regression model, except that the vector of disturbances ε_k has a singular distribution. If the vector ε_k is normally distributed,[19] the maximum likelihood estimator of the unknown parameters in the complete model is equivalent to the estimator obtained by dropping one equation, estimating the remaining $N - 1$ equations by maximum likelihood, and then deriving estimates of the parameters of the omitted equation from estimates of the parameters for the $N - 1$ equations not omitted.[20] Consider a model where one equation has been dropped; this reduced model is a linear multivariate regression model so that the unique, minimum variance, unbiased estimator of the unknown parameters γ_1, γ_2 and Γ_3 is obtained by applying ordinary least squares to each equation separately.

To link the parameters γ_1, γ_2 and Γ_3 to the parameters of the translog model of aggregate consumer behavior we first observe that the parameters of the translog model can be identified only up to a normalization, since multiplying all of the parameters by the same nonzero constant leaves the expenditure shares unchanged. The usual normalization is $\iota' \alpha_p = -1$, giving the unknown parameters the same sign as those in the translog indirect utility function. Second, without loss of generality we can take the prices of all goods to be equal to unity for a particular period of time. In the application to a single cross section we take all prices at the date of the survey to be equal to unity. The prices for all other time periods are expressed relative to prices of this base period.

Given the normalization of the parameters and the choice of base period for measurement of the prices, we obtain the following correspondence between the unknown parameters of the cross section model and the parameters of the translog model of aggregate consumer behavior

$$\gamma_1 = -\alpha_p$$

$$\gamma_2 = B_{pp}\iota \qquad (145)$$

$$\Gamma_3 = -B_{pA}$$

The constants α_p and the parameters associated with demographic characteristics of individual households B_{pA} can be estimated from a single cross section. The parameters associated with total expenditure $B_{pp}\iota$ can also be estimated from a single cross section. The remaining parameters, those associated with prices, can be estimated from time series data on aggregate expenditure patterns.

Since the model is linear in parameters for a cross section, we can use ordinary least squares regression to estimate the impact of the demographic structure on aggregate expenditure patterns. This feature characterizes exact aggregation models in general, as indicated in Section II. The resulting linearity greatly simplifies computations.

After correction for heteroscedasticity the translog model of aggregate consumer behavior is given by:

$$\rho_t w_t = \frac{\rho_t}{D_t}(\alpha_p + B_{pp} \ln p_t) - \frac{\rho_t}{D_t} B_{pp} \iota \frac{\sum_{k=1}^{K} M_{kt} \ln M_{kt}}{\sum_{k=1}^{K} M_{kt}}$$

$$+ \frac{\rho_t}{D_t} B_{pA} \frac{\sum_{k=1}^{K} M_{kt} A_k}{\sum_{k=1}^{K} M_{kt}} + \rho_t \varepsilon_t \qquad (t = 1, 2, \ldots, T) \qquad (146)$$

where

$$D_t = -1 + \iota' B_{pp} \ln p_t \qquad (t = 1, 2, \ldots, T)$$

and ε_t is a vector of unobservable random disturbances. We have time series observations on prices p_t, the expenditure statistic $\sum M_{kt} \ln M_{kt} / \sum M_{kt}$, the vector of attribute-expenditure statistics $\{\sum M_{kt} A_{kt} / \sum M_{kt}\}$, and the heteroscedasticity correction $\rho_t (t = 1, 2, \ldots, T)$.

The translog model in (146) might appear to be a nonlinear regression model with additive errors, so that nonlinear regression techniques could be employed.[21] However, the existence of supply functions for all commodities makes it more appropriate to treat some of the right side variables as endogenous. For example, due to demand-supply interactions shifts in prices should be treated as endogenous. To obtain a consistent estimator for this model we could specify supply functions for all commodities and estimate the complete model by full information maximum likelihood.

Alternatively, to estimate the model in (146) we can consider limited information techniques utilizing instrumental variables. In particular, we can introduce a sufficient number of instrumental variables to identify all parameters. We estimate the model by nonlinear three stage least squares (NL3SLS).[22] Application of NL3SLS to our model would be straightforward except for the fact that the covariance matrix of the disturbances is singular. We obtain NL3SLS estimators of the complete system by dropping one equation and estimating the resulting system of $N - 1$ equations by NL3SLS; we derive an estimator for parameters of the remaining equation from the conditions for summability. The parameter estimates are invariant to the choice of the equation omitted in the model for aggregate time series data and the model for individual cross section data.

In the analysis of the model to be applied to cross section data on individual expenditure patterns, we have assumed that individual disturbances and individual total expenditure are uncorrelated. If aggregate demand-supply interactions induce shifts in the distribution of expenditure, the zero correlation assumption cannot be strictly valid for all consumers at the individual level. However, the cross section is a random sample that includes a minute percentage of the total population, so that it is reasonable to assume that the correlations between total expenditure and disturbances at the individual level are negligible.

The NL3SLS estimator can be employed to estimate all parameters of the model of aggregate expenditures, provided that these parameters are identified. Since we wish to obtain a detailed characterization of the impact of changes in the demographic structure of the population, the model (146) contains a large number of parameters and requires a large number of time series observations for identification. The technical conditions for identification are quite complicated. A sufficient condition for underidentification is that the number of instruments is less than the number of parameters. For the translog model of aggregate consumer behavior, this occurs if:

$$(N - 1)(1 + S) x \frac{(N + 1)N}{2} - 1 > (N - 1) x \min (V, T) \quad (147)$$

where N is the number of commodities, S is the number of components of A_{kt} and V is the number of instruments. The left-hand side of (147) is the number of free parameters of the translog model under symmetry of the matrix B_{pp} and the right-hand side is the number of instruments, assuming that no collinearity exists among the instruments.

Condition (147) is met in our application, so that not all parameters are identified in the model for aggregate time series data. We next consider methods utilizing individual cross section data together with aggregate time series data to obtain identification. As we have seen, cross section data can be used to identify the constant α_p, the coefficients of total expenditure $-B_{pp}\iota$ and the demographic coefficients B_{pA}. Only the price coefficients B_{pp} must be identified from aggregate time series data.

A necessary condition for identification of these parameters is:

$$\frac{(N-1)\,N}{2} < (N-1)\min(V, T) \tag{148}$$

or

$$\frac{N}{2} < \min(V, T) \tag{149}$$

This condition is met in our application. Sufficient conditions are given in the next section; these amount to the nonlinear analogue of the absence of multicollinearity. These conditions are quite weak and hold in our application.

In order to pool cross section and time series data, we combine the model for individual expenditures and the model for aggregate expenditures and apply the method of NL3SLS to the whole system. The instruments for the cross section model are the micro data themselves; for the aggregate model the instruments are variables that can be taken to be distributed independently of the aggregate disturbances. A list of the aggregate instrumental variables is given in Appendix II. The data sets are pooled statistically, where estimates of the covariance matrix of the aggregate disturbances from time series data and the covariance matrix of the individual disturbances from cross section data are used to weight aggregate and cross section data, respectively. The resulting estimator is consistent and asymptotically efficient in the class of instrumental variable estimators utilizing the instruments we have chosen. We next describe the pooled estimation procedure, together with the simplification of computations that results from exact aggregation.

C.   Pooling Time Series and Cross Sections

The pooled estimation of the translog model of aggregate consumer behavior requires application of the method of nonlinear three stage least squares (NL3SLS). The linearity of the cross section model results in a number of simplifications of the NL3SLS estimator. Our objective is to estimate the unknown parameters α_p, B_{pp}, B_{pA} subject to the restrictions implied by summability, symmetry, monotonicity, the exact aggregation conditions, and the normalization $\iota'\alpha_p = -1$. By dropping the equation for one commodity in both cross section and time series models, we can eliminate the restrictions implied by summability. We employ these restrictions in estimating the parameters that occur in the equation that has been dropped.

We impose the restrictions implied by the exact aggregation conditions and the normalization $\iota'\alpha_p = -1$ by imposing these restrictions on the function D_t in expression (135) for the individual expenditure shares. Second, we impose the restrictions implied by symmetry by requiring that the matrix B_{pp} is symmetric. The restrictions implied by summability, symmetry, exact aggregation, and the normalization take the form of equalities. The restrictions implied by monotonicity take the form of inequalities. The matrix B_{pp} has an inverse B_{pp}^{-1} that is strictly merely positive subdefinite, so that all the elements of this inverse matrix are nonpositive and the matrix B_{pp} has exactly one negative Cholesky value, δ_5, and four positive Cholesky values—δ_1, δ_2, δ_3, δ_4. In Section V.C we have expressed these restrictions in terms of the Cholesky factorization of the matrix B_{pp}. We discuss the estimation of the unknown parameters α_p, B_{pp}, B_{pA} subject to monotonicity restrictions below.

Since we have taken the base period for all prices and time as the period corresponding to the cross section survey, we can write the cross section model in the form:

$$y_1 = X\beta_1 + \varepsilon_1$$

$$y_2 = X\beta_2 + \varepsilon_2 \qquad (150)$$

$$\cdots$$

$$y_{N-1} = X\beta_{N-1} + \varepsilon_{N-1}$$

where y_i ($i = 1, 2, \ldots, N - 1$) is the vector of observations on the individual expenditure shares of the ith commodity for all individuals, X is a matrix of observations on $2 + S$ independent variables, including a dummy variable corresponding to the constant term in each equation, the logarithm of total expenditure, and dummy variables corresponding to individual attributes and ε_i ($i = 1, 2, \ldots, N - 1$) is a vector of unobservable random disturbances.

We can stack the equations in (150) in the usual way, obtaining:

$$y = [I \otimes X] \beta + \varepsilon \qquad (151)$$

where

$$y = \begin{bmatrix} y_1 \\ y_2 \\ \vdots \\ y_{N-1} \end{bmatrix}, I \otimes X = \begin{bmatrix} X & 0 & \cdots & 0 \\ 0 & X & \cdots & 0 \\ \vdots & \vdots & & \vdots \\ 0 & 0 & \cdots & X \end{bmatrix}, \beta = \begin{bmatrix} \beta_1 \\ \beta_2 \\ \vdots \\ \beta_{N-1} \end{bmatrix}, \varepsilon = \begin{bmatrix} \varepsilon_1 \\ \varepsilon_2 \\ \vdots \\ \varepsilon_{N-1} \end{bmatrix} \qquad (152)$$

By the assumptions listed in Section VI.B, above, the matrix X is of full rank and the random vector ε is distributed normally with mean zero and covariance matrix $\Sigma_\varepsilon \otimes I$, where Σ_ε is obtained from the covariance matrix Ω_ε in (138) by striking the row and column corresponding to the omitted equation.

Similarly, we can write the time series model in the form

$$v_1 = f_1(\beta, \gamma) + v_1$$

$$v_2 = f_2(\beta, \gamma) + v_2 \tag{153}$$

$$\cdot \quad \cdot \quad \cdot$$

$$v_{N-1} = f_{N-1}(\beta, \gamma) + v_{N-1}$$

where v_i $(i = 1, 2, \ldots, N - 1)$ is the vector of observations on the aggregate expenditure shares of the ith commodity for all time periods, transformed to eliminate heteroscedasticity, f_i $(i = 1, 2, \ldots, N - 1)$ is a vector of nonlinear functions of the parameters β that enter the cross section model and the remaining parameters γ that enter the time series model, and v_i $(i = 1, 2, \ldots, N - 1)$ is a vector of unobservable random disturbances, transformed to eliminate heteroscedasticity.

As before, we can stack the equations in (153), obtaining

$$v = f(\beta, \gamma) + v \tag{154}$$

$$= f(\delta) + v$$

where

$$v = \begin{bmatrix} v_1 \\ v_2 \\ \vdots \\ v_{N-1} \end{bmatrix}, f = \begin{bmatrix} f_1 \\ f_2 \\ \vdots \\ f_{N-1} \end{bmatrix}, \delta = \begin{bmatrix} \beta \\ \gamma \end{bmatrix}, v = \begin{bmatrix} v_1 \\ v_2 \\ \vdots \\ v_{N-1} \end{bmatrix}$$

By the assumptions listed in Section VI.B the random vector v is distributed normally with mean zero and covariance matrix $\Sigma_v \otimes I$, where Σ_v is obtained from the covariance matrix Ω in (143) by striking the row and column corresponding to the omitted equation.

The maximum likelihood estimator of β from the cross section model is

$$\hat{\beta} = [I \otimes (X'X)^{-1} X'] y \tag{155}$$

or

$$\hat{\beta}_i = (X'X)^{-1} X' y_i \qquad (i = 1, 2, \ldots, N - 1)$$

which is equivalent to the least squares estimator applied to each equation individually. This estimator has covariance matrix

$$V(\hat{\beta}) = \Sigma_\varepsilon \otimes (X'X)^{-1} \tag{156}$$

The least squares estimator is a consistent estimator of the vector of unknown parameters β; the probability limit of this estimator as the number of cross section observations K tends to infinity is equal to β.

The nonlinear three stage least squares (NL3SLS) estimator for the aggregate model is obtained by minimizing the weighted sum of squared residuals:

$$\text{SSR}(\delta) = [v - f(\delta)]'[\hat{\Sigma}_v^{-1} \otimes Z(Z'Z)^{-1} Z'][v - f(\delta)] \qquad (157)$$

with respect to the vector of unknown parameters δ, where Z is the matrix of time series observations on the R instrumental variables. Provided that the parameters are identified from the aggregate model, we can apply the Gauss-Newton method to minimize (157). First, we can linearize the model, obtaining:

$$v = f(\delta_0) + \frac{\partial f}{\partial \delta}(\delta_0) \, \Delta \, \delta + u \qquad (158)$$

where δ_0 is the initial value of the vector of unknown parameters δ and

$$\Delta \, \delta = \delta_1 - \delta_0$$

where δ_1 is the revised value of this vector. The fitted residuals u depend on the initial and revised values.

To revise the initial values we apply Zellner and Theil's (1962) three stage least squares method to the linearized model, obtaining

$$\Delta\delta = \left\{ \frac{\partial f}{\partial \delta}(\delta_0)' \, (\hat{\Sigma}_v^{-1} \otimes Z(Z'Z)^{-1}Z') \frac{\partial f}{\partial \delta}(\delta_0) \right\}^{-1} \cdot$$

$$\frac{\partial f}{\partial \delta}(\delta_0)'\{\hat{\Sigma}_v^{-1} \otimes Z(Z'Z)^{-1}Z'\}[v - f(\delta_0)] \qquad (159)$$

If $\text{SSR}(\delta_0) > \text{SSR}(\delta_1)$, a further iteration is performed by replacing δ_0 by δ_1 in (158) and (159), resulting in a further revised value, say δ_2, and so on. If this condition is not satisfied, we divide the revision $\Delta\delta$ by two and evaluate the criteria $\text{SSR}(\delta)$ again; we continue reducing the revision $\Delta\delta$ until the criterion improves or the consequence criterion $\max_j \Delta\delta_j/\delta_j$ is less than some pre-specified limit. If the criterion improves, we continue with further iterations. If not, we stop the iterative process and employ the current value of the vector of unknown parameters δ as our NL3SLS estimator.

The final step in estimation of the aggregate model is to minimize the criterion function (157) subject to the restrictions implied by monotonicity of the individual expenditure shares. We have eliminated the restrictions implied by summability, symmetry, the exact aggregation conditions, and the normalization $\iota'\alpha_p = -1$; these restrictions take the form of equalities. Monotonicity of the individual expenditure shares implies the inequality restrictions given in Table 2 and the restrictions (133) and

(134). We can represent these restrictions in the form:

$$\phi_r(\delta) \geqq 0 \qquad (r = 1, 2, \ldots, R) \tag{160}$$

where R is the number of restrictions. We obtain the inequality constrained nonlinear three stage least squares estimator for the aggregate model by minimizing the criterion function subject to the constraints (160). This estimator corresponds to a saddlepoint of the Lagrangian function:

$$\pounds = \text{SSR}(\delta) + \lambda'\phi \tag{161}$$

where λ is a vector of R Lagrange multipliers and ϕ is a vector of R constraints. The Kuhn-Tucker (1951) conditions for a saddlepoint of this Lagrangian are the first-order conditions:

$$\frac{\partial \pounds}{\partial \delta} = \frac{\partial \text{SSR}(\delta)}{\partial \delta} + \lambda' \frac{\partial \phi}{\partial \delta} = 0 \tag{162}$$

and the complementary slackness condition:

$$\lambda'\phi = 0, \lambda \geq 0 \tag{163}$$

To find a saddlepoint of the Lagrangian (161) we begin by linearizing the aggregate model (154) as in (158). Second, we linearize the constraints as:

$$\phi(\delta) = \frac{\partial \phi}{\partial \delta}(\delta_0) \Delta \delta + \phi(\delta_0) \tag{164}$$

where δ_0 is a vector of initial values of the unknown parameters. We apply Liew's (1976) inequality constrained three stage least squares method to the linearized model, obtaining

$$\Delta\delta^* = \Delta\delta + \left\{ \frac{\partial f}{\partial \delta}(\delta_0)'(\hat{\Sigma}_v^{-1} \otimes Z(Z'Z)^{-1}Z') \frac{\partial f}{\partial \delta}(\delta_0) \right\}^{-1} \frac{\partial \phi}{\partial \delta}(\delta_0)' \lambda^* \tag{165}$$

where $\Delta\delta$ is the change in the value of the parameters (159) and λ^* is the solution of the linear complementarity problem

$$\frac{\partial \phi}{\partial \delta}(\delta_0) \left\{ \frac{\partial f}{\partial \delta}(\delta_0)'(\hat{\Sigma}_v^{-1} \otimes Z(Z'Z)^{-1} Z') \frac{\partial}{\partial \delta}(\delta_0) \right\}^{-1} \frac{\partial \phi}{\partial \delta}(\delta_0) \lambda$$

$$+ \frac{\partial \phi}{\partial \delta}(\delta_0) \Delta\delta - \phi(\delta_0) \geqslant 0$$

where

$$\left\{ \frac{\partial \phi}{\partial \delta}(\delta_0) \left[\frac{\partial f}{\partial \delta}(\delta_0)'(\hat{\Sigma}_v^{-1} \otimes Z(Z'Z)^{-1}Z') \frac{\partial f}{\partial \delta}(\delta_0) \right]^{-1} \frac{\partial \phi}{\partial \delta}(\delta_0) \right\} \lambda$$

$$+ \frac{\partial \phi}{\partial \delta}(\delta_0) \Delta\delta - \phi(\delta_0)]' \lambda = 0, \lambda \geqslant 0$$

Given an initial value of the unknown parameters δ_0 that satisfies the R constraints (160), if $SSR(\delta_1) < SSR(\delta_0)$ and δ_1 satisfies the constraints, the iterative process continues by linearizing the model (154) as in (159) and the constraints (160) as in (164) at the revised value of the vector of unknown parameters $\delta_1 = \delta_0 + \Delta\,\delta$. If not, we shrink $\Delta\,\delta$ as before, continuing until an improvement is found subject to the constraints or $\max_j \Delta\delta_j/\delta_j$ is less than a convergence criterion.

The conditions for identifiability of the vector of unknown parameters δ in the aggregate model are equivalent to the nonsingularity of the following matrix in a neighborhood of the true parameter vector:

$$\frac{\partial f}{\partial \delta}(\delta)'\,(\Sigma_v^{-1} \otimes Z(Z'Z)^{-1}\,Z')\,\frac{\partial f}{\partial \delta}(\delta) \tag{166}$$

The condition (147) given above is sufficient for the singularity of this matrix, as well as the singularity of the matrix evaluated at each iteration in (159).

The pooled NL3SLS estimator is found by minimizing the following function with respect to δ:

$$SSR(\delta) = (y - Y\delta)'\,(\hat{\Sigma}_\varepsilon^{-1} \otimes I)\,(y - Y\delta) \tag{167}$$
$$+ \,[v - f(\delta)]'\,[\hat{\Sigma}_v^{-1} \otimes Z(Z'Z)^{-1}Z']\,[v - f(\delta)]$$

where

$$Y = \begin{bmatrix} I \otimes X & 0 \\ 0 & 0 \end{bmatrix} \tag{168}$$

is a matrix of observations on the variables that determine the individual expenditure shares in the cross section model.

To find a minimum of the criterion function $SSR(\delta)$ in (167) we began by linearizing the pooled system (151) and (153) as

$$y - Y\delta_0 = Y\Delta\,\delta + e \tag{169}$$
$$v - f(\delta_0) = \frac{\partial f}{\partial \delta}(\delta_0)\,\Delta\delta + u$$

where δ_0 is a vector of initial values of the unknown parameters. As before, we apply ordinary three stage least squares to the linearized model, obtaining:

$$\Delta\delta = \left\{ Y'(\hat{\Sigma}_\varepsilon^{-1} \otimes I)\,Y + \frac{\partial f}{\partial \delta}(\delta_0)'\,[\hat{\Sigma}_v^{-1} \otimes Z(Z'Z)^{-1}\,Z']\,\frac{\partial f}{\partial \delta}(\delta_0) \right\}^{-1} \cdot$$
$$\left\{ Y'(\hat{\Sigma}_\varepsilon^{-1} \otimes I)(y - Y\delta_0) \right.$$
$$\left. + \frac{\partial f}{\partial \delta}(\delta_0)'[\hat{\Sigma}_v^{-1} \otimes Z(Z'Z)^{-1}Z'][v - f(\delta_0)] \right\} \tag{170}$$

If $SSR(\delta_1) < SSR(\delta_0)$, the iterative process continues by linearizing the model at the revised value of the parameters $\delta_1 = \delta_0 + \Delta \delta$. If not, we shrink $\Delta \delta$ as before, dividing $\Delta \delta$ by two and re-evaluating the criterion function and continuing until an improvement is found or $\max_j \Delta\delta_j/\delta_j$ is less than a convergence criterion.

The nonlinear three stage least squares estimator obtained by minimizing the criterion function (167) is a consistent estimator of the vector of unknown parameters δ; note that this requires taking the probability limit of the NL3SLS estimator as the number of cross section observations K and the number of time series observations T tend to infinity. This estimator has asymptotic covariance matrix

$$V(\hat{\delta}) = \left\{ Y'(\Sigma_\varepsilon^{-1} \otimes I)\, Y + \frac{\partial f}{\partial \delta}(\delta)'[\Sigma_\nu^{-1} \otimes Z(Z'Z)^{-1}Z']\frac{\partial f}{\partial \delta}(\delta) \right\}^{-1} \quad (171)$$

We obtain an estimator of this matrix by inserting the estimators $\hat{\delta}$, $\hat{\Sigma}_\varepsilon$, and $\hat{\Sigma}_\nu$ in place of the parameters δ, Σ_ε, and Σ_ν. The conditions for identifiability of the vector of unknown parameters δ in the model for pooling time series and cross section data are equivalent to nonsingularity of the following matrix in the neighborhood of the true parameter vector:

$$Y'\,(\Sigma_\varepsilon^{-1} \otimes I)\, Y + \frac{\partial f}{\partial \delta}(\delta)'\,(\Sigma_\nu^{-1} \otimes Z(Z'Z)^{-1}Z')\frac{\partial f}{\partial \delta}(\delta) \quad (172)$$

Under the following regularity conditions

$$\lim_{K\to\infty} \frac{X'X}{K} = \Sigma_{X'X}$$

$$\lim_{T\to\infty} \frac{Z'Z}{T} = \Sigma_{Z'Z} \quad (173)$$

$$\lim_{T\to\infty} \frac{1}{T}Z'\frac{\partial f_i}{\partial \delta_i} = \Sigma_{Z'\partial f_i/\partial \delta_i} \quad (i = 1, 2, \ldots, N)$$

where $\Sigma_{X'X}$, $\Sigma_{Z'Z}$ and $\Sigma_{Z'\partial f_i/\partial \delta_i}$ $(i = 1, 2, \ldots, N)$ are positive definite matrices, the NL3SLS estimator is asymptotically efficient in the class of instrumental variables estimators using X and Z as instrumental variables.

Up to this point we have presented the pooled estimator for cross section and time series models as a standard application of the NL3SLS estimator. The linearity of the cross section model resulting from exact aggregation implies that the computations can be simplified. First, the moment matrix of the cross section model takes the form:

$$Y'\,(\hat{\Sigma}_\varepsilon^{-1} \otimes I)\, Y = \hat{\Sigma}_\varepsilon^{-1} \otimes X'X \quad (174)$$

which depends on $\hat{\Sigma}_\varepsilon$ and on $X'X$, the moment matrix of the independent variables in the cross section model. Similarly, the vector of moments involving the dependent variables of the cross section model takes the form:

$$Y' \, (\hat{\Sigma}_\varepsilon^{-1} \otimes I) \, (y - Y\delta) = \hat{\Sigma}_\varepsilon^{-1} \otimes (X'y - X'X \, \delta) \qquad (175)$$

which depends on $\hat{\Sigma}_\varepsilon$, $X'X$, and on $X'y$, the vector of moments involving the dependent variables of the cross section model.

The final step in pooled estimation of the unknown parameters of the translog model of aggregate consumer behavior is to estimate these parameters subject to the inequality restrictions implied by monotonicity of the individual expenditure shares. We minimize the criterion (167) subject to the restrictions (160). As before, this is a concave programming problem. We apply inequality constrained three stage least squares to the linearized model, obtaining

$$\Delta\delta^* = \Delta\delta + \left\{ Y'(\hat{\Sigma}_\varepsilon^{-1} \otimes I)Y \right.$$

$$\left. + \frac{\partial f}{\partial \delta} (\delta_0)'(\hat{\Sigma}_\nu^{-1} \otimes Z(Z'Z)^{-1}Z) \frac{\partial f}{\partial \delta} (\delta_0) \right\}^{-1} \frac{\partial \phi}{\partial \delta} (\delta_0)\lambda^* \qquad (176)$$

where $\Delta \delta$ is the change in the value of the parameters for unconstrained three stage least squares (170) and λ^* is the solution of the linear complementarity problem

$$\frac{\partial \phi}{\partial \delta} (\delta_0) \left\{ Y'(\hat{\Sigma}_\varepsilon^{-1} \otimes I)Y + \frac{\partial f}{\partial \delta} (\delta_0)'(\hat{\Sigma}_\nu^{-1} \otimes Z(Z'Z)^{-1}Z') \frac{\partial f}{\partial \delta} (\delta_0) \right\}^{-1} \frac{\partial \phi}{\partial \delta} (\delta_0) \lambda$$

$$+ \frac{\partial \phi}{\partial \delta} (\delta_0) \Delta \delta - \phi (\delta_0) \geq 0$$

where

$$\left[\frac{\partial \phi}{\partial \delta} (\delta_0) \left\{ Y'(\hat{\Sigma}_\varepsilon^{-1} \otimes I)Y + \frac{\partial f}{\partial \delta} (\delta_0)'(\hat{\Sigma}_\nu^{-1} \otimes Z(Z'Z)^{-1}Z') \frac{\partial f}{\partial \delta} (\delta_0) \right\}^{-1} \frac{\partial \phi}{\partial \delta} (\delta_0) \lambda \right.$$

$$\left. + \frac{\partial \phi}{\partial \delta} (\delta_0) \Delta \delta - \phi (\delta_0) \right]' \lambda = 0, \lambda \geq 0$$

Given an initial value of the unknown parameters δ_0 that satisfies the constraints, if $SSR(\delta_0) < SSR(\delta)$ and δ_1 satisfies the constraints, the iterative process continues by linearizing the model as in (169) and the constraints as in (164) at the revised value of the vector of unknown parameters $\delta_1 = \delta_0 + \Delta \delta$. If not, we shrink $\Delta\delta$ as before, continuing until an improvement is found subject to the constraints or $\max_j \Delta\delta_j/\delta_j$ is less than a convergence criterion.

We assume that the restrictions associated with monotonicity of the individual expenditure shares are valid or, more precisely, that the vector of unknown parameters δ is an interior point of the set of parameters defined by the constraints. Under this assumption the inequality constrained nonlinear three stage least squares estimator is a consistent estimator of the vector of unknown parameters. This estimator has the same asymptotic covariance matrix (171) as the estimator pooling time series and cross section data.[23] As before, we obtain an estimator of this matrix by inserting the estimators δ, $\hat{\Sigma}_\epsilon$, and $\hat{\Sigma}_\nu$ in place of the parameters δ, Σ_ϵ, and Σ_ν. The conditions for identifiability of the vector of unknown parameters δ is the nonsingularity of the matrix (172) in the neighborhood of the true parameter vector.

D.   Summary and Conclusion

In this Section we have discussed the econometric implementation of the translog model of aggregate consumer behavior presented in Section V. To formulate an econometric model of individual consumer behavior we add a stochastic component to the functions that determine the individual expenditure shares. The interpretation of the individual disturbances is that the individual consuming unit maximizes utility, subject to a budget constraint, but that the expenditure shares are chosen with a random disturbance.

We assume that the individual disturbances have expected value equal to zero. Since the individual expenditure shares for all commodities sum to unity for each consuming unit in each time period, the unobservable random disturbances for all commodities sum to zero. As a consequence, these disturbances are not distributed independently. We assume that the covariance matrix of the individual disturbances has rank equal to $N - 1$, where N is the number of commodities. Finally, we assume that disturbances corresponding to distinct observations are uncorrelated.

The aggregate expenditure shares at any point of time are equal to the individual shares multiplied by the ratio of individual expenditure to aggregate expenditure. Although the data for individual consuming units and for the aggregate of all consuming units are based on the same definitions, the methods of measurement are not the same. Accordingly, we introduce an additional random component in the equations for the aggregate expenditure shares. This component corresponds to errors of measurement in the observations on individual expenditure shares that underly the observations of the aggregate expenditure shares.

We assume that the errors of measurement that underly the aggregate expenditure shares have expected value equal to zero. These errors of measurement, like the individual disturbances, sum to zero for each unit in each time period and are not distributed independently. We assume that the covariance matrix of the errors of observation has rank equal to $N - 1$. Finally, we assume that the errors of measurement corresponding to distinct observations are uncorrelated.

The aggregate disturbances are weighted averages of the individual disturbances and the errors of measurement. As a consequence, the aggregate disturbances corresponding to different time periods are heteroscedastic. We can correct for heteroscedasticity by transforming the observations on the aggregate expenditure shares. The transformed aggregate disturbances have expected value equal to zero for all observations and have a covariance matrix with rank $N - 1$. We assume that the errors of measurement corresponding to distinct observations are uncorrelated, so that the aggregate disturbances for distinct observations are also uncorrelated.

In our application of the translog model of aggregate consumer expenditure presented in Section VII, we pool cross section data on individual expenditure patterns with time series data on aggregate expenditure patterns. We first estimate the parameters of a model for single cross section of observations on individual expenditure patterns, assuming that the prices for all consumers are the same for all individuals. This model can be regarded as a linear, multivariate, regression model, so that the parameters that can be identified from a single cross section can be estimated by applying ordinary least squares to each equation separately. These parameters are associated with total expenditures and demographic characteristics of individual households.

The second step in pooling individual cross section data with aggregate time series data is to estimate the parameters of a model for a time series of observations on aggregate expenditure patterns. In this model we treat the prices and the expenditure statistic $\Sigma M_k \ln M_{kt}/\Sigma M_{kt}$ as jointly dependent variables. A second complication is that too few time series observations are available to identify all the parameters of the model of aggregate consumer behavior.

To identify the unknown parameters we combine cross section and time series data. We introduce a sufficient number of instrumental variables to identify all parameters. Given the identification of the parameters from the model combining time series and cross section data, we apply the methods of inequality constrained nonlinear three stage least squares to obtain an estimator of the parameters of the complete model. The resulting estimator is consistent and asymptotically efficient in the class of instrumental variables estimators utilizing the instruments we have chosen.

A substantial simplification in the computations required for the estimator pooling cross section and time series data results from the theory of exact aggregation. The iterative process for the pooled estimator depends only on moments computed as part of the evaluation of the least squares estimator for the cross section model. The individual observations from the cross section data are not required for the pooled estimator, provided that the ordinary least squares estimator of the cross section model is computed first to obtain an initial estimator of the parameters of this model.

VII. AGGREGATE CONSUMER BEHAVIOR IN THE UNITED STATES, 1958–1974

In this Section we present the empirical results of implementing the econometric model of aggregate consumer behavior discussed in Section VI. For this purpose we employ cross section observations on individual expenditure patterns in the United States during the year 1972. We combine these cross section data with time series observations on aggregate expenditure patterns in the United States for the period 1958–1974. We first employ a model of individual expenditure allocation as a basis for estimating the parameters that can be identified from cross section data alone. We then employ a model of aggregate expenditure allocation as a basis for estimating the remaining parameters of the model from time series, holding the values of parameters estimated from cross section data fixed. Finally, we pool time series and cross section data to estimate all of the parameters of our model of aggregate consumer behavior.

We begin by discussing the allocation of consumer expenditures among commodity groups. We next consider the classification of consuming units by demographic characteristics. We then describe the data sources we have employed and the assumptions we have imposed in combining the data sources. We present estimates of the parameters of the transcendental logarithmic model of aggregate consumer behavior. To characterize these estimates we analyze changes in patterns of individual expenditures with changes in demographic characteristics of individual consuming units. We also describe differences in expenditure and price elasticities of demand for consuming units with different demographic characteristics.

A.   Commodities and Consuming Units

Total consumer expenditure is defined as the sum of all expenditures on nondurable goods and services, plus the services of durable goods. We analyze patterns of consumer expenditures as flows of goods and services with purchases of durables treated as investment, increasing the stock of durables and replacing elements of the stock as they wear out. We divide consumer expenditures into five broad categories:

1. *Energy*. Expenditures on electricity, gas, heating oil, and gasoline.
2. *Food and clothing*. Expenditures on food, beverages and tobacco, clothing expenditures, and other related expenditures.
3. *Consumer services*. Expenditures on services, such as entertainment, maintenance and repairs of automobiles and housing, tailoring, cleaning, and insurance.
4. *Capital services*. The service flow from consumer durables as well as the service flow from housing.
5. *Other nondurable expenditure*. The remainder of the budget, which includes transportation and trade margins from other expenditures.

Our allocation of the consumer budget into five commodity groups embodies a set of restrictions on the allocation of expenditures within each commodity group. We assume that the direct utility function is homothetically separable in goods within each commodity group. This implies that the indirect utility function is homothetically separable in the prices of goods within each group. More specifically, we assume that the price for each commodity group is a homogeneous translog function of its components, so that:

$$\ln p_n = \ln p^{n'} \alpha_p^n + \tfrac{1}{2} \ln p^{n'} B_{pp}^n \ln p^n \qquad (177)$$

where

$\ln p^n = (\ln p_{n1}, \ln p_{n2} \ldots \ln p_{nM_n})$ Vector of logarithms of prices for the M_n goods within the nth commodity group,

and the vector α_p^n and the matrix B_{pp}^n satisfy the restrictions

$$\iota' \alpha_p^n = -1$$

$$\iota' B_{pp}^n = 0$$

The price index

$$\Delta \ln p_n = \bar{w}^{n'} \Delta \ln p^n, \qquad (178)$$

is exact for the homogeneous translog functions,[24] where

$\bar{w}^n = (\bar{w}_{n1}, \bar{w}_{n2}, \ldots, \bar{w}_{nM_n})$ Vector of average budget shares for the M_n goods within the nth commodity group,

and

$$\bar{w}_{nm} = \tfrac{1}{2}(w_{nm,t} + w_{nm,t-1}) \qquad (m = 1, 2, \ldots, M_n)$$

The basic consuming unit employed in this study is the household. Unrelated individuals are considered to be households of size one. All consuming units are classified by attributes that reflect differences in preferences among consuming units. We employ the following demographic characteristics as attributes of households:

1. Family size: 1, 2, 3, 4, 5, 6, and 7 or more persons.
2. Age of head: 15–24, 25–34, 35–44, 45–54, 55–65, 65 and over.
3. Region of residence: Northeast, North Central, South and West.
4. Race: White, nonwhite.
5. Type of residence: Urban, rural.

Each household is assigned to one of the categories for each of the five demographic characteristics. Since these categories are discrete, integer-valued variables are required to represent the attributes.

Under exact aggregation all attributes appear linearly in the functions that determine shares of individual expenditures. We impose no *a priori* restrictions on the form of the impact on expenditure patterns of variations in demographic characteristics among consuming units. If, for example, we were to include an integer-valued variable with value equal to family size as a determinant of individual expenditure patterns, we would implicitly impose a constraint on the effects of different family sizes. To avoid these implicit constraints, we represent each family size by a qualitative or dummy variable, so that the precise pattern of the impacts of changes in family size can be estimated. To avoid singularity of the matrix of dummy variables we take all variables to be zero for unrelated individuals, age 15–24, living in the Northeast, white in race, and living in an urban area. This leaves 16 qualitative variables to be treated as separate consumer attributes in representing the effects of demographic characteristics on preferences of consuming units.

We next turn to a discussion of data sources for our study. For time series observations on aggregate expenditure patterns we take data on personal consumption expenditures from the U.S. Interindustry Transactions Accounts for the period 1958–1974.[25] These data are very similar to data from the National Income and Product Accounts (NIPA) with two exceptions. First, we consider purchases of durable goods to be investment rather than consumption; the corresponding service flow from the stock of durables is the appropriate measure of personal consumption.[26] Second, trade and transportation margins are separated from final purchases, so that all goods and services are evaluated at producers' prices.

We employ data on household expenditure patterns for the year 1972 from the 1972–1973 Survey of Consumer Expenditures (CES), collected and published by the Bureau of Labor Statistics.[27] The CES data categories correspond fairly closely to those within the NIPA accounts, so that we were able to employ a bridge between the U.S. Interindustry Accounts and the U.S. National Income and Product Accounts[28] to transform observations on individual expenditures to appropriate commodity groups.

A key feature of the exact aggregation approach is the incorporation of the distribution of individual expenditures into the determination of aggregate expenditure patterns. We have a detailed description of the distribution of total expenditures in 1972, the year of our cross section survey, plus a detailed tabulation of before tax income for all years from *Current Population Reports, Series P-60, Consumer Income.*[29] To construct the statistics of the joint distribution of attributes and expenditures required for our model of aggregate consumer behavior, we have constructed a mapping from the distribution of before tax income to the distribution of total expenditure, using the detailed information about these distributions available from our cross section data.[30]

First, we characterize the tax structure in each year empirically by means of a mapping between the before tax and after tax income distributions. This mapping is not exact so that the tax rates for demographically identical families with the same income are measured with a residual. However, the mapping is sufficiently detailed to provide statistics of the after tax income distribution from those of the before-tax income distribution. Second, we map the distribution of after-tax income into the distribution of expenditure, by using the permanent income model. We assume that income and expenditure are joint log normally distributed, so that the marginal distribution of expenditure is lognormal. On the basis of similar assumptions for groups of the population classified by demographic characteristics we determine the distribution of expenditure over groups from the distribution of income over groups.

The translog model of aggregate consumer behavior requires variables that depend only on the distribution of individual expenditures:

$$\frac{\sum_{k=1}^{K} M_{kt} \ln M_{kt}}{\sum_{k=1}^{K} M_{kt}} = \mu_M + \sigma_M^2 \qquad (t = 1, 2, \ldots, T) \qquad (179)$$

where the logarithm of expenditure M has a normal distribution with mean μ_M and variance σ_M^2, and variables that depend on the distribution of individual attributes and expenditures of the form

$$\frac{\sum_{k=1}^{K} M_{kt} A_{kt}}{\sum_{k=1}^{K} M_{kt}} \qquad (t = 1, 2, \ldots, T) \qquad (180)$$

Finally, we require the heteroscedasticity correction ρ_t of Section VI, which takes the form:

$$\rho_t = \frac{\left(\sum_{k=1}^{K} M_{kt}\right)^2}{\sum_{k=1}^{K} M_{kt}^2} = \sqrt{K}\, e^{-1/2\, \sigma_M^2} \qquad (t = 1, 2, \ldots, T) \qquad (181)$$

where, without loss of generality, we normalize population size to one in 1972. Together with the time series of prices and aggregate expenditure shares, the variables (179–181) form a complete set of aggregate data for the translog model for the period 1958–1974.

B.   Estimation Results

The translog model of individual expenditures described in Section VI can be represented in the form:

$$w_{kt} = \frac{1}{D_t}\left(\alpha_p + B_{pp}\ln p_t - B_{pp}\iota \ln M_{kt} + B_{pA}A_k\right) + \varepsilon_{kt}$$

$$(k = 1, 2, \ldots, K;\, t = 1, 2, \ldots, T) \qquad (182)$$

where

$$D_t = -1 + \iota' B_{pp}\ln p_t \qquad (t = 1, 2, \ldots, T)$$

w_{kt} is the vector of observed budget shares, M_{kt} is expenditure for the kth consuming unit at time t, $\ln p_t$ is the vector of logarithms of prices at time t, and A_k is the vector of attributes of the kth consuming unit. The unobservable random disturbance ε_{kt} is distributed normally with mean zero and covariance matrix Ω_ε.

The cross section model for a sample of size K' in 1972 with all prices equal to unity and time equal to zero is:

$$w_{k,1972} = -\alpha_p + B_{pp}\iota \ln M_{k,1972} - B_{pA}A_k + \varepsilon_{k,1972}$$

$$(k = 1, 2, \ldots, K') \qquad (183)$$

where we have set $\iota'\alpha_p = -1$; the disturbance term $\varepsilon_{k,1972}$ is assumed to be uncorrelated among consuming units.

The translog model of aggregate expenditures, corrected for heteroscedasticity, is:

$$\rho_t w_t = \rho_t \frac{\sum_{k=1}^{K} M_{kt}w_{kt}}{\sum_{k=1}^{K} M_{kt}} = \frac{1}{D_t}\left[\alpha_p\rho_t + B_{pp}\rho_t \ln p_t - B_{pp}\iota\, \rho_t \frac{\sum_{k=1}^{K} M_{kt}\ln M_{kt}}{\sum_{k=1}^{K} M_{kt}}\right]$$

$$+ B_{pA}\rho_t \frac{\displaystyle\sum_{k=1}^{K} M_{kt}A_k}{\displaystyle\sum_{k=1}^{K} M_{kt}} + \rho_t\varepsilon_t \quad (t = 1, 2, \ldots, T) \quad (184)$$

where the unobservable random disturbance $\rho_t\varepsilon_t$ is normally distributed with mean zero and covariance matrix Ω_v; we assume that this disturbance is uncorrelated over time.

In our application we have five commodity groups so that we estimate four equations. As unknown parameters we have four elements of the vector α_p, four expenditure coefficients of the vector $B_{pp}\iota$, sixteen attribute coefficients for each of the four equations in the matrix B_{pA}, plus ten price coefficients in the matrix B_{pp}, which is symmetric. We have a total of 82 unknown parameters to be estimated. Since there are only seventeen time series data points and we utilize fourteen instrumental variables, not all of the parameters can be identified from time series data alone. Since there is no price variation in the cross section, the remaining parameters of the matrix B_{pp} cannot be identified from the cross section model alone.

We first estimate the cross section model by ordinary least squares from data on individual expenditures, as outlined in Section VI. We present the results in Appendix I. Next, we estimate the complete model, subject to the inequality restrictions implied by monotonicity of the individual expenditure shares, pooling time series and cross section data. The results are given in Table 3. We now turn to a detailed discussion of the inequality constrained pooled results, utilizing the cross section results only for comparison.

We begin our discussion of the pooled estimation results by comparing the final estimates of the impact of total expenditure and demographic characteristics to those obtained from the cross section model alone. Next, we analyze the impact of changes in total expenditure and demographic characteristics. Finally, we present price and expenditure elasticities calculations to illustrate the character of our pooled results. As an overview of the pooled estimates, we see that most of the unknown parameters are estimated very precisely. This is largely due to the enormous quantity of data that enters the pooling process. The price coefficients that appear in the numerators of the functions giving expenditure shares for commodity groups have relatively large standard errors by comparison with the attribute coefficients; this is to be expected, since there is no price variation in the cross section data. By contrast the price coefficients that appear in the denominators are estimated very precisely. These coefficients are estimated by pooling time series and cross section data.

The patterns of demographic effects, such as increases in the shares of food and clothing with increases in family size, are the same in the estimates from cross section alone and the pooled estimates. This invalidates the usual criticism of pooling cross section and aggregate time-series, namely, that the aggregate data reflect only short run determinants of expenditure patterns, resulting in smaller effects in the time series than the cross section.[31] It appears to be very likely that the demographic effects in the aggregate data capture the underlying dynamics of the processes determining changes in aggregate expenditure patterns.[32]

C.   Individual Expenditure Patterns

We next turn to a discussion of the impact of change in expenditure and demographic characteristics on individual expenditure patterns. In

Table 3.   Pooled Estimation Results

Notation:

W	budget share
ln p	log price

In order to designate the proper good to which W or ln p refers, we append the following subscripts where appropriate:

EN	energy
FC	food and clothing
O	other nondurable goods
CAP	capital services
SERV	consumer services

Further notation is given as:

ln M	log total expenditure
F2	dummy for family size 2
F3	dummy for family size 3
F4	dummy for family size 4
F5	dummy for family size 5
F6	dummy for family size 6
F7	dummy for family size 7 or more
A30	dummy for age class 25–34
A40	dummy for age class 35–44
A50	dummy for age class 45–54
A60	dummy for age class 55–64
A70	dummy for age class 65 and older
RNC	dummy for region North Central
RS	dummy for region South
RW	dummy for region West
RNW	dummy for nonwhite head
RUR	dummy for rural residence

$$D(p) = -1 - .01814 \ln p_{EN} - .06201 \ln p_{FC} - .03097 \ln p_{O}$$
$$ (.000660) \quad\quad (.00137) \quad\quad\quad (.00123)$$
$$+ .1507 \ln p_{CAP} - .03965 \ln p_{SERV}$$
$$(.00308) \quad\quad\quad (.00286)$$

Table 3. continued

Equation	Variable	Numerator Coefficient	Standard Error
WEN	Constant	−.1845	.00601
	ln p_{EN}	.02659	.0125
	ln p_{FC}	−.02255	.0254
	ln p_0	.005458	.0191
	ln p_{CAP}	−.008346	.0207
	ln p_{SERV}	−.01929*	.0243*
	ln M	.01814	.000660
	F2	−.01550	.000974
	F3	−.01900	.00114
	F4	−.02201	.00125
	F5	−.02209	.00143
	F6	−.02524	.00173
	F7	−.02372	.00182
	A30	−.001581	.00134
	A40	−.003679	.00144
	A50	−.005671	.00138
	A60	−.008287	.00137
	A70	−.007465	.00133
	RNC	−.008694	.000910
	RS	−.007465	.000908
	RW	.004283	.000978
	RNW	.003624	.00116
	RUR	−.01767	.000978
WFC	Constant	−.7155	.0126
	ln p_{EN}	−.02255	.0254
	ln p_{FC}	.07251	.110
	ln p_0	.01702	.0906
	ln p_{CAP}	−.1083	.0514
	ln p_{SERV}	−.02069*	.0900*
	ln M	.06201	.00137
	F2	−.03461	.00203
	F3	−.05254	.00239
	F4	−.06782	.00260
	F5	−.08293	.00299
	F6	−.08945	.00361
	F7	−.1148	.00380
	A30	−.02209	.00281
	A40	−.04021	.00302
	A50	−.04769	.00288
	A60	−.04689	.00287
	A70	−.03444	.00279
	RNC	.01792	.00189
	RS	.01216	.00189
	RW	.01381	.00204
	RNW	−.01138	.00242
	RUR	.007507	.00188

Table 3.   continued

Equation	Variable	Numerator Coefficient	Standard Error
WO	Constant	− .4452	.0110
	ln p_{EN}	.005458	.0191
	ln p_{FC}	.01702	.0906
	ln p_0	.1723	.123
	ln p_{CAP}	− .1710	.0362
	ln p_{SERV}	− .05472*	.0357*
	ln M	.03097	.00123
	F2	− .01588	.00182
	F3	− .02667	.00214
	F4	− .03366	.00234
	F5	− .03707	.00268
	F6	− .04314	.00324
	F7	− .05565	.00341
	A30	− .01318	.00252
	A40	− .01646	.00270
	A50	− .01928	.00258
	A60	− .01746	.00257
	A70	− .003344	.00250
	RNC	.009577	.00170
	RS	− .0001790	.00169
	RW	.008988	.00183
	RNW	− .004260	.00217
	RUR	− .0001298	.00169
WCAP	Constant	1.0906	.0273
	ln p_{EN}	− .008346	.0207
	ln p_{FC}	− .1083	.0514
	ln p_0	− .1710	.0362
	ln p_{CAP}	.5929	.0481
	ln p_{SERV}	− .1544*	.0540*
	ln M	− .1507	.00308
	F2	.006422	.00456
	F3	.01695	.00537
	F4	.02416	.00585
	F5	.02668	.00671
	F6	.03810	.00811
	F7	.06580	.00853
	A30	.03668	.00632
	A40	.04184	.00678
	A50	.04674	.00646
	A60	.03187	.00645
	A70	− .002706	.00627
	RNC	− .04193	.00426
	RS	− .02927	.00425
	RW	− .01785	.00458
	RNW	.02118	.00543
	RUR	− .04590	.00423

Table 3. continued

Equation	Variable	Numerator Coefficient	Standard Error
WSERV	Constant	−.7452*	.0255*
	ln p_{EN}	−.01929*	.0243*
	ln p_{FC}	−.02069*	.0900*
	ln p_0	−.05472*	.0357*
	ln p_{CAP}	−.1544*	.0540*
	ln p_{SERV}	.2094*	.105*
	ln M	.03965*	.00286*
	F2	.05958*	.00424*
	F3	.08126*	.00500*
	F4	.09934*	.00545*
	F5	.1154*	.00625*
	F6	.1197*	.00755*
	F7	.1284*	.00794*
	A30	.0001850*	.00588*
	A40	.01851*	.00631*
	A50	.02590*	.00602*
	A60	.04076*	.00600*
	A70	.04795*	.00584*
	RNC	.02313*	.00397*
	RS	.02474*	.00396*
	RW	−.009231*	.00426*
	RNW	−.009156*	.00506*
	RUR	.05620*	.00394*

Estimate of Covariance Matrix Σ_v

	WEN	*WFC*	*WO*	*WCAP*
WEN	.000009436			
WFC	−.000003545	.00008021		
WO	−.000002289	−.00001017	.000007800	
WCAP	−.00001444	.00002593	−.000005464	.00004371

SSR = 32626.58.
Gauss Newton algorithm.
Convergence criterion = .01.
Convergence achieved after one iteration.

*Derived from estimated coefficients.

addition to the estimated coefficients we present the results graphically in order to bring out their implications more clearly. In the graphs employed to depict individual expenditure patterns we use a "typical" consumer unit with family size five, age of head 35–44 years, living in the Northeast, white in race, with an urban residence, having a total expenditure of $9,000 as a basis for comparison. The choice of another base case would shift the curves vertically, but would leave the relative impact of changes in demographic characteristics unchanged.[33]

1. *Total Expenditure*

In Figure 1 we display the effects of changing expenditure on individual expenditure patterns on each commodity. We see that as expenditure increases, the share devoted to capital services increases, while all other shares decrease. The effect is quite strong for low expenditure values and diminishes as total expenditure grows.[34] The overall behavior of the individual expenditure shares with respect to changes in expenditure corresponds quite closely to what might be expected. The goods energy and food and clothing correspond most closely to basic necessities. As expenditure increases, the shares of energy and food and clothing decline. The dramatic growth of the capital services share as expenditure increases indicates that capital services are a luxury good. The individual expenditure shares of consumer services and other nondurables diminish at a much lower rate than those for energy and food and clothing as expenditure increases, and remain fairly constant over a large range of expenditure. This indicates that the expenditures on services and other nondurables grow at approximately the same rate as total expenditure.

Nonnegativity in our model is equivalent to the condition that all budget shares are between zero and unity. Since the equations for individual expenditure shares are linear in the logarithms of expenditure, there is a range of expenditure for each share and for each set of attributes where nonnegativity holds. We investigate the range of total expenditure for which nonnegativity holds for 1972 by presenting two sets of calculations. First, we calculate the range of admissible shares for a typical family in 1972, of family size five, age of head 35–44, Northeast region, white race, and urban residence. Second, we calculate the greatest lower bound on expenditure and the least upper bound which allows the share to fall between zero and unity. These calculations are presented in Table 4.

For our typical family, we see that nonnegativity will hold for expenditures between $2,427 and $112,198. This range certainly includes almost all families with the typical attributes. The large lower bound is due to the capital services equation. At any rate, for the typical set of attributes, the proportion of the population on which nonnegativity fails is quite small. The greatest lower bound is $3,997 from capital services, for families of size seven or more, head age 35–44, living in the urban Northeast, and nonwhite in race. Thus nonnegativity fails for large nonwhite families with income less than $3,997. The least upper bound is $11,981, for single nonwhites, age 20 living in the urban West. Except for consumer services, all upper bounds are generated by unrelated in-

Figure 1. Expenditure Shares as Functions of Total
Expenditure, 1972*

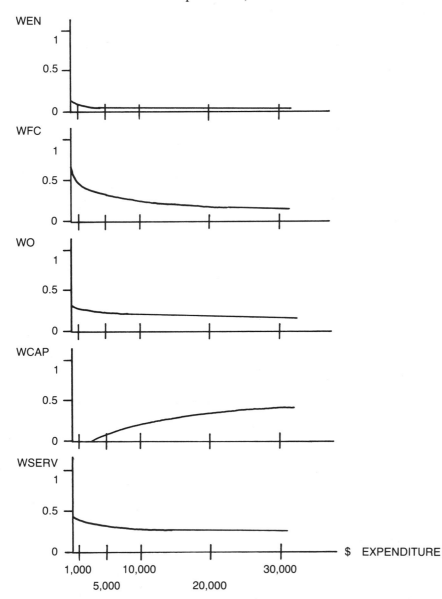

* Reference family has: family size = 5, age = 35–44, region = Northeast, race = white,
  residence = urban.

Table 4.   Nonnegativity Bounds, 1972*

Share	Lower Bound	Upper Bound
WEN	1.0×10^{-18}	112,198
WFC	0.15	492,820
WO	1.2×10^{-7}	8,588,666
WCAP	2,427	1,386,632
WSERV	9.8×10^{-8}	4,880,149

* Reference family has: family size = 5, age = 35–44; region = Northeast, race = white, residence = urban.

Greatest Lower Bounds, 1972

Share	Bound	Attributes
WEN	6.2×10^{-18}	FS = 7, A = 55–64, R = NC, RC = White, RES = Rural
WFC	0.40	FS = 7, A = 35–44, R = NE, RC = White, RES = Urban
WO	3.7×10^{-7}	FS = 7, A = 35–44, R = S, RC = Nonwhite, RES = Urban
WCAP	3,997	FS = 7, A = 35–44, R = NE, RC = Nonwhite, RES = Urban
WSERV	0.01	FS = 1, A = 15–24, R = W, RC = Nonwhite, RES = Urban

Least Upper Bounds, 1972

Share	Bound	Attributes
WEN	11,981	FS = 1, A = 15–24, R = W, RC = Nonwhite, RES = Urban
WFC	28,640	FS = 1, A = 15–24, R = NC, RC = Nonwhite, RES = Rural
WO	604,564	FS = 1, A = 15–24, R = NC, RC = White, RES = Rural
WCAP	403,061	FS = 1, A = 15–24, R = NC, RC = White, RES = Rural
WSERV	198,986	FS = 7, A = 65 and over, R = S, RC = White, RES = Rural

dividuals of age 15–24. Again, except for consumer services, all lower bounds are generated by families of size seven or more.

2. *Family Size.*

Figure 2 depicts the effects of family size on relative expenditure shares. We see that as family size changes from one to seven or more, the shares of energy, food and clothing, and other nondurable expend-

Figure 2. Expenditure Shares as Functions of Family Size, 1972*

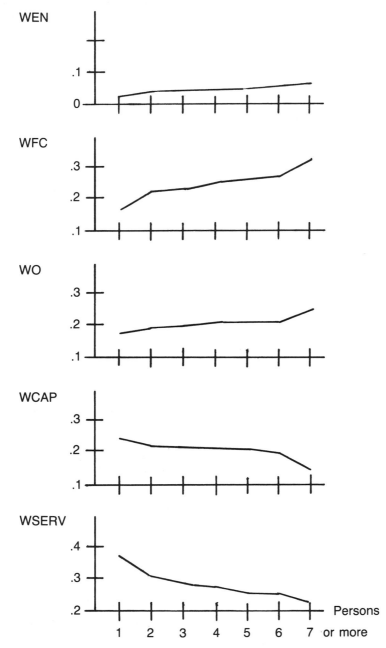

* Reference family has: expenditure = $9,000, age = 35–44, region = Northeast, race = white, residence = urban.

itures increase, whereas the shares of capital services and consumer services decrease. A striking feature of these graphs is the abrupt changes from family size one to two and from six to seven or more. For families of sizes two to six the share of energy remains roughly constant, food and clothing and other nondurable expenditure show a monotonic increase, matched by smooth decreases in capital and consumer services. Larger families buy more food and clothing and employ fewer services, such as entertainment.

The movement from family size one to two involves a substantial alteration of expenditure patterns. Two person families spend a much larger proportion of their budget on necessities than unrelated individuals and spend less on capital services and consumer services with the same total expenditure. Similarly, the movement from family size six to seven or more involves a sizable change in expenditure patterns, especially in food and clothing. Expenditures on food and clothing are higher, expenditure shares of energy and other nondurable expenditures are relatively large, and expenditure shares devoted to capital services and consumer services are quite small. The abruptness of the change in expenditure patterns results from the fact that the size category seven or more includes not only families of size seven or eight, but also those of larger size, such as twelve and fifteen.

3. Age of Head

The impact of age of head of families on expenditure patterns is depicted in Figure 3.[35] We see that the age of head has impacts that are not monotonic. The energy shares increases a small amount, food and clothing grows until approximately age 40, levels off and then decreases. The capital services share shows the opposite profile to food and clothing. Consumer services decline relatively smoothly and other nondurable expenditures rise and then fall a small amount. A plausible explanation of this behavior is that the age of head is highly correlated with the ages of children in the family. When the head is young, so are the children and so relatively small amounts are allocated to food and clothing. As the head ages, the children need more food for growth and more clothing; the family allocates more expenditure to food and clothing. This is associated with a decrease in the shares of capital services and consumer services. The food and clothing share peaks, levels off, and drops as the head ages further.

4. Region and Race

In Figure 4 we present the impact of demographic characteristics—region, race, and type of residence. The region effects are rather small for energy and other nondurables, but households living in North Central

Figure 3.　Expenditure Shares as Functions of Age of Head, 1972*

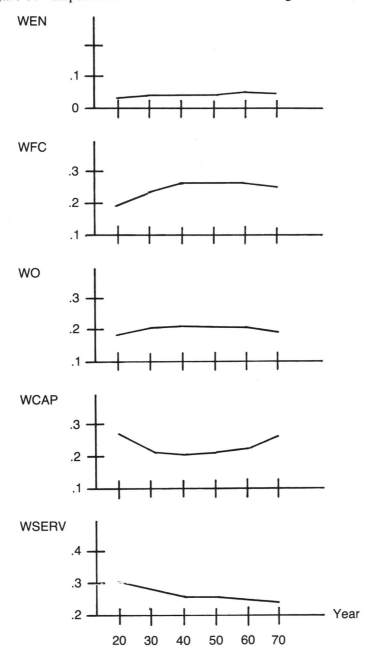

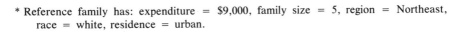

* Reference family has: expenditure = \$9,000, family size = 5, region = Northeast, race = white, residence = urban.

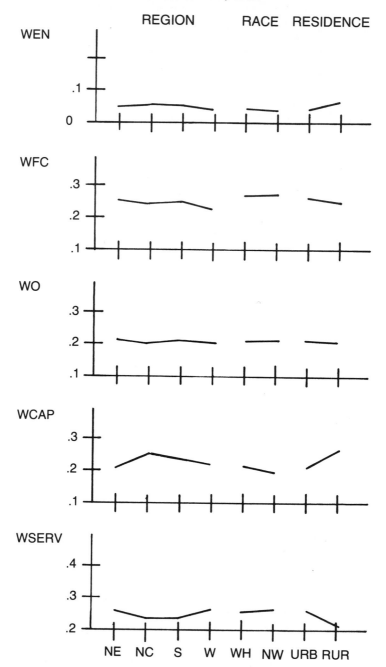

Figure 4. Expenditure Shares as Functions of Region, Race, and Residence, 1972*

* Reference family has: expenditure = $9,000, family size = 5, region = Northeast, race = white, residence = urban.

and Southern regions use relatively more capital services from homes and automobiles. Increased use of capital is accompanied by a small increase in energy use. These increases are associated with a fall in the share of consumer services. The Northeast and West regions are virtually indistinguishable in individual expenditure patterns with only a slight increase in capital services and consumer services and a slight decrease in food and clothing for the West. The white-nonwhite distinction has no substantial effect on the shares of energy, food and clothing, or other nondurable expenditures. The only difference between whites and non-whites is a smaller share devoted to capital services and a larger share devoted to consumer services for nonwhites.

5. *Type of Residence*

The final difference in demographic characteristics that we analyze, type of residence, is also depicted in Figure 4. Food and clothing and other nondurable expenditure shares are smaller for rural families; the shares of capital services and energy are much larger and the consumer services share is much smaller for these families. Except for food and clothing, these impacts are exactly as expected. Being relatively distant from urban areas, rural families tend to employ much more capital services in the form of homes and automobiles. In order to use the increased capital services, more energy is acquired. This is associated with a reduced share of consumer services, which are less available to rural locations.

We are left with the problem of explaining the decrease in the share of food and clothing for rural households. Some of the food consumed by the family may be produced at home and may be underreported in our data. Under this interpretation it is quite likely that rural families have expenditure greater than the $9,000 indicated in Figure 4. The large increase in the share of capital services may be partly due to differences in consumption patterns and partly due to larger expenditure. Similar remarks would apply to the share of consumer services. The energy share also shows a marked difference; the effect of increased expenditure would lessen rather than increase it.

6. *Elasticity Calculation*

As a further illustration of the differences in preferences among individual consuming units represented in our model, we give budget shares, price elasticities, and expenditure elasticities for all commodities in Table 5. Different budget shares, price elasticities, and expenditure elasticities are given by the model for each set of total expenditure levels and demographic characteristics. By varying total expenditure and each demographic characteristic, we obtain an indication of the variation in elasticities among consuming units. Unless otherwise indicated we con-

Table 5.   Estimated Budget Shares, Price and Expenditure
Elasticities, 1972*

Expen-diture	$5,000	$10,000	$15,000	$20,000	$25,000	$30,000	$35,000
			BUDGET SHARES				
EN	0.055802	0.043229	0.035874	0.030655	0.026607	0.023300	0.020504
FC	0.310471	0.267483	0.242337	0.224496	0.210657	0.199350	0.189790
O	0.234992	0.213524	0.200967	0.192057	0.185146	0.179500	0.174726
CAP	0.125156	0.229674	0.290813	0.334191	0.367838	0.395330	0.418574
SERV	0.273579	0.246090	0.230010	0.218601	0.209751	0.202520	0.196407
			INCOME ELASTICITIES				
EN	0.674924	0.580371	0.494335	0.408253	0.318229	0.221455	0.115277
FC	0.800247	0.768144	0.744086	0.723748	0.705600	0.688902	0.673231
O	0.868205	0.854955	0.845892	0.838743	0.832724	0.827462	0.822747
CAP	2.204792	1.656527	1.518502	1.451200	1.409927	1.381420	1.360240
SERV	0.855037	0.838844	0.827577	0.818578	0.810924	0.804173	0.798078
			PRICE ELASTICITIES				
EN	−1.494684	−1.633294	−1.759418	−1.885610	−2.017580	−2.159447	−2.315099
FC	−1.295595	−1.333133	−1.361265	−1.385047	−1.406268	−1.425794	−1.444118
O	−1.764320	−1.838050	−1.888480	−1.928261	−1.961754	−1.991034	−2.017266
CAP	−5.586618	−3.430767	−2.888035	−2.623392	−2.461103	−2.349010	−2.265725
SERV	−1.805281	−1.890805	−1.950310	−1.997838	−2.038265	−2.073918	−2.106111

Family Size	1	2	3	4	5	6	7 or more
			BUDGET SHARES				
EN	0.023044	0.038553	0.042048	0.045057	0.045140	0.048289	0.046764
FC	0.191084	0.225695	0.243628	0.258906	0.274017	0.280543	0.305953
O	0.179716	0.195603	0.206391	0.213384	0.216787	0.222865	0.235371
CAP	0.240472	0.234050	0.223513	0.216312	0.213787	0.202370	0.174666
SERV	0.365684	0.306100	0.284419	0.266340	0.250268	0.245932	0.237246
			INCOME ELASTICITIES				
EN	0.212801	0.529477	0.568586	0.597398	0.598138	0.624345	0.612096
FC	0.675444	0.725215	0.745442	0.760464	0.773673	0.778938	0.797297
O	0.827669	0.841666	0.849942	0.854860	0.857138	0.861035	0.868418
CAP	1.627045	1.644252	1.674622	1.697080	1.705315	1.745104	1.863287
SERV	0.891549	0.870438	0.860562	0.851097	0.841535	0.838741	0.832836
			PRICE ELASTICITIES				
EN	−2.172133	−1.707903	−1.650570	−1.608333	−1.607248	−1.568831	−1.586787
FC	−1.441531	−1.383332	−1.359680	−1.342115	−1.326668	−1.320512	−1.299044
O	−1.989877	−1.911994	−1.865942	−1.838579	−1.825902	−1.804222	−1.763138
CAP	−3.314841	−3.382500	−3.501918	−3.590228	−3.622607	−3.779064	−4.243776
SERV	−1.612444	−1.723941	−1.776101	−1.826091	−1.876594	−1.891351	−1.922535

Table 5. continued

Age of Head	15–24	25–34	35–44	45–54	55–64	65 & over
			BUDGET SHARES			
EN	0.041461	0.043043	0.045140	0.047132	0.049748	0.048926
FC	0.233801	0.255901	0.274017	0.281497	0.280692	0.268242
O	0.200322	0.213512	0.216787	0.219610	0.217789	0.203667
CAP	0.255627	0.218941	0.213787	0.208882	0.223749	0.258334
SERV	0.268788	0.268603	0.250268	0.242878	0.228022	0.220831
			INCOME ELASTICITIES			
EN	0.562479	0.578559	0.598138	0.615123	0.635362	0.629235
FC	0.734743	0.757651	0.773673	0.779687	0.779055	0.768800
O	0.845396	0.854947	0.857138	0.858975	0.857796	0.847935
CAP	1.589871	1.688711	1.705315	1.721877	1.673910	1.583690
SERV	0.852453	0.852351	0.841535	0.836713	0.826074	0.820411
			PRICE ELASTICITIES			
EN	− 1.659523	− 1.635950	− 1.607248	− 1.582350	− 1.552681	− 1.561662
FC	− 1.372190	− 1.345404	− 1.326668	− 1.319636	− 1.320375	− 1.332366
O	− 1.891238	− 1.838096	− 1.825902	− 1.815683	− 1.822244	− 1.877112
CAP	− 3.168664	− 3.557318	− 3.622607	− 3.687730	− 3.499118	− 3.144363
SERV	− 1.818929	− 1.819466	− 1.876594	− 1.902060	− 1.958249	− 1.988159

Region	Northeast	North Central	South	West
		BUDGET SHARES		
EN	0.045140	0.053835	0.052606	0.040856
FC	0.274017	0.256097	0.261848	0.260199
O	0.216787	0.207210	0.216966	0.207799
CAP	0.213787	0.255727	0.243058	0.231645
SERV	0.250268	0.227131	0.225522	0.259500
		INCOME ELASTICITIES		
EN	0.598138	0.663044	0.655172	0.556001
FC	0.773673	0.757836	0.763155	0.761654
O	0.857138	0.850535	0.857256	0.850959
CAP	1.705315	1.589641	1.620376	1.650940
SERV	0.841535	0.825392	0.824146	0.847172
		PRICE ELASTICITIES		
EN	− 1.607248	− 1.512100	− 1.523641	− 1.669020
FC	− 1.326668	− 1.345187	− 1.338967	− 1.340723
O	− 1.825902	− 1.862642	− 1.825246	− 1.860285
CAP	− 3.622607	− 3.167763	− 3.288614	− 3.408797
SERV	− 1.876594	− 1.961853	− 1.968432	− 1.846820

Table 5. concluded

Race and Residence	White	Nonwhite	Urban	Rural
		BUDGET SHARES		
EN	0.045140	0.041516	0.045140	0.062818
FC	0.274017	0.285407	0.274017	0.266510
O	0.216787	0.221047	0.216787	0.216917
CAP	0.213787	0.192606	0.213787	0.259689
SERV	0.250268	0.259424	0.250268	0.194065
		INCOME ELASTICITIES		
EN	0.598138	0.563058	0.598138	0.711228
FC	0.773673	0.782705	0.773673	0.767298
O	0.857138	0.859892	0.857138	0.857224
CAP	1.705315	1.782879	1.705315	1.580644
SERV	0.841535	0.847127	0.841535	0.795641
		PRICE ELASTICITIES		
EN	− 1.607248	− 1.658674	− 1.607248	− 1.441464
FC	− 1.326668	− 1.316107	− 1.326668	− 1.334123
O	− 1.825902	− 1.810581	− 1.825902	− 1.825426
CAP	− 3.622607	− 3.927601	− 3.622607	− 3.132384
SERV	− 1.876594	− 1.847056	− 1.876594	− 2.118979

* Reference family has: expenditure = \$9,000, family size = five, age = 35–44, region = Northeast, race = white, residence = urban.

sider consuming units with expenditure of \$9,000, family size five, age of head 35–44 years, living in the Northeast region, white, and having an urban residence.

We see that as total expenditure increases, expenditure allocation becomes significantly less sensitive to changes in total expenditure and more sensitive to changes in all prices except the price of capital services. Expenditure elasticities of demand decrease with total expenditure for all commodity groups and price elasticities of demand increase with total expenditure for all commodity groups except for capital services. Variations in family size are almost, but not quite, a mirror image of variations in total expenditure. As family size increases, the expenditure elasticities of demand increase for all commodity groups except consumer services and for all family sizes except the largest. The expenditure elasticity of demand for consumer services declines with family size, possibly indicating that some services available in the market are performed within the household by members of large families. The expenditure elasticity of demand for energy peaks at family size six and declines for families of size seven or more. Price elasticities of demand decrease for all commodity groups except capital services and consumer services and for all family sizes except the largest. The price elasticity of demand for energy reaches a minimum at family size six.

Variations in the age of head of household result in smaller changes in expenditure and price elasticities than variations in total expenditure or family size. The expenditure elasticity of demand for energy increases up to age of head 55–64 and then declines for age of head 65 and older. The pattern for food and clothing is similar. The expenditure elasticities of demand for other nondurables and capital services peak at age of head 45–54. The expenditure elasticity of demand for consumer services declines monotonically with age of head of household. The price elasticity of demand for energy falls to age of head 55–64 and then rises for age of head 65 and over. Price elasticities for food and clothing and other nondurables fall to age of head 45–54 and then rise. The price elasticity of demand for capital services reaches a peak at age 45–54 and then falls. The price elasticity of demand for consumer services increases monotonically with age of head of household.

Expenditure and price elasticities of demand vary with region, race, and type of residence. Expenditure elasticities of demand for energy are highest in the North Central and Southern regions, the expenditure elasticity for food and clothing is highest in the Northeast, while the expenditure elasticity for other nondurables is highest in the South. The expenditure elasticity of demand for capital services is highest in the Northeast, while the expenditure elasticities for consumer services are highest in the Northeast and Western regions. Price elasticities of demand for energy are lowest in the North Central and Southern regions, the price elasticity of demand for food and clothing is lowest in the North East, and the price elasticity for other nondurables is lowest in the Northeast and Southern regions. The price elasticity of demand for capital services is lowest in the North Central regions while the price elasticity of demand for consumer services is lowest in the West.

The expenditure elasticity of demand for energy is lower for whites than for nonwhites. For all other commodity groups the expenditure elasticities of demand are lower for nonwhites than for whites. Price elasticities of demand for energy and capital services are higher for nonwhites than for whites, while price elasticities for food and clothing, other nondurables, and consumer services are higher for whites. Finally, expenditure elasticities of demand for energy and other nondurables are lower for urban residents than for rural residents, while expenditure elasticities of demand for food and clothing, capital services, and consumer services are lower for rural residents. Price elasticities of demand for energy, other nondurables, and capital services are higher for urban than for rural residents. Price elasticities for food and clothing and consumer services are higher for rural residents. Our overall conclusion is that both expenditure and price elasticities of demand vary considerably with total expenditure and with demographic characteristics of the household.

D.   Summary and Conclusion

In this Section we have presented the results of implementing the translog model of aggregate consumer behavior. For this purpose we have divided consumer expenditures among five broad commodity groups—energy, food and clothing, consumer services, capital services, and other nondurable expenditure. We assume that the direct utility function is homothetically separable in goods within each category, so that we can construct price indexes for each commodity group. We define the quantity consumed for each group as the ratio of expenditure on that group to the corresponding price index.

We employ households as consuming units. Expenditures within the household are allocated so as to maximize a household welfare function, so that the household behaves in the same way as an individual maximizing a utility function. All consuming units are classified by five demographic characteristics that result in differences in preferences among households—family size, age of head, region of residence, race, and type of residence. For each of these characteristics, households are classified into exhaustive and mutually exclusive groups. Each group is represented by a qualitative or dummy variable, equal to unity when a household is in the group and zero otherwise.

Our time series observations are based on data on personal consumption expenditures from the U.S. Interindustry Transactions Accounts for the period 1958–1974. Our cross section observations are for the year 1972 from the 1972–1973 Survey of Consumer Expenditures. We employ data on the distribution of expenditures over all households and among demographic groups based on the Current Population Survey. To complete our time series data set we require data for our heteroscedasticity adjustment, also based on the Current Population Survey.

We first estimate the model for individual expenditures by ordinary least squares. We then estimate the combined model by pooling time series and cross section data. We discuss the pooled estimates in detail, introducing the results from cross section data alone only to provide additional perspective. Most of the unknown parameters in the pooled model for cross section and time series data are estimated very precisely.

The impacts of changes in total expenditures and in demographic characteristics of the household that appear in the numerators of the functions determining the allocation of expenditures are estimated more precisely than the impacts of changes in prices. This reflects the fact that estimates of the expenditure and demographic effects incorporate a relatively large quantity of cross section data while estimates of the price effects incorporate a much smaller quantity of time series data on prices. The impacts of changes in prices that appear in the denominators of the functions determining the allocation of expenditures are estimated very precisely, reflecting the fact that these changes incorporate both time series and cross section data. The sign and order of magnitude of the expenditure and demographic effects are very similar in the cross section and the pooled estimates.

We characterize the impact of changes in expenditure, demographic characteristics of the household, and prices on individual expenditure patterns by considering a consumer unit with five members, age of head 35–44 years, living in the Northeast, white in race, and with an urban residence, having a total expenditure of $9,000 for the year 1972. We then vary total expenditure and each of the demographic characteristics, holding constant all the demographic characteristics and total expenditure and the remaining demographic characteristics, respectively.

Individual expenditure shares for capital services increase with total expenditure, while all other shares decrease with total expenditures. As family size increases, the shares of energy, food and clothing, and other nondurable expenditures increase, while the shares of capital services and consumer services decrease. The energy share increases with age of head, while the consumer services share declines. The shares of food and clothing and of other nondurables increase and then decrease with age of head, while capital services has the opposite profile.

The effects of region of residence on patterns of individual expenditures is small for energy and other nondurables. Households living in North Central and Southern regions use relatively more capital services and slightly more energy; these households use less consumer services. The only difference between whites and nonwhites is a smaller share of capital services and a larger share of consumer services for nonwhites. Finally, shares of food and clothing, consumer services, and other nondurables are smaller for rural families, while the shares of capital services and energy are much larger.

As a final illustration of differences in preferences among individual consuming units, we have presented price and expenditure elasticities for different consuming groups. Again we consider units with five members, age of head 35–44 years, living in the Northeast, white in race, and with an urban residence, having a total expenditure of $9,000 for the year 1972. Increases in total expenditure decrease expenditure elasticities and increase price elasticities, except for capital services. Increases in family size for a given total expenditure result in decreases in price elasticities and increases in expenditure elasticities of demand, except for consumer services. Differences in price and expenditure elasticities associated with age of head, region of residence, race, and type of residence are also substantial.

APPENDIX I.

Cross Section Estimation Results

Equation	Variable	Coefficient	Standard Error
WEN	Constant	−.18047	.00572
	ln M	.01750	.00066
	F2	−.01550	.00097
	F3	−.01900	.00115
	F4	−.02201	.00125
	F5	−.02209	.00143
	F6	−.02524	.00173
	F7	−.02372	.00182
	A30	−.00158	.00134
	A40	−.00367	.00144
	A50	−.00567	.00138
	A60	−.00828	.00137
	A70	−.00746	.00134
	RNC	−.00869	.00091
	RS	−.00746	.00091
	RW	.00428	.00098
	RNW	.00362	.00116
	RUR	−.01767	.00090

R^2 = 0.2057.
S.E. = 0.0283.
Number of observations = 8,049.

Equation	Variable	Coefficient	Standard Error
WFC	Constant	−.65939	.01193
	ln M	.06286	.00138
	F2	−.03461	.00203
	F3	−.05254	.00239
	F4	−.06782	.00261
	F5	−.08293	.00299
	F6	−.08945	.00362
	F7	−.11486	.00381
	A30	−.02210	.00281
	A40	−.04021	.00302
	A50	−.04769	.00288
	A60	−.04689	.00287
	A70	−.03444	.00279
	RNC	.01792	.00190
	RS	.01216	.00189
	RW	.01381	.00204
	RNW	−.01138	.00242
	RUR	.00750	.00189

R^2 = .2909.
S.E. = .0591.
Number of observations = 8,049.

APPENDIX I. continued

Equation	Variable	Coefficient	Standard Error
WO	Constant	−.42202	.01070
	ln M	.03105	.00124
	F2	−.01588	.00182
	F3	−.02667	.00215
	F4	−.03366	.00234
	F5	−.03706	.00268
	F6	−.04314	.00324
	F7	−.05565	.00341
	A30	−.01319	.00252
	A40	−.01646	.00270
	A50	−.01928	.00258
	A60	−.01746	.00257
	A70	−.00334	.00250
	RNC	.00957	.00170
	RS	−.00018	.00170
	RW	.00899	.00183
	RNW	−.00426	.00217
	RUR	−.00013	.00169

R^2 = 0.1159.
S.E. = .0530.
Number of observations = 8,049.

Equation	Variable	Coefficient	Standard Error
WCAP	Constant	1.09550	.02680
	ln M	−.15184	.00310
	F2	.00642	.00457
	F3	.01695	.00538
	F4	.02415	.00587
	F5	.02668	.00672
	F6	.03808	.00813
	F7	.06580	.00855
	A30	.03668	.00632
	A40	.04183	.00678
	A50	.04674	.00647
	A60	.03187	.00645
	A70	−.00270	.00627
	RNC	−.04194	.00426
	RS	−.02927	.00425
	RW	−.01785	.00458
	RNW	.02118	.00544
	RUR	−.04590	.00424

R^2 = .2827.
S.E. = .1327.
Number of observations = 8,049.

APPENDIX I. concluded

Equation	Variable	Coefficient	Standard Error
WSERV	Constant	− .83361	.02496
	ln M	.04041	.00289
	F2	.05958	.00425
	F3	.08126	.00501
	F4	.09934	.00546
	F5	.11541	.00626
	F6	.11976	.00757
	F7	.12843	.00796
	A30	.00018	.00588
	A40	.01852	.00631
	A50	.02591	.00602
	A60	.04076	.00600
	A70	.04795	.00584
	RNC	.02313	.00397
	RS	.02474	.00396
	RW	− .00923	.00427
	RNW	− .00915	.00506
	RUR	.05620	.00395

R^2 = 0.2052.
S.E. = .1236.
Number of observations = 8,049.

Estimate of Covariance Matrix Σ_ϵ

	WEN	WFC	WO	WCAP
WEN	.0008032			
WFC	− .0001561	.003494		
WO	.00002166	.001951	.002812	
WCAP	.0001231	− .002970	− .003694	.01763

Number of observations = 8,049.

APPENDIX II

Aggregate Instrumental Variables

The variables used as instruments for the aggregate time series portion of the model are as follows:

> Constant
> TL—effective tax rate, labor services
> TCR—effective tax rate, noncompetitive imports
> LH—time available for labor services
> P—U.S. population, millions of individuals

APPENDIX II.   concluded

PL—implicit deflator, supply of labor service
PLG—implicit deflator, government purchases of labor services
EL-HR-RT—exogenous income, which equals government transfers to persons (excepting social insurance) less personal transfers to foreigners and personal nontax payments to government
W(−1)—private national wealth, lagged one period
LH·(1 + H)^T—potential time for labor services; H—rate of Harrod neutral change
Total imports
PCR—implicit deflator, noncompetitive imports
PL/(1 + H)^T—corrected deflator for labor services
T—time, set to 0 in 1972

NOTES

1.   Note that when we consider only a single commodity or a single consumer, we can suppress the corresponding commodity or individual subscript. This is done to keep the notation as simple as possible; any omission of subscripts will be clear from the context.

2.   Note the power of the assumption that $F(p, M_1 + M_2, A_1 + A_2)$ is single-valued. In general, $F(p, M_1 + M_2, A_1 + A_2) = f_1(p, M_1, A_1) + f_2(p, M_2, A_2)$ is a correspondence; for fixed A_1 and A_2, there is an infinite number of possible combinations of M_1 and M_2 corresponding to every aggregate expenditure $M_1 + M_2$; aggregate demands are given by

$$f_1(p,M_1,A_1) + f_2(p,M_2,A_2) = f_1(p,M_1,A_1) + f_2(p,(M_1 + M_2) - M_1, A_2)$$

Since M_1 is free to change, aggregate demand can take many different values for the same value of aggregate expenditure.

3.   See, for example, Houthakker (1957) and the references given there.

4.   Alternative approaches to the representation of the effects of household characteristics on expenditure allocation are presented by Barten (1964), Gorman (1976), and Prais and Houthakker (1955). Empirical evidence on the impact of variations in demographic characteristics on expenditure allocation is given by Lau, Lin, and Yotopoulos (1978), Muellbauer (1977), Parks and Barten (1973) and Pollak and Wales (1980). A review of the literature is presented by Deaton and Muellbauer (1980b), pp. 191–213.

5.   Alternative approaches to the representation of the effects of total expenditure on expenditure allocation are reviewed by Deaton and Muellbauer (1980b), pp. 148–160. Gorman (1981) shows that Engel curves for an individual consumer that are linear in certain functions of total expenditure, as required in the theory of exact aggregation considered below, involve at most three linearly independent functions of total expenditure. Evidence from budget studies on the nonlinearity of Engel curves is presented by Leser (1963), Muellbauer (1976b), Pollak and Wales (1978), and Prais and Houthakker (1955).

6.   See, for example, Blackorby, Boyce, and Russell (1978) and the references given there.

7.   We omit the proof of this theorem, referring the interested reader to Lau (1977b).

8.   Alternative approaches to the representation of the effects of prices on expenditure allocation are reviewed by Barten (1977), Deaton and Muellbauer (1980b), pp. 60–85, and Lau (1977a). The indirect translog utility function was introduced by Christensen, Jorgen-

son, and Lau (1975) and was extended to encompass changes in preferences over time by Jorgenson and Lau (1975).

9. The specification of a system of individual demand functions by means of Roy's Identity was first implemented empirically in a pathbreaking study by Houthakker (1960). A detailed review of econometric models of consumer behavior based on Roy's Identity is given by Lau (1977a).

10. Note that this derivation does not require differentiability of either the individual or aggregate demand functions.

11. Summability requires that $\Sigma_{n=1}^{N} p_n h_{n2}(p) = 0$, which implies $h_{n2}(p) = 0$, ($n = 1, 2, \ldots, N$). For the power function case, the system of individual demand functions may not be nonnegative under summability.

12. Summability requires that $\Sigma_{n=1}^{N} p_n h_{n2}^{*}(p) = 0$, which implies that at least one function $h_{n2}^{*}(p)$ is negative for some prices. This is consistent with the condition $h_{n2}^{*}(p) \ln h_{n1}^{*}(p) \geqq 0$, since for that function and those prices $\ln h_{n1}^{*}(p)$ can be negative.

13. See Jorgenson and Lau (1979), p. 131.

14. For details, see Jorgenson and Lau (1979). The second-order interpolation property is discussed by Lau (1977a).

15. See Samuelson (1956) for details.

16. These conditions are implied by the Fundamental Theorem of Exact Aggregation presented in Section I, above.

17. The concepts of equivalent and compensating variations are due to Hicks (1942). Measures of compensating variations based on the translog indirect utility functions under exact aggregation were introduced by Jorgenson, Lau, and Stoker (1980). The corresponding measures of equivalent variations were introduced by Jorgenson, Lau, and Stoker (1981). Net equivalent variations correspond to Samuelson's (1974) concept of "money metric utility." Further discussion and references to the literature are provided by Deaton and Muellbauer (1980b), pp. 184–190.

18. Chipman and Moore (1976, 1980) have shown that in the absence of restrictions on price variations a necessary and sufficient condition for net compensating variations to provide a unique ordering among a number of alternative policies is that individual preferences are homothetic. These conditions are also necessary and sufficient for Hicksian and Marshallian measures of consumer's surplus to provide a unique ordering among alternative policies. In the absence of restrictions on price variations or on preferences, they recommend net equivalent variations, based on an econometric model of individual consumer expenditure allocation, to provide an ordering among policies.

19. Since budget shares are bounded dependent variables, the normality assumption cannot be strictly valid.

20. See Barten (1969).

21. See Malinvaud (1970), Chapter 9, for a discussion of these techniques.

22. Nonlinear two stage least squares estimators were introduced by Amemiya (1974). Subsequently, nonlinear three stage least squares estimators were introduced by Jorgenson and Laffont (1974). For detailed discussion of nonlinear three stage least squares estimators, see Amemiya (1977), Gallant (1977), and Gallant and Jorgenson (1979).

23. See Malinvaud (1970), pp. 366–368, for more detailed discussion.

24. See Diewert (1976) for a detailed justification of this approach to price index numbers.

25. The preparation of these data is described in detail in Jack Faucett Associates (1977).

26. In the U.S. National Income and Product Accounts consumers' durables purchases are included in personal consumption expenditures.

27. The cross section data are described by Carlson (1974).

28.   The application of the bridge to the cross section data involves four steps. First, the cross section expenditure categories are associated with expenditure categories of the National Income and Product Accounts (NIPA). Second, the expenditure allocated to each commodity group is divided among five components—energy, food and clothing, trade and transportation, durables, and consumer services—on the basis of the proportion of the corresponding NIPA commodity group allocated to each Interindustry Transactions group. Third, these expenditures are added across commodity groups, providing energy, food and clothing, trade and transportation, durables purchases, and consumer services for each consumer. Finally, durables purchases are scaled to a durables service rate using the aggregate ratio of durables service flow to durables purchases. The durables service rate is added to the estimated annual rental value for owner-occupied housing to give the flow of capital services. Total expenditure is then defined as the sum of expenditures for energy, food and clothing, trade and transportation, consumer services, and durables.

Mean total expenditure in 1972 in the aggregate data was found to be $10,326, while the cross section value was $9,369, resulting in a discrepancy of 9.3 percent. This can be partly attributed to underreporting of expenditures in the cross section data, and partly to the inclusion of institutional purchases in the time series data. Therefore, we normalized the time series of mean total expenditure to match the cross section in 1972, making the assumption that aggregate budget shares are the same across for families and institutions. The cross section data contain 8,049 observations and the time series data 17 observations from 1958 to 1974.

29.   This series is published annually by the U.S. Bureau of the Census. For our study, numbers 33, 35, 37, 39, 41, 43, 47, 51, 53, 59, 60, 62, 66, 72, 75, 79, 80, 84, 85, 90, 96, 97, and 101 were employed together with technical report numbers 8 and 17.

30.   For details, the interested reader is referred to Stoker (1979).

31.   This viewpoint is presented by Kuh and Meyer (1957).

32.   Alternative approaches to the representation of changes in expenditure allocation over time are presented by Darrough, Pollak, and Wales (1980), Houthakker and Taylor (1970), Jorgenson and Lau (1975), and Phlips (1974).

33.   Attributes have a constant effect on the budget shares. Also, it should be kept in mind that the figures are constructed for 1972 and will differ for other years.

34.   This is due to our reliance on ln M as the expenditure variable in the share equations; this choice is supported by the results of Leser (1963) and Muellbauer (1976b).

35.   The reader should bear in mind that the figures are constructed holding all demographic dimensions constant except the one under study. This is particularly important for age, which holds expenditure constant at $9,000. Thus the decrease in capital services over the age range 15–44 does not imply that this behavior is typical for families whose expenditure grows with age. When expenditure is not held constant, the share for capital services increases as expected over the age range 15–44.

REFERENCES

Amemiya, T. (1974). The nonlinear two-stage least squares estimator, *Journal of Econometrics 2*, 105–110.

————— (1977). The maximum likelihood estimator and the nonlinear three-stage least squares estimator in the general nonlinear simultaneous equation model, *Econometrica 45*, 955–968.

Barten, A.P. (1964). Family composition, prices, and expenditure patterns, in P. Hart, G. Mills, and J.K. Whitaker (eds.), *Econometric Analysis for National Economic Planning: 16th Symposium of the Colston Society*, London, Butterworth, pp. 277–292.

_____ (1969). Maximum likelihood estimation of a complete system of demand equations, *European Economic Review 1*, 7–23.

_____ (1977). The systems of consumer demand functions approach: A review, in M.D. Intriligator (ed.), *Frontiers of Quantitative Economics*, IIIA, Amsterdam, North-Holland, 23–58.

Berndt, E.R., M.N. Darrough, and W.E. Diewert (1977). Flexible functional forms and expenditure distributions: an application to Canadian consumer demand functions, *International Economic Review 18*, 651–676.

Blackorby, C., R. Boyce, and R.R. Russell (1978). Estimation of demand systems generated by the Gorman polar form: a generalization of the S-branch utility tree, *Econometrica 46*, 345–364.

Bureau of the Census (various annual issues). *Current Population Reports, Consumer Income, Series P-60*, Washington, D.C., U.S. Department of Commerce.

Carlson, M.D. (1974). The 1972–1973 consumer expenditure survey, *Monthly Labor Review 97*, 16–23.

Chipman, J.S., and J.C. Moore (1976). The scope of consumer's surplus arguments, in A.M. Tang et al. (eds.), *Evolution, Welfare and Time in Economics: Essays in Honor of Nicholas Georgescu-Roegen*, Lexington, Heath-Lexington Books, 69–123.

_____ (1980). Compensating variation, consumer's surplus, and welfare, *American Economic Review 70*, 933–949.

Christensen, L.R., D.W. Jorgenson, and L.J. Lau (1975). Transcendental logarithmic utility functions, *American Economic Review 65*, 367–383.

Cottle, R.W., and J.A. Ferland (1972). Matrix-theoretic criteria for the quasi-convexity and pseudo-convexity of quadratic functions, *Linear Algebra and Its Applications 5*, 123–136.

Darrough, M., R.A. Pollak and T.J. Wales (1980). Taste change and stochastic structure: an analysis of three time series of household budget studies, unpublished manuscript, September.

Deaton, A., and J.S. Muellbauer (1980a). An almost ideal demand system, *American Economic Review 70*, 312–326.

_____ (1980b). *Economics and Consumer Behavior*, Cambridge, Cambridge University Press.

Diewert, W. Erwin (1976). Exact and superlative index numbers, *Journal of Econometrics 4*, 115–146.

_____ (1977). Generalized Slutsky conditions for aggregate consumer demand functions, *Journal of Economic Theory 15*, 353–362.

Faucett, Jack, and Associates (1977). *Development of 35 order input-output tables, 1958–1974*, Final Report, Washington, Federal Emergency Management Agency.

Gallant, A.R. (1977). "Three-stage least squares estimation for a system of simultaneous, nonlinear, implicit equations, *Journal of Econometrics 5*, 71–88.

Gallant, A.R. and D.W. Jorgenson (1979). Statistical inference for a system of simultaneous, nonlinear, implicit equations in the context of instrumental variable estimation, *Journal of Econometrics 11*, 275–302.

Gorman, W.M. (1953). Community preference fields, *Econometrica 21*, 63–80.

_____ (1976). Tricks with utility functions, in M.J. Artis and A.R. Nobay (eds.), *Essays in Economic Analysis: Proceedings of the 1975 AUTE Conference, Sheffield*, Cambridge, Cambridge University Press, 211–243.

_____ (1981). Some Engel curves, in A.S. Deaton (ed.), *Essays in the Theory and Measurement of Consumer Behaviour* New York, Cambridge University Press, (forthcoming).

Hicks, J.R. (1942). Consumers' surplus and index-numbers, *Review of Economic Studies 9*, 126–137.

Houthakker, H.S. (1957). An international comparison of household expenditure patterns commemorating the centenary of Engel's Law, *Econometrica 25*, 532–551.

——— (1960). Additive preferences, *Econometrica 28*, 244–257.

Houthakker, H.S. and L.D. Taylor (1970). *Consumer Demand in the United States, Analyses and Projections*, 2nd ed., Cambridge, Mass., Harvard University Press.

Jorgenson, D.W. and J.-J. Laffont (1974). Efficient estimation of nonlinear simultaneous equations with additive disturbances, *Annals of Social and Economic Measurement 3*, 615–640.

Jorgenson, D.W. and L.J. Lau (1975). The structure of consumer preferences, *Annals of Economic and Social Measurement 4*, 49–101.

——— (1977). Statistical tests of the theory of consumer behavior, in H. Albach, E. Helmstädter, and R. Henn (eds.), *Quantitative Wirtschaftforschung*, Tubingen, J.C.B. Mohr, 383–394.

——— (1979). The integrability of consumer demand functions, *European Economic Review 12*, 115–147.

Jorgenson, D.W., L.J. Lau, and T.M. Stoker (1980). Welfare comparison under exact aggregation, *American Economic Review 70*, 268–272.

——— (1981). Aggregate consumer behavior and individual welfare, in D. Currie, R. Nobay, and D. Peel (eds.), *Macroeconomics Analysis*, London, Croon-Helm, pp. 35–6).

Klein, L.R. and H. Rubin (1947–1948). A constant-utility index of the cost of living, *Review of Economic Studies 15*, 84–87.

Kuh, E. and J. Meyer (1957). How extraneous are extraneous estimates? *Review of Economics and Statistics 39*, 380–393.

Kuhn, H.W. and A.W. Tucker (1951). Nonlinear Programming, in J. Neyman (ed.), *Proceedings of the Second Berkeley Symposium on Mathematical Statistics and Probability*, Berkeley, Ca., University of California Press, 481–492.

Lau, L.J. (1977a). Complete systems of consumer demand functions through duality,'' in M.D. Intriligator (ed.), *Frontiers of Quantitative Economics* IIIA, Amsterdam, North-Holland, 59–86.

——— (1977b). Existence conditions for aggregate demand functions, Technical Report No. 248, Institute for Mathematical Studies in the Social Sciences, Stanford University, Stanford, Ca. (Revised, February 1980).

Lau, L.J., W.L. Lin, and P.A. Yotopoulos (1978). The linear logarithmic expenditure system: an application to consumption-leisure choice, *Econometrica 46*, 843–868.

Leser, C.E.V. (1963). Forms of Engel functions, *Econometrica 31*, 694–703.

Liew, C.K. (1976). A two-stage least-squares estimator with inequality restrictions on parameters, *Review of Economics and Statistics 58*, 234–238.

Malinvaud, E. (1970). *Statistical Methods of Econometrics*, 2nd. ed., Amsterdam, North-Holland.

Martos, B. (1969). Subdefinite matrices and quadratic forms, *SIAM Journal of Applied Mathematics 17*, 1215–1223.

Muellbauer, J.S. (1975). Aggregation, income distribution, and consumer demand, *Review of Economic Studies 42*, 525–543.

——— (1976a). Community preferences and the representative consumer, *Econometrica 44*, 979–999.

——— (1976b). Economics and the representative consumer, in L. Solari and J.N. Du Pasquier, (eds.) *Private and Enlarged Consumption*, Amsterdam, North-Holland, 29–54.

——— (1977). Testing the Barten model of household composition effects and the cost of children, *Economic Journal 87*, 460–487.

Parks, R.W. and A.P. Barten (1973). A cross country comparison of the effects of prices, income, and population composition on consumption patterns, *Economic Journal 83*, 834–852.

Phlips, L. (1974). *Applied Consumption Analysis*, Amsterdam, North-Holland.

Pollak, R.A. and T.J. Wales (1978). Estimation of complete demand systems from household budget data: the linear and quadratic expenditure systems, *American Economic Review 68*, 348–359.

———————— (1980). Comparison of the quadratic expenditure system and translog demand systems with alternative specifications of demographic effects, *Econometrica 48*, 595–612.

Prais, S.J. and H.S. Houthakker (1955). *The Analysis of Family Budgets*, Cambridge, Cambridge University Press (2nd ed., 1971).

Roy, R. (1943). *De l'Utilité: Contribution a la Theorie des Choix*, Paris, Herman.

Samuelson, P.A. (1956). Social indifference curves, *Quarterly Journal of Economics 70*, 1–22.

———————— (1974). Complementarity—an essay on the 40th anniversary of the Hicks-Allen revolution in demand theory, *Journal of Economic Literature 12*, 1255–1289.

Schultz, H. (1938). *The Theory and Measurement of Demand* Chicago, Il.: University of Chicago Press.

Sonnenschein, H. (1973). The utility hypothesis and market demand theory, *Western Economic Journal 11*, 404–410.

Stoker, T.M. (1979). *Aggregation Over Individuals and Demand Analysis*, Ph.D. Dissertation, Harvard University.

Stone, Richard (1954a). Linear expenditure systems and demand analysis: An application to the pattern of British demand, *Economic Journal 64*, 511–527.

———————— (1954b). *Measurement of Consumers' Expenditures and Behavior in the United Kingdom 1*, Cambridge, Cambridge University Press.

Wold, H.O.A. and L. Jureen (1953). *Demand Analysis: A Study in Econometrics*, New York, John Wiley.

Working, H. (1943). Statistical laws of family expenditure, *Journal of the American Statistical Association 38*, 43–56.

Zellner, A. and H. Theil (1962). Three-stage least squares: simultaneous estimation of simultaneous equations, *Econometrica 30*, 54–78.

PART II
STUDIES IN ECONOMETRIC
THEORY

ESTIMATION OF REGRESSION COEFFICIENTS FROM A DECISION THEORETIC VIEWPOINT

Takeaki Kariya

I. INTRODUCTION

Recently Bock and Judge (1978) extensively treated the problem of estimating regression coefficients based on the mean quadratic error or the risk with a quadratic loss. This article also considers the same problem from a decision theoretic viewpoint and contains some expository aspects. The arguments here are closely related to those in the problem of estimating mean vector of a normal distribution, originated by Stein (1956). However, as will be shown in Section IV, there is a structural difference between the two problems, which makes the problem in regression more difficult. This point is reflected in Chapter 10 of Bock and Judge (1978). An idea to avoid this difficulty is to estimate the risk function unbiasedly, which is offered by Efron and Morris (1976).

Advances in Econometrics, volume 1, pages 241–265.
Copyright © 1982 by JAI Press Inc.
All rights of reproduction in any form reserved.
ISBN: 0-89232-138-5

In Section II, a decision theoretic framework of the problem is prepared. A discussion on the choice of a loss function is made and sufficiency principle is applied. In Section III, the OLSE (ordinary least squares estimator) is reexamined. First it is pointed out that in economic analyses unbiasedness, by which OLSE claims its dominant position, is not the most important property for an estimator to have. Second, it is pointed out that the linearity of an estimator in regression may not be so natural as we expect; further, the relationship between the linearity of an estimator and the invariant structure is considered. The class of linear unbiased estimators is contained in the class of invariant estimators, and the OLSE is shown to be the best invariant estimator. Further, under normality, since the class of unbiased estimators based on a sufficient statistic consists of the OLSE alone, and since the class of invariant estimators based on a sufficient statistic contains more estimators including the OLSE, it is more meaningful to say that the OLSE is the best invariant estimator. In Section IV, the criteria for selection of an estimator are discussed. From a decision theoretic viewpoint, minimaxity and admissibility are chosen as basic criteria. However, since no admissible and minimax estimator has been found for our problem, minimaxity, together with some other properties, is adopted as our criterion. Some decision theoretic concepts are reviewed. We often use Sacks' (1963) result that in such a problem as we are considering any estimator that is not generalized Bayes is inadmissible. In Section V, applying the ideas of Efron and Morris (1976) and Berger (1976) to our problem, we give a broad class of minimax estimators. This part is comparable to Chapter 10 of Bock and Judge (1978), where a rather complicated evaluation of the risk is pursued. Further, we give a condition for which a minimax estimator under one risk function is also minimax under another risk function. The results in this section are partly reported in Kariya (1977). In Section VI, the problem concerning a preliminary test estimator is treated. Following the basic idea due to Toro-Vizcarrondo and Wallace (1968) but estimating the risk function unbiasedly, an alternative critical point for the F (or t) test is proposed. In our criterion, whatever the degrees of freedom are, the restricted estimator is accepted if the F statistic is less than approximately 2. Then, after some remarks on the arguments concerning preliminary test estimators, we show how to have a preliminary test estimator that is minimax.

II. FRAMEWORK

In this section, a decision theoretic framework for our problem is given. Let

$$y = X\beta + \varepsilon \qquad (\beta: k \times 1) \qquad (1)$$

be a linear regression model where X is an $n \times k$ fixed matrix of rank k; unless otherwise stated, for error term ε normality is assumed

$$\varepsilon \sim N(0, \sigma^2 I_n) \tag{2}$$

Here the sample space is $\mathcal{X} = R^n$, the space of y, and the parameter space is $\Theta = R^k \times R_+$, the space of (β, σ^2), where $R_+ = \{x > 0\}$. Since the estimation problem for β is considered, the action space is $\Delta = R^k$, the range space of an estimator for β. We adopt as a loss function a quadratic loss

$$L[a, (\beta, \sigma^2) : Q] = (a - \beta)' Q (a - \beta) / \sigma^2, \tag{3}$$

where $Q \in \mathcal{S}(k)$ is a fixed matrix and so it is independent of (β, σ^2). Here $\mathcal{S}(k)$ denotes the set of $k \times k$ positive definite matrices. Since this is a convex function of a, without loss of generality only nonrandomized estimators of β are considered (see Ferguson, 1967, Chapter 3). Hence the class of all estimators of β is the set of all Borel functions $\phi: \mathcal{X} \to \Delta$, and this class is denoted by $\mathcal{T}$. For $\phi \in \mathcal{T}$, the risk function of ϕ is defined by

$$R[\phi, (\beta, \sigma^2) : Q] = EL[\phi(y), (\beta, \sigma^2) : Q] \tag{4}$$

where E indicates expectation. This is regarded as a weighted mean quadratic error. Although risk (4) depends on (β, σ^2) in general, our problem is to find an estimator ϕ in $\mathcal{T}$ that minimizes (4) in some sense. Since the risk of the constant estimator $\phi_0(y) \equiv 0$ is 0 when $\beta = 0$, there exists no estimator that minimizes (4) uniformly in $(\beta, \sigma^2) \in \Theta$. But the next definition is basic when estimator comparisons are based on risks.

Definition 1. If for two estimators $\hat{\beta}_1, \hat{\beta}_2 \in \mathcal{T}$

$$R[\hat{\beta}_2, (\beta, \sigma^2) : Q] \leq R[\hat{\beta}_1, (\beta, \sigma^2) : Q] \tag{5}$$

holds for all $(\beta, \sigma^2) \in \Theta$, and if for some $(\beta, \sigma^2) \in \Theta$, the inequality is strict, then $\hat{\beta}_2$ is said to be better than $\hat{\beta}_1$. If for $\hat{\beta}_1 \in \mathcal{T}$, there exists a $\hat{\beta}_2 \in \mathcal{T}$ such that $\hat{\beta}_2$ is better than $\hat{\beta}_1$, $\hat{\beta}_1$ is said to be inadmissible. An estimator that is not inadmissible is said to be admissible.

This definition implies that from the viewpoint of risk, without loss of generality, inadmissible estimators can be discarded from the choice set. That is, the class of estimators to which we pay attention is the class of admissible estimators, which is denoted by $\mathcal{A}$. However, even in $\mathcal{A}$ there are uninteresting estimators, such as $\phi(y) \equiv$ const. This means that admissibility is a necessary property for an estimator to have, but it is not a sufficient property for an estimator to be chosen.

Under the normality (4), as is well known, the pair

$$b = (X'X)^{-1} X'y \quad \text{and} \quad v = (y - Xb)'(y - Xb) \tag{6}$$

is a sufficient statistic, where b is the OLSE (ordinary least squares estimator). The next lemma is an application of the Rao-Blackwell Theorem.

Lemma 1. For any $\hat{\beta}_1 \in \mathcal{T}$

$$R[\hat{\beta}_1, (\beta,\sigma^2):Q] = R[\hat{\beta}_2,(\beta,\sigma^2):Q] + E(\hat{\beta}_1 - \hat{\beta}_2)'Q(\hat{\beta}_1 - \hat{\beta}_2)/\sigma^2$$

where $\hat{\beta}_2 = E[\hat{\beta}_1 (y) \mid (b,v)]$, the conditional expectation of $\hat{\beta}_1$ given (b,v). The second term of the right side is 0 if and only if $\hat{\beta}_1 (y) = \hat{\beta}_2$ (b,v) a.e. (almost everywhere).

This lemma means that any estimator that is not a function (a.e.) of (b,v) is inadmissible. Consequently, it is necessary and sufficient to consider the subclass of estimators in $\mathcal{T}$ based on the sufficient statistic (b,v), that is, the class of all Borel functions $\mathcal{D} = \{\phi:R^k \times R_+ \to \Delta \equiv R^k\}$. Then the model becomes

$$\begin{cases} b \sim N[\beta,\sigma^2(X'X)^{-1}] , & v \sim \sigma^2\chi_m^2 \\ b \text{ and } v \text{ are independent} \end{cases} \qquad (7)$$

where $m = n - k$ and χ_m^2 denotes χ^2-distribution with d.f. (degrees of freedom) m.

Finally, we consider the choice of the weight matrix Q. Needless to say, the choice of Q depends on the problem concerned. In some cases, reasonable choices will be (1) $Q = I$ and (2) $Q = X'X$. In case (1), the loss function becomes

$$L[a, (\beta,\sigma^2):I] = \|a - \beta\|^2/\sigma^2 \qquad (8)$$

and this is intuitively appealing, where $\|a\|^2 = a'a$. In the case (2), the loss is

$$L[a, (\beta,\sigma^2):X'X] = (a - \beta)'X'X(a - \beta)/\sigma^2 = \|Xa - X\beta\|^2/\sigma^2 \qquad (9)$$

Since (b,v) is a sufficient statistic and $b \sim N[\beta,\sigma^2 (X'X)^{-1}]$, (9) is regarded as the loss normalized by var $(b) = \sigma^2 (X'X)^{-1}$. Except for constant terms, the regression coefficients in economic analyses often have such physical units as an increase per unit increase (e.g., propensity to consume) and they do not have the same physical units as y. That is, the statistic for which β serves as a location parameter is not y but b, and since var $(b) = \sigma^2 (X'X)^{-1}$, (9) may be regarded as a natural loss function. Technically speaking, $Q = X'X$ is the easiest case to treat. If $Q \neq X'X$, an invariant structure the problem owns is lost and in Section V, as will be discussed a technical difficulty is brought into the problem (see also, for example, Bock, Yancy, and Judge, 1973).

III. OLSE

In this section, to set up a criterion for selection, the properties of the OLSE (7), which dominates applications, are reexamined. As is well known, under normality (2), the OLSE is the unique estimator that minimizes in the ordering of nonnegative definiteness the risk matrix

$$\bar{R}(\hat{\beta},\beta) = E[\hat{\beta}(y) - \beta][\hat{\beta}(y) - \beta]'/\sigma^2 \tag{10}$$

in the class of unbiased estimators

$$\mathcal{U} = \{\hat{\beta} \in \mathcal{T} | E[\hat{\beta}(y)] = \beta\} \tag{11}$$

However, exactly in the same way as Lemma 1, it is shown that even for the risk matrix (10) it is necessary and sufficient to consider the class of estimators based on the sufficient statistic (b,v), that is, $\mathcal{D}$. Since (b,v) is also a complete statistic, the above fact merely notes that in the class $\mathcal{D}$ there exists no unbiased estimator except the OLSE b (a.e.). That is, it only states

$$\mathcal{D} \cap \mathcal{U} = \{b\} \quad \text{(a.e.)} \tag{12}$$

This result is not directly dependent on the normality, but rather on the sufficiency and completeness of (b,v). The relation (12) implies that in the class $\mathcal{D} \cap \mathcal{U}$ there is no need to minimize (10) since it contains only one estimator. It should be noted that with no relation to unbiasedness, it is necessary to restrict the class of estimators $\mathcal{T}$ to the class $\mathcal{D}$, and the unbiasedness in $\mathcal{D}$ yields the unique estimator b. Hence, unless unbiasedness is an indispensable property for an estimator to have, it may be better to consider competitors that may have other optimal properties rather than impose unbiasedness, and thus have the OLSE. As is well known, unbiasedness simply requires the mean of the sample distribution of an estimator $\hat{\beta}$ to coincide with "true value" β. Although unbiasedness is a desirable property, it does not seem that it dominates other properties, such as the property of minimizing the risk (3). Rather, in economic analyses where repeated experiments are impossible, the author thinks that as a criterion for selection of estimators, the property that an estimator is close to the true value on the average precedes to the unbiasedness that the mean of the distribution of an estimator coincides with the true value. Of course, the question of what kind of risk function (or quadratic loss function) should be chosen is a different problem, and the arbitrariness of the risk or the nonuniqueness of optimal estimators under a risk function does not necessarily justify unbiasedness. It is considered appropriate that the choice of a risk function is based on each specific individual problem.

The preceding argument is based on the assumption of normality even though it does not directly depend upon it. On the other hand, as far as $E(\varepsilon) = 0$ and $E(\varepsilon\varepsilon') = \sigma^2 I_n$, without normality, the OLSE minimizes the risk matrix (10) in the class of linear and unbiased estimators

$$\mathscr{L} \cap \mathscr{U} = \{A \in \mathscr{L} \mid AX = I_k\} \tag{13}$$

where $\mathscr{L}$ is the class of all linear estimators

$$\mathscr{L} = \{A \mid A \text{ is a } k \times n \text{ matrix}\} \tag{14}$$

This result does not depend on the distribution of ε, and there (b,v) may not be a sufficient statistic. The reason why the class of linear estimators is considered is sometimes based on the intuitive judgment that a given model has linear structure. However the intuitive understanding of linearity is not the same as the invariance principle that formalizes it mathematically. Let us consider the relationship between linearity and invariance more closely. The property that an estimator $\hat{\beta}$ is linear in y means that an observation of $\alpha_1 y_1 + \alpha_2 y_2$ in the sample space implies as an estimate of β, $\alpha_1\hat{\beta}(y_1) + \alpha_2\hat{\beta}(y_2)$. But as stated in Section II, apart from experimental designs, in economic analyses the parameter β does not have the same physical unit as y, and the hereditary property that the change of y is linearly transformed into the estimate does not seem so natural as it is generally thought.

Next, we consider the invariance principle. (For invariance, the readers are referred to Ferguson, 1967, Chapter 4.) Usually a real-valued risk function such as (3) is chosen when invariance is applied. But since the argument below does not depend on values of the weight matrix Q, we choose the risk matrix (10) as a risk function. For the risk matrix (10), we take the group of transformations $G = R^k \times R_+$, for $(g,\alpha) \in G$, transform a point y in the sample space by

$$y \rightarrow \alpha y + Xg \tag{15}$$

and correspondingly transform a point $(\beta,\sigma^2) \in \Theta$ in the parameter space and a point $a \in \Delta$ in the action space by

$$\beta \rightarrow \alpha\beta + g, \qquad \sigma^2 \rightarrow \alpha^2\sigma^2 \tag{16}$$

and

$$a \rightarrow \alpha a + g \tag{17}$$

respectively. Then the estimation problem for β is left invariant. Here, since the distribution of ε is arbitrary except for $E(\varepsilon) = 0$ and $E(\varepsilon\varepsilon') = \sigma^2 I$, it is necessary to assume that the distribution of y obtained from that of ε is invariant under (15) and (16). This assumption is not restrictive, since it simply means that the distribution of ε is invariant under $\varepsilon \rightarrow \alpha\varepsilon$ and $\sigma \rightarrow \alpha\sigma$. Hence when the probability density function (pdf), say h, of ε exists, h is of the form $h(\varepsilon) = f(\varepsilon/\sigma)$ for some f, where f is independent of σ. In particular, when $\varepsilon_1, \ldots, \varepsilon_n$ are independently distributed such that the pdf of ε_i is of the form $f_i(\varepsilon_i/\sigma)$ where f_i does not depend on σ, then the assumption is satisfied. Now according to the invariance principle, estimating β by a when y is observed in the sample space is regarded as equivalent to estimating $\alpha\beta + g$ by $\alpha a + g$ when $\alpha y + Xg$ is observed. Consequently, in this case, as a natural structure for an estimator ϕ to satisfy

$$\phi(\alpha y + Xg) = \alpha\phi(y) + g \quad \text{for all } (g,\alpha) \in G \tag{18}$$

is required, and an estimator ϕ that satisfies (18) is called an invariant (or equivariant) estimator. By $\mathscr{I}$ we shall denote the class of invariant estimators. An invariant estimator ϕ in (18) is not linear in y and so invariance is different from linearity. Suppose a linear estimator $A \in \mathscr{L}$ is an invariant estimator. Then from (18)

$$A(\alpha y + Xg) = \alpha Ay + g$$

must be satisfied for all y and $(g,\alpha) \in G$. This is clearly equivalent to $AX = I_k$. Therefore the class of linear invariant estimators is equal to the class of linear unbiased estimators. That is

$$\mathscr{L} \cap \mathscr{I} = \mathscr{L} \cap \mathscr{U} \tag{19}$$

However, for example, a nonlinear estimator

$$\phi_0(y) = b + \|y - Xb\| a_0 \tag{20}$$

belongs to $\mathscr{I}$ where a_0 is any $k \times 1$ fixed vector, and so $\mathscr{L} \cap \mathscr{I} \neq \mathscr{I}$. Hence $\mathscr{L} \cap \mathscr{U} \subset \mathscr{I}$. That is, the class of invariant estimators $\mathscr{I}$ does not contain the class of linear estimators, but it contains the class of linear unbiased estimators $\mathscr{L} \cap \mathscr{U}$. On the other hand, the estimator in (20) is not unbiased and so $\mathscr{I}$ is not contained in $\mathscr{U}$.

Finally we shall show that the OLSE is the best invariant estimator. In addition to the assumption of the invariance of the distribution of y under (15) and (16), we assume $P(\varepsilon = 0) = 0$. Setting $g = b$ and $y = 0$ in (18) yields $\phi(0) = 0$. Further, replacing y by Ny with $N = I - X(X'X)^{-1}X'$ and setting $g = 0$ and $\alpha = \|Ny\|^{-1}$ yield $\phi(Ny) = \|Ny\| \phi(Ny/\|Ny\|)$. Hence substituting Ny for y and $g = b$ in (18) produces

$$\phi(y) = \|Ny\| \phi(Ny/\|Ny\|) + b, \quad \phi(0) = 0 \tag{21}$$

The class of estimators that satisfy (21) is $\mathscr{I}$. Next, since there exist orthogonal matrices $\rho_1 \in \mathcal{O}(n)$ and $\rho_2 \in \mathcal{O}(k)$ such that

$$\rho_1 X \rho_2 = \begin{bmatrix} D \\ 0 \end{bmatrix} \quad (D: k \times k, \text{ diagonal})$$

letting $\zeta = \rho_1 \varepsilon = (\zeta_1' \zeta_2')'$ $[\zeta_1: k \times 1, \zeta_2: (n - k) \times 1]$ yields

$$b - \beta = (X'X)^{-1} X'\varepsilon = \rho_2 D^{-1} \zeta_1 , \quad Ny = \rho_1 \begin{Bmatrix} 0 \\ \zeta_2 \end{Bmatrix} \qquad (22)$$

where $\mathcal{O}(k)$ denotes the set of $k \times k$ orthogonal matrices. From (22),

$$E\left[(b - \beta) \|N\varepsilon\| \phi\left\{ \frac{N\varepsilon}{\|N\varepsilon\|} \right\} \right] = \rho_2 D^{-1} E\left[\zeta_1 \|\zeta_2\| \phi\left\{ \rho_1 \begin{Bmatrix} 0 \\ \zeta_2 \end{Bmatrix} / \|\zeta_2\| \right\}' \right] \qquad (23)$$

is obtained. The left side of (23) is 0 at least when

$$E[\zeta_1 \mid \zeta_2] = 0 \qquad (24)$$

or

$$\text{the distribution of } (\zeta_1, \zeta_2) \text{ is equal to that of } (-\zeta_1, \zeta_2) \qquad (25)$$

For example, when ε has a spherical pdf $h(\varepsilon) = q(\|\varepsilon\|^2/\sigma^2)$ for some q, then both (24) and (25) are satisfied. Of course, the normal distribution is a special case. When the distribution of $\zeta = \rho_1 \varepsilon$ satisfies (24) or (25), the risk matrix of an invariant estimator ϕ is evaluated as

$$E[\phi(y) - \beta][\phi(y) - \beta]' \geq \sigma^2 (X'X)^{-1} + E[\phi(N\varepsilon)\phi(N\varepsilon)'] \qquad (26)$$

in the ordering of nonnegative definiteness, where $\phi(N\varepsilon) = \|N\varepsilon\|\phi(N\varepsilon/\|N\varepsilon\|)$. The equality in (26) holds if and only if $\phi(Ny) = \phi(N\varepsilon) = 0$ or $\phi(y) = b$. Therefore we obtain

Theorem 1. Suppose (1) $E(\varepsilon) = 0$ and $E(\varepsilon\varepsilon') = \sigma^2 I_n$, (2) the distribution of ε is invariant under $\varepsilon \to \alpha\varepsilon$ and $\sigma \to \alpha\sigma$ for $\alpha > 0$, and (3) $P(\varepsilon = 0) = 0$. Further assume (24) or (25). Then OLSE b is the best invariant estimator. That is, b minimizes the risk matrix (26) in the class of invariant estimators, which contains the class of linear unbiased estimators $\mathcal{L} \cap \mathcal{U}$.

Corollary 1. If ε has a spherical pdf $h(\varepsilon) = q(\|\varepsilon\|^2/\sigma^2)$ for some q with $E\|\varepsilon\|^2 < \infty$, then the OLSE is the best invariant estimator.

Although $\mathcal{I} \supset \mathcal{L} \cap \mathcal{U}$, the condition on the sphericity of the pdf of ε is rather restrictive.

When the normality for ε is assumed, (b,v) is a sufficient statistic. Since $b \sim N[\beta, \sigma^2(X'X)^{-1}]$ and $v \sim \sigma^2\chi^2_{n-k}$, the estimation problem is invariant under the group $G = R^k \times G_+$ where G acts on (b,v) and (β,σ^2) by

$$b \to \alpha b + g , \quad v \to \alpha^2 v$$

and

$$\beta \to \alpha\beta + g, \qquad \sigma^2 \to \alpha^2\sigma^2$$

for $(g,\alpha) \in G$. In this case an estimator in $\mathscr{D}$ is invariant if and only if

$$\phi(\alpha b + g, \alpha^2 v) = \alpha\phi(b) + g \qquad (27)$$

which in turn holds if and only if

$$\phi(b,v) = b + (v)^{1/2}a \qquad (28)$$

where a is a $k \times 1$ fixed vector. In fact, setting $b = 0$ and $v = 1$ in (27) yields (28). This implies that under normality, the class of unbiased estimators based on the sufficient statistic

$$\mathscr{D} \cap \mathscr{U} = \{b\} \subset \mathscr{D} \cap \mathscr{I} \qquad \text{(a.e.)}$$

Therefore, the following theorem is more meaningful than stating that b is the best unbiased estimator (in $\mathscr{D}$).

Theorem 2. When $\varepsilon \sim N(0,\sigma^2 I_n)$, the OLSE is the best invariant estimator. That is, it minimizes the risk matrix (26) in the class of estimators of the form (28).

IV.   CRITERIA FOR SELECTION OF ESTIMATORS

Selection of estimators is basically based on the risk function (3). However, as has been seen, there exists no estimator in $\mathscr{D}$ that uniformly minimizes the risk. An approach to a solution of this indeterminacy is to restrict by a certain criterion the class $\mathscr{D}$ to a subclass of $\mathscr{D}$, in which we try to find an estimator that minimizes the risk as much as possible or whose risk function behaves well for the purpose of an analysis. This procedure usually helps to exclude such uninteresting estimators in $\mathscr{D}$ as constant estimators $\phi(b,v) \equiv c$. Criteria to restrict $\mathscr{D}$ to a subclass of $\mathscr{D}$ may be categorized as follows:

1. Like unbiasedness and consistency, desirable sampling properties for an estimator are imposed independently of risk.
2. Like linearity, an estimator is required to have a special structure independently of risk, and only classes of estimators having that structure are considered.
3. Like invariance, associated with the decision-theoretic structure of a problem concerned, a natural structure is required for estimators.
4. Like minimaxity, as we shall see later, an optimal property is required for the behavior of a risk function, and only classes of estimators whose risk functions satisfy this property are considered.

As our basic standpoint in this article, we adopt criterion (4), but we do not completely neglect the other criteria.

In the rest of this section, we state our viewpoint on the criteria for selections and, based on our problem, we review the relationships among the concepts of admissibility, Bayes, generalized Bayes, and minimaxity. In the definition below we fix Q arbitrarily and write $R[\hat{\beta},(\beta,\sigma^2)] \equiv R[\hat{\beta},(\beta,\sigma^2):Q]$.

Definition 2. An estimator $\phi_0 \in \mathcal{T}$ is said to be minimax if

$$\sup_{(\beta,\sigma^2)} R[\phi_0,(\beta,\sigma^2)] = \inf_{\phi} \sup_{(\beta,\sigma^2)} R[\phi,(\beta,\sigma2^2)] < \infty \qquad (29)$$

We shall denote by $\mathcal{M}$ the class of minimax estimators *in* $\mathcal{D}$. Let ℓ be the right side of (29). Then if $\hat{\beta} \in \mathcal{M}$,

$$R[\hat{\beta},(\beta,\sigma^2)] \leq \ell \qquad \text{for all } (\beta,\sigma^2) \in \Theta \qquad (30)$$

hence no estimator whose risk goes over ℓ for some (β,σ^2) is contained in $\mathcal{M}$. For example, neither constant estimators nor linear biased estimators can be minimax. In fact, for a linear estimator $\phi(y) = Ay$

$$R[\phi,(\beta,\sigma^2)] = \text{tr } AA'Q + \beta'(I - AX)'Q(I - AX)\beta/\sigma^2 \qquad (31)$$

and so unless $AX = I_k$, $R[\phi,(\beta,\sigma^2)]$ can go to infinity. Since the OLSE b minimizes (31) under $AX = I$ and since $R[b,(\beta,\sigma^2)] = \text{tr } (X'X)^{-1}Q$, the value ℓ of the right side of (29) is not greater than tr $(X'X)^{-1}Q$. Actually, in the next section, $\ell = \text{tr } (X'X)^{-1}Q$ is shown. Hence if we presume this, the class of minimax estimators in $\mathcal{D}$ is described as

$$\mathcal{M} = \{\phi \in \mathcal{D} | R[\phi,(\beta,\sigma^2)] \leq \text{tr } (X'X)^{-1}Q, \quad (\beta,\sigma^2) \in \Theta\}, \qquad (32)$$

which of course includes the OLSE b. Consequently unless a minimax estimator is equal to the OLSE (a.e.), it is (uniformly) better than the OLSE. On the other hand, minimaxity is a weak condition on the behavior of the risk function, and under the assumption that there is no specific information on the structure of the parameter space, all estimators of our concern seem to belong to this class. In this sense, it can be said that the class of estimators for selections is the class of admissible and minimax estimators in $\mathcal{D}$, i.e., $\mathcal{A} \cap \mathcal{M}$. But if $\mathcal{A} \cap \mathcal{M}$ contains more than one estimator, it will be difficult to give a general criterion for selection of a single estimator in the class. In fact, when $\hat{\beta} \in \mathcal{A} \cap \mathcal{M}$, the risk of $\hat{\beta}$ is not greater than tr $(X'X)^{-1}Q$, and there exists no better estimator than $\hat{\beta}$ (Definition 1). This implies with the continuity of the risk function of $\hat{\beta}$ that for any $\hat{\beta}_1 \in \mathcal{T}$ such that $\hat{\beta}_1 \neq \hat{\beta}$ (a.e.), there exists a neighborhood Θ_0 of a point $(\beta,\sigma^2) \in \Theta$ such that

$$R[\hat{\beta},(\beta,\sigma^2)] < R[\hat{\beta}_1,(\beta,\sigma^2)] \quad \text{for all} \quad (\beta,\sigma^2) \in \Theta_0 \qquad (33)$$

Hence, when no information on the parameter space is available, from the viewpoint of risk it is impossible to put an ordering on the estimators in $\mathcal{A} \cap \mathcal{M}$ that leads to the selection of a single estimator. That is, as a general criterion for selection of an estimator, it seems necessary and sufficient that an estimator belongs to the class $\mathcal{A} \cap \mathcal{M}$, and the selection of an estimator depends on each specific problem. However, it is difficult to not only describe the class $\mathcal{A} \cap \mathcal{M}$ itself, but also to find an estimator that belongs to $\mathcal{A} \cap \mathcal{M}$.

The preceding criterion is regarded as an ideal one only when the argument is strictly based on the viewpoint of risk, and needless to say, there are other criteria that fit the purpose of a specific problem.

As a method to find an estimator in $\mathcal{A}$, there is the concept of Bayes. Regarding the parameter space $\Theta = R^k \times R_+$ as a Borel space, let us consider a probability measure π on Θ. Such a measure π is called a prior distribution and the set of all prior distributions shall be denoted by Π. As is well known, for $\hat{\beta} \in \mathcal{T}$ and $\pi \in \Pi$ the Bayes risk of $\hat{\beta}$ with respect to π is defined as

$$r(\hat{\beta},\pi) = \int R[\hat{\beta},(\beta,\sigma^2)] \, d\pi(\beta,\sigma^2) \tag{34}$$

Definition 3. If for $\pi \in \Pi$, $\hat{\beta} \in \mathcal{T}$ satisfies

$$r(\hat{\beta},\pi) = \inf_{\phi \in \mathcal{T}} r(\phi,\pi) < \infty \tag{35}$$

$\hat{\beta}$ is said to be a Bayes estimator with respect to π. If an estimator $\hat{\beta}$ satisfies (35) for some $\pi \in \Pi$, $\hat{\beta}$ is simply said to be a Bayes estimator.

Let $\hat{\beta}$ be a Bayes estimator with respect to $\pi \in \Pi$, and define $\hat{\beta}_0(b,v) = E[\hat{\beta}(y)|(b,v)]$. Then from Lemma 1 and Definition 2

$$R[\hat{\beta}_0,(\beta,\sigma^2)] \leq R[\hat{\beta},(\beta,\sigma^2)]$$

and

$$r(\hat{\beta}_0,\pi) = r(\hat{\beta},\pi)$$

hold. Hence from Lemma 1, when the class of Bayes estimators is considered, it is necessary and sufficient to consider the class of Bayes estimators based on the sufficient statistic (b,v). We denote this class by $\mathcal{B}$. Denoting by $\pi(\beta,\sigma^2|b,v)$ the conditional distribution of (β,σ^2) given (b,v), which is called the posterior distribution of (β,σ^2), a Bayes estimator $\hat{\beta}$ with respect to π is uniquely determined by

$$\hat{\beta}(b,v) = \frac{\int_\Theta (\beta/\sigma^2) d\pi(\beta,\sigma^2|b,v)}{\int_\Theta (1/\sigma^2) d\pi(\beta,\sigma^2|b,v)} \tag{36}$$

It is noted that the weight matrix Q is assumed to be independent of (β,σ^2).

Lemma 2. (Ferguson, 1967, p. 60). A unique Bayes estimator is admissible.

This implies $\mathcal{B} \subset \mathcal{A}$ and hence $\mathcal{B} \cap \mathcal{M} \subset \mathcal{A} \cap \mathcal{M}$. Hence a method to find an estimator that belongs to $\mathcal{A} \cap \mathcal{M}$ is to find an estimator that belongs to $\mathcal{B} \cap \mathcal{M}$.

Next, a necessary condition for an estimator to belong to $\mathcal{A} \cap \mathcal{M}$ is considered. Let Π^* denote the set of all σ-finite measures on Θ. For $\pi \in \Pi^*$, the estimator $\hat{\beta}(b,v)$ defined by (36) is said to be a generalized Bayes estimator with respect to π when $\|\hat{\beta}(b,v)\| < \infty$ (a.e.). By $\mathcal{B}^*$, the class of generalized Bayes estimators is denoted. Sacks (1963) has shown that under the risk of mean square errors a limit of a sequence of Bayes estimators (with respect to a certain topology), is a generalized Bayes estimator. This result implies $\mathcal{A} \subset \mathcal{B}^*$ and hence $\mathcal{A} \cap \mathcal{M} \subset \mathcal{B}^* \cap \mathcal{M}$. That is, an estimator that is not generalized Bayes is not admissible and hence it does not belong to $\mathcal{A} \cap \mathcal{M}$.

Finally, to make a bridge between the concepts of Bayes and minimaxity, the concept of extended Bayes is defined. If an estimator $\hat{\beta}_0 \in \mathcal{T}$ satisfies that for any $\eta > 0$ there exists $\pi \in \Pi$ such that

$$r(\hat{\beta}_0,\pi) \leq \inf_\phi r(\phi,\pi) + \eta < \infty$$

$\hat{\beta}_0$ is said to be extended Bayes. A Bayes estimator is extended Bayes.

Lemma 3. (Ferguson, 1967, p. 91). An extended Bayes estimator with constant risk is minimax.

V.   A CLASS OF MINIMAX ESTIMATORS

First we show that the OLSE b is minimax. Since $R[b(\beta,\sigma^2):Q] = \text{tr}\,(X'X)^{-1}Q$, by Lemma 3, it suffices to show that b is extended Bayes. Taking a prior distribution π in (36) such that $\beta \sim N[0,a(X'X)^{-1}]$ and $\sigma^2 \equiv 1$ yields the Bayes estimator $\phi(b,v) = (a/a + 1)b$, and then the Bayes risk is

$$r(\phi,\pi) = \{[a/(a + 1)]^2 + [a/(a + 1)^2]\}\,\text{tr}\,(X'X)^{-1}Q$$

Clearly, for any $\eta > 0$, there exists $a > 0$ (large) such that $r(b,\pi) \leq r(\phi,\pi) + \eta$. Hence b is extended Bayes and so $b \in \mathcal{M}$.

Theorem 3. $\varepsilon \sim N(0,\sigma^2 I_n)$. Then when $k = 1$ and $k = 2$, the OLSE *b* is the unique (a.e.) admissible and minimax estimator, i.e., $\mathcal{A} \cap \mathcal{M}$ = {*b*} (a.e.).

Proof. Since $b \in \mathcal{M}$ and $R[b,(\beta,\sigma^2):Q]$ = const., if $b \in \mathcal{A}$, $\mathcal{M}$ = {*b*} a.e. follows. The proof for $b \in \mathcal{A}$ can be performed in a similar manner as in James and Stein (1961).

Consequently, in the case of a simple regression, our criterion also yields the OLSE *b*. However, for $k \geq 3$, the OLSE is not admissible. To show $b \notin \mathcal{A}$, it suffices to show that there is another minimax estimator in $\mathcal{M}$. Hence it is desirable to describe or characterize the class $\mathcal{M}$ itself in (33), but so far this has not been solved. In this section, we extend the result of Berger (1976) based on the approach of Efron and Morris (1976) and give a relatively large subclass of $\mathcal{M}$. Although the argument is closely related to the estimation problem of mean vector of normal distribution, the approaches before Efron and Morris' (1976) approach aim at a direct evaluation of the risk function so that except for the case of $Q = X'X$ or $X'X = I_k$, they are hard to apply. On this point, readers are referred to Bock, Yancy, and Judge (1973, p. 109). This difficulty lies in the fact that in the case of $Q \neq X'X$ and $X'X = I_k$, an invariant structure on which the estimation problem of mean of normal distribution holds is lost. For example, when $Q = X'X$, for the sufficient statistic (b,v), the transformation

$$b \to \alpha Cb \quad \text{and} \quad v \to \alpha^2 v$$

where $\alpha > 0$ and $C \in \{C: k \times k | CX'XC' = X'X\} \equiv \mathcal{C}$, leaves the problem invariant, and this problem is reduced to the usual estimation problem of mean vector of normal distribution. However, in the case of $Q \neq X'X$ and $X'X \neq I_k$, the invariant structure with respect to group $\mathcal{C}$ above disappears and for this reason, a subclass of minimax estimators has not been given in a satisfactory form. More specifically, in case of $Q = X'X$, the risk function of an invariant estimator is a function of a single parameter $\lambda = \beta'X'X\beta/\sigma^2$ only, while in the case of $Q \neq X'X$ and $X'X \neq I_k$, the risk function depends on X and Q in a complicated way, which makes it difficult to make an analytical comparison of risk functions by the usual approach. It should be noted that in a problem of the invariant structure, a minimax estimator can be found in the class of invariant estimators. This is a result due to Kudo (1955) and Kiefer (1957). Bock and Judge (1978, Chapter 10) evaluate the risk directly.

On the other hand, the approach due to Efron and Morris (1976) estimates the risk function of an estimator unbiasedly and compares it with the risk of the OLSE. This approach is not only convenient in finding a minimax estimator in the noninvariant problem, but also it gives a relatively large class of minimax estimators. More specifically, suppose that a unique unbiased estimate of the risk function $R[\hat{\beta},(\beta,\sigma^2):Q]$ of an estimator $\hat{\beta} \in \mathcal{D}$, say

$$\hat{R}(\hat{\beta}:Q) \equiv \hat{R}(\hat{\beta}:Q)\,(b,v)$$

is obtained and it satisfies

$$\hat{R}(\hat{\beta}:Q) \leq \operatorname{tr}(X'X)^{-1}Q = R[b,(\beta,\sigma^2):Q] \quad \text{(a.e.)} \tag{37}$$

Then since taking expectations from both sides of (37) produces $R[\hat{\beta},(\beta,\sigma^2):Q] \leq R[b,(\beta,\sigma^2):Q]$ for all (β,σ^2), $\hat{\beta}$ belongs to $\mathcal{M}$ in (33) or $\hat{\beta}$ is minimax. The class of estimators we consider is not the class of all estimators satisfying (37) but a subclass of it in which an estimator is of the form

$$\hat{\beta}(Q) \equiv \hat{\beta}(Q)\,(b,v) = b - [c_0 h(T)/T]\,Q^{-1}X'Xb \tag{38}$$

where $h:[0,\infty) \to R^1$ is a Borel function

$$T = b'X'XQ^{-1}X'Xb/v \quad \text{and} \quad c_0 = (k-2)/(n-k+2) \tag{39}$$

The form in (38) is an analogy to the form Berger (1976) considered in the estimation problem of mean of normal distribution.

Theorem 4. Let $\varepsilon \sim N(0,\sigma^2 I_n)$, $k \geq 3$ and $n - k > 1$. Then an estimator of the form (38) is minimax if (1), (2) and (3) are satisfied, i.e.

(1) For all $T \geq 0$, $0 \leq h(T) \leq 2$.
(2) For all T such that $h(T) < 2$, $T^{(k-2)/2}\,h(T)/[2 - h(T)]^{1+2c_0}$ is nondecreasing.
(3) If there exist T_1 such that $h(T_1) = 2$, $h(T) = 2$ for all $T \geq T_1$.

Further, if $h(T)$ is an absolute continuous function with derivative $h'(T)$ (a.e.), the unique unbiased estimate of the risk function of an estimator in (38) is given by

$$\hat{R}(\hat{\beta}:Q)\,(T) = \ell - \{c_0\,(k-2)[h(T)/T][2 - h(T)]$$

$$+ 4c_0 h'(T)[1 + c_0 h(T)]\} \tag{40}$$

where $\ell = \operatorname{tr}(X'X)^{-1}Q$, $R[\hat{\beta},(\beta,\sigma^2):Q] < \infty$ and the expectation of each term in (40) is assumed to exist.

The proof is given at the end of this section. If h is absolutely continuous and satisfies (1), (2), and (3), then $\hat{R}(\hat{\beta}:Q)$ in (40) clearly satisfies (37) and so $\hat{\beta}$ is minimax.

Corollary 3. $k \geq 3$ and $n - k \geq 1$. Then $\hat{\beta}(Q)$ in (38) is minimax if it satisfies

(4) $0 \leqslant h(T) \leqslant 2$ and $h(T)$ is nondecreasing

Proof. In (2) of Theorem 4, $h/(2 - h)^{1+2c_0}$ is nondecreasing when (4) holds. Hence the result follows.

Example 1. $h(T) = a$ (const.), $0 \leqslant a \leqslant 2$. Then from Corollary 2

$$\hat{\beta}_a = b - (c_0 a/T)Q^{-1}X'Xb$$

is minimax and the unbiased estimate of the risk of $\hat{\beta}_a$ is given by

$$\hat{R}(\hat{\beta}_a:Q) = \ell - (k - 2)c_0 a(2 - a)T \tag{41}$$

where c_0 is given in (39). This estimate is uniformly minimized if and only if $a = 1$, and then the estimator

$$\hat{\beta}_1 = [I - (c_0/T)Q^{-1}X'X]b \tag{42}$$

shall be called the Stein-type estimator. When $Q = X'X$,

$$b_1 = [1 - (c_0/F)]b \qquad \text{where} \qquad F = b'X'Xb/v$$

is the so-called Stein estimator. But it is known that the "positive part estimator" $b_2 = [1 - (c_0/F)]^+ b$ is better than b_1 where for a real number a, $a^+ = \max(0,a)$. Further it is also known that these estimators including (42) are inadmissible because these can not be generalized Bayes estimators.

Example 2. $h(T) = aT/(T + c_0 a)$, $0 \leqslant a \leqslant 2$. From Corollary 2, $\hat{\beta}(Q)$ with this h is minimax. Again, this estimator is inadmissible since this can not be generalized Bayes. When $a = 1$ and $Q = X'X$ with $c_1 = k/(n - k)$, it becomes

$$\phi_1(b,v) = g(F)b \tag{43}$$

where $g(F) = c_1 F/(c_1 F + c_0)$ and $F = b'X'Xb/c_1 v$.

This estimator is again considered in the next section. Here we consider the implication of the form (43). First note that F in (43) is an F statistic for testing $\beta = 0$ and distributed as $F(\lambda:k, n - k)$, a noncentral F with d.f. $(k, n - k)$ and noncentral parameter $\lambda = \beta'X'X\beta/2\sigma^2$. Since $g(F)$ is an increasing function of F, as a test statistic, $g(F)$ is equivalent to F. Since $0 \leqslant g(F) \leqslant 1$, $\phi_1(b,v)$ can be regarded as the estimator that gives the probability $[1 - g(F)]$ to the null hypothesis $\beta = 0$ and the probability $g(F)$ to b. On the other hand, since F has the monotone likelihood ratio property for λ (Lehmann, 1959, p. 68), the larger λ is, that is, the farther β goes from the hypothesis $\beta = 0$, the larger values F and so $g(F)$ tend to take stochastically. Hence ϕ_1 always estimates β smaller than b, but when λ gets larger, ϕ_1 tends to be closer to b.

Example 3. $h(T) = a\, I_{(c_0a,\infty)}\,(T)$, $0 \le a \le 2$, where $I_A(x) = 1$ if $x \in$ A and $I_A(x) = 0$ if $x \notin A$. Then the estimator in (38) is minimax. In this case, h is not absolutely continuous.

Theorem 4 gives a sufficient condition for which an estimator of the form (38) is minimax, but it is hard to set up a general criterion to choose an estimator even among the minimax estimators of this form. As has been discussed, we are interested in the class $\mathcal{A} \cap \mathcal{M}$ of admissible and minimax estimators, but it is difficult to find an estimator in $\mathcal{A} \cap \mathcal{M}$. In the problem of estimating μ of $N(\mu,\sigma^2 I_n)$, when σ^2 is unknown, no admissible and minimax estimator has been found. Alam's (1975) proof for claiming this seems incorrect. In fact, in the proof of admissibility, he applies Theorem 5.6.1 in Brown (1971). But the set in the parameter space he chooses is not compact, which violates a condition required in Theorem 5.6.1. For this reason, we may take a compromised criterion in which an estimator is chosen from the class $\mathcal{M}$, based on some other rules. As such rules of thumb in this case, for example, the derivation can be well explained, the computation is not too complicated, and an estimator chosen has some sample optimal properties, etc.

An estimator in (38) depends on the weight matrix Q. If h satisfies (4) in Corollary 2, then $\hat{\beta}(Q)$ is minimax under the risk function $R[\cdot,(\beta,\sigma^2):Q]$. The next theorem gives a sufficient condition for which $\hat{\beta}(Q)$ is also minimax under a different risk $R[\cdot,(\beta,\sigma^2):Q^*]$.

Theorem 5. Suppose an estimator $\hat{\beta}(Q)$ in (38) satisfies (4) in Corollary 2. Let $\lambda_1 \ge \ldots \ge \lambda_k > 0$ be the latent roots of $Q^{-1}Q^*$ and let $m = \sup h(T)$. Then $\hat{\beta}(Q)$ is also minimax under the risk $R[\cdot,(\beta,\sigma^2):Q^*]$ if

$$2 \sum_{i=1}^{k} \lambda_i - [4 + (k - 2)m]\lambda_1 \ge 0.$$

The proof is deferred to the end of this section.

For example, a Stein-type estimator $\hat{\beta}_1(Q)$ in Example 1 is also minimax under $R[\cdot,(\beta,\sigma^2):Q^*]$ if the condition of Theorem 5 is satisfied. In particular, the Stein estimator $b_1 \equiv \hat{\beta}_1(X'X)$ is minimax under $R[\cdot,(\beta,\sigma^2):I]$ if $2\mathrm{tr}\,(X'X)^{-1} - (k + 2)\lambda_1^* \ge 0$ where λ_1^* is the largest latent root of $(X'X)^{-1}$.

The condition in Theorem 5 for which $\hat{\beta}(Q)$ is minimax under $R[\cdot,(\beta,\sigma^2):Q^*]$ depends on the roots of $Q^{-1}Q^*$ and the supremum of $h(T)$ only. If we denote by $\beta(Q)$ any estimator with $a = 1$ in Examples 1–3, then any such estimator is minimax under $R[\cdot,(\beta,\sigma^2):Q^*]$ as far as Q belongs to the set

$$a = \{Q > 0 | 2\mathrm{tr}\,Q^{-1}Q^* - (k + 2)\lambda_1 \ge 0\}$$

In fact, any estimator with $a = 1$ in these examples satisfies $m = \sup$

$h(T) = 1$. On the other hand, an estimator with $m = 2$, the set a contains only one element $Q = Q^*$. A more general result for Theorem 5 is stated as follows.

Theorem 6. Suppose an estimator $\hat{\beta}(Q)$ in (38) satisfies the following conditions (1), (2), and (3).

(1) $0 \leq h(T) \leq 2$
(2) $h(T)$ is absolutely continuous with $h'(T)$ (a.e.)
(3)   For all (b,v)

$$\left[\frac{h(T)}{T}\right]\left[2\mathrm{tr}\, Q^{-1}Q^* - 4\frac{S}{T} - (k - 2)\frac{h(T)S}{T}\right]$$
$$+ 4\left[\frac{h'(T)S}{T}\right][1 + c_0 h(T)] \geq 0 \quad (44)$$

where each term in (44) is assumed to have finite expectation and

$$S = b'X'XQ^{-1}Q^*Q^{-1}X'Xb/v \quad (45)$$

Then $\hat{\beta}(Q)$ is minimax under risk $R[\cdot,(\beta,\sigma^2):Q^*]$.

Now we shall prove Theorems 4, 5, and 6. First we shall prove Theorem 6. The risk function of $\hat{\beta}(Q)$ under $R[\cdot,(\beta,\sigma^2):Q^*]$ is given by

$$E[b - \beta - g(T)Q^{-1}X'Xb]'Q^*[b - \beta - g(T)Q^{-1}X'Xb]/\sigma^2$$
$$= \mathrm{tr}\,(X'X)^{-1}Q^* - 2E[g(T)b'X'XQ^{-1}Q^*(b - \beta)/\sigma^2] \quad (46)$$
$$+ E[g^2(T)b'X'XQ^{-1}Q^*Q^{-1}X'Xb/\sigma^2]$$

where $g(T) = c_0 h(T)/T$. Let $u = (X'X)^{1/2}b \sim N(\tau,\sigma^2 I_k)$ with $\tau = (X'X)^{1/2}\beta$

$$A = (X'X)^{1/2}\, Q^{-1}Q^*Q^{-1}\,(X'X)^{1/2} \quad (47)$$
$$B = (X'X)^{1/2}\, Q^{-1}Q^*(X'X)^{-1/2} \quad (48)$$
$$C = (X'X)^{1/2}\, Q^{-1}\,(X'X)^{1/2} \quad (49)$$

Then the second term of the right side in (46) is

$$E[g(T)u'\,B(u - \tau)/\sigma^2] = E\left[g(T)\sum_{i=1}^{k}\sum_{j=1}^{k} b_{ij}\,u_i\,(u_j - \tau_j)/\sigma^2\right]$$
$$= \sum_{i=1}^{k}\sum_{j=1}^{k}\left\{E\left[g'\,(T)\left\{\frac{\partial T}{\partial u_j}\right\}b_{ij}\,u_i\right] + E[g(T)b_{ij}\,\delta_{ij}]\right\}$$
$$= E[2g'(T)u'Au/v + g(T)\mathrm{tr}\, B] \quad (50)$$

where $\delta_{ii} = 1$ and $\delta_{ij} = 0\ (i \neq j)$. Here the second equality follows from the fact that when $z \sim N(\theta,\sigma^2)$, $E[(z - \theta)h(z)] = \sigma^2 E[h'(z)]$, and the third equality follows from $T = u'Cu/v$ and $BC = A$. Since $S = u'Au/v$ from (45) and (47), the third term of the right side in (46) is evaluated as

$$E[g^2(T)u'Au/\sigma^2] = E[g^2(T)Sv/\sigma^2]$$

$$= (n - k)\, E[g^2(T)S] + 2E\left\{v\frac{\partial}{\partial v}[g^2(T)S]\right\} \qquad (51)$$

$$= E[(n - k)g^2(T)S - 4g(T)\, g'(T)TS - 2g^2(T)S]$$

where the second equality follows from the fact that when $w \sim \alpha\chi^2_m$, $E[(w - m\alpha)h(w)] = 2\alpha E[wh'(w)]$. Therefore, since (b,v) is complete, from (50) and (51), the unique unbiased estimate of the risk $R[\hat{\beta}(Q), (\beta,\sigma^2):Q^*]$, say $R^{\,\hat{}}[\hat{\beta}(Q):Q^*]$, is given by

$$\hat{R}[\hat{\beta}(Q):Q^*] = R^*_0 - 2[2g'(T)S' + g(T)\mathrm{tr}Q^{-1}Q^*]$$

$$+ [(n - k)g^2(T)S - 4g(T)g'(T)TS - 2g^2(T)S] \quad (52)$$

where $R_0 = \mathrm{tr}(X'X)^{-1}Q^*$. Substituting $g'(T) = [c_0 h'(T)/T] - [c_0 h(T)/T^2]$ into (52) yields

$$\hat{R}[\hat{\beta}(Q):Q^*] = R^*_0 - c_0\{[h(T)/T][2\mathrm{tr}\, Q^{-1}Q^* - 4(S/T)$$

$$- (k - 2)h(T)S/T] + 4[h'(T)/TS + c_0 h(T)S']\} \quad (53)$$

Since $R^*_0 = R[b,(\beta,\sigma^2):Q^*]$ is the minimax value under Q^*, a sufficient condition for which $\hat{\beta}(Q)$ is minimax under the present risk is $\hat{R}[\hat{\beta}(Q):Q^*] \leq R^*_0$. This is satisfied if and only if the inside of { } is nonnegative, which proves Theorem 6. To prove Theorem 5, first assume $h(T)$ is absolutely continuous. Since $h(T)$ is assumed to be nondecreasing, this implies $h'(T) \geq 0$. Hence from (53), a sufficient condition for which $\hat{R}[\hat{\beta}(Q):Q^*] \leq R^*_0$ is

$$2\,\mathrm{tr}\, Q^{-1}Q^* - 4S - (k - 2)h(T)S$$

$$= u'[2C\,\mathrm{tr}\, Q^{-1}Q^* - 4A - (k - 2)h(T)A]\, u \geq 0 \quad (54)$$

for all u. From (47) and (49) this is equivalent to

$$\{2I\,\mathrm{tr}\, Q^{-1}Q^* - [4 + (k - 2)h(T)]Q^{-1/2}Q^*Q^{-1/2}\} \geq 0$$

which is guaranteed by the assumption of Theorem 5. Hence Theorem 5 is proved in the case that h is absolutely continuous. When $h(T)$ is not absolutely continuous, approximate $h(T)$ by a sequence of nondecreasing absolutely continuous functions $h_m(T)$ since $h(T)$ is nondecreasing. Then using the bounded convergence theorem yields the result.

Finally, to prove Theorem 4, set $Q^* = Q$ in (53) and assume h is absolutely continuous. Then $\hat{R}[\hat{\beta}(Q):Q] \leq R_0 = \ell = \text{tr}(X'X)^{-1}Q$ if and only if the inside of { } is nonnegative. But the inside is expressed as $2c_0 T^{-(k-2)/2}[2 - h(T)]^{2+2C_0} \psi'(T)$ where $\psi(T) = T^{(k-2)/2} h(T)/[2 - h(T)]^{1+2C_0}$. Hence it is nonnegative if and only if $\psi'(T) \geq 0$ for all T such that $h(T) < 2$. When h is not absolutely continuous, take a sequence of nondecreasing absolutely continuous functions ψ_m such that $\lim \psi_m = \psi$ and define $0 \leq h_m(T) < 2$ by $\psi_m(T) = T^{(k-2)/2} h_m(T)/[2 - h_m(T)]^{1+2C_0}$. This is possible since $\psi(T)$ is nondecreasing. Since h_m satisfies (1), (2), and (3) in Theorem 4, $\hat{\beta}_m(Q)$ with h_m in (38) satisfies (37). Using the bounded convergence theorem, Theorem 4 follows.

VI. PRELIMINARY TEST ESTIMATOR

It is rather common practice to perform preliminary tests for selections of regression variables or specifications of models before a specific model is chosen. And then, assuming that a selected model is "correct" or "true," it is often said that the OLSE or other estimators have such optimal properties as best linear unbiased, etc. However, these statements are effective only if the selected model is true. This section concerns the problems on such preliminary test estimators. In the normal regression model (1), let us consider the problem of testing a general linear hypothesis

$$H:R\beta = r \quad \text{versus} \quad K:R\beta \neq r \tag{55}$$

where $R:q \times k$ with rank $(R) = q$. In this case, the parameter space of β is $\Theta = \Theta_H \cup \Theta_K$ where

$$\Theta_H = \{\beta \in R^k | R\beta = r\} \quad \text{and} \quad \Theta_K = \{\beta \in R^k | R\beta \neq r\} \tag{56}$$

In the hypothesis testing theory, it is checked whether a maintained hypothesis is consistent with data in hand, and the result there is just a posterior judgment (decision). Hence, without respect to the result of a test, the "true" parameter β is conceptually taken as a point in $\Theta = R^k$. Let

$$\delta = R\beta - r \tag{57}$$

denote a specification error due to the acceptance of H. If $\delta = 0$ or H is true, the restricted LSE

$$\hat{\beta} = b - A(Rb - r) \tag{58}$$

where

$$A = (X'X)^{-1} R'[R(X'X)^{-1}R']^{-1} \tag{59}$$

is the best unbiased estimator, and for this reason, under H $\hat{\beta}$ is usually chosen. Since

$$\hat{\beta} \sim N\{\beta - A\delta, \sigma^2[(X'X)^{-1} - AR(X'X)^{-1}]\} \qquad (60)$$

if $\delta = 0$, $\hat{\beta}$ is a biased estimator. But whatever value δ may be, cov $(b) - \text{cov}(\hat{\beta}) \geq 0$. We first consider the problem of selection of variables based on this trade-off.

Different critical values of preliminary F test (or t test) for regression coefficients have been proposed by Toro-Vizcarrondo and Wallace (1968), Wallace (1972), Sawa and Hiromatsu (1973), and Toyoda and Wallace (1976). Here, following the basic viewpoint of Toro-Vizcarrondo and Wallace (1968) but estimating the MSE (mean square error) function unbiasedly instead of testing specific values of noncentral parameter, we derive alternative critical values. Let

$$T = (n - k) (Rb - r) [R(X'X)^{-1}R']^{-1} (Rb - r)/qv \qquad (61)$$

be the usual F test statistic where $v = (y - Xb)'(y - Xb)$ and $T \sim F(\lambda:q,n - k)$ with noncentral parameter

$$\lambda = \delta'[R(X'X)^{-1}R']^{-1} \delta/2\sigma^2 \qquad (62)$$

In the criterion of Toro-Vizcarondo and Wallace (1968), for values of (β,σ^2) satisfying

$$E(\hat{\beta} - \beta) (\hat{\beta} - \beta)' \leq E(b - \beta) (b - \beta)' \qquad (63)$$

$\hat{\beta}$ is chosen and otherwise b is chosen. Wallace (1972) called this the stronger MSE criterion. They showed that the set of (β,σ^2) satisfying (63) is the set of (β,σ^2) for which $\lambda \leq 1/2$ where λ is given by (62), and reduced the problem of choice between $\hat{\beta}$ and b to the problem of testing $\lambda \leq 1/2$ instead of the usual hypothesis $\lambda = 0$. We take the risk with $Q = X'X$ as a criterion function

$$R[a,(\beta,\sigma^2):X'X] = E(a - \beta)'X'X(a - \beta)/\sigma^2 \qquad (64)$$

and estimate (64) unbiasedly. And if the unbiased estimates, say $\hat{R}(\hat{\beta}:X'X)$ and $\hat{R}(b:X'X)$, satisfy

$$\hat{R}(\hat{\beta}:X'X) \leq \hat{R}(b:X'X) \qquad (65)$$

then $\hat{\beta}$ is chosen.

Lemma 4. The unique unbiased estimator $\hat{R}(\hat{\beta}:Q)$ for $R[\hat{\beta},(\beta,\sigma^2):Q]$ is given by

$$\hat{R}(\hat{\beta}:Q) = \text{tr}\,(X'X)^{-1}Q - 2\text{tr}\,(X'X)^{-1}QAR$$
$$+ (n - k + 2) (Rb - r)'A'QA(Rb - r)/v \qquad (66)$$

Proof

$$R[\hat{\beta}, (\beta,\sigma^2):Q] = E[b - \beta - A(Rb - r)]'\, Q[b - \beta - A(Rb - r)]/\sigma^2$$
$$= \mathrm{tr}\,(X'X)^{-1}Q - 2E(b - \beta)'\, QA(Rb - r)/\sigma^2$$
$$+ E(Rb - r)'\, A'QA(Rb - r)/\sigma^2$$

The second term of the right side is

$$2\mathrm{tr}\; E\{QA[R(b - \beta) + R\beta - r]\,(b - \beta)'/\sigma^2\} = 2\mathrm{tr}\,(X'X)^{-1}QAR$$

Since $(n - k - 2)E(1/v) = 1/\sigma^2$ and since b and v are independent, replacing $1/\sigma^2$ by $(n - k - 2)(1/v)$ yields (66). The uniqueness follows from the completeness of the sufficient statistic (b,v).

Since $R[b,(\beta,\sigma^2):Q] = \mathrm{tr}\,(X'X)^{-1}Q$, $\hat{R}(b:X'X) = k$. Hence the criterion for choice of $\hat{\beta}$ in (65) is equivalent to

$$(n - k - 2)(Rb - r)'\, A'QA(Rb - r)/v \leqslant 2\,\mathrm{tr}\,(X'X)^{-1}QAR \qquad (67)$$

Setting $Q = X'X$ in (67) gives

$$T \leqslant 2(n - k)/(n - k - 2) \qquad (68)$$

Therefore we obtain

Theorem 7. The criterion that $\hat{\beta}$ is chosen if (65) holds and b is chosen otherwise is equivalent to the criterion that $\hat{\beta}$ is chosen if the usual F statistic T satisfies (68) and b is chosen otherwise.

The preceding criterion means that if the F statistic (or t statistic) is not greater than approximately 2 (or $\sqrt{2}$, respectively), $\hat{\beta}$ is chosen without respect to the degrees of freedom. In the case of $q = 1$, this corresponds to 16–18% F value (or t value) for testing $\lambda = 0$. Since T is regarded as the ratio of sample variances per one degree of freedom, it is not so surprising that the criterion does not depend on degrees of freedom. On the other hand, the above criterion depends on the choice $Q = X'X$. In order to try to obtain a criterion that does not depend on Q, we may require $\hat{R}(\hat{\beta}:Q) \leqslant \hat{R}(b:Q)$ for all $Q \in \mathcal{S}\,(k)$, which implies (63). Then from (67), this is equivalent to

$$\sup_{Q} \frac{(n - k - 2)\,(Rb - r)'A'QA(Rb - r)}{2v\,\mathrm{tr}\,(X'X)^{-1}QAR} \leqslant 1 \qquad (69)$$

However, a matrix Q attaining this supremum depends on the data and so no criterion is obtained through it.

We want to comment on the argument that the null hypothesis $R\beta = r$ is eventually rejected as n goes to infinity and therefore the usual testing procedure based on a significance level is misleading. It should be noted that in the usual testing theory a check is made of whether or not a hypothesis is consistent with data in hand for each finite sample; and since information on the true parameter increases with sample size, it is natural to require a test to judge the null hypothesis more strictly with sample size increasing. In this sense, the consistency seems a necessary property for a test to have. We believe it to be incorrect to require modification of the usual testing scheme to achieve a consistent test, by supposing the situation in which n is limitlessly large, leading to eventual rejection of the null hypothesis. If there is a problem, it is the hypothesis testing theory itself, and if one thinks the theory inappropriate, he should choose or formalize other procedures.

We also want to comment on the preliminary test estimators. As is well known, before the F test based on T is performed, we have chosen the estimator

$$\tilde{\beta} = I_{(0,c)}(T)\hat{\beta} + I_{(c,\infty)}(T)b \tag{70}$$

where c is a critical point and $I_A(x)$ is the indicator function of A. An estimator of this form is called a preliminary estimator. Sample properties of this estimator are extensively studied in Bock and Judge (1978). The nonminimaxity and inadmissibility of this estimator for the case of $Q = X'X$ can be translated from the results in Sclove, Morris, and Radhakrishnan (1972). From (70), $\tilde{\beta}$ is a nonlinear and biased estimator of β. Further, since $\tilde{\beta}$ cannot be generalized Bayes (see Section IV), $\tilde{\beta}$ is not admissible when $q \geq 3$ or $k - q \geq 3$. And in a similar manner as in Sclove et al. (1972), it is shown to be not minimax. However, these considerations are based on the viewpoint that $\tilde{\beta}$ is regarded as an estimator of β in the class of all estimators and that there is no such prior information available as $R\beta$ may be closer to r. There the nonoptimality of $\tilde{\beta}$ in the class of all estimators is the result of neglecting the prior information in the argument. In this sense, although $\tilde{\beta}$ does not have optimal properties in the class of all estimators, the choice of $\tilde{\beta}$ should not be argued based on such optimal properties.

Associated with this, we consider finally the problem of estimating β under the situation that $R\beta$ may be close to r. In the usual case, as stated earlier, the preliminary estimator (70) is chosen before a test is performed. Since (70) implies that with probability $I_{(0,c)}(T)$, which is 0 or 1, $\hat{\beta}$ is chosen and with probability $1 - I_{(0,c)}(T)$, b is chosen before data are observed, a generalization of this idea is a randomization. Specifically, since T is regarded as a statistic measuring how strongly the relationship $R\beta = r$ holds, choosing a nondecreasing function h such that

$$h(0) = 0, \quad h(\infty) = 1, \quad \text{and} \quad 0 \leq h(T) \leq 1 \tag{71}$$

we define the estimator

$$\tilde{\beta} = [1 - h(T)]\hat{\beta} + h(T)b \tag{72}$$

Then this estimator chooses $\hat{\beta}$ with probability $1 - h(T)$ and b with probability $h(T)$ before data are observed. A general argument on the selection of the function h is rather difficult. As an example, we can take Example 2. There the null hypothesis is $\beta = 0$ and so the estimator in (71) becomes

$$\tilde{\beta}_1 = [1 - h(F)]0 + h(F)b = h(F)b \tag{73}$$

where $h(F) = c_1 F/(c_1 F + c_0)$, $c_0 = (k - 2)/(n - k + 2)$ $c_1 = k/(n - k)$, and $F = b'X'Xb/c_1 v$. As has been shown, this is minimax in the class of all estimators. Analogously for the hypothesis $R\beta = r$, we may take

$$\tilde{\beta}_2 = [1 - h_2(T)]\hat{\beta} + h_2(T)b \quad \text{with} \quad h_2(T) = T/(T + d) \tag{74}$$

where $d = (n - k)(k - 2)/q(n - k + 2)$. However, the problem of selecting h including (74) will be discussed elsewhere. Here the derivation of (73) given in Kariya and Tokoyama (1977) is introduced. First for any $Q \in \mathscr{S}(k)$, we consider the risk of a *linear form Ay*

$$R[A,(\beta,\sigma^2):Q] = E(Ay - \beta)' Q(Ay - \beta)/\sigma^2 \tag{75}$$
$$= [\text{tr } QA(\sigma^2 I + X\beta\beta'X')A' - 2\text{tr } QAX\beta\beta' + \text{tr } Q\beta\beta']/\sigma^2$$

and find A, which minimizes this uniformly. Here, Ay is called a linear form rather than a linear estimator so that we may allow A to depend on (β,σ^2). Differentiating (75) with respect to A gives the minimizer

$$A_0 \equiv A_0(\beta,\sigma^2) = \beta\beta'X'/(\sigma^2 + \beta'X'X\beta) \tag{76}$$

and the risk of $A_0 y$ is

$$R[A_0, (\beta,\sigma^2):Q] = \beta'Q\beta/(\sigma^2 + \beta'X'X\beta) \tag{77}$$

Naturally, the risk of $A_0 y$ is uniformly smaller than the risk of any linear estimator Ay. In fact, $R[A, (\beta,\sigma^2):Q] - R[A_0, (\beta,\sigma^2):Q]$ is evaluated as

$$\text{tr } (A - A_0)' Q(A - A_0)(\sigma^2 I + X\beta\beta'X')/\sigma^2 \tag{78}$$

which is strictly positive except in the case that $A \equiv 0$ and $\beta = 0$. Further, since A_0 does not depend on Q, A_0 also minimizes (75) uniformly in Q. That is, A_0 minimizes the risk matrix $E(Ay - \beta)(Ay - \beta)'/\sigma^2$. The fact that A_0 does depend on (β,σ^2) shows that A_0 is sensitive to the value of (β,σ^2). But, since (β,σ^2) is unknown, we replace it by $(b,\alpha v)$ to obtain

$$\tilde{\beta} \equiv \tilde{\beta}(\alpha) = A_0(b,\alpha v)y = \frac{b'X'Xb}{b'X'Xb + \alpha v} b \tag{79}$$

where α is a normalizer for v. Choosing $\alpha = c_0$ yields (73). Such an estimator is sometimes called an adaptive estimator. It is noted that the derivation does not depend on the distribution of the error term ε.

REFERENCES

Alam, K. (1973). A family of admissible minimax estimators of the mean of a multivariate normal distribution, *Ann. Statist. 1*, 517–525.

Alam, K. (1975). Minimax and admissible minimax estimators of the mean of a multivariate normal distribution for unknown covariance matrix, *J. Multi. Analysis 5*, 83–95.

Baranchik, A. J. (1970). A family of minimax estimators of the mean of a multivariate normal distribution, *Ann. Math. Statist. 41*, 642–645.

Baranchik, A. J. (1973). Inadmissibility of maximum likelihood estimators in some multiple regression problems with three or more independent variables, *Ann. Statist. 1*, 312–321.

Berger, J. (1974). Admissible minimax estimation of a multivariate normal mean with arbitrary quadratic loss, *Ann. Statist. 4*, 223–226.

Berger, J. (1976). Admissibility results for generalized Bayes estimators of coordinates of a location vector, *Ann. Statist. 4*, 334–356.

Bock, M. E. (1975). Minimax estimators of the mean of a multivariate normal distribution, *Ann. Statist. 3*, 209–218.

Bock, M. E. and G. G. Judge (1978). *Preliminary Estimators and Stein-rule Estimator in Econometrics*, Amsterdam: North-Holland.

Bock, M. E., T. A. Yancy, and G. G. Judge (1973). Statistical consequences of preliminary test estimators in regression, *JASA 68*, 109–116.

Brown, L. (1971). Admissible estimators, recurrent diffusions, and insoluble boundary value problems, *Ann. Math. Statist. 42*, 855–904.

Efron, B. and C. Morris (1973). Stein's estimation rule and its competitors—An empirical Bayes approach, *JASA 68*, 117–130.

Efron, B. and C. Morris (1976). Families of minimax estimators of a multivariate normal distribution, *Ann. Statist. 4*, 11–21.

Ferguson, T. S. (1967). *Mathematical Statistics—A Decision Theoretic Approach*, New York: Academic Press.

James, W. and C. Stein (1961). Estimation with quadratic loss, *Proc. Fourth Berk. Symp. Math. Statist. Prob. 1*, 361–379, Berkeley: University of California Press.

Kariya, T. (1977). A class of minimax estimators in a regression model with arbitrary quadratic loss, *J. Japan Statist. Soc. 7*, 67–73.

Kariya, T. and K. Tokoyama (1977). An alternative estimator in a linear regression model. (Mimeograph).

Kiefer, J. (1957). Invariance, minimax sequential estimation and continuous time process, *Ann. Math. Statist. 28*, 573–601.

Kudo, H. (1955). On minimax invariant estimates of the transformation parameter, *Natural Science Report 6*, 31–73, Ochanomizu University.

Lehmann, E. L. (1959). *Testing Statistical Hypothesis*, New York: Wiley.

Sacks, J. (1963). Generalized Bayes solution in estimation problems, *Ann. Math. Statist. 34*, 752–768.

Sawa, T. and T. Hiromatsu (1973). Minimax regret significance points for a preliminary test in regression analysis, *Econometrica 41*, 1903–1101.

Sclove, S. L., C. Morris, and R. Radhakrishnan (1972). Nonoptimality of preliminary test estimators for the mean of a multivariate normal distribution, *Ann. Math. Statist. 43*, 1481–1490.

Stein, C. (1956). Inadmissibility of the usual estimator for the mean of a multivariate normal distribution, *Proc. Third Berk. Symp. Math. Statist. Prob. 1,* 197–206, Berkeley: University of California Press.

Strawderman, W. E. (1971). Proper Bayes minimax estimators of the multivariate normal mean, *Ann. Math. Statist. 42,* 385–388.

Toro-Vizcarrondo, C. and T. D. Wallace (1968). A test of the mean squared error criterion for restrictions in linear regression, *JASA 63,* 558–572.

Toyoda, T. and T. D. Wallace (1976). Optimal critical values for pre-testing in regression, *Econometrica 44,* 365–375.

Wallace, T. D. (1972). Weaker criteria and tests for linear restrictions in regression, *Econometrica 40,* 689–709.

ON MONTE CARLO ESTIMATES OF MOMENTS THAT ARE INFINITE

J. D. Sargan

I. INTRODUCTION

This article consists of three parts. The first is a comparatively general discussion giving rather crude approximations to the distribution of the Monte Carlo estimate of an infinite moment; the second, for a rather special case, gives a considerably more detailed discussion. Both are concerned with the classical case where an estimator $\hat{\beta}$ is a function of a set of sample second moments of the basic variables. Assuming a simultaneous equation model with nonstochastic exogenous variables and normally distributed errors, it is usually simplest to rewrite the estimators as functions of the unconstrained ordinary least squares (OLS) estimates of reduced form coefficients and the corresponding estimates of the variance matrix of the errors on the reduced form equation. Denote the OLS estimates expressed as a vector by p, and the elements of the estimated variance matrix by w, writing $q' = (p', w')$ and $\bar{q} = E(q)$, then

Advances in Econometrics, volume 1, pages 267–299.
ISBN: 0-89232-138-5

in the first section it is shown that if the estimator under consideration is a continuous function of q in some neighborhood of $\bar{q}$ and if T is the sample size (i.e., the basic sample size for the sample defining the econometric estimator $\hat{\beta}$), and N is the number of Monte Carlo replications defining the Monte Carlo estimate of the moment of $\hat{\beta}$, then it is possible to allow N and T both to tend to infinity simultaneously in such a way that the Monte Carlo estimate of the moment differs from the Nagar approximation with final term of order $(T^{-k/2})$ with random errors of probabilistic order less than $T^{-k/2}$ on assumptions equivalent to those of Sargan (1975). More practically, bounds can be put on the various errors to show that for reasonable values of T and N, the fact that the moment does not exist has only a very slight effect on the distribution of the Monte Carlo estimates.

In order to illustrate these theoretical results, a Monte Carlo study is made of the just-identified instrumental variable estimator first and second moments. The moments are computed both before and after censoring (Windsorizing). It is clear that truncating the distributions does improve the moments as estimates of the equivalent Nagar approximations, but the general theoretical conclusions (that if N and T are appropriately chosen, good estimates of the Nagar moments can be made) are justified.

II. A GENERAL BOUND

Suppose

$$\hat{\beta} - \beta = \phi(q - \bar{q}),$$

where $\hat{\beta}$ is the scalar estimator and

$$\bar{q} = E(q) = \plim_{T \to \infty} (q)$$

We assume that ϕ is continuous in some neighborhood of the origin and that $\phi(0) = 0$, so that $p \lim \hat{\beta} = \beta$.

The set of singular points S in q space, such that $q_0 \in S$ if $\phi(q - \bar{q})$ is unbounded in every neighborhood of q_0, will be called the zero set following my notation in Sargan (1974). Define a set $\tilde{S}(\varepsilon)$ such that $q \in \tilde{S}(\varepsilon)$ if $\|q - q_0\| > \varepsilon$ for all $q_0 \in S$. We also need to bound q, so that we define H as the hypersphere center $\bar{q}$, radius R, and define $\tilde{S}(\varepsilon,R) = H \cap \tilde{S}(\varepsilon)$. Now $\phi(q - \bar{q})$ is bounded on $S(\varepsilon,R)$. For if the converse is assumed it is possible to find a sequence such that $\phi(q - \bar{q})$ is tending to either $+\infty$ or $-\infty$ and a subsequence of this sequence, which is tending to a limit point q^+ in the closure of $\tilde{S}(\varepsilon,R)$. But then in every neighborhood of q^+, $\phi(q - \bar{q})$ is unbounded, but q^+ cannot be in S, leading to a contradiction. Also denoting the probability that $q \notin \tilde{S}(\varepsilon,R)$ by

$Q(\varepsilon,R)$, if we assume that S is of measure zero, it follows that $\lim_{R\to\infty}$ $\lim_{\varepsilon\to\infty} Q(\varepsilon,R) = 0$. However the assumption that S is of measure zero is not necessary for the subsequent results of this section.

Now we define

$$F(x) = p[\phi(q - \bar{q}) \leq x]$$

and

$$F_2(x) = P[\phi(q - \bar{q}) \leq x \quad \text{and} \quad q \notin \bar{S}(\varepsilon,R)]/Q(\varepsilon,R)$$

$F_2(x)$ is thus defined as the conditional probability that $\hat{\beta} - \beta \leq x$ given $q \notin \bar{S}(\varepsilon,R)$. If $F_1(x)$ is defined similarly as the conditional probability that $\hat{\beta} - \beta \leq x$ given $q \in \bar{S}(\varepsilon,R)$ then we have

$$F(x) = (1 - Q)F_1(x) + QF_2(x)$$

But since ϕ is bounded if $q \in \bar{S}(\varepsilon,R)$ the range of the $F_1(x)$ distribution is bounded and $F_1(x)$ has moments of all orders. And clearly $F_2(x)$ has its hth order moments finite if and only if $F(x)$ has its hth order moments finite. We can now regard $F(x)$ as being a mixture of the two distributions $F_1(x)$ and $F_2(x)$. It is clearly of some interest to establish the behavior of Q as a function of ε, R, and T. In Appendix A it is proved that $Q = 0(e^{-\kappa T/2})^1$ where κ is a constant that depends on the type of estimator and the parameters of the mode, but is uniform for large R and small ε.

Now, since the distribution of x is precisely the same as that generated by the mixture of the $F_1(x)$ and $F_2(x)$ distributions, we can discuss the behavior of any sample moment by using the mixture model.

Suppose then that we are interested in the distribution of

$$m_h = \left(\sum_{r=1}^{N} x_r^h\right)/NT^{h/2}$$

where the x_r are independent drawings from the mixture model. Write Φ_s for the proposition that s of the $(\hat{\beta} - \beta)_r$ are drawn from $F_2(x)$. Then note that

$$P\left(\sum_{r=1}^{N} x_r^h \leq \xi\right) = P(\Phi_0)P_1\left(\sum_{r=1}^{N} x_r^h \leq \xi\right) + \sum_{s=1}^{N} P(\Phi_s)P(\sum x_r^h \leq \xi/\Phi_s) \tag{1}$$

$$< P(\Phi_0)P_1\left(\sum_{r=1}^{N} x_r^h \leq \xi\right) + 1 - P(\Phi_0)$$

and also that

$$P\left(\sum_{r=1}^{N} x_r^h \leq \xi\right) \geq P(\Phi_0)P_1\left(\sum_{r=1}^{N} x_r^h \leq \xi\right) \tag{2}$$

where P_1 denotes the probability distribution function conditional upon x_r being drawn from $F_1(x)$.

Thus, defining $\eta = \xi/(NT^{h/2})$

$$[1 - P(\Phi_0)]P_1(m_h \leq \eta) \leq P(m_h \leq \eta) - P_1(m_h \leq \eta) \tag{3}$$

$$< [1 - P(\Phi_0)][1 - P_1(m_h \leq \eta)]$$

Now

$$P(\Phi_0) = (1 - Q)^N$$

and

$$1 - P(\Phi_0) = 1 - (1 - Q)^N$$

Thus if N and T tend to infinity with N a function of T, we can write

$$1 - P(\Phi_0) = 0(Ne^{-\kappa T/2}) \tag{4}$$

It is now necessary to show that the moment of $F_1(x)$ can be approximated to any order of magnitude in T by the moments of suitable Edgeworth approximations to $F(x)$, which in turn coincide with the Nagar approximations to the moments of $F(x)$. A general way of doing this is to extend the results of Theorem 1 of Sargan (1975). Translating the notation of Sargan (1975) slightly we can state a more general version of the theorem where q, p, w, and ϕ are defined as in the previous section.

Theorem 1.

Assumption 1. For some $k > h$ and all integers $j \leq k + 2$, there exists a neighborhood of $\bar{q}$, such that $\phi(q - \bar{q})$ has continuous jth order derivatives uniformly bounded in the neighborhood as $T \to \infty$, and $\phi(0) = 0$.

Assumption 2. Denoting the vector of first derivatives with respect to p at $q = \bar{q}$ by ϕ_p, $\phi_p'\phi_p$ is bounded above zero as $\to \infty$.

Assumption 3. Denoting similarly the vector of first derivatives with respect to w by ϕ_w, $\phi_w = 0(T^{-1/2})$ as $T \to \infty$.

On the above assumption

$$F(x/\sqrt{T}) = I(x/\sigma) + I_1(x/\sigma) \sum_{r=1}^{k-1} \psi_r(x)T^{-r/2} + R(x) \tag{5}$$

where σ^2 is the asymptotic variance of $\sqrt{T} \phi(q - \bar{q})$, $I(x/\sigma)$ is the cumulative normal distribution function, $I_1(x/\sigma)$ is its first derivative, the

$\psi_r(x)$ are suitable polynomials with bounded coefficients as $T \to \infty$, and $|R(x)| < BT^{-k/2}$, for all $|x| < cT^{1/(k+1)}$.

This statement extends Theorem 1 of Sargan (1975) in three ways. It takes in the extension stated immediately after the proof of the theorem in the previous article to ensure that the error in the approximation is $0(T^{-k/2})$, but it also considers the uniformity of the error with respect to x and allows x to depend on T, rather than be constant. The proof of the extension with respect to all x in an interval of $0(T^{1/(k+1)})$ follows by repeating the previous proof and noting that at each stage of the proof the orders of magnitude of the errors and residuals are as before (provided that ε^* of the theorem equals $1/(k + 1)$) and are also uniform with respect to x in the stated interval.

It follows in particular from the stated theorem and the order of magnitude of the Edgeworth approximation for $x = \pm cT^{1(k+1)}$ that

$$F(x/\sqrt{T}) = 0(T^{-k/2}) \text{ if } x = -cT^{1/(k+1)}$$

and

$$1 - F(x/\sqrt{T}) = 0(T^{-k/2}) \text{ if } x = +cT^{1/(k+1)}$$

Suppose now that the range over which $F_1(x)$ has a nonzero density is $(-a, b)$, and that $F(x)$ and $F_1(x)$ are uniformly continuous over $(-a, b)$. Then by integration by parts

$$\int_{-a\sqrt{T}}^{b\sqrt{T}} x^h dF_1(x) = \int_{cT^{1/(1+k)}}^{b\sqrt{T}} x^h dF_1(x) + \int_{-a\sqrt{T}}^{-cT^{1/(1+k)}} x^h dF_1(x)$$

$$+ c^h T^{h/(1+k)} F_1[cT^{1/(1+k)}] - (-c)^h T^{h/(1+k)} F_1[-cT^{1/(1+k)}]$$

$$- h \int_{-cT^{1/(1+k)}}^{cT^{1/(1+k)}} x^{h-1} F_1(x) dx$$

Now writing $F_k^*(x)$ for the Edgeworth approximation to $F(x)$ of order $T^{-k/2}$, provided $N = c(T^{h+1})$ then

$$F_1(x) - F_k^*(x) = 0(T^{-k/2})$$

uniformly in the central domain of integration.
Similarly

$$\int_{-\infty}^{\infty} x^h dF_k^*(x) = \int_{cT^{1/(1+k)}}^{\infty} x^h dF_k^*(x) + \int_{-\infty}^{-cT^{1/(1+k)}} x^h dF_k^*(x)$$

$$+ c^h T^{h/(1+k)} F_k^*[cT^{1/(1+k)}] - (-c)^h T^{h/(1+k)} F_k^*[-cT^{1/(1+k)}]$$

$$- h \int_{-cT^{1/(1+k)}}^{cT^{1/(1+k)}} x^{h-1} F_k^*(x) dx$$

Subtracting and particularly taking account of

$$\left| \int_{cT^{1/(1+k)}}^{b\sqrt{T}} x^h dF_1(x) \right| \leqslant b^h T^{h/2} \{1 - F_1[cT^{1/(1+k)}]\}$$

$$= 0(T^{-(k-h)/2})$$

we have that

$$\mu_{1h} - \mu_{kh}^* = 0(T^{-(k-h)/2})$$

where μ_{1h} and μ_{kh}^* are the moments of degree h for $F_1(x)$ and $F_k^*(x)$ distributions. But then considering directly the moments of the two Edgeworth expansions we have

$$\mu_{(k-h)h}^* - \mu_{kh}^* = 0(T^{-(k-h)/2})$$

so that

$$\mu_{1h} - \mu_{(k-h)h}^* = 0(T^{-(k-h)/2}) \tag{6}$$

We can reformulate this by noting that $\mu_{1h} - \mu_{rh}^* = 0(T^{-r/2})$, provided that the conditions of the theorem apply for $k = r + h$. Now clearly conditionally on Φ_0, $\sqrt{N}(m_k - \mu_{1k})$ is asymptotically normally distributed as $N \to \infty$, so that if $N = c^*(T^r)$, and we consider a confidence interval with asymptotic probability of falling outside the interval equal to p, then using (6) we can find d such that

$$P_1(|m_h - \mu_{rh}^*| > dT^{-r/2}) < p$$

where P_1 signifies the probability conditional on Φ_0.

But now clearly from (3)

$$P(|m_h - \mu_{rh}^*| < dT^{-r/2}) \leqslant p$$

if $\lim_{T \to \infty} P(\Phi_0) = 1$, and from (4) if $N = c^*(T^r)$

$$P(\Phi_0) \to 1$$

Thus

$$m_h = \mu_{rh}^* + 0(T^{-r/2})$$

where 0 here signifies stochastic order of magnitude.

This gives a rigorous limiting result as T and $N \to \infty$, but in practice it is difficult to specify how N and T should vary so that the Monte Carlo estimate of the Nagar approximation has only a small error. The required values of T and N are sensitive to the model specification, and in particular, whatever the simultaneous equation estimator, if the model is almost unidentified κ will be small. Suitable values of N and T are most easily achieved for small r. For example, if $r = 1$, and $T = 50$, it is suggested that $N = 100$ or 250 might be used, with the expectation that the bias of order $(1/T)$ corresponding to the terms in the Edgeworth expansion of $0(T^{-1/2})$ might be well approximated. In order that the condition that $Ne^{-\kappa T/2}$ is small be satisfied, note that with $N = 200$, $T = 50$, $Ne^{-\kappa T/2} < .01$ if $\kappa \geqslant .396$. This does not seem a particularly strong requirement.

A slight extension of the preceding argument can be used to discuss the case where the Monte Carlo estimation is made more efficient by the use of a control variate (Hendry and Harrison, 1974). In this case there is no difficulty in showing that if

$$m_k^* = \mu_k^* + \sum(x_r^k - x_r^{*k})/N$$

where x_r^* is the control variate, and $\mu_k^* = E(x_r^{*k})$, then by suitable choice of the control variate one can arrange that $x_r^k - x_r^{*k} = 0(1/T^{1/2})$, and that $(NT)^{1/2}(m_k^* - \mu_k)$ has an asymptotic normal distribution as $T \to \infty$ and $N \to \infty$. Thus in this case it is appropriate to take

$$N = c^*(T^{r-1})$$

to approximate the Nagar moment with error of order $T^{-r/2}$.

III. MORE DETAILED CONSIDERATIONS FOR INSTRUMENTAL VARIABLE ESTIMATORS

From the results of Richardson (1968), Sargan and Mikhail (1971), or Mariano and Sawa (1972), it is clear that for two-stage least squares (2SLS), instrumental variable, and limited-information maximum likelihood (LIML) estimators of the coefficients of equations containing two endogenous variables, the cumulative distribution function can be approximated on the tails of the distribution by

$$P[\sqrt{T}(\hat{\beta} - \beta) > r) = \left(\frac{1}{r}\right)^{s+1} (\alpha_0 + \alpha_1/r + \alpha_2/r^2 + \ldots)$$

$$\text{for } r > 0$$

(7)

$$P[\sqrt{T}(\hat{\beta} - \beta) < r] = \left|\frac{1}{r}\right|^{s+1} (\alpha_0 + \alpha_1/r + \alpha_2/r^2 + \ldots)$$

$$\text{for } r < 0$$

(8)

where s is the degree of overidentification of the equation for 2SLS or three-stage least squares (3SLS), or zero for maximum likelihood estimators, and $\alpha_0 > 0$ and all $\alpha_i = 0(e^{-\kappa T/2})$ for some κ as $T \to \infty$. Consider now density functions of the following form

$$g_{1s}(x,x_0) = |x_0/x|^{s+2} \qquad |x| > x_0$$
$$= 1 \qquad |x| \leq x_0$$
$$g_{2s}(x,x_0) = (x_0/x)^{s+2} \qquad x > x_0$$
$$= -|x_0/x|^{s+2} \qquad x < -x_0$$
$$= (x/x_0) \qquad |x| \leq x_0$$

Suppose as before that we are interested in the moment of degree h of x. Corresponding to the preceding density functions, we have cumulative functions

$$G_{1s}(x,x_0) = x_0^{s+2}|x|^{-(s+1)}/(s + 1) \qquad\qquad x < -x_0$$

$$= x_0/(s + 1) + (x + x_0) \qquad\qquad |x| \leq x_0$$

$$= 2(s + 2)x_0/(s + 1) - x_0^{s+2}|x|^{-(s+1)}/(s + 1) \qquad x > x_0$$

$$G_{2s}(x,x_0) = -x_0^{s+2}|x|^{-(s+1)} \qquad\qquad |x| > x_0$$

$$= -x_0/(s + 1) + \frac{1}{2}x^2/x_0 - \frac{1}{2}x_0 \qquad\qquad |x| \leq x_0$$

Now let us write

$$F(x) = \sum_{k=0}^{h-(s/2)} (2k + s + 1)\,\alpha_{2k}G_{1(2k+s)}/x_0^{2k+s+2}$$

$$+ \sum_{k=1}^{h+(s/2)-s} (2k + s)\,\alpha_{2k-1}G_{2(2k+s-1)}/x_0^{2k+s+1} + F^+(x)$$

where

$$(s/2) = s/2 \qquad \text{if } s \text{ is even}$$
$$= (s + 1)/2 \text{ if } s \text{ is odd}$$

Note that the terms in the G_{1s} and G_{2s} have been subtracted so that $F^+(x)$ should have moments of degree $2h$. If $F(x)$ has a continuous density function, so has $F^+(x)$ and

$$\lim_{x \to -\infty} F^+(x) = 0, \ \lim_{x \to +\infty} F^+(x) = 1 - \sum_{k=0}^{h-(s/2)} 2(2k + s + 2)\alpha_{2k}/x_0^{2k+s+1}$$

Consider next the distribution function for x^h, which is clearly dependent on whether h is odd or even. If h is odd we have

$$P(x^h \leq r) = P(x \leq r^{1/h})$$

and write this

$$F_h(r) = \sum_{k=0}^{h-(s/2)} (2k + s + 1)\alpha_{2k}G_{1(2k+s)}(r^{1/h})/x_0^{2k+s+2}$$

$$+ \sum_{k=1}^{h+(s/2)-s} (2k + s)\alpha_{2k-1}G_{2(2k+s-1)}(r^{1/h})/x_0^{2k+s+1} + F^+(r^{1/h})$$

If on the other hand h is even, we have

$$F_h(r) = P(x^h \leq r) = P(|x| \leq r^{1/h}) = P(x \leq r^{1/h}) - P(x \leq -r^{1/h})$$

$$= \sum_{k=0}^{h-(s/2)} (2k + s + 1)\alpha_{2k}G^*_{1(2k+s)}(r^{1/h})/x_0^{2k+s+2} + \bar{F}(r^{1/h})$$

where

$$G^*_{1s}(x) = 2x \qquad 0 \leq x < x_0$$

$$= 2(s + 2)x_0 - x_0^{s+2}/x^{-(s+1)})/(x + 1) \qquad \text{if } x \geq x_0$$

and

$$\bar{F}(x) = F^+(x) - F^+(-x)$$

Consider now the corresponding characteristic functions. Define

$$\psi_{1s}(t) = \int_{-\infty}^{\infty} e^{ixt} dG_1(x^{1/h}) = \frac{2}{h} \int_{x_0^h}^{\infty} \cos(xt)(x_0^h/x)^{(s+2)/h} x^{1/h-1} dx$$

$$+ \frac{2}{h} \int_0^{x_0^h} \cos(xt)x^{1/h-1} dx$$

Note that we are considering $0 \leq s < 2h$.

First consider the case where $s + 1 \neq h$ and $s + 1 \neq 2h$. Then we can integrate the first integral by parts to get

$$\psi_{1s}(t) = \frac{2}{s + 1} \cos(x_0^h t)x_0^{s+2}x_0^{-(s+1)}$$

$$- \frac{2t}{s + 1} \int_{x_0^h}^{\infty} \sin(xt)x_0^{s+2}x^{-(s+1)/h} dx$$

$$+ \frac{2}{h} \int_0^{x_0^h} \cos(xt)x^{1/h-1} dx$$

Now either $s + 1 \gtrless h$.

Consider first the possibility that $s + 1 < h$. Then the preceding equals

$$\psi_{1s}(t) = \frac{2x_0}{s+1} \cos(x_0^h t) + \frac{2t}{s + 1} \int_0^{x_0^h} \sin(xt)x_0^{s+2}x^{-(s+1)/h} dx$$

$$+ \frac{2}{h} \int_0^{x_0^h} \cos(xt) x^{1/h-1} \, dx \tag{9}$$

$$- \frac{2tx_0^{s+2}}{s+1} \, \mathrm{Im} \int_0^{\infty} e^{ixt} x^{-(s+1)/h} \, dx$$

Now if $t > 0$, the last integral can be evaluated by using a contour integral as shown in Figure 1.

It can be shown that both integrals around the quadrants of radius R and δ can be neglected as $\delta \to 0$ and $R \to \infty$, so that

$$\int_0^{\infty} e^{ixt} x^{-(s+1)/h} \, dx = - \int_0^{\infty} e^{-yt} \, (e^{\pi i/2} \, y)^{-(s+1)/h} \, i \, dy$$

$$= - \exp[(\pi i/2)(h - s - 1)/h] t^{-(h-s-1)/h} \Gamma[(h - s - 1)/h]$$

Now in the first two integrals expanding $\cos xt$ and $\sin xt$ as power series and integrating term by term, one finds that the characteristic function may be written

$$\psi_{1s}(t) = \frac{2x_0}{s+1} \cos(x_0^h t) + \frac{2t^2 x_0}{s+1} \sum_{j=0}^{\infty} \frac{(-t^2)^j \, x_0^{(2j+2)h}}{(2j+1)! \, [2j + 2 - (s+1)/h]}$$

$$+ \frac{2}{h} \sum_{j=0}^{\infty} \frac{(-t^2)^j \, x_0^{2jh+1}}{2j! \, [2j + (1/h)]} \tag{10}$$

$$+ \frac{2x_0^{s+2}}{(s+1)} \sin \frac{h-s-1}{2h} \, \pi \, |t|^{(s+1)/h} \, \Gamma\left(\frac{h-s-1}{h}\right)$$

The last term follows because changing the sign of t clearly does not affect the original formula for the characteristic function. Note that apart from this last term, the characteristic function is analytic at the origin.

If now $h < s + 1 < 2h$, we can integrate by parts again to obtain for the characteristic function

$$\psi_{1s}(t) = \frac{2x_0}{s+1} \cos(x_0^h t) - \frac{2thx_0^h \sin(x_0^h t)}{(s+1)(s+1-h)}$$

$$- \frac{2t^2 hx_0^{s+2}}{(s+1)(s+1-h)} \int_{x_0^h}^{\infty} \cos(xt) x^{-(s+1-h)/h} \, dx$$

$$+ \frac{2}{h} \int_0^{x_0^h} \cos(xt) x^{-(h-1)/h} \, dx$$

But using the same technique as before we prove easily that

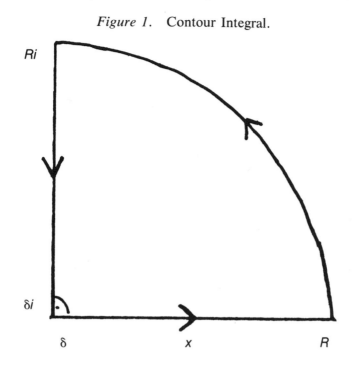

Figure 1. Contour Integral.

$$\int_{x_0^h}^{\infty} \cos(xt)x^{-(s+1-h)/h}\,dx = \cos\left(\frac{s+1}{2h}\right)\pi\,\Gamma[2 - (s+1)/h]|t|^{[(s+1)/h-2]}$$

$$- \int_0^{x_0^h} \cos(xt)x^{-(s+1-h)/h}\,dx$$

and the last integral can be replaced by a power series in t by expanding $\cos xt$ in a power series. Thus again we can write

$$\psi_{1s}(t) = -\frac{2|t|^{(s+1)/h}}{h}\Gamma[-(s+1)/h]\cos\left[\left(\frac{s+1}{2h}\right)\pi\right]x_0^{s+2} + \psi_{1s}^{*}(t) \quad (11)$$

where $\psi_{1s}^{*}(t)$ is analytic for all values of t. Comparing (10) and (11) we see that the result is the same for all $0 \le s \le 2h - 2$.

Now considering the two omitted cases, suppose first that $s = h - 1$, so that

$$\psi_{1s}(t) = \frac{2x_0^{h+1}}{h}\int_{x_0^h}^{\infty}\cos(xt)x^{-2}dx + \frac{2}{h}\int_0^{x_0^h}\cos(xt)x^{-(h-1)/h}\,dx$$

$$= \frac{2x_0}{h}\cos(x_0^h t) - \frac{2x_0^{h+1} t}{h}\int_{x_0^h}^{\infty}[(\sin xt)/x]dx$$

$$+ \frac{2}{h}\int_0^{x_0^h}\cos(xt)x^{-(h-1)/h}\,dx$$

$$= -\frac{\pi}{h}|t|x_0^{h+1} + \frac{2x_0}{h}\cos(x_0^h t) + \frac{2x_0^{h+1} t}{h}\int_0^{x_0^h}\frac{\sin xt}{x}dx$$

$$+ \frac{2}{h}\int_0^{x_0^h}\cos(xt)x^{1/h-1}\,dx$$

since

$$\frac{2}{\pi}\int_0^{\infty}[(\sin xt)/x]dx = +1 \qquad \text{if } t > 0$$
$$= -1 \qquad \text{if } t < 0$$

Finally, if $s = 2h - 1$

$$\psi_{1s}(t) = \frac{2x_0^{2h+2}}{h}\int_{x_0^h}^{\infty}\cos(xt)x^{-3}dx + \frac{2}{h}\int_0^{x_0^h}\cos(xt)x^{1/h-1}dx$$

$$= \frac{x^0}{h}\cos(x_0^h t) - \frac{tx_0^{2h+1}}{h}\int_{x_0^h}^{\infty}\frac{\sin xt}{x^2}\,dx\cdot$$

$$+ \frac{2}{h}\int_0^{x_0^h}\cos(xt)x^{1/h-1}\,dx$$

and

$$\int_{x_0^h}^{\infty}\frac{\sin xt}{x^2}\,dx = \mathrm{Im}\int_{x_0^h}^{\infty}(e^{ixt}/x^2)dx$$

and assuming $t > 1$

$$\int_{x_0^h}^{\infty}(e^{ixt}/x^2)dx = \int_{x_0^h}^{\infty}\frac{(e^{ixt}-1)-t(e^{ix}-1)}{x^2}\,dx + \frac{1}{x_0^h}$$

$$+ t\int_{x_0^h}^{\infty}\left(\frac{e^{ix}-1}{x^2}\right)dx$$

$$= \frac{1}{x_0^h} + t\int_{x_0^h}^{\infty}\left(\frac{e^{ix}-1}{x^2}\right)dx$$

$$- \int_0^{x_0^h}\frac{(e^{ixt}-1)-t(e^{ix}-1)}{x^2}\,dx$$

$$+ \int_0^\infty \frac{(e^{ixt} - 1) - t(e^{ix} - 1)}{x^2} \, dx$$

Now

$$\int_\delta^\infty \frac{(e^{ixt} - 1) - t(e^{ix} - 1)}{x^2} \, dx = \int_\delta^\infty \left(\frac{e^{ixt} - 1}{x^2} \right) dx - t \int_\delta^\infty \frac{e^{ix} - 1}{x^2} \, dx$$

$$= t \int_{t\delta}^\infty \frac{e^{ix} - 1}{x^2} \, dx - t \int_\delta^\infty \frac{e^{ix} - 1}{x^2} \, dx$$

where in the first integral (tx) has been replaced by x

$$= -t \int_\delta^{t\delta} \frac{e^{ix} - 1}{x^2} \, dx$$

Now expanding e^{ix} in power series and integrating term by term, we have that this equals

$$- it \log t + 0(\delta)$$

Thus for $t > 1$

$$\int_{x_0^h}^\infty \frac{\sin xt}{x^2} \, dx = t \int_{x_0^h}^\infty \frac{\sin x \, dx}{x^2} - \int_0^{x_0^h} \frac{\sin tx - t \sin x \, dx}{x^2} - t \log t$$

and note that the first two terms are analytic in t. A similar method proves the same result for $0 < t < 1$, and for t negative

$$\int_{x_0^h}^\infty \frac{\sin xt}{x^2} \, dx = - \int_{x_0^h}^\infty \frac{\sin (x|t|)}{x^2} \, dx$$

so that we can write

$$\int_{x_0^h}^\infty \frac{\sin xt \, dx}{x^2} = t \int_{x_0^h}^\infty \frac{\sin x}{x^2} - \int_0^{x_0^h} \frac{(\sin tx - t \sin x) dx}{x^2} - t \log |t|$$

Finally then

$$\psi_{1s}(t) = \frac{-x_0^{2h+1}}{h} t^2 \log |t| + \psi_{1s}^*(t) \qquad \text{if } s = 2h - 1$$

where ψ_{1s}^* is analytic for all t.

If we consider $\psi_{2s}(t) = \int e^{ixt} \, dG_2(x)$ in the same way, we find

$$\psi_{2s}(t) = - \frac{2it}{h} |t|^{(s+1)/h - 1} \Gamma\left[-\left(\frac{s+1}{h} \right) \right] \sin \left[\left(\frac{s+1}{2h} \right) \pi \right] x_0^{s+2} + \psi_{2s}^*(t)$$

where $\psi_{2s}^*(t)$ is analytic in t, if $s \neq h - 1$ or $2h - 1$.

If $s = h - 1$, we obtain

$$\psi_{2s}(t) = -\frac{2ix_0^{h+1}}{h} t \log|t| + \psi_{2s}^*(t)$$

if $s = 2h - 1$

$$\psi_{2s}(t) = -\frac{i\pi}{2h} x_0^{2h+1} t |t| + \psi_{2s}^*(t)$$

Similar characteristic function transforms can be obtained for the $G_{1s}^*(x)$ functions and we can summarize by saying that in all cases we have one term that is nonanalytic added to a function that is analytic. The nonanalytic terms take one of the forms: $|t|^\alpha$, $t|t|^\alpha$, $t \log|t|$, $|t| \log|t|$, $t^2 \log|t|$: for α of the form k/h, where k is a positive integer less than $2h$.

Consider now the characteristic function $\psi(t)$ corresponding to $F_h(r)$, we can write this in the form of a sum of terms of the preceding type, each multiplied by a corresponding α_k, selected from the set $k = 0,. . .,2h - s$, plus a characteristic function that possesses a continuous second derivative at the origin, corresponding to the property that $f^+(x)$ possesses a finite second moment.

Let us suppose that we can write

$$\psi(t) = \psi_1(t) + \psi_2(t)$$

where $\psi_2(t)$ is the characteristic function corresponding to the nonanalytic terms and $\psi_1(t)$ is a function that possesses a second derivative at the origin.

Then we can write

$$\log \psi_1(t) = \theta_0 + \theta_1 t + (\theta_2 + \theta_2^*)t^2$$

where θ_1 and θ_2 are the first and second derivatives at the origin and θ_2^* is zero at $t = 0$.

We assume that $\lim_{T \to \infty} \theta_2 = \bar{\theta}_2$ is finite. Since $\psi(0) = 1$

$$e_0^\theta = \psi_1(0) = 1 - \psi_2(0)$$

We assume that for large T, the α_k can be written of the same order of magnitude, so that $\psi_2(0)$ is of the same order of magnitude in T, and θ_0 is also of the same order of magnitude.

We consider the distribution of

$$\eta = \sum_{r=1}^{N} (x_r^h - \theta_1)/\sqrt{N}$$

Clearly the characteristic function for η can be written

$$\psi^*(t) = \exp\left[N\theta_0 + (\theta_2 + \theta_2^*)t\right] \left(1 + \frac{\psi_2(t/\sqrt{N})}{\psi_1(t/\sqrt{N})}\right)^N$$

Now the convergence criterion for distribution functions only requires that for any t the characteristic function converges to a limiting function that is a characteristic function. This will certainly be achieved if N and T tend to infinity in such a way that

$$\text{(1) } N\theta_0 \to 0 \qquad \text{(2) } \theta_2^* \to 0 \qquad \text{(3) } \lim \left(1 + \frac{\psi_2(t/\sqrt{N})}{\psi_1(t/\sqrt{N})}\right)^N = 1$$

If all $\alpha_k = 0(e^{-\kappa T/2} T^\rho)$ for some ρ, then for given t, $\psi_2(t/\sqrt{N})$ is at most of the same order in T, and $\psi_1(t/\sqrt{N}) \to 1$: if N is a function of T such that condition (1) is satisfied as $T \to \infty$, and θ_1 and θ_2 are bounded as $T \to \infty$. Now using the mean value theorem to consider the limit of $N\{\log[1 + \psi_2(t/\sqrt{N})/\psi_1(t/\sqrt{N})]\}$, a sufficient condition for (3) is that $\lim_{T\to\infty} (Ne^{-\kappa T} T^\rho) = 0$, and this is clearly also sufficient for (1). Thus convergence to a normal distribution with variance θ_2 will be achieved if

$$\lim_{\substack{T\to\infty \\ N\to\infty}} (Ne^{-\kappa T/2} T^\rho) = 0$$

and θ_2 has a finite limit as $T \to \infty$.

Clearly the conclusions of this section are very similar to those of the previous section. The value of κ defined here is closely related to that of Section II. Appendix B discusses appropriate values for κ for a general instrumental estimator. It is to be expected that if the values of the α_j were known, more exact estimates of the errors in the various approximations could be estimated by the methods of this section than by the cruder approximations of Section II. However, even for the general instrumental variable estimator, the formulae for the α_j in terms of the model parameters are very complicated, and even κ is difficult to evaluate, as Appendix B demonstrates. It is clear that κ and the α_j are quite sensitive to changes in the values of the model's parameters.

IV. A MONTE CARLO STUDY

The results of this article are easily illustrated by conducting a Monte Carlo study, and since the purpose of this is largely illustrative, it was decided to use the just-identified two-equation model. Suppose we are estimating by 2SLS the equation that can be written

$$y_1 = \beta y_2 + Z_1\gamma + u$$

where y_1, y_2, and u are $T \times 1$ vectors of endogenous variables and random errors, respectively, and Z_1 is a $T \times (m - 1)$ matrix of non-stochastic exogenous variables included in the equation with unconstrained coefficients. Write z as a $T \times 1$ vector of exogenous variables excluded from the equation. Then the 2SLS estimator can be regarded as defined by

$$z'y_1 = \hat{\beta}(z'y_2) + (z'Z_1)\hat{\gamma}$$
$$z'_1y_1 = \hat{\beta}(Z'_1y_2) + (Z'_1Z_1)\hat{\gamma}$$

and considering only $\hat{\beta}$ we can write

$$\hat{\beta} = \frac{[z'y_1 - (z'Z_1)(Z'_1Z_1)^{-1} Z'_1y_1]}{[z'y_2 - (z'Z_1)(Z'_1Z_1)^{-1} Z'_1y_2]}$$

We now write the reduced form equation for y_2 as

$$y_2 = p_1z + Z_1p_1 + v = \bar{y}_2 + v$$

where v is the random error on the reduced form and $\bar{y}_2$ is the systematic part of y_2.

Now write $v = \delta u + w$, where w is independent of u, and so $\delta = \rho\sigma_v/\sigma_u$, where $E(u_t^2) = \sigma_u^2$, $E(v_t^2) = \sigma_v^2$, $E(u_tv_t) = \rho\sigma_u\sigma_v$. Also define $z^{*'} = z' - (z'Z_1)(Z'Z_1)^{-1}Z'_1$. Then

$$\hat{\beta} - \beta = \frac{z^{*'}u}{z^{*'}\bar{y}_2 + z^{*'}w + \delta z^{*'}u}$$

Define

$$\xi = \frac{(\hat{\beta} - \beta)z^{*'}\bar{y}_2}{\sigma_u(z^{*'}z^*)^{1/2}}$$

$$p = \frac{z^{*'}u}{\sigma_u(z^{*'}z^*)^{1/2}}$$

$$q = \frac{z^{*'}w}{\sigma_v[(1 - \rho^2)z^{*'}z^*]^{1/2}}$$

$$\gamma_1 = \frac{\sigma_v[(1 - \rho^2)z^{*'}z^*]^{1/2}}{z^{*'}\bar{y}_2}$$

$$\gamma_2 = \rho\sigma_v \frac{(z^{*'}z^*)^{1/2}}{(z^{*'}\bar{y}_2)}$$

Then we can write

$$\xi = \frac{p}{1 + \gamma_1q + \gamma_2p}$$

and note that p and q are identically and independently distributed $N(0, 1)$. Given that both γ_1 and γ_2 are $0(T^{-1/2})$ it is clear that ξ is asymptotically equivalent to p so that ξ is asymptotically distributed $N(0, 1)$. It was decided to generate Monte Carlo samples by generating p and q directly. This allows up to 5000 replications for each model (corresponding to a given pair of numbers γ_1 and γ_2) to be generated very quickly.

We also generate Monte Carlo control variates. Clearly p is a control variate for ξ, and p^2 a control variate for ξ^2. Thus we consider

$$\eta_1 = \xi - p + \gamma_2$$

γ_2 is the Nagar approximation of $0(T^{-1/2})$ to the bias of ξ, so that η_1 is zero bias to this order of Nagar approximation. Writing

$$\eta_2 = \xi^2$$

$$\eta_3 = \xi^2 - p^2 - 3\gamma_1^2 - 9\gamma_2^2$$

$$= -\frac{2p^2(\gamma_1 q + \gamma_2 p) + p^2(\gamma_1 q + \gamma_2 p)^2}{(1 + \gamma_1 q + \gamma_2 p)^2} - 3\gamma_1^2 - 9\gamma_2^2$$

it is clear that the Nagar approximation to the bias of η_3 is zero to $0(T^{-3/2})$. Thus we consider

$$\bar{\xi} = \sum_{j=1}^{N} \xi_j/N$$

$$\bar{\eta}_1 = \sum_{j=1}^{N} \eta_{1j}/N$$

$$\bar{\eta}_2 = \sum_{j=1}^{N} \eta_{2j}/N$$

$$\bar{\eta}_3 = \sum_{j=1}^{N} \eta_{3j}/N$$

In fact for each sample of 5000 replications, we divide up into subsamples so that $N = 50, 100, 250, 500, 1000$. Then we would expect $\bar{\xi}$, $\bar{\eta}_1$, $\bar{\eta}_2$, $\bar{\eta}_3$ to be approximately normally distributed for large T and N [with γ_1 and γ_2 $0(T^{-1/2})$], with zero mean and variances of order $N^{-1/2}$, $(NT)^{-1/2}$, $N^{-1/2}$, and $(NT)^{-1/2}$, respectively. The γ_1 and γ_2 were chosen to correspond to only two ratios $\gamma_1/\gamma_2 = 5$ or $.5$. The corresponding ρ are $.196$ or $.898$. By regarding $(1 + \gamma_1 q + \gamma_2 p)^2/(\gamma_1^2 + \gamma_2^2)$ as a noncentral χ^2 of one degree of freedom, it is clear that the noncentrality parameter for this case is $1/(\gamma_1^2 + \gamma_2^2)$.

To compare this study with the discussion of Sargan and Mikhail (1971), note that in that article K was defined to equal $T\sigma_v^2(z^{*\prime}z^*)/(z^{*\prime}\bar{y}_2)^2$ and that in discussing the sample size necessary for a given accuracy in approximation, a standard value for K was taken to be one, based on values found in the estimated Klein–Goldberger model. From these definitions $T = K/(\gamma_1^2 + \gamma_2^2)$. Six cases were simulated and the cases, corresponding to different values of γ_1, γ_2 were selected so that pairs of cases with roughly the same $(\gamma_1^2 + \gamma_2^2)$ but different ρ ($\rho = .2$ or $.9$) could be compared. In fact, the six cases considered were defined as in Table 1.

Table 1. Six Simulations in Monte Carlo Study

Case	1	2	3	4	5	6
ρ	.196	.196	.196	.898	.898	.898
γ_1	.40	.20	.15	.18	.09	.07
γ_2	.08	.04	.03	.36	.18	.14
$\gamma_1^2 + \gamma_2^2$	.1664	.0416	.0234	.162	.0405	.0245
T	6.0	24.0	42.7	6.2	24.7	40.8
α_0	.1171	5.67×10^{-5}	8.78×10^{-9}	.0334	1.92×10^{-5}	9.98×10^{-9}
Nagar Approximation to Arithmetic Mean						
$\bar{\xi}$	$-.40$	$-.20$	$-.15$	$-.18$	$-.09$	$-.07$
$\bar{\eta}_2$	1.5376	1.1344	1.0756	2.2636	1.3159	1.1911
Asymptotic Variance						
$\bar{\eta}_1$	.1728	.0432	.0243	.2916	.0729	.0441
$\bar{\eta}_3$	2.3040	.5760	.3240	8.1648	2.0412	1.2348

The values of T in Table 1 correspond to $K = 1$. It can be shown that the probability density in this case is given by probability density function

$$\text{p.d.f.}\,\xi = \frac{\exp\{-\frac{1}{2}\xi^2/[1 - 2\gamma_1\xi + (\gamma_1^2 + \gamma_2^2)\xi^2]\}}{\sqrt{2\pi}[1 - 2\gamma_1\xi + (\gamma_1^2 + \gamma_2^2)\xi^2]}$$

$$\times \left[\frac{|1 - \gamma_1\xi|}{[1 - 2\gamma_1\xi + (\gamma_1^2 + \gamma_2^2)\xi^2]^{1/2}} I\left(\frac{|1 - \gamma_1\xi|}{\gamma_2[1 - 2\gamma_1\xi + (\gamma_1^2 + \gamma_2^2)\xi^2]^{1/2}} \right) \right.$$

$$\left. + (2\gamma_2^2/\pi)^{1/2} \exp\left(-[1 - \gamma_1\xi]^2/\{2\gamma_2^2[1 - \gamma_1\xi + (\gamma_1^2 + \gamma_2^2)\xi^2]\}\right) \right]$$

where

$$I(z) = \frac{1}{\sqrt{2\pi}} \int_{-z}^{z} \exp(-\frac{1}{2}x^2)dx$$

Note that with γ_1 and γ_2 both $0(T^{-1/2})$ $I(\cdot) = 1 - 0(e^{-\kappa T})$, for some κ, and the tails of the expansion for large T can be asymptotically approximated by

$$\frac{\gamma_1 \exp\{-1/[2(\gamma_1^2 + \gamma_2^2)]\}}{\sqrt{2\pi}(\gamma_2^2 + \gamma_2^2)^{3/2}|\xi|}$$

so that in the expansions of Section III

$$\alpha_0 = \gamma_1 \exp[-1/2(\gamma_1^2 + \gamma_2^2)]/[\sqrt{2\pi}(\gamma_2^2 + \gamma_2^2)^{3/2}]$$

This is given in Table 1. Note that α_i, $i > 0$, are of the same order of magnitude, and the condition for the good approximation of the distribution of the moment by the asymptotic distribution devised in Section

III, that $\lim_{T \to \infty} N\theta_0 = 0$, makes it clear that we must choose N such that $N\alpha_0$ is small. Thus we would not expect a good approximation for Cases 1 and 4 even for N as small as 50 but that for the other cases the approximation might be expected to be good for $N < 10,000$.

The asymptotic distributions of these Monte Carlo estimators is discussed in Sargan (1977). From this discussion we conclude that ξ can be regarded as approximately normally distributed with mean $-\gamma_1$ and variance $1/N$, $\bar{\eta}_1$ with mean zero and variance $(\gamma_1^2 + 2\gamma_2^2)/N$, $\bar{\eta}_2$ with mean $1 + 3(\gamma_1^2 + 3\gamma_2^2)$ and variance $2/N$, and $\bar{\eta}_3$ with mean zero and variance $12(\gamma_1^2 + 5\gamma_2^2)/N$. The appropriate means are listed in the rows of Table 1 headed "Nagar Approximations to Arithmetic Means," and $(\gamma_1^2 + 2\gamma_2^2)$ and $12(\gamma_1^2 + 5\gamma_2^2)$ are given in the last rows of Table 1. Note that to this asymptotic approximation it will only be more efficient to use the control variate approach to estimating the variance (i.e., to use $\bar{\eta}_3$ rather than $\bar{\eta}_2$) if $12(\gamma_1^2 + 5\gamma_2^2) < 2$. So comparing the numbers in the last row of Table 1 with 2, it is clear that we would expect that the control variate estimate would be no better for cases 1 and 5, and a good deal worse for case 4.

Since for $N = 50$ and 100, we have, respectively, 100 and 50, subsamples by suitably subdividing our sample of 5000 replications, it is possible to undertake a detailed comparison with these distributions. In fact for $\bar{\xi}$ and $\bar{\eta}_2$, comparisons were made with crude asymptotic approximations in which the mean of $\bar{\xi}$ was set equal to zero and the mean for $\bar{\eta}_2$ was set equal to one. In each case the numbers occurring between limits set at ± 2.58, ± 1.96, ± 1.64, ± 0.67, and 0, multiplied by the asymptotic standard errors, were compared with the expected numbers from the asymptotic distributions. In order to conserve space, Tables 2 and 3 give the results for $N = 50$ and 100, respectively, for cases 2, 3, 5, and 6. The approximations for cases 1 and 4 were very poor. On the other hand, the approximations for the remaining cases were reasonable. The biases in the $\bar{\xi}$ and $\bar{\eta}_2$ were in the expected directions. Clearly the control variate estimates ($\bar{\eta}_1$ and $\bar{\eta}_3$) distributions are better approximated by the asymptotic distributions than the corresponding $\bar{\xi}$ and $\bar{\eta}_2$ distributions, and the approximation is better for small ρ (cases 2 and 3) than for large ρ. Considering only cases 2 and 3, there seems to be neither relatively little difference between the goodness of approximation for $N = 50$ and $N = 100$ nor a great deal of difference between the results for (.20, .04) and (.15, .03) when considering $\bar{\eta}_1$ and $\bar{\eta}_3$. For $\bar{\eta}_2$ the (.15, .03) case gives a better result on the top tail. Note however that from this we can conclude that it is always better to use, for small ρ, the control variates $\bar{\eta}_1$ and $\bar{\eta}_3$, since the Monte Carlo results suggest a lower variance. Similarly although with the control variates the approximation to the asymptotic distribution is apparently no worse for $N = 50$ than for $N = 100$, the fact that the asymptotic variance for

Table 2. $N = 50$. Distributions of 100 Replications

Asymptotic distribution	.20, .04				.15, .03				.09, .18				.07, .14			
	$\bar{\xi}$	$\bar{\eta}_1$	$\bar{\eta}_2$	$\bar{\eta}_3$	$\bar{\xi}$	$\bar{\eta}_1$	$\bar{\eta}_2$	$\bar{\eta}_3$	$\bar{\xi}$	$\bar{\eta}_1$	$\bar{\eta}_2$	$\bar{\eta}_3$	$\bar{\xi}$	$\bar{\eta}_1$	$\bar{\eta}_2$	$\bar{\eta}_3$
.5	0	5	0	1	0	1	0	0	23	13	0	0	7	8	0	2
1.0	0	5	0	1	0	3	0	1	35	17	0	1	11	9	0	2
2.5	5	9	0	2	4	4	0	2	41	24	0	3	17	12	1	3
5.0	5	10	1	4	7	10	3	5	55	30	0	6	25	15	2	6
25.1	34	29	16	35	29	22	18	36	78	56	7	20	61	38	16	39
50	58	51	30	51	49	50	42	60	88	75	17	34	76	60	31	58
74.9	82	78	53	64	77	74	66	75	98	86	23	48	96	76	49	69
95.0	95	94	65	84	95	92	88	90	100	99	33	65	99	96	67	84
97.5	98	97	73	88	99	96	93	93	100	100	44	72	100	99	75	85
99.0	99	97	85	90	100	99	96	95	100	100	49	80	100	100	77	88
99.5	100	97	91	90	100	100	97	96	100	100	51	82	100	100	82	90
100	100	100	100	100	100	100	100	100	100	100	100	100	100	100	100	100

Table 3. N = 100. Distribution of 50 Replications

Asymptotic distribution	.20, .04				.15, .03				.09, .18				.07, .14			
	$\bar{\xi}$	$\bar{\eta}_1$	$\bar{\eta}_2$	$\bar{\eta}_3$	$\bar{\xi}$	$\bar{\eta}_1$	$\bar{\eta}_2$	$\bar{\eta}_3$	$\bar{\xi\xi}$	$\bar{\eta}_1$	$\bar{\eta}_2$	$\bar{\eta}_3$	$\bar{\xi}$	$\bar{\eta}_1$	$\bar{\eta}_2$	$\bar{\eta}_3$
.25	0	1	0	0	0	0	0	0	25	7	0	0	4	7	0	1
.50	1	1	0	0	0	1	0	1	28	12	0	0	8	7	0	2
1.25	1	5	0	1	1	3	0	4	32	16	0	0	12	8	0	2
2.50	4	8	0	1	4	4	0	5	36	20	0	2	19	9	0	3
12.57	15	14	6	12	15	11	9	16	45	34	1	6	38	21	5	18
23	27	25	13	23	29	26	21	28	50	43	2	11	47	29	14	26
37.43	44	38	19	31	40	38	27	36	50	46	4	16	50	40	20	31
47.50	50	48	25	41	48	46	44	44	50	50	7	28	50	48	30	43
48.75	50	49	32	42	49	48	46	46	50	50	9	32	50	49	32	43
49.50	50	50	38	44	50	49	48	49	50	50	12	35	50	50	36	46
49.75	50	50	40	45	50	49	49	49	50	50	15	38	50	50	38	46
50	50	50	50	50	50	50	50	50	50	50	50	50	50	50	50	50

$N = 100$ is half that for $N = 50$ ensures that in some cases it would be better to use $N = 100$ to obtain adequate accuracy.

Considering now the cases (.09, .18) and (.07, .14), the expected bias in the asymptotic distribution of $\bar{\xi}$ is apparent, but it is clear that $\bar{\eta}_1$ also has a downward bias. Even so, taking account of the much lower asymptotic variances, the use of the control variate is very worthwhile. Similarly $\bar{\eta}_2$ and $\bar{\eta}_3$ are both biased upward, but the bias is much less for $\bar{\eta}_3$. However, for $\bar{\eta}_3$, the upper tail approximation is still rather poor unless using a T corresponding to (.07, .14) rather than (.09, .18). The advantage in using $N = 100$ rather than $N = 50$ is well represented by the ratio of asymptotic variances.

For $N = 250$ and $N = 500$, where the number of replications is only 20 or 10, respectively, this elaborate comparison of the Monte Carlo sample distribution with the asymptotic distribution is not possible. For $\bar{\xi}$ and $\bar{\eta}_1$, where the form of the difference between the true distribution and the asymptotic distribution function was not obvious, it was decided to consider only the first and third quartiles of the observed distribution for $N = 250$, and these are reported in Table 4. For these, given only a sample of 20 replications, the standard error of estimate of the quartiles is relatively large and can be approximated by .019 for the quartiles of $\bar{\xi}$ for all cases, and by .019 multiplied by the square root of the last but one line in Table 1 for the quartiles of $\bar{\eta}_1$. It is clear that it is worthwhile to use the control variate rather than the $\bar{\xi}$ estimator. For $\bar{\eta}_1$ for cases 1 and 4, the results are poor in the sense that $\bar{\eta}_1$ gives no better estimates in 50% of the simulations than taking zero as the mean of $\bar{\xi}$. For the other cases, $\bar{\eta}_1$ gives satisfactory and relatively unbiased estimates. It is confirmed that there is a negative bias in $\bar{\eta}_1$ for (.09, .18) and (.07, .14) but this is relatively small compared with the bias in $\bar{\xi}$, so that it is certainly worthwhile to use the control variate to estimate the bias.

Considering now $\bar{\eta}_2$ and $\bar{\eta}_3$, it seemed on initial inspection and is to be expected on *a priori* grounds that the large outliers would be predominantly positive so that the distributions are biased upward. It was decided that an adequate representation of the bias is given by looking at the median. The results are reported in Table 5 for $N = 250$ and $N = 500$. Clearly there are very strong upward biases for cases 1 and 4 for both N. The standard errors for the medians of $\bar{\eta}_3$ are approximately obtained by multiplying .018 by the square root of the last line of Table 1. The medians of $\bar{\eta}_3$ for cases 2, 3, and 6 are not significantly different from zero, but in case 5, for both $N = 250$ and 500, the median is significantly greater than zero, when using asymptotic approximations to the standard errors of the medians. Even so, for this latter case, the use of $\bar{\eta}_3$ would give a much better estimate of the bias on the average than the assumption that the bias is zero.

Table 4. $N = 250$. First and Third Quartiles for $\bar{\xi}$ and $\bar{\eta}_1$

		.40, .08	.20, .04	.15, .03	.18, .36	.09, .18	.07, .14
$\bar{\xi}$	Q_1	−.28	−.070	−.060	−.83	−.28	−.161
	Q_3	.08	.017	.031	.00	−.19	−.100
$\bar{\eta}_1$	Q_1	−.14	−.019	−.003	−.39	−.045	−.023
	Q_3	.10	.009	.006	.40	−.021	−.004

A final straightforward analysis of this latter point was made by considering the proportion of the Monte Carlo replications for which either (1) the Nagar approximation to the first moment $-\gamma_2$ was better approximated by zero than by (a) $\bar{\xi}$ or, (b) $(\bar{\eta}_1 - \gamma_2)$, (2) the Nagar approximations to the second moment, $1 + 3(\gamma_1^2 + 3\gamma_2^2)$, was better approximated by one than by (c) $\bar{\eta}_2$ or (d) $\bar{\eta}_3 + 1 + 3(\gamma_1^2 + 3\gamma_2^2)$. Tables 6, 7, 8, and 9 record the proportions satisfying these conditions. We note the following generalizations. First with respect to $\bar{\xi}$ and $\bar{\eta}_1$, the Monte Carlo results are relatively poor for cases 1 and 4, (.40, .08) and (.18, .36). For the other cases it appears true that the larger N, the lower the proportion that lies outside the intervals, although the effective sample sizes for each case are small for $N = 500$ and 1000. Even so for $\bar{\eta}_1$, there seems little point in increasing N above 100, and the asymptotic variance gives a reasonable guide to the accuracy with which the Nagar approximation first moment is estimated. For $\bar{\eta}_2$ and $\bar{\eta}_3$, the Monte Carlo results are extremely poor for cases 1 and 4. For the other cases, somewhat larger N is indicated for good results. Clearly it is marginally worthwhile to use the control variate $\bar{\eta}_3$ in the cases 2, 3, 5, and 6 where good estimates of Nagar approximate moments can be made. The accuracy is sensitive to ρ, and with $\bar{\eta}_3$, $N = 250$ seems appropriate if ρ is small or K is relatively small, but otherwise $N = 500$ should be used.

V. TRUNCATED MONTE CARLO ESTIMATES

The results of the last section are of some interest in justifying the theoretical conclusions of the earlier sections. However there may be practical reasons why we would want to produce Monte Carlo estimates

Table 5. Medians for $N = 50$ and $N = 500$

N		.40, .08	.20, .04	.15, .03	.18, .36	.09, .18	.07, .14
250	$\bar{\eta}_2$	5.53	1.180	1.076	59.0	1.560	1.224
	$\bar{\eta}_3$	3.95	.019	−.007	56.7	.215	.016
500	$\bar{\eta}_2$	4.61	1.174	1.068	43.9	1.520	1.181
	$\bar{\eta}_3$	3.12	.015	−.008	141.6	.169	−.002

Table 6.   Proportion of $\bar{\xi}$ that lie in the Interval $(0, -2\gamma_2)$

N	.40, .08	.20, .04	.15, .03	.18, .36	.09, .18	.07, .14
50	.27	.20	.13	.50	.66	.61
100	.30	.32	.28	.46	.82	.86
250	.40	.50	.45	.40	.95	1.00
500	.60	.90	.40	.30	1.00	1.00
1000	.40	1.00	.60	.60	1.00	1.00

of the Nagar approximations to the moments, and it is clear that we might expect to do this more efficiently if we made use of a censored or truncated distribution for $\xi = \sqrt{T}(\hat{\beta} - \beta)/\sigma_\beta$ in estimating its moments. Thus if we know that x is asymptotically distributed as a t ratio, we can censor the distribution by making use of the normal distribution. The proposal is then that we define a new variable ξ^+ such that

$$
\begin{aligned}
\xi^+ &= \xi & &\text{if } |\xi| \leqslant \xi_1 \\
&= \xi_2 & &\text{if } \xi > \xi_1 \\
&= -\xi_2 & &\text{if } \xi < -\xi_1
\end{aligned}
$$

From this we can define

$$
\begin{aligned}
\eta_1^+ &= \xi^+ - p + \gamma_2 \\
\eta_2^+ &= \xi^{+2} \\
\eta_3^+ &= \xi^{+2} - p^2 - 3\gamma_1^2 - 9\gamma_2^2
\end{aligned}
$$

by analogy with our previous definitions, and the corresponding simulation sample means $\bar{\xi}^+$, $\bar{\eta}_1^+$, $\bar{\eta}_2^+$, $\bar{\eta}_3^+$. The results clearly depend on the choice of ξ_1 and ξ_2. In fact, the Monte Carlo simulations were carried out for four different combinations of ξ_1 and ξ_2. In the first pair it was decided to use the relatively crude choice of ξ_2 such that $\xi_2 = \xi_1$, and to choose $\xi_1 = 2.58$ or 3.00; 2.58 was chosen to correspond to the symmetric 99% confidence interval for the normal distribution and 3.00 corresponds to the symmetric 99.73% confidence interval. As an alternative the choice of $\xi_2 = \xi_1 + (1/\xi_1)$ was also considered and simulated for $\xi_1 = 2.58$ and 3.00. This was motivated by noting that

Table 7.   Proportion of $\bar{\eta}_1$ that lie in the Interval $(-\gamma_2, +\gamma_2)$

N	.40, .08	.20, .04	.15, .03	.18, .36	.09, .18	.07, .14
50	.31	.75	.78	.57	.98	.99
100	.36	.90	.92	.48	.98	1.00
250	.45	.95	1.00	.35	1.00	1.00
500	.60	1.00	1.00	.30	1.00	1.00
1000	.40	1.00	1.00	.60	1.00	1.00

Table 8. Proportion of $\bar{\eta}_2$ that lie in the Interval $[1, 1+6(\gamma_1^2+3\gamma_2^2)]$

N	.40, .08	.20, .04	.15, .03	.18, .36	.09, .18	.07, .14
50	.34	.36	.26	.27	.60	.42
100	.16	.38	.18	.12	.58	.50
250	.05	.65	.60	.00	.70	.85
500	.10	1.00	1.00	.00	.80	.80
1000	.00	1.00	1.00	.00	.80	1.00

$$\frac{1}{\sqrt{2\pi}} \int_\xi^\infty x^h e^{-\frac{x^2}{2}} dx = \frac{1}{\sqrt{2\pi}} e^{-\frac{\xi^2}{2}} \xi^{h-1} \{[1 + (h-1)/\xi^2] + 0(\xi^{-4})\}$$

using the standard asymptotic expansion derived by integration by parts. Thus writing

$$I(\xi) = \frac{1}{\sqrt{2\pi}} \int_{-\infty}^\xi \exp(-\frac{1}{2}x^2) dx, \qquad \int_\xi^\infty x^h I_1(x) dx - [\xi + (1/\xi)]^h [1 - I(\xi)]$$

$$= 0[I_1(\xi)\xi^{h-5}]$$

where

$$I_r(x) = \left(\frac{d}{dx}\right)^r I(x)$$

There is no problem in showing similarly that

$$\int_\xi^\infty x^h I_r(x) dx + \left(\xi + \frac{1}{\xi}\right)^h I_{(r-1)}(\xi) = 0[I_{r-1}(\xi)\xi^{h-4}]$$

It follows that for any Edgeworth expansion the error in truncating at $x = \xi_1$ and then using $\xi_2 = (\xi_1 + 1/\xi_1)$ as representative value on the truncated tail produces errors of relative order ξ_1^{-4} in any finite moment and so would be expected to produce rather better approximations to Nagar moment approximations than the setting of $\xi_2 = \xi_1$.

Table 9. Proportion of $\bar{\eta}_3$ that lie in the Interval $-3(\gamma_1^2+3\gamma_2^2)$, $3(\gamma_1^2+3\gamma_2^2)$

N	.40, .08	.20, .04	.15, .03	.18, .36	.09, .18	.07, .14
50	.36	.70	.58	.27	.53	.55
100	.16	.80	.72	.12	.70	.82
250	.05	.80	.90	.00	.65	.85
500	.10	1.00	1.00	.00	.90	.80
1000	.00	1.00	1.00	.00	.80	.80

Table 10. Sample Distributions for Truncated η_1^+ and η_3^+. $N = 50$, 100 Replications, $\gamma_1 = .04$, $\gamma_2 = .20$

Asymptotic Distribution	$\bar{\eta}_1^+$					$\bar{\eta}_3^+$					
ξ_1	∞^a	2.58	2.58	3.00	3.00	∞^a	2.58	2.58	2.58	3.00	3.00
ξ_2	∞	2.58	2.97	3.00	3.33	∞	2.58	2.58	2.97	3.00	3.33
.5	5	1	2	2	2	1	0	0	0	1	1
1	5	1	3	3	4	1	0	0	0	1	1
2.5	9	3	5	5	6	2	5	5	2	2	2
5	10	5	10	7	10	4	10	10	4	6	4
25.1	29	29	33	23	27	35	38	38	29	41	34
50	51	52	51	47	50	51	68	68	51	63	56
74.9	78	69	72	77	77	64	87	87	80	76	71
95	94	91	89	94	94	84	98	98	90	98	89
97.5	97	94	93	97	97	88	99	99	91	99	94
99	97	99	99	98	97	90	100	100	95	100	98
99.5	97	100	100	99	97	90	100	100	96	100	99
100	100	100	100	100	100	100	100	100	100	100	100

[a] These columns are the same as those for the untruncated distributions in Table 2.

Table 11. Sample Distributions for Truncated η_1^+ and η_3^+ $N = 50$, 100 Replications, $\gamma_1 = .18$, $\gamma_2 = .09$

Asymptotic Distribution	η_1^+					η_3^+				
ξ_1	∞^a	2.58	2.58	3.00	3.00	∞^a	2.58	2.58	3.00	3.00
ξ_2	∞	2.58	2.97	3.00	3.33	∞	2.58	2.97	3.00	3.33
.5	13	0	0	0	0	0	0	0	0	0
1	17	0	0	0	0	1	2	0	2	1
2.5	24	0	1	1	5	3	7	4	5	3
5	30	0	4	4	10	6	16	9	10	5
25.1	56	5	22	19	32	20	69	51	42	31
50	75	25	42	43	57	34	90	70	73	61
74.9	86	49	68	70	79	48	100	87	92	80
95	99	90	93	97	99	65	100	100	99	96
97.5	100	96	98	99	100	72	100	100	100	99
99	100	98	99	100	100	80	100	100	100	99
99.5	100	100	100	100	100	82	100	100	100	100
100	100	100	100	100	100	100	100	100	100	100

[a] The columns for $\xi_1 = \infty$, $\xi_2 = \infty$ correspond to the untruncated distributions of Table 2. Note that the asymptotic distributions of $\bar\eta_1$ and $\bar\eta_3$ are worst approximated by the sample distribution of $\bar\eta_1$ and $\bar\eta_3$ when $\gamma_1 = .18$ and $\gamma_2 = .09$, and that the sample distribution of $\bar\eta_1$ has a long negative skew tail, and the sample distribution of $\bar\eta_3$ has a long positive skew tail. Clearly truncation with $\xi_1 = 3$, $\xi_2 = 3.33$ corrects this rather well, and there seems no obvious bias in the approximations of the actual distribution by the asymptotic distribution in this case, and the results for the (.04, .20) case seems also quite good.

293

In fact the general results of the Monte Carlo simulation justified these theoretical arguments, but the results would take rather a large amount of space to display. However the results for the (.40, .08) and (.18, .36) cases were still very poor, and the results for (.15, .03) and (.07, .14) cases were sufficiently good when not truncated that truncation did not produce a major improvement. Thus the only tables given are for the $N = 50$, (.20, .04) and (.09, .18) cases (Tables 10 and 11), which should be compared with Table 2. Only sample distributions for $\bar{\eta}_1^+$ and $\bar{\eta}_3^+$ are given, since our previous results, and these Monte Carlo results made it clear that these control variates were more efficient than the crude $\bar{\xi}^+$, $\bar{\eta}_2^+$ estimates.

However, a narrower truncation may be preferable. Indeed if we are not particularly concerned with whether the sample distribution approximates well the asymptotic distributions but rather consider the probability of being within a given symmetric confidence interval, then there are some initial indications that it may pay to use a smaller ξ_1. However there is no uniformity between different cases and different confidence intervals. Clearly truncation is better than no truncation but the result is insensitive to the truncation limits used if they are within the limits discussed here.

VI.   GENERAL COMMENTS AND CONCLUSIONS

The author has devoted some effort to discussing a phenomenon that should not arise, since if a moment is known to be infinite there seems little point in estimating it by Monte Carlo methods. However the estimated Nagar moments are of interest because they throw light on the coefficients of the Edgeworth expansion for the distribution function, and so indirectly on the distribution function itself. Thus there may be some point in deliberately considering Monte Carlo estimates of infinite moments.

APPENDIX A

The Order of Magnitude of $Q(\varepsilon, R)$ as $T \to \infty$

Accepting the definitions of Section II of this article, we discuss the order of magnitude of Q by defining a suitable seminorm. We can clearly simplify our discussion without loss of generality by linearly transforming the endogenous variables so that the variance matrix of the errors on the reduced form equations is the unit matrix. Denoting the $T \times n$ data matrix of endogenous variables by Y, and the $T \times m$ matrix of exogenous variables by Z, we assume that the exogenous variables have also been linearly transformed so that $Z'Z = TI_m$. Then if the reduced form equations are written in the form

$$y' = PZ' + V'$$

and if $\hat{P}$ are the unconstrained OLS estimates of P so that

$$\hat{P} = (Y'Z)(Z'Z)^{-1}$$

then we define

$$p = \text{vec}(\hat{P} - P)$$

and p is then a vector of nm independent identically distributed normal variates with mean zero, variance $1/T$. Defining

$$W = [Y'Y - (Y'Z)(Z'Z)^{-1}(Z'Y)]/(T - m),$$

W is an $n \times n$ Wishart matrix of degrees of freedom $T - m$, and variance matrix I. Denote by w the vector of diagonal and superdiagonal elements of W, and assume that q of Section II is made up of p and w. Then a suitable seminorm in q space is defined by

$$D(q) = \max[p'p, \text{tr} (W - I) - \log \det W]$$

$D(q)$ obviously has the two properties

(1) $D(q) \geqslant 0$,   all q
(2) $D(q) = 0$ if and only if $q = \bar{q}$, where $\bar{q} = E(q)$

Now define

$$D_0 = \inf [D(q){:}q \in S)$$

where S is the zero set, and

$$D_\varepsilon = \inf [D(q){:}q \notin \tilde{S}(\varepsilon)]$$

where $\tilde{S}(\varepsilon)$ is defined in Section II.

Clearly since $\phi(q - \bar{q})$ is continuous in some neighborhood of $q = \bar{q}$, we have $D_0 > 0$. Also by choosing ε sufficiently small we can ensure that $|D_\varepsilon/D_0 - 1| < h$ for any positive h. Consider the set S^* defined by $q \in S^*$ if $D(q) \geqslant D_\varepsilon$. Clearly if $q \notin \tilde{S}(\varepsilon)$ then $D(q) \geqslant D_\varepsilon$. Also if $q \notin \tilde{S}(\varepsilon,R)$ then $q \notin \tilde{S}(\varepsilon)$ or $q \notin H$. Now define D_R by $D_R = \inf [D(q){:}q \notin H]$. Clearly this is a strictly increasing function of R, so that it is possible to choose R so that $D_R > D_\varepsilon$. It follows that if we denote the complement of a set by $\sim$, $\sim H \subset S^*$, and $\sim \tilde{S}(\varepsilon) \subset S^*$, so that $\sim \tilde{S}(\varepsilon,R) \subset S^*$. Thus

$$Q \geqslant P(q \in S^*)$$

Now S^* is defined as the union of points where $p'p \geqslant D_\varepsilon$ or $\text{tr} (W$

$- I) - \log \det W \geqslant D_\varepsilon$. Denote tr $(W - I) - \log \det W = \psi(w)$. Since p and w are statistically independent

$$P(q \in S^*) = P(p'p \geqslant D_\varepsilon) + P[\psi(w) \geqslant D_\varepsilon]$$

$$- P(p'p \geqslant D_\varepsilon)P[\psi(w) \geqslant D_\varepsilon] \quad \text{(A1)}$$

Since $T(p'p)$ is distributed as a χ^2 of nm degrees of freedom, $P(p'p \geqslant D_\varepsilon)$ can be approximated by the first term of the expansion for the tail of the χ^2

$$P(p'p \geqslant D_\varepsilon) \, [= \text{UR}] \, (\tfrac{1}{2}TD_\varepsilon)^{(nm - 1)/2} \exp(-\tfrac{1}{2}TD_\varepsilon)/\Gamma(\tfrac{1}{2}nm) \quad \text{(A2)}$$

Now considering $P[\psi(w) \geqslant D_\varepsilon]$, write the probability density function for W as $p(W)$ so that

$$P[\psi(w) \geqslant D_\varepsilon] = \int_{\phi(w) \,\geqslant\, D_\varepsilon} p(W)dW$$

Then if $T^* = T - m$

$$p(W) = (T^*/2)^{Tn/2}/\{\pi^{n(n - 1)/2} \prod_{k=0}^{n-1} \Gamma[\tfrac{1}{2}(T^* - k)]\}$$

$$(\det W)^{(T^* - n - 1)/2} \exp\left(-\tfrac{1}{2}T^* \text{ tr } W\right)$$

Define

$$k^* = (T^*/2)^{Tn/2}/\{\pi^{n(n - 1)/2} \prod_{k=0}^{n-1} \Gamma[\tfrac{1}{2}(T^* - k)]\}$$

Now choose a small positive λ less than 1, and define $\eta = 1 - \lambda$. Note that if

$$\text{tr } (W - I) - \log \det W \geqslant D_\varepsilon$$

then

$$p(W) \leqslant k^* \exp[-\tfrac{1}{2}\lambda T^*; h + D_\varepsilon](\det W)^{(\eta T^* - n - 1)/2}\exp(-\tfrac{1}{2}\eta T^* \text{ tr } W)$$

and

$$P[\psi(w) \geqslant D_\varepsilon] \leqslant k^* \exp[-\tfrac{1}{2}\lambda T^*(n + D_\varepsilon)]$$

$$\times \int (\det W)^{(\eta T^* - n - 1)/2}\exp(-\tfrac{1}{2}\eta T^* \text{ tr } W)dW$$

where we now relax the restriction to integrate over the region where $\psi(w) \geqslant D_\varepsilon$, and instead consider integration over the whole set such that W is nonnegative definite. Making use of the well-known result for the integral of the Wishart distribution choosing λ so that T^* is an integer, we find that

$$P[\psi(w) \geqslant D_\varepsilon] \leqslant \exp(-\frac{1}{2}\lambda D_\varepsilon T^*)\left(\left[(T^*/2)^{\lambda T^* n/2}/\eta^{\eta T^* n/2}\right]\left\{\prod_{k=0}^{n-1}\Gamma[\frac{1}{2}(\eta T^* - \text{k})]\right.\right.$$

$$\left.\left./\Gamma[\frac{1}{2}(T^* - k)]\}\exp(-\frac{1}{2}\lambda T^* n)\right)\right.$$

But using the Stirling approximation for large z, we can prove that

$$\prod_{k=0}^{n-1}\log\Gamma[\frac{1}{2}(z - k)] = \frac{1}{2}n[(z - n - 1)\log\frac{1}{2}z - z + \log 2\pi] + 0(1/z)$$

$$\text{as } z \to \infty$$

so that

$$\frac{1}{2}\lambda T^* n \log\frac{1}{2}T^* - \frac{1}{2}\eta T^* n \log \eta - \sum_{k+0}^{n-1}\{\log\Gamma[\frac{1}{2}(T^* - k)] - \log I$$

$$= -\frac{1}{2}n(n + 1)\log \eta + 0(1/T^*)$$

Clearly if $\lambda < h$, then we can conclude that

$$P[\psi(w) \geqslant D_\varepsilon) = 0\{\exp[-\frac{1}{2}T(1 - h)D_\varepsilon]\} \qquad \text{as } T \to \infty \qquad \text{(A3)}$$

Substituting (A1) and (A3) into (A2), we conclude that

$$Q = 0\left(e^{-T(1-h)D_\varepsilon/2}\right)$$

Since $\lim_{\varepsilon \to 0} D_\varepsilon = D_0$, we can conclude that for any $h > 0$, provided ε is sufficiently small

$$Q = 0\left(e^{-T(1-h)D_0/2}\right)$$

The seminorm used above obviously facilitates the discussion of the probability relating to W. D_0 will be small when there is a point of the zero set close to $\bar{q}$, and by considering each econometric estimator separately, we find this corresponds to models where the equation is almost unidentified.

APPENDIX B

The Tails of the Instrumental Variable Distribution

In Sargan and Mikhail (1971), formulae are given for the exact coefficient of the inverse powers of r in formulae (7) and (8) of this article for α_0, α_1, α_2, for estimation of a simultaneous equation that contains two endogenous variables.

The equation to be estimated can be written

$$y_1 = \beta y_2 + Z_1\gamma + u \tag{B1}$$

as in Section IV of this article, and we can write for the reduced form equation for y_2

$$y_2 = Z_1 p_1 + Z_2 p_2 + Z_4 p_4 + v \tag{B2}$$

where, as in Sargan and Mikhail (1971), we assume that $(Z_1 Z_2)$ are used as instrumental variables and that an initial linear transformation of the exogenous variables has been carried out so that if $Z = (Z_1 : Z_2 : Z_4)$, $Z'Z = TI$. The asymptotic behavior of the formulae of Sargan and Mikhail (1971) can be considered by noting that in the integrals defined there $D = 0(T^{-1/2})$ and that the range of integration can in the limit be taken as $\pi/2 \leqslant \theta \leqslant \pi$, and $-\infty \leqslant s \leqslant \infty$. The resulting asymptotic approximation is

$$P(\hat{\beta} - \beta > r) = \frac{\exp{(-kT)}}{(r - \delta)^N} \left(\frac{\delta}{2}\right)^N \frac{(kT)^{N/2}}{\Gamma[(N/2) + 1]}$$

$$\left[1 - \frac{k\delta T}{(r - \delta)} + \frac{\delta^2 kT}{(N + 2)} \frac{[kT(N + 3) - (N + 1)]}{(r - \delta)^2}\right]$$

where

$$k = \frac{1}{2}\left(\frac{p_2' p_2}{\sigma_v^2}\right) \quad \text{and} \quad \delta = \rho\sigma_u/\sigma_v$$

Clearly k is model dependent and can be regarded as small when the equation is badly identified.

It is quite difficult to extend this to the case where there are more than two endogenous variables in the equation. This is partly because the large T approximation given in Sargan (1976) only covers the part of the multivariate tail distribution where $2\omega'(b - \beta) < \sigma^2$, and the notation is that of the quoted article, and in particular β, y_{2t}, and v_t are now vectors and b is the instrumental variable estimate of β, and $E(u_t^2) = \sigma^2$, $E(u_t v_t) = \omega$. However, it is not too difficult to obtain a similar formula for an asymptotic approximation to the joint density for values of b where $2\omega'(b - \beta) > \sigma^2$, and then to integrate out so as to obtain the marginal distribution for one element of the vector on its tails. However an explicit formula for a particular b_i element tail distribution is difficult (the available formula involves a complicated multiple integral). However as a simplification we can consider an inequality involving the smallest latent root λ_m of the equation

$$\det|R - \lambda\Omega| = 0$$

where R and Ω are defined as in Sargan (1976), Ω being $E(v_t v_t')$, and the definition of R is obscured by the transformation of the exogenous variables used in Sargan (1976), but can be most easily defined verbally from the remark that $\sigma^2 R^{-1}/T$ is the asymptotic variance matrix of the instrumental variable estimator. Then the result that can be proved without too much difficulty is that

$$P(b_i > r) = c_i/r^{N+1} + 0(r^{N+2}) \qquad \text{for } r \to \infty$$

where $c_i = 0(e^{-\kappa T/2})$ *as* $T \to \infty$ for any $\kappa < \lambda_m$. Of course λ_m can be regarded as a measure of the extent to which the instrumental variables identify the equation.

NOTE

1. The order of magnitude $Q = 0(e^{-\kappa T/2})$ means that $Qe^{\kappa T/2}$ is bounded as $T \to \infty$.

REFERENCES

Hendry, D. F. and R. W. Harrison (1974). Monte Carlo methodology and the small sample behaviour of ordinary and two-stage least-squares *Journal of Econometrics 2*, 151–174.

Mariano, R. S. and T. Sawa (1972). The exact finite-sample distribution of the limited-information maximum likelihood estimator in the case of two included exogenous variables, *J.A.S.A. 67*, 159–163.

Richardson, D. H. (1968). The exact distribution of a structural coefficient estimator, *J.A.S.A. 63*, 1214–1226.

Sargan, J. D. and Mikhail, W. M. (1971). A General Approximation to the Distribution of Instrumental Variables Estimates, *Econometrica 39*, 131–169.

Sargan, J. D. (1975). Gram-Charlier approximations applied to t-ratios of k-class estimators, *Econometrica 43*, 327–346.

Sargan, J. D. (1974). The moments of the 3SLS estimates of the structural coefficients of a simultaneous equation model, Cowles Foundation Discussion Paper No. 370.

Sargan, J. D. (1976). Econometric estimators and the Edgeworth approximation, *Econometrica 44*, 421–448.

Sargan, J. D. (1977). Asymptotic properties of control variates in Monte Carlo studies, Unpublished Working Paper.

A TEST FOR SIMILARITY BETWEEN TWO GROUPS OF GROWTH CURVES OF ECONOMIC TIME SERIES VARIABLES

Takeaki Kariya

This article provides a test for similarity between two groups of growth curves of p economic time-series variables. The problem is reduced to the MANOVA problem.

I. PROBLEM

In such fields as economic development or international economics, it may be important to determine whether two scalar or vector groups of economic time-series growth curves are similar as well as congruent. For example, in economic development it may be interesting to investigate the similarity of the two growth curves of GNP series between one period in Japan and another period in West Germany. This article

Advances in Econometrics, volume 1, pages 301–310.
Copyright © 1982 by JAI Press Inc.
All rights of reproduction in any form reserved.
ISBN: 0-89232-138-5

contrives a test for such similarity in the following hypothesis-testing problems.

A. Problem I

Suppose that two economic time-series variables $y_i(t)(i = 1,2)$ are independently distributed as

$$y_i(t) \sim N[\mu_i(t), \sigma_i^2] \quad (i = 1,2) \tag{1}$$

where, as random samples, $y_1(t)$ and $y_2(t)$ are observed at $t = t_1, \ldots, t_n$ and $t = s_1, \ldots, s_m$, respectively. The problem is to test, based on $[y_1(t_1), \ldots, y_1(t_n); y_1(s_1), \ldots, y_2(s_m)]$, the hypothesis that $\mu_1(t)$ and $\mu_2(t)$ are similar figures.

B. Problem II

Suppose that two groups of p economic time-series variables, denoted by vectors $y_i(t) = [y_{i1}(t), \ldots, y_{ip}(t)]'$ $(i = 1,2)$, are independently distributed as

$$y_i(t) \sim N_p(\mu_i(t), \Sigma_i) \quad (i = 1,2) \tag{2}$$

where, as random samples, $y_1(t)$ and $y_2(t)$ are observed at $t = t_1, \ldots, t_n$ and $t = s_1, \ldots, s_m$, respectively. The problem is to test the hypothesis of simultaneous similarity of $\mu_1(t)$ and $\mu_2(t)$ based on $[y_1(t), \ldots, y_1(t_n); y_2(s_1), \ldots, y_2(s_m)]$. Clearly Problem I is a special case of Problem II, but the two problems are treated separately for heuristic purposes. Since $\mu_i(t)$ in each problem is unknown, it is approximated by a polynomial of degree less than $\min(n,m)$. Further $\sigma_1^2 = a^2\sigma_2^2$ and $\Sigma_1 = a^2\Sigma_2$ are assumed in Problems I and II, respectively, where a is the ratio of the similarity in each problem. And Problem I is reduced to the problem of testing a general linear hypothesis in linear regression and Problem II is reduced to a special case of the MANOVA (multivariate analysis of variance) problem. Hence the test we propose is an F test in Problem I, and in Problem II, it is one of (1) Roy's maximal root test, (2) Rawley–Hotelling's trace test, (3) Pillai's trace test, or (4) LRT (likelihood ratio test).

II. PROBLEM I

In this section we treat Problem I. First it is assumed that for the unknown path $\mu_i(t)$, it is approximated by a polynomial of degree $k - 1$

$$\mu_i(t) = \beta_{i0} + \beta_{i1}t + \ldots + \beta_{ik-1}t^{k-1} \quad \text{for } i = 1,2 \tag{3}$$

The choice of k is discussed in Section IV. Now suppose that the two paths $\mu_1(t)$ and $\mu_2(t)$ are similar, as illustrated in Figure 1, in the sample periods $t = t_1, \ldots, t_n$ and $t = s_1, \ldots, s_m$. Assuming the polynomials (3) for $\mu_i(t)$'s, let us derive the conditions on the coefficient β_{ij}'s ($j = 0,\ldots, k - 1; i = 1,2$) for which $\mu_1(t)$ and $\mu_2(t)$ are similar. In Figure 1, let $(0,0)$ and (c,d) be the coordinates of the origin 0 and the center of the similarity, respectively. Without loss of generality, this can be done by defining a historical time point to be zero, and $t_1,\ldots,t_n$ and $s_1,\ldots,s_m$ are assumed to be scaled from the origin 0. The coordinate (c,d) of the center of the similarity is measured with respect to this origin and in this section it is assumed to be known. The determination of c and d are also discussed in Section IV. Next for $\mu_1(t)$ and $\mu_2(t)$, we make the following parallel translations so that the origin 0 moves to the center of the similarity $0'$

$$\eta_i(t) = \mu_i(t + c) - d \quad (i = 1,2) \tag{4}$$

Let a be the ratio of the similarity. Since the determination of a is given in Section IV, we assume here that a is known. From Figure 1 and (4), $a = \eta_1(0)/\eta_2(0)$, and $[at, a\eta_2(t)] = [at, \eta_1(at)]$ for all t or

$$a\eta_2(t) = \eta_1(at) \quad \text{for all } t \tag{5}$$

The relation (5) with (3) and (4) is equivalent to

$$a[\beta_{20} + \beta_{21}(t + c) + \ldots + \beta_{2\,k-1}(t + c)^{k-1}] - ad$$

$$= \beta_{10} + \beta_{11}(at + c) + \ldots + \tag{6}$$

$$\beta_{1\,k-1}(at + c)^{k-1} - ad \quad \text{for all } t$$

Figure 1. Two Possible Unknown Paths

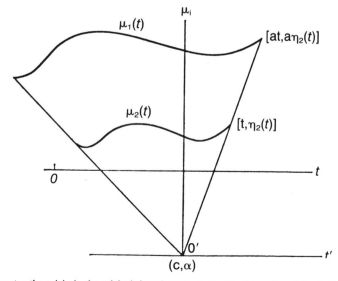

0 denotes the origin in the original time domain. $0'$ denotes the center of the similarity.

Comparing the coefficients in both sides of (6), we obtain

$$a[\beta_{20} + \beta_{21}c + \ldots + \beta_{2\,k-1}c^{k-1} - d]$$

$$= \beta_{10} + \beta_{11}c + \ldots + \beta_{1\,k-1}c^{k-1} - d$$

$$a[\beta_{21} + \binom{2}{1}\beta_{22}c + \ldots + \binom{k-1}{1}\beta_{2\,k-1}c^{k-2}]$$

$$= \beta_{11}a + \binom{2}{1}\beta_{12}ac + \ldots + \binom{k-1}{1}\beta_{1\,k-1}ac^{k-2}$$

$$\vdots$$

$$a\beta_{2\,k-1} = a^{k-1}\beta_{1\,k-1}$$

(7)

Here we let

$$e_{ij} = \binom{j-1}{i-1}c^{j-i} \quad (j \geq i;\ i,j = 1,\ldots,k-1),$$ (8)

$$R_1 = \begin{pmatrix} e_{11} & e_{12} & \ldots & e_{1k} \\ 0 & e_{22} & \ldots & e_{2k} \\ \vdots & & & \vdots \\ 0 & \ldots & 0 & e_{kk} \end{pmatrix} : k \times k$$ (9)

$$D_a = \begin{pmatrix} 1 & & & 0 \\ & a & & \\ & & a^2 & \\ & & & \ddots & \\ 0 & & & & a^{k-1} \end{pmatrix} : k \times k$$

$$\tilde{d} = (d,0,\ldots,0)' : k \times 1 \text{ and } \beta_i = (\beta_{i0},\beta_{i1},\ldots,\beta_{i\,k-1})' : k \times 1$$ (10)

Then the relations in (7) are written as

$$aR_1\beta_2 - a\tilde{d} = D_aR_1\beta_1 - \tilde{d}$$ (11)

Hence if we let

$$\beta = (\beta_1',\beta_2')', \quad R = (-D_aR_1, aR_1), \text{ and } r = a\tilde{d} - \tilde{d}$$ (12)

(11) is expressed as the general linear hypothesis

$$R\beta = r$$ (13)

On the other hand, to express the model in matrix notation, we let

$$y_1 = [y_1(t_1),\ldots,y_1(t_n)]', \quad y_2 = [y_2(s_1),\ldots,y_2(s_m)]',$$

$$X_1 = \begin{pmatrix} 1 & t_1 & t_1^2 & \cdots & t_1^{k-1} \\ 1 & t_2 & t_2^2 & \cdots & t_2^{k-1} \\ \vdots & \vdots & \vdots & & \vdots \\ 1 & t_n & t_n^2 & \cdots & t_n^{k-1} \end{pmatrix} : n \times k, \quad X_2 = \begin{pmatrix} 1 & s_1 & s_1^2 & \cdots & s_1^{k-1} \\ 1 & s_2 & s_2^2 & \cdots & s_2^{k-1} \\ \vdots & \vdots & \vdots & & \vdots \\ 1 & s_m & s_m^2 & \cdots & s_m^{k-1} \end{pmatrix} : m \times k \tag{14}$$

$$u_1 = [u_1(t_1), \ldots, u_1(t_n)]', \quad u_2 = [u_2(s_1), \ldots, u_2(s_m)]'$$

$$y = \begin{pmatrix} y_1 \\ y_2 \end{pmatrix}, \quad X = \begin{pmatrix} X_1 & 0 \\ 0 & X_2 \end{pmatrix}, \quad u = \begin{pmatrix} u_1 \\ u_2 \end{pmatrix}, \text{ and } \Sigma = \begin{pmatrix} \sigma_1^2 I_n & 0 \\ 0 & \sigma_2^2 I_m \end{pmatrix}$$

Then the model (1) with (3) is expressed as

$$y = X\beta + u \quad u \sim N(0, \Sigma) \tag{15}$$

Thus the problem of testing similarity is reduced to the problem of testing the linear hypothesis (13) in the linear model (15). Since the covariance matrix Σ of the error term u is of heteroskedastic structure, we distinguish two cases.

Case 1. $\sigma_1^2 = a^2 \sigma_2^2$. Since this means that the ratio of the standard deviations of $y_1(t)$ and $y_2(t)$ equals the ratio of similarity, it will be reasonable. A test for checking this is available (see Section IV). Anyway, in this case, Σ is written as

$$\Sigma = \sigma_2^2 A^2 \quad \text{where } A = \begin{pmatrix} aI_n & 0 \\ 0 & I_m \end{pmatrix} \tag{16}$$

Since A is known by assumption, we let

$$\bar{y} = A^{-1}y, \quad \bar{X} = A^{-1}X, \text{ and } \bar{u} = A^{-1}u, \tag{17}$$

and rewrite the model (15) as

$$\bar{y} = \bar{X}\beta + \bar{u} \quad \bar{u} \sim N(0, \sigma_2^2 I_{n+m}) \tag{18}$$

Now, as is well known, a uniformly most powerful invariant test for testing (13) under the model (18) is the test that rejects the hypothesis for large values of

$$T = \frac{(n + m - 2k)(Rb - r)'[R(\bar{X}'\bar{X})^{-1}R']^{-1}(Rb - r)}{k(\bar{y} - \bar{X}b)'(\bar{y} - \bar{X}b)} \tag{19}$$

where $b = (\bar{X}'\bar{X})^{-1}\bar{X}'\bar{y}$ (see Lehemann, 1959, Chapter 6 or Theil, 1971, pp. 143–145). This is an F test and T in (19) is distributed as $F(k, n + m - 2k; \lambda)$, F distribution with degrees of freedom k and $n + m - 2k$ and noncentral parameter λ where

$$\lambda = (R\beta - r)'[R(\bar{X}'\bar{X})^{-1}R']^{-1}(R\beta - r)/2\sigma_2^2 \tag{20}$$

Case 2. $\sigma^2_1 \neq a^2\sigma^2_2$. This case corresponds to the Behrens–Fisher problem and it is difficult to treat (see Lehemann, 1959). Here we just indicate the preceding procedure with

$$A = \begin{pmatrix} \hat{\sigma}_1 I & 0 \\ 0 & \hat{\sigma}_2 I \end{pmatrix}$$

and use the test based on T in (19) for large n and m compared to $2k$, although T is no longer F distributed. The estimates $\hat{\sigma}_i^2$ ($i = 1,2$) are $\hat{\sigma}_i^2 = y_i'[I - X_i(X_i'X_i)^{-1}X_i']y_i/n_i$ ($i = 1,2$) where $n_1 = n$ and $n_2 = m$.

III. PROBLEM II

To treat Problem II, we assume polynomials for $\mu_{ij}(t)$, the jth element of $\mu_i(t)$ ($i = 1,2; j = 1, \ldots, p$)

$$\mu_{ij}(t) = \beta_{ij0} + \beta_{ij1}t + \ldots + \beta_{ijk_j-1}t^{k_j-1} \tag{21}$$

Let $k = \max(k_1, \ldots, k_p)$ and allowing β_{ijk_j-1} to be zero, let $k_1 = \ldots = k_p = k$. Then the models of two groups of economic time-series variables are expressed as

$$Y_i = X_iB_i + U_i \quad (i = 1,2) \tag{22}$$

where X_i's are given by (14)

$$Y_1 = \begin{pmatrix} y_1'(t_1) \\ \vdots \\ y_1'(t_n) \end{pmatrix} : n \times p, \quad Y_2 = \begin{pmatrix} y_2'(s_1) \\ \vdots \\ y_2'(s_m) \end{pmatrix} : m \times p, \quad \text{and}$$

$$B_i = \begin{pmatrix} \beta_{i10} & \cdots & \beta_{ip0} \\ & \vdots & \\ \beta_{i1k-1} & \cdots & \beta_{ipk-1} \end{pmatrix} : k \times p \tag{23}$$

for $i = 1,2$. Of course, U_i are of the same form as Y_i ($i = 1,2$). Now suppose that the two groups of variables are simultaneously similar figures with the ratio of similarity a, as was supposed in Problem I. Then for each column of B_i, the arguments used in (3)–(10) hold and the hypothesis of similarity is expressed as

$$aR_1B_2 - aD = D_aR_1B_1 - D \quad \text{where } D = [d, \ldots, d] : k \times p \tag{24}$$

or

$$RB = R_0 \tag{25}$$

where

$$R = (-D_aR_1, aR_1), \quad R_0 = aD - D \text{ and } B = \begin{pmatrix} B_1 \\ B_2 \end{pmatrix}$$

$$Y = \begin{pmatrix} Y_1 \\ Y_2 \end{pmatrix}, \quad X = \begin{pmatrix} X_1 0 \\ 0 \ X_2 \end{pmatrix}, \quad \text{and } U = \begin{pmatrix} U_1 \\ U_2 \end{pmatrix} \tag{26}$$

Then the problem is reduced to the problem of testing (25) under the model

$$Y = XB + U, \quad U \sim N_{(n + m)p}(0, \Sigma), \quad \text{where } \Sigma = \begin{pmatrix} I_n \otimes \Sigma_1 & 0 \\ 0 & I_m \otimes \Sigma_2 \end{pmatrix} \tag{27}$$

Since it is difficult to treat the case $\Sigma_1 \neq a^2\Sigma_2$, we treat the case

$$\Sigma_1 = a^2\Sigma_2 \tag{28}$$

The assumption (28) can be tested (see Section IV), but it will be a reasonable assumption from the property of the problem at present. Under (28), Σ in (27) is written as $\Sigma = A^2 \otimes \Sigma_2$ where A is given by (16). In the same manner as in Problem I, we let $\tilde{Y} = A^{-1}Y$, $\tilde{X} = A^{-1}X$ and $\tilde{U} = A^{-1}U$. Then the problem is now to test the general linear hypothesis (25) under the multivariate regression model

$$\tilde{Y} = \tilde{X}B + \tilde{U} \quad \tilde{U} \sim N(0, I_{n + m} \otimes \Sigma_2) \tag{29}$$

This is nothing but the MANOVA problem and as is well known (see Anderson, 1958 or Giri, 1977), the following tests are proposed:

1. Roy's maximal root test with c.r. (critical region)

$$ch_1(S_1 S^{-1}) > c_1$$

2. Rawley–Hotelling's trace test with c.r.

$$\text{tr} S_1 S^{-1} > c_2$$

3. Pillai's trace test with c.r.

$$\text{tr} S_1(S_1 + S)^{-1} > c_3$$

4. The LRT with c.r.

$$|S_0|/|S| > c_4,$$

where $S = \tilde{Y}'[I - \tilde{X}(\tilde{X}'\tilde{X})^{-1}\tilde{X}']\tilde{Y}$, $S_0 = S + S_1$ and with $\hat{B} = (\tilde{X}'\tilde{X})^{-1}\tilde{X}'\tilde{Y}$, $\hat{B}_0 = \hat{B}_0 = \hat{B} - C(R\hat{B} - R_0)$ and $C = (\tilde{X}'\tilde{X})^{-1}R'[R(\tilde{X}'\tilde{X})^{-1}R']^{-1}$, $S_0 = (\tilde{Y} - \tilde{X}\hat{B}_0)'(\tilde{Y} - \tilde{X}\hat{B}_0)$. In test (1), $ch_1(\cdot)$ denotes the maximal latent root of a matrix. Tables for these tests are provided by Heck (1960), Pillai (1960), and Davis (1971). Some optimalities of these tests are shown by Das Gupta, Anderson, and Mudholkar (1964), and Schwartz (1967).

In the case of $\Sigma_1 \neq a^2\Sigma_2$, we again propose these tests with

$$A = \begin{pmatrix} \hat{\Sigma}_1^{1/2} & 0 \\ 0 & \hat{\Sigma}_2^{1/2} \end{pmatrix}$$

in the definition of $\tilde{Y}$, $\tilde{X}$, and $\tilde{U}$ in (29), instead of A in (16), when n and m are large compared to k. Here $\hat{\Sigma}_i = Y_i'[I_{n_i} - X_i(X_i'X_i)^{-1}X_i']Y_i/n_i$ with $n_1 = n$ and $n_2 = m$, and $(\hat{\Sigma}_i^{1/2})^2 = \hat{\Sigma}_i (i = 1,2)$.

IV.   CHOICES OF c, d, AND k, AND TESTS FOR $\sigma_1^2 = a^2\sigma_2^2$ AND $\Sigma_1 = a^2\Sigma_2$

In the preceding sections, the center of the similarity (c,d) is assumed to be known. In each practical problem, the determination of (c,d) will not be treated in a unified manner, but the following idea will help. First, to determine c, we choose the starting points t_1 and s_1 and the endpoints t_n and s_m of the two (groups of) time series. Usually such points correspond to some specific points so long as the similarity is considered between the two periods (t_1,t_n) and (s_1,s_m). For example, for the GNP series in Japan and West Germany, s_1 and t_1 may correspond to the end of World War II and the end of World War I, respectively. As is illustrated in Figure 2, the similarity implies

$$|t_n - s_m|/|c - s_m| = |t_1 - s_1|/|c - s_1| \tag{30}$$

from which c is determined. Then the ratio of the similarity a is determined by

Figure 2.   Determination of Center of Similarity

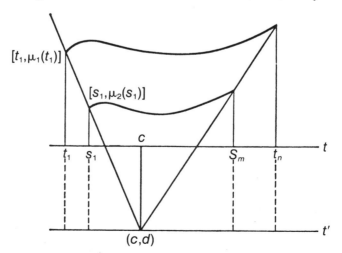

$$a = |t_n - c|/|s_m - c| = |c - t_1|/|c - s_1| \tag{31}$$

Hence it is not so restrictive to assume that c and a are known. However, it is difficult to determine d without letting d depend on data. From Figure 2, for $[t_1, \mu_1(t_1)]$ and $[s_1, \mu_2(s_1)]$

$$a = \{(c - t_1)^2 + [d - \mu_1(t_1)]^2\}^{1/2}/\{(c - s_1)^2 + [d - \mu_2(s_1)]^2\}^{1/2} \tag{32}$$

To determine d from (32), we need to know the values of $\mu_1(t_1)$ and $\mu_2(s_1)$, which are unknown. One possibility to determine d from (32) is to use the values of $y_1(t_1)$ and $y_2(s_1)$ for $\mu_1(t_1)$ and $\mu_2(s_1)$ and test the hypothesis of similarity based on $[y_1(t_2), \ldots, y_1(t_n); y_2(s_2), \ldots, y_2(s_m)]$ where $y_1(t_1)$ and $y_2(s_1)$ are deleted.

Another problem left out is the problem of choices of the degree of polynomials. As a matter of a fact, there is no systematic method for choices of k. One possibility is to increase the degree k one by one from $k = 1$ and stop at k if none of the polynomials improve significantly by increasing the degree from k to $k + 1$. That is, each time we test that the coefficients of highest degree β_{ik-1}'s are all zero, and when we accept this hypothesis, we stop there. But when k is too big, the degrees of freedom in residuals are small and the results of tests may not be stable. Hence it may be desirable that k is less than, say $\min(n, m)/2$.

We remark that in Problem II, the choice of d suggested earlier depends on the variable chosen from p time-series variables.

Finally, we remark that tests for $\sigma_1^2 = a^2\sigma_2^2$ and for $\Sigma_1 = a^2\Sigma_2$ are nothing but tests for equality of variances and for equality of covariance matrices based on $[y_1(t_1), \ldots, y_1(t_n); ay_2(s_1), \ldots, ay_2(s_m)]$ and $[y_1(t_1), \ldots, y_1(t_n); ay_2(s_1), \ldots, ay_2(s_m)]$, respectively. For these problems, the readers are referred to Anderson (1958), Chapter 10 and Giri (1977), pp. 233–236.

REFERENCES

Anderson, T. W. (1958). *An Introduction to Multivariate Statistical Analysis*. New York: Wiley.

Chow, G. C. (1960). Tests of equality between sets of coefficients in two linear regressions. *Econometrica 28*, 591–695.

Das Gupta, S., T. W. Anderson, and G. S. Mudholkar (1964). Monotonicity of the power functions of some tests of the multivariate linear hypothesis. *Ann. Math. Statist. 35*, 200–205.

Davis, A. W. (1971). Percentile approximations for a class of likelihood criteria. *Biometrika 58*, 349–356.

Giri, N. (1977). *Multivariate Statistical Inference*. Academic Press, New York.

Heck, D. L. (1960). Charts of some upper percentage points of the distribution of the characteristic root. *Ann. Math. Statist. 31*, 625–642.

Johnson, N. L. and S. Kotz (1972). *Distributions in Statistics: Continuous Multivariate Distributions*. New York: Wiley.

Lehemann, E. L. (1959). *Testing Statistical Hypotheses.* Wiley, New York.

Pillai, K. C. S. (1960). *Statistical Tables for Tests of Multivariate Hypotheses.* Manila Statist. Center, Univ. of Phillipines.

Schwartz, R. (1967). Local minimax tests. *Ann. Math. Statist. 38,* 340–360.

Theil, H. (1971). *Principles of Econometrics.* New York: Wiley.